Wildwood

Roger Deakin, who died in August 2006, shortly after completing the manuscript for *Wildwood*, was a writer, broadcaster and film-maker with a particular interest in nature and the environment. He lived for many years in Suffolk, where he swam regularly in his moat, in the River Waveney and in the sea, in between travelling widely through the landscapes he writes about in his book. *Waterlog*, the predecessor to *Wildwood*, recounts his swimming adventures and has been hailed as a classic of nature writing.

A writer needs a strong passion to change things, not just to reflect or report them as they are. Mine is to promote a feeling for the importance of trees through a greater understanding of them, so that people don't just think of 'trees' as they mostly do now, but of each individual tree, and each kind of tree.

Roger Deakin

Praise for *Waterlog*

'A simply wonderful book . . . A delightfully eccentric masterpiece' Craig Brown, *Mail on Sunday*

'A delicious, cleansing, funny, wise and joyful book, so wonderfully full of energy and life. I love it' Jane Gardam

'Deakin's evocation of place is superb' Robert McCrum

'A triumph of topographical and naturalist writing . . . to weave environmental and cultural concerns so deftly together in this enchanting and original travel book is a real achievement' *Independent*

Wildwood

A Journey Through Trees

ROGER DEAKIN

HAMISH HAMILTON

an imprint of

PENGUIN BOOKS

HAMISH HAMILTON

Published by the Penguin Group
Penguin Books Ltd, 80 Strand, London WC2R ORL, England
Penguin Group (USA) Inc., 375 Hudson Street, New York, New York 10014, USA
Penguin Group (Canada), 90 Eglinton Avenue East, Suite 700, Toronto, Ontario, Canada M4P 2Y3
(a division of Pearson Penguin Canada Inc.)
Penguin Ireland, 25 St Stephen's Green, Dublin 2, Ireland
(a division of Penguin Books Ltd)
Penguin Group (Australia), 250 Camberwell Road, Camberwell, Victoria 3124, Australia
(a division of Pearson Australia Group Pty Ltd)
Penguin Books India Pvt Ltd, 11 Community Centre, Panchsheel Park, New Delhi – 110 017, India
Penguin Group (NZ), 67 Apollo Drive, Rosedale, North Shore 0632, New Zealand
(a division of Pearson New Zealand Ltd)
Penguin Books (South Africa) (Pty) Ltd, 24 Sturdee Avenue, Rosebank, Johannesburg 2196, South Africa

Penguin Books Ltd, Registered Offices: 80 Strand, London WC2R ORL, England

www.penguin.com

First published 2007
6

Text copyright © The Estate of Roger Deakin, 2007
Illustrations copyright © David Holmes, David Nash, Mary Newcomb, 2007

Original chapter illustrations throughout by David Holmes, excluding illustration on p. 151 by David Nash and
illustration on p. 179 by Mary Newcomb.

Every effort has been made to trace and contact copyright-holders. The publishers will be pleased
to make good any omissions or rectify any mistakes brought to their attention at the earliest opportunity.

The moral right of the author has been asserted

Set in 12/14.75 pt Monotype Dante
Typeset by Rowland Phototypesetting Ltd, Bury St Edmunds, Suffolk
Printed in Great Britain by Clays Ltd, St Ives plc

A CIP catalogue record for this book is available from the British Library

ISBN: 978-0-241-14184-7

www.greenpenguin.co.uk

Penguin Books is committed to a sustainable future
for our business, our readers and our planet.
The book in your hands is made from paper
certified by the Forest Stewardship Council.

For Alison

Contents

Contents

Introduction

For a year I travelled amphibiously about the country, swimming in the wild, literally immersing myself in the landscape and in the elements, in particular the primal element of water, in an attempt to discover for myself that 'third thing' D. H. Lawrence puzzled about in his poem of that title. Water, he wrote, is something more than the sum of its parts, something more than two parts hydrogen and one of oxygen. In writing *Waterlog*, the account of my meanderings, swimming was a metaphor for what Keats called 'taking part in the existence of things'.

Now it seemed logical to plunge into what Edward Thomas called 'the fifth element': the element of wood. Swimming in the Helford River, where the oaks stretch out their branches level with the water to dip into it at high tide, or on Dartmoor, going against the current with the running salmon in the steeply wooded Dart, I realized the logic of Patrick Leigh Fermor's superb *Between the Woods and the Water*. In the woods, there is a strong sense of immersion in the dancing shadow play of the leafy depths, and the rise and fall of the sap that proclaims the seasons is nothing less than a tide, and no less influenced by the moon.

It is through trees that we see and hear the wind: woodland people can tell the species of a tree from the sound it makes in the wind. If *Waterlog* was about the element of water, *Wildwood* is about the element of wood, as it exists in nature, in our souls, in our culture and in our lives.

To enter a wood is to pass into a different world in which we ourselves are transformed. It is no accident that in the comedies of Shakespeare, people go into the greenwood to grow, learn and change. It is where you travel to find yourself, often, paradoxically, by getting lost. Merlin sends the future King Arthur as a boy into the greenwood to fend for himself in *The Sword in the Stone*. There, he falls asleep and dreams himself, like a chameleon, into the lives of the animals and the trees. In *As You Like It*, the banished Duke Senior goes to live in the Forest of Arden like Robin Hood, and in *Midsummer Night's Dream* the magical metamorphosis of the lovers takes place in a wood 'outside Athens' that is quite obviously an English wood, full of the faeries and Robin Goodfellows of our folklore.

Pinned on my study wall is a still from Truffaut's *L'Enfant Sauvage*. It shows Victor, the feral boy, clambering through the tangle of branches of the dense deciduous woods of the Aveyron. The film remains one of my touchstones for thinking about our relations with the natural world: a reminder that we are not so far away as we like to think from our cousins the gibbons, who swing like angels through the forest canopy, at such headlong speed that they almost fly like the tropical birds they envy and emulate in the music of their marriage-songs at dawn in the treetops. To begin where I began, my mother's name was Wood. The third of my father's three Christian names was Greenwood: Alvan Marshall Greenwood Deakin. My great-grandfather had the timber yard in Walsall: Wood's of Walsall. So I am one of the Wood tribe, and, although I have read Thomas Hardy's *The Woodlanders* many times over, the story of Marty South, Giles Winterbourne and Grace Melbury always moves me more than anything else I know. I am a wood-lander; I have sap in my veins. My great-uncle on my father's side was Joseph Deakin, framed and imprisoned at the age of twenty by Lord Salisbury's government in 1892 as one of the Walsall

Anarchists. He became Librarian at Parkhurst Prison on the Isle of Wight, where he continued his self-education with the help of William Morris, George Bernard Shaw, Edward Carpenter, Sidney and Beatrice Webb and other early socialists. He was a true defender of the greenwood spirit of democratic freedom, and I always think of him as belonging to the outlaw tradition of Robin Hood.

In Suffolk, where I live, I have begun to coppice the wood I planted twenty years ago. It is now home to a family of foxes, deer lie up in it, and this year I was proud to discover some discreetly set rabbit snares: I had my first poachers. The wood has come of age. An ancient green lane and a mile of old hedgerows surround my fields. When I first came to Suffolk thirty years ago, I found my Tudor oak-framed farmhouse and spent a year rebuilding it myself. The house was so ruinous that I camped in the garden while I worked, and when I eventually moved in, the creatures and plants that had grown used to wandering in and out through all the holes in the walls just carried on as usual. Swallows still nest in the chimney, bats fly through the upstairs bedrooms on summer nights when the windows are flung open, and a leg count of the household spiders would run into hundreds. At the time of rebuilding, I even had a timber-framed car, the ash-framed Morgan Plus Four. Then I constructed the wooden barn, using oak beams and pegs and no nails. I have a lathe and a workshop in there where I sometimes make furniture and turn wood, mostly into bowls. I once made a living by making and mending chairs, selling them on a stall in the Portobello Road. Later, I worked for Friends of the Earth, campaigning for whales, woods and rainforests, and founded Common Ground, which still champions old orchards and the 6,000 varieties of apple recorded in our land.

The Chinese count wood as the fifth element, and Jung considered trees an archetype. Nothing can compete with these larger-than-life organisms for signalling the changes in the natural world. They are our barometers of the weather and the changing seasons. We tell the time of year by them. Trees have the capacity to rise to the heavens and to connect us to the sky, to endure, to renew, to bear fruit, and to burn and warm us through the winter. I know of nothing quite as elemental as the log fire glowing in my hearth, nothing that excites the imagination and the passions quite as much as its flames. To Keats, the gentle cracklings of the fire were whisperings of the household gods 'that keep / A gentle empire o'er fraternal souls'. Most of the world still cooks on wood fires, and the vast majority of the world's wood is used as firewood. In so far as 'Western' people have forgotten how to lay a wood fire, or its fossil equivalent in coal, they have lost touch with nature. Aldous Huxley wrote of D. H. Lawrence that 'He could cook, he could sew, he could darn a stocking and milk a cow, he was an efficient woodcutter and a good hand at embroidery, fires always burned when he had laid them and a floor after he had scrubbed it was thoroughly clean.' As it burns, wood releases the energies of the earth, water and sunshine that grew it. Each species expresses its character in its distinctive habits of combustion. Willow burns as it grows, very fast, spitting like a firecracker. Oak glows reliably, hard and long. A wood fire in the hearth is a little household sun.

When Auden wrote, 'A culture is no better than its woods', he knew that, having carelessly lost more of their woods than any other country in Europe, the British generally take a correspondingly greater interest in what trees and woods they still have left. Woods, like water, have been suppressed by motorways and the modern world, and have come to look like the subconscious of the landscape. They have become the guardians of our dreams of greenwood liberty, of our wildwood, feral, childhood selves, of Richmal Crompton's Just William and his outlaws. They hold the merriness of Merry England, of yew longbows, of Robin Hood and his outlaw band. But they are also repositories of the ancient stories, of the Icelandic myths of Ygdrasil the Tree of Life, Robert Graves's 'The Battle of the Trees' and the myths of Sir James Frazer's *Golden Bough*. The enemies of woods are always the enemies of culture and humanity.

Wildwood is a quest for the residual magic of trees and wood that still touches most of us not far beneath the surface of our daily lives.

Human beings depend on trees quite as much as on rivers and the sea. Our intimate relationship with trees is physical as well as cultural and spiritual: literally an exchange of carbon dioxide for oxygen. Once inside a wood, you walk on something very like the seabed, looking up at the canopy of leaves as if it were the surface of the water, filtering the descending shafts of sunlight and dappling everything. Woods have their own rich ecology, and their own people, woodlanders, living and working in and around them. A tree itself is a river of sap: through roots that wave about underwater like sea anemones, the willow pollard at one end of the moat where I swim in Suffolk draws gallons of water into the leaf-tips of its topmost branches every day; released as vapour into the summer air, this water then rises invisibly to join the clouds, and the falling raindrops ripple out into every tree ring.

PART ONE

Roots

Staying Put

While the rest of the world has been playing musical chairs all around me, I have stayed put in the same house for more than half my life. It's not that I don't like to wander, but somehow I feel easier in my freewheeling knowing that this place is here, a fixed point. I am located by it, just as Donne's lovers are the twin points of compasses in his poem *A Valediction, Forbidding Mourning*:

> Thy firmness draws my circle just,
> And makes me end where I begun.

The adventures of my mother's family, the Woods, all nine of them, were the stuff of my bedtime stories. My mother never seemed to read to me but recounted instead the many tales of the Wood tribe. I grew up in a strictly oral tradition of home-grown folklore peopled almost entirely by my mother's siblings. Welsh Grandma Jones, silver-haired Grandpa Wood, with his one left hand and a steel hook for his right, two dashing uncles and four aunts. My grandparents had upheld our sylvan traditions by christening two of them Ivy Wood and Violet Wood. My mother was always thankful nobody had thought of Primrose.

Wood family history is ingrained in me, just as memory and

history are ingrained into the timbers of Walnut Tree Farm. Each post and beam has its own particular story and once grew free. If you take a cross-section of any beam, close study of the pattern of its annual rings by a dendrochronologist would reveal exactly when it grew up from the acorn or the coppice stool, and exactly when it was cut down.

The house sits at a dizzy 174 feet above sea level, enough to keep my patch islanded when the promised flood comes. But I am part-islanded already by a moat and a round cattle pond that juts out into the common, one of twenty-four that are strung around it and connected by an ancient system of moats and drains. The jungled hedges that surround my four meadows comprise a necessary rampart to the winds that cut across the open wheat prairies beyond. They have vaulted the ditches, creating a secret leaf-mould world of ferny tunnels. There's a little wood too, and an old droving road that flanks the land to the west.

All of this lies on the shores of a great inland sea of rippling grasses that rises like a tide towards haymaking in July, obscuring my neighbour's farm on its far side. It stretches a mile to the west of this place, the biggest grazing common in Suffolk. So, although the sea is twenty-five miles due east at Walberswick, I can still enjoy some of the pleasures of living beside it: the big skies and wide, dramatic sunsets. In Suffolk we have daydream mountains too: the volcanic cumulus clouds of harvest time.

Why have I stayed so long? Not because I was born here or have Suffolk roots, but because of all the hard work, and the accumulated history. I mean my own, mixed up with the people I love. For three years I taught English at the old grammar school in Diss, putting more roots down among the local students and families who became my friends. There is no more intimate way of getting to know your neighbours than by teaching their children. Then there were the Barsham Fairs and the *Waveney Clarion*, the community newspaper of the Waveney Valley, which I helped write, plan and distribute, as a whole extended family of us quasi-hippies did, from Diss to Bungay to Beccles to Lowestoft. The rural culture we built together then during the 1970s and early 1980s, based firmly on the values of the *Whole Earth Catalogue*, Friends of the Earth, Cobbett's *Cottage Economy* and John Seymour's *The Fat of the Land*, flushed out all the pioneer immigrants busy settling in Suffolk – rough carpenters, dirt farmers, musicians, poets, ditchdiggers and drivers of timber-framed Morris Minor estate cars – and put us all to work together building what for a golden moment became a grand tradition of Suffolk fairs, ephemeral, dreamlike, gypsyish shanty capitals in fields full of folk. Again, it was work – creative, bold, imaginative but at the same time hard, manual and physical – that drew us together. A shared experience of risk too: you never knew what the weather would do or if anyone would turn up at the gate and pay for it all. Dancing and music played a big part. We had our own local heroes, our own Suffolk Bob Dylans and Willie Nelsons, and any number of ceilidh bands sawing away in village halls on Friday nights.

The house was a ruin when I found it in 1969. I noticed a chimney rising just above the treetops of a spinney of ash, maple, hazel, elder, blackthorn, ivy and bramble, and what was left of a cottage orchard of walnut, greengage and apple. Like everyone else in the village, Arthur Cousins, the owner, clearly thought the house had crept away to hide itself and discreetly die, like an old cat. He lived across the fields at Cowpasture Farm with his daughters Beryl and Precious, keeping pigs in the old house downstairs, chickens upstairs. The roof was a patchwork of flapping corrugated iron, and the remaining damp, composting thatch was so verdant with grass and moss it could have been turf. I love ruins because they are always doing what everything really wants to do all the time: returning themselves to the earth, melting back into the landscape. And though it is long since I moved in, nature has refused to relinquish all kinds of ancient rights of way through the place.

For several weeks I paid court to Arthur at Cowpasture Farm, and eventually he consented to sell me the house and twelve acres. We went on to become the best of friends, even sharing Heather, a big-eyed Guernsey house-cow, whom we took turns to milk.

Arthur was one of the last generation of the old Suffolk horse men. For most of his life he had been an independent timber-hauler with his own gang of heavy horses and carts, plying the roads between Norwich and Ipswich, hauling timber from the woods to the saw-mills, timber yards and shippers. He worked hard, saved up and bought his farm before the war, when land was cheap. He still hung hagstones, Suffolk's flint version of the evil eye, in his stables and cowsheds to ward off the nightmare who might disturb his animals as they slept in their stalls. He was my tutor in husbandry, animal lore and village politics.

Slowly, I stripped the house to its skeleton of oak, chestnut and ash, repairing it with oak timbers gleaned from a barn one of the local farmers had demolished. I lived in the back of a Volkswagen van for a while, then made a bivouac around the big central fireplace and slept beside a wood fire with two cats for company. The hearth became the most sacred, numinous place in the house. It lies at its centre, and is the only part that still opens to the skies. In spring, I moved upstairs into what felt like a tree house, sleeping under the stars as I repaired the open rafters in a perch with a canvas roof. Soon the wood-pigeons roosting in the ash tree at eye level grew used to me. The tree felt then, as it does now, like a guardian of the house, arching up over the roof in a kind of embrace, and I fought the council building inspector tooth and nail to retain it.

I found myself then, as I still do deep down, in love with the place as a ruin and therefore partly at odds with myself as its healer. I liked the way the wattle-and-daub walls, baked by the sun to a biscuit, were cratered all over where they faced south, like the peepholes of a Yemeni city, by nesting mason bees or solitary wasps. I appreciated the inquisitive tendrils of ivy that poked their heads in through the cracks in the rotted windows, fogged green with algae, patterned by questing snails. I welcomed the sparrows and starlings fidgeting in the thatch or under the tin, and the bats that later flitted through the tented open rafters as I lay dozing in bed, limbs aching sweetly from a long day's labour. I wanted to repair the walls, but at the same time to foster the passepartout menagerie that refused to recognize them. Somehow, through the sum of minor inefficiencies in a handmade wood-framed house, I succeeded.

Having personally shaped or repaired every single one, I have ended up on terms of the greatest intimacy with all the beams, posts and pegged joints in the place. I have perhaps also earned some kinship with the people who, twenty years or so before Shakespeare was born, originally built the house and probably dug out the moat. Uncovering the carpenters' coded inscriptions on the rafters and floor beams was like finding a lost manuscript. They were carved when the oak or sweet chestnut was still green and the house under prefabricated construction in a kind of kit form at the carpenters' shop, ready to be carted to the site and raised, whole walls at a time, by the combined muscle of dozens of villagers. The proportions of everything, measured in feet and inches, impressed on me the organic nature of the entire structure. The proportions of each room, and of the house as a whole, were predicated on the natural proportions of the trees available. Suffolk houses like mine tend to be about eighteen feet wide, because that is about the average limit of the straight run of the trunk of a youngish oak suitable in girth for making a major crossbeam of eight inches by seven. The bigger barns tend to twenty-one feet wide, with slightly bigger timbers. Uprights too are of tree height, the idea being to select trees or coppice poles of about the right cross-section, so they can be squared with an adze with the minimum of work.

This is the beam count in my house. Kitchen: 44. Sitting room: 50. Study: 32. Upstairs landing, bathroom and study: 22. Small bedroom: 23. Big bedroom: 72. Total: 243. If I add all 30 hidden beams in the kitchen, as well as 50-odd rafters, the total is 323 beams. So some 300 trees were felled to build this house: a small wood. The bark is still on many of these timbers after 400 years, and so is the sapwood here and there. The timber was always worked in its green, unseasoned condition, when it is easiest to cut, drill or shape into joints. Once assembled into the hardwood frame, the timbers would gradually season in situ, often twisting or curving as they did so and creating the graceful undulations so characteristic of old houses. One of the saddest things to witness in Suffolk today is the number of fine old timber houses that have been straightened out by builders. The last generation of Suffolk builders understood the old houses well, approaching them as structures that are engineered as much as built. Evolved rather than designed, the timber frame is intended to sit lightly on the sea of shifting Suffolk clay like an upturned boat and ride the earth's constant movement.

The House-sheds: Camping

I have a weakness for sheds or huts of all kinds, no doubt inherited from the bothy my father built for me and my animal familiars at the end of the garden when I was about six. Thoreau would have approved of the name we gave it: 'Cosy Cabin', emblazoned on a tin sign above the door. I used to spend hours in there conversing with the lodgers: an assortment of beetles or woodlice in match-boxes, rabbits, guinea pigs, white mice and toads, all grateful to have a roof over their heads. In summer I was allowed to sleep up there too. No wonder we called it cosy. Later a crow moved in, even a few homely pigeons. My father, who had his own shed on the allotment, was fond of quoting William Cobbett on the pigeons: 'Very interesting in their manners; they are an object to delight *children* and to give them the *early habit* of fondness for animals and of *setting a value* on them, which, as I have often had to observe, is a very great thing.'

These days, my cosy cabin is a shepherd's hut in the lee of a south-facing Suffolk hedge and a big ash tree a field away from the house. Perched on iron wheels, it is lined with close-grained pine boards stained a deep honey-amber by years of woodsmoke seeping from the stove. There's a simple chair and table where I often work, oil lamps and candles, sun-faded curtains, and a wooden bed with a space underneath where sheepdogs and orphan lambs would once have curled up, gently warming the slumbering shepherd above. The hut has a barrelled tin roof and wooden ceiling, so when it rains the whole vessel resounds to the tattoo. Sleep through that, and you could still be woken early by magpies clattering along the corrugated rooftop like Cajun washboard-players, or an ill-bred bluetit noisily investigating the eaves. Across the field is the cabin I built for *my* son. I like to think it will always be like this: future cities of unofficial shanties stretching away across the country, down the generations.

28 May

Lying in bed in the shepherd's hut is an out-of-body experience in which you are suspended six feet above the bottom of a wooden boat, gazing into its wooden hull and along the line of its keel. Everything is upside down, of course, but it is such another world in there that anything is possible. You gaze out of the open door at a wake of bubbling cow-parsley and the green depths of a hedge in May. Lift your face up to a porthole and you can survey the green waters of Cowpasture Meadow coming up to meet you as you voyage across doldrums of Sargasso buttercups in lazy pools, or navigate towards the beacon of a solitary green-winged orchid.

13 June

I slept in the shepherd's hut last night after an evening swim in the moat, now beginning to weed up, under an almost-full moon. It was so bright, you could hardly call it proper darkness at all. At ten to four I was awoken by a blackcap hopping along the tin roof, then striking up the most exquisite warbling, at first utterly solo in the half-light, soon joined by other birds. It sang its heart out, moving about the roof now and then between phrases or cadenzas to a new vantage point, eventually ascending into the ash tree that overhangs the hut and the pond beside it. You hear everything in the hut: the foxes barking down the lane, even the rabbits thumping their hind legs on the ground sometimes. Easing myself up on one elbow about twenty past four, I inched back the curtain and surveyed the meadow. Yellow pools of buttercup, and here and there a pyramidal orchid, or a lush, intensely purple patch of the southern marsh orchid, the huge flowers stacked and layered like wedding cakes. A crow was flying in big circles above the pasture, climbing steeply, then gliding down for pure pleasure.

I dozed back to sleep, but was awoken by a most violent rumbling and shaking of the whole hut, then a sound of loud scratching. For a moment I thought a cat must have leapt in, somehow, through an open window and on to my bed. Then, looking out of the window in some alarm, I realized what it was: a roe-deer rubbing herself against one corner of the hut, inches away from my pillow. A clamour of hooves as she and two others bounced off through the standing hay. The birdsong was by now too loud for sleep, so I adjourned to the house across the dew for breakfast.

10 *August*

I'm lying in the shepherd's hut on a wooden bed under a boarded roof like a pine tent, between walls panelled with pine, tongued and grooved horizontally. Each time a nail has pierced the deep amber wood it has bled a black rusty stain that has crept along the grain and blurred, as though the wood or the wagon itself were travelling at speed. A woodpecker shrieks across the field. A wasp worries the windowpane, then zigzags above the bed and eventually blunders into the outer air. The open door frames a wall of green: the hawthorn, maple, blackthorn hedge, the dipping wands of an ash, nettles, graceful flowers of grasses. All stir in the hot breeze. Dust motes flicker and drift in the window-light. In the far corner, the stainless-steel stove-pipe rises like a new stem from the rusty little stove. On the other side of the doorway is the pine corner-cupboard I bodged out of skip-wood containing spare blankets and Bushmills for cold nights. Across the common, cows have been lowing all night. Perhaps the weather will change. I sleep coffined in pine.

Why do I sleep outdoors? Because of the sound of the random dripping of rain off the maples or ash trees over the roof of the railway wagon, or the hopping of a bird on the wet felt of the roof, or the percussion of a twig against the steel stove-chimney. Out there, I hear the yawn of the wind in the trees along Cowpasture Lane. I feel in touch with the elements in a way I never do indoors.

Sleeping one time in Burgate Wood on the moated island of the old hall, I put my cheek against the loam and the cool ground ivy. When I closed my eyes I saw the iceberg depths of the wood's root-world. Walking there, picking my way through the trees, I had thought of it as perpendicular until I lay down and entered the ground-world. This is the part of a wood that only reveals itself occasionally after a big storm, when the trees have keeled over and the roots are thrown suddenly upright, clutching earth and stones. How deep do roots go?

I also have a railway wagon, which I hauled into one of my fields years ago. Working or sleeping in my railway wagon is like embarking on a journey. An ash tree growing just behind it strokes the roof and plays tunes on the stove-pipe chimney with its branches whenever the wind blows. Wind rattles the heavy wooden sliding door and seeps in through small gaps between the boards. The entire structure is of wood: an oak frame strengthened by bolted iron straps and brackets, and by double walls of sturdy pine boards, all secured by screws, running horizontally inside and vertically outside to shed rain better. The roof is barrel-vaulted with oak, boarded above, with thick tarred roofing felt on top. When I bought the wagon it had no floor, so I made a wooden one, insulated beneath and damp-proofed by building paper.

There's so much room inside, you could happily live in the wagon. It is fifteen feet by eight, with an airy ceiling nine feet high. At each end, a tiny foot-square window in a corner opens by sliding up a wooden shutter and propping it with a stick. The wagon is sunk so deep in the massive hedge that the light seeping in is pure green. The interior is painted cream, and the sliding front door faces south. This will open to a width of six feet, so plenty of light comes in, reflected off the blond, drying hay of the meadow. Opposite the entrance is a cast-iron Tortoise stove with a stainless-steel chimney pipe that runs up inside the wagon and heats it in winter. When the stove is going full tilt, the hot metal sometimes glows red in the dark, and it is burnished rainbow blues and reds from the passage and oxidation of the hot gases. Outside on the roof, the chimney is topped with a jaunty steel Chinaman's hat to keep the rain off. Most of one end of the wagon is occupied by a wooden bed whose ends I rescued in a damaged state from the auction sheds at Diss and repaired. When I light the candles in the three Moroccan lanterns, I think of something the artist Roger Ackling said to me, quoting Thoreau: 'Electricity kills darkness, candlelight illuminates it.'

In the warm embrace of the wagon's wood, I always sleep like a cat for eight hours at a time. It is almost as if I were actually being rocked and lulled by the rhythm of its wheels on a nocturnal *Night Mail* journey. What is it about being enclosed by wood that is so comforting? Is this some kind of Reichian orgone box? Or is it simply a matter of feng shui: that the bed is oriented in the right way for deep sleep? I think it more likely that it is the symbolic act of leaving worldly things behind in the house, walking a hundred-yard winding path through a hay meadow and climbing aboard the uncluttered wagon, sunk deep into the leaf-purified air of an unruly Suffolk hedgerow that calms me down and encourages the dreams. It is a version of the wild, and always a return: every cabin is a version of all other cabins, dens, treehouses and nests. I leave the door open, with just a swaying curtain to keep the moths away from the lanterns.

19 *August*

Sleeping in the railway wagon. 'Have you got your ticket?' said A, as I went off over the field. There is plenty of wind, bashing the ash branches against the stove-pipe chimney, playing a tune on it. Wind creates a soothing sound I'm quite accustomed to, like the creaking of ship's timbers, so it actually sends me to sleep. Going out into the dark meadow at night, it would be easy to mistake the outlines of the young walnut trees for deer.

29 *August*

In the railway wagon I hang a pale cotton curtain at the open door, and the sun filters through it. In the mornings I lie in bed watching the shadow puppet show of insects. Last night owls sounded their cool oboe-notes along the hedges. Theirs is such a soothing note for such murderous birds. Owls and the moon work hand in hand; accomplices in the killing of voles and shrews. I lay listening to the nightly shrewicides in the meadow and along the lane.

Sleeping north–south does seem to improve the quality of my slumbers. 'They had been denied the hospitality of sound sleep,' says Saint-Exupéry in *Terre des Hommes*. The beds in the house are all east–west, but the beds in the railway wagon and the shepherd's hut are both north–south. But to sleep half a field away from the house, tucked into a hedge, with an open door facing south into the meadow and plenty of cool night air, must surely add very much to the chances of sleep. The closing of the door on all the daytime stuff in the house, and so little in the shed to encumber the thoughts: just a few rugs, a stove, a bed, a table and chair.

There's more truth about a camp than a house. Planning laws need not worry the improvising builder because temporary structures are more beautiful anyway, and you don't need permission for them. There's more truth about a camp because that is the position we are in. The house represents what we ourselves would like to be on earth: permanent, rooted, here for eternity. But a camp represents the true reality of things: we're just passing through.

Study

I swear there's a singing newt in my study. It generally bursts into song around ten at night and seems to live somewhere near the wood-stove, possibly behind the mantelpiece. Its song is a high-pitched squeak like a piece of clockwork machinery in need of a spot of oil. I have heard it before rising out of the bottoms of drains, or the rainwater traps at the bottoms of drainpipes. In one instance I tracked down a plaintive newt-song I kept hearing in the garden to the flooded depths of a pipe sunk in the lawn with a water stopcock at the bottom. I lay down and plunged in my arm as far as I could and actually succeeded in capturing the tiny songster, a common newt, and liberated it in the vegetable garden. A few nights later, however, it was back again in its damp atelier, practising scales. The song of the newt must count as the most subtle, and the least known, in nature, coming close to the ideal of some of the modern schools of composition: utter silence.

Working in the study and regularly pausing to feed the stove another log is like working on the footplate of a steam locomotive. I am the fireman, teamed with my other self, the driver. This is the pleasure of wood: that it warms you so many times over. First when you fell it, then when you cart it back to the woodpile and again when you saw it into logs. Then it warms you again as you cart it and stack the woodshed to the roof with willow and ash, and again as you barrow it to the hearth. Then, at last, the final warming in front of the fire, the climax and finale of the whole exercise, the sum of so much work, so many hours lost in thought.

Building the new desk under the window in the study, looking south across the garden to the moat. Perfectionism kicks in and all the same self-critical criteria that go into a piece of writing. I make a yew bracket to peg to the oak wall post and support the top, a slab of fine-grained Oregon pine, and a careful wooden sub-frame or chassis. I fill some open cracks in the grain with plaster, smooth it down and carefully stain it pale blue using a delicate watercolour brush. I hollow out one of the old bolt-holes in the top to accommodate a smooth, round flattened pebble from the Hebrides, like a tiny curling stone. It is a sort of worry-bead.

At one end of my desk sits the laminated hub of an early wooden aeroplane propeller. It is a massive thing, with the two linen-skinned blades amputated at their stems. It has been constructed beautifully from ten planks of walnut a foot wide and three-quarters of an inch thick, originally glued and clamped together. I came across it years ago at a Norfolk country auction and was immediately reminded of the Venus de Milo by the deliberate incompleteness of its form, by the way the sawn-off, imaginary arms turned it into something sculptural. I wasn't the only one thus smitten by its mystery that day, and remember holding on tight as the price went into a steep climb. Four lines of coded capitals were carved into the wood where it swept into the convex cleavage between the two blades. I made a brass-rubbing of them on a sheet of typing paper with a 4B pencil and read:

> LUCIFER
> DRG P3153
> DIA 7–9
> PIT 5–5

Decoded, this means that the propeller was designed for one of Bristol Aircraft's Lucifer aero engines, and therefore made around 1925 or soon after. DRG stands for the drawing number of the original propeller design and DIA is the diameter of the propeller: seven feet nine inches. PIT is its pitch, the number of degrees through which the blades have been twisted out of direct alignment.

I use the muscular propeller-hub on my desk as a bookend. It contains stories I shall never know. It belongs to the era of Antoine de Saint-Exupéry, when every flight was an adventure, and, in its long sleep, it probably relives the spinning elation of an aerial life, like a cat dreaming of chasing its tail.

I sit at my desk on the elm seat of a Windsor smoker's bow chair. It is nineteen and a half inches square, cut from a single inch-and-a-quarter plank, elegantly rounded at the corners and tough enough to anchor the beech legs as well as eight hand-turned chair backs that support the bowed arm and backrest. It is probably not far off a hundred years old, and the seat, originally adzed and spokeshaved into shape, has been subtly worn, polished and rendered even more comfortable by generations of shifting bottoms. Its design is entirely traditional, yet the infinite variations of every handmade component give each chair its individuality and a kind of intimate informality that could never be achieved by the techniques of modern mass production. Its beech components were most likely turned by bodgers working out of doors on foot-treadle pole-lathes in the steep hangars of the Chilterns above High Wycombe. As with the elm hub of a cart wheel, or the elm keel of a wooden ship, it is the elm seat that holds together the chair. Elm always seems to be the axis of things. When bells ring out from the church tower, they swing on massive timber stocks of elm.

I belong to the generation that grew up with elm. The big tree at the bottom of our back garden was an elm, and I once knew every crevice in its latticed bark. I even tried to cut it down as a small boy, aiming a hatchet at a minuscule notch over what seemed like several years, barely making an impression, while my parents benignly turned the other way. The tree was one of a long crescent of elm and oak almost certainly planted in the eighteenth century around the perimeter of the old Pinner Park, spaced close enough to keep the squirrels airborne. I rode my bike to school past Long Elms, another eighteenth-century elm avenue planted on the old Chantry Estate, leading to Hatch End.

My prep school was in Hatch End, a suburb of Pinner, and it was there that I acquired my first slow-worms from a boy called George Porges. Porges had arrived a term late in our class, so had ground to make up socially. He set about creating a myth of himself on Day One by showing us the bullet scar on his back, acquired, as he explained, when he was shot by border guards as he fled his mother country, Czechoslovakia. He spoke faultless English without a trace of an accent, and I am pretty sure in retrospect that the scar was a birthmark.

Porges lived a few miles away on the Piccadilly Line at Rayners Lane, where there was a confluence of tube lines with a triangular island of long grass and brambles between them. In our young minds, it came to resemble Czechoslovakia, surrounded on all sides by an Iron Curtain of live electric rails. Porges claimed this was the source of his slow-worms. He alone was able to capture them by dint of death-defying expeditions across the live rails. Porges knew all about the marketing concept of Added Value. So desirable were these reptiles that Porges was willing to pay the ultimate price for them. The Rayners Lane island grew in our imaginations into a Galapagos, cut off from the rest of suburbia by the Scylla and Charybdis of live rails and the Railway Police, who would impose unspeakable penalties if you hadn't already been fried.

Thus snatched from under the nose of Death by the heroic Porges, the slow-worms themselves seemed to carry electricity in their metallic bodies, arcing when they touched, sending shivers of envy through the entire class. They had all the macabre glamour of black mambas with none of the risk. Everyone now jostled after break-time to sit next to Porges, and most of us wanted his slow-worms too. He commanded outrageous prices. Now and again we would go into secret conclave and work out ways to cross the railway lines ourselves wearing several pairs of wellington boots, waders and rubber gloves, but it was pure bravado.

Porges had us mesmerized, and we were all beginning to suffer loss of concentration in our craving. On top of this, I had a few problems at home. It was my white mice. They were doubling their numbers almost daily, and there was a queue for the treadmill. I mentioned very casually to Porges that I might have a mouse or two available for sale. To my amazement, he took the bait, offering me his reptiles but naming his price in rodents in double figures. This suited me perfectly, but prep school had already taught me enough by the age of seven not to hand over the mice without a pained expression.

Our classroom might as well have been an East End pub for all the wheeling and dealing that went on. Another boy, Smith, offered to the highest bidder a stone axe-head he claimed was Mohawk Indian and deadly, its edge having been impregnated with rattle-snake poison. Even to touch it could mean a slow, painful death. Again, my secret liquidity in mice paid off, and the axe-head was mine. This stone axe-head was the very first tool I owned and, as it happens, pretty much the first owned by *Homo sapiens*. As a relic from my own Stone Age, it has always been more of a talisman than anything of much practical use, except as reserve schoolboy currency. I still have it on my desk, and it hasn't killed me yet.

The ants outside my study swarmed this afternoon at 3 p.m. exactly, all the young queens climbing up blades of grass and taking off, escorted by excited workers scattering in every direction. A warm, humid afternoon.

The virgin queen ants fly off south-west, the workers racing about as air-traffic control, chivvying the nervous princesses into unsteady flight. They send them up a small cow-parsley plant to get some extra lift and take off from the dizzy top.

I'm looking at one of the black-and-white photographs that feature in the gallery on my study wall. My younger self is there in plimsolls, khaki shorts and elastic snake-buckle belt, standing on

Campsite Track beside a donkey. I'm holding up my butterfly net like a semaphore flag, and a knapsack, probably full of collecting jars, is slung over one shoulder. Campsite Track led across the heath to our tents, sheltered and concealed within a series of hollows in a range of gorse-topped, gravel dunes above a railway cutting on the Bournemouth line.

This is where I first came to know the New Forest, returning several times to camp at Beaulieu Road during the school holidays with the Botany and Zoology sixth form and our Biology teacher Barry Goater, who was in his first teaching job, in charge of the school Biology Department. A formidable lepidopterist, ornithologist and all-round naturalist, Barry infected us all with his wild enthusiasm.

Although he would modestly deny it, Barry Goater was the instigator of an extraordinary educational experiment. In a quiet corner of the New Forest, he established a camp for the detailed study and mapping of the natural history of a stretch of the wild forest woodland, bog and heath surrounding Beaulieu Road by his Biology sixth form. The camp became something of an institution at our school in the relatively treeless Cricklewood. It was traditional for each generation of us sixth form naturalists to return there again and again and taste the intoxicating pleasure of exploration and discovery in the wild for ourselves. Each of us had a particular project, literally a field of inquiry, and the work we were doing was genuinely original. We learnt the scientific disciplines of botany, zoology and ecology, and we kept our eyes open as all-round naturalists. What we discovered was particular to the place, and, best of all, it belonged to us.

Beaulieu Road was our America, we were pioneers, and the map we jointly drew and refined through gradual accretions of personal observation represented not only the complex natural ecology of the place but also an ambitious and entirely novel cooperation between several generations of the sixth form botanists and zoologists of our school. Through our cumulative endeavours we were charting the relationships between the plants and animals of the place. But the records we kept were also a testament to our own human relationships as naturalists, botanists and zoologists. We were learning at first-hand how exploration and scholarship can evolve and progress in time through cooperation and the free exchange of ideas. Small wonder that the experience influenced so many of our lives so profoundly. Over the course of a total of twenty-four camps from April 1955 to the spring of 1961, everything any of us discovered or recorded was logged in two extraordinary volumes known as the Beaulieu Tomes.

Just as in *Swallows and Amazons*, Richard Jefferies's *Bevis*, Shackleton's accounts of the Antarctic or any explorer's journal, we enthusiastically set about naming all the topographical features of our wild haunts at Beaulieu Road on a handmade map. Of the almost 100,000 acres that now constitute the New Forest, our chosen territory of water, bog, dry heath and woodland was a rough oblong three miles by two straddling north and south of the road from Lyndhurst to Beaulieu. We had naturally adopted, or adapted, the old names where they existed, and made up our own where they didn't. We drew our water in green canvas buckets from a pure spring under the railway embankment known simply as the Spring, or Campsite Spring. Beyond it, in a gentle valley across Black Down, lay the source of the Beaulieu River at a confluence of its wooded headwaters, the Matley Stream, Deerleap Stream and Matley Stream Tributary. Interesting ferns, liverworts and mosses grew under the Matley Stream Bridge where the waters passed under the railway, and verdant *lawns* lay along the banks of the infant river. 'Lawns' is the New Forest term for the strips of grazing you come across in woodland clearings and along the banks of streams, close-cropped by deer, rabbits and ponies.

Over by Station Heath lay the boggy Gentian Valley with its marsh gentians, and First Bog, snowed with the fluffy tops of cotton grass. Beyond it was the huge expanse of Second Bog, perfumed by bog myrtle bushes at night and bounded by an ancient bank, the Bishop of Winchester's Dyke, known to us as the Bishop of Winchester's Bottom. South of the dyke lay Woodfidley, full of old oaks, holly, beeches and fritillaries on its sunny rides: an outback like the wildwood of *Wind in the Willows*, to be respected in the dark. To the west of it were the shady depths of Denny Wood. On the other side of the railway, through Botrychium Bridge (named after the moonwort that grew on the bank near by) and Second Bog Outflow, was the mysterious Great Bog, where the snipe lay so close they could go off like landmines from under your boot. The bridge, christened after the ferns that grew on it, would have been Moonwort Bridge had it not been for our mentor's general preference for Linnaean accuracy over poetry. Ceterach Bridge, a couple of miles to the north in Matley Wood, was named after another fern, the rustyback, discovered and recorded in the Tomes in August 1958 by a schoolboy naturalist called George Peterken. Peterken's contribution is entitled 'Distribution of Ferns on the Railway Bridges' and records the 735 ferns of seven different species he found growing on or around the eleven bridges at Beaulieu Road that summer.

We also evolved our own vernacular for some of the Beaulieu plants and animals. The cream-striped caterpillars of the broom moth that lived on the bushes by our tents were always known as 'Bournemouth Belle caterpillars' after the brown and cream-liveried carriages of the famous train that used to steam through the cutting beside our camp each day.

Gradually over the years, from camp to camp, several generations of sixth formers wrote a detailed account of the Natural History of Beaulieu Road, including a flora listing 353 species of flowering plants, over 100 mosses, 21 liverworts and George Peterken's 735 ferns. We would arrive by train from Waterloo laden with camping kit, field guides, nets and collecting jars at a station that was little more than a halt in the wild centre of the forest. Campers would generally number anything between ten and twenty, and each of us worked in a particular field of study, setting off each morning to explore the territory, often lugging about with us our hefty copies of Clapham, Tutin and Warburg's *Flora of the British Isles*. Learned papers were written and presented over the campfire or in the bar of the Beaulieu Road Hotel, finds passed round for inspection and the day's discoveries written up for the Tomes. Some were important enough for wider publication. A rare type of cuckoo flower was found by B. Fitzgerald growing in Shatterford Bottom, close to the railway line. It had no sexual organs, no stamens and no carpels, only petals, so could multiply by vegetative reproduction alone. The schoolboy botanist's drawing of the plant and its sterile flower was eventually published in the journals of the Hampshire Naturalists, and of the Botanical Society of the British Isles.

We soon picked up the standard techniques of ecological survey-ing, casting foot-square frames about on the heath or woodland floor at random and noting the variety and numbers of species within them. During the mapping of First Bog in September 1960, we waded or squelched about for days on end counting plants, flinging round our transect frames like abstract land artists. Barry Goater was unfailing in his insistence that close observation, often involving hours of patient counting and recording, was the founda-tion of all good science and truly original discovery. He himself was insatiably curious about everything, climbing trees to inspect birds' nests, getting up at daybreak to check the tilley-lamp moth trap or leading night patrols across the heather armed with torches and nets to sweep it for moths and caterpillars. Much of the work was physically demanding, and Barry, who ran for Shaftesbury Harriers and had been the RAF half-mile champion during his national service, seemed to have endless energy.

Some of our projects, as logged in the Tomes, read almost like Swift's accounts of the scientists' experiments on Laputa in *Gulliver's Travels*: 'He had been eight years upon a project for extracting sun-beams out of cucumbers, which were to be put into vials hermetically sealed, and let out to warm the air in raw inclement summers.' We peered down a microscope and identified the seven species of mite parasitic in a blackbird's nest, conducted a census of the local leeches and patiently analysed the plant communities of pony-dung. One famous Beaulieu research project sparked itself off when somebody idly broke open several seedpods of the needle whin, *Genista anglica*, growing on Dyke Heath, and discovered the seeds being devoured by a weevil hidden inside. A specimen was hurried off to R. T. Thompson, the weevil specialist at the Natural History Museum, where it was identified as *Apion genistae*. The mystery was that the infested pods all looked perfectly developed from the outside and showed no sign of perforation. How the weevils had got inside was a mystery. A big needle whin pod-counting operation began, and, out of the 1,668 pods we boy detectives doggedly opened, well over half had been attacked by the weevil. About a fifth of the infested seedpods also contained the larvae of a small chalcid wasp, *Spintherus leguminium*, parasitic on the hapless weevils. The seed was devoured by the weevil, and the weevil by the wasp: the pods were like Russian dolls.

Another of our Laputian experiments centred on the pony corrals across the road from the little outback station and the remote Beaulieu Road Hotel, where we used to buy our supplies of gourmet food: beans, bread, bacon, eggs, tomatoes and Mars bars. Three times a year, in late summer and autumn, the tough little wild ponies and their foals were rounded up from all over the New Forest by the commoners and driven into the corrals at Beaulieu to be auctioned. The pony sales take place in August, September and October. For the rest of the year, the wooden-railed corrals and the auctioneer's podium at the centre stand deserted.

In April one year Stephen Waters, the camp's resident expert on mosses and liverworts, discovered large quantities of mousetail, *Myosurus minimus*, the smallest member of the buttercup family, growing in the corrals. It is a scarce plant and an exciting find anywhere, but for some reason it was thriving here and nowhere else in the forest, not even immediately beyond the pens. By September the same year there was not a trace of it, yet in the spring of the following year it was back again in the same profusion.

We got down on our hands and knees in every one of the fifty-six corrals and recorded the numbers of each plant species we found by repeating the process over the course of the year, and gradually we boy detectives uncovered the life story of *Myosurus minimus*.

The secret, we found, lay in the heavy trampling and manuring of the ground during the pony sales. Mousetail is an annual, setting the seed in early summer. It was later trodden in by the ponies at the sales, and germinated the following spring. The trampling of the ground destroyed the other competing plants without burying the *Myosurus* seeds too deeply, and the plant seemed to thrive in the copious manure, as did we as we warmed to our quest. The wetter and more flooded the corrals, the better the mousetail liked it. Where it occurred, it was in almost pure patches on otherwise bare ground. Here was a plant that had discovered its perfect niche. Here too was a wonderfully accidental lesson in the ways of ecology: a perfect wedding between the tiniest of the buttercup family, an ancient custom of the New Forest commoners and the wild ponies.

Tucked away in the botanical Tomes is another account of a survey of the algae of Beaulieu by my friend Ian Baker and me in which we took samples in phials from 47 different watery locations and laboured over microscopes to identify 17 different genera of algae. We would both have been sixteen at the time. In that same August week, under 'Other interesting records', is one of the many footnotes about our day-to-day encounters: 'A young nightjar was found by R. Deakin among the heather in a stony place opposite the campsite on the east side of the railway. About half grown, it was extremely well camouflaged.' The well-oiled, liquid churring of these oddly moth-like birds was a continuous background to our summer evenings and nights in the camp, like taxis waiting with engines ticking over. They were never far away and sometimes flitted before us on the paths through the heather at dusk. We lay in our tents on beds of heather and bracken, listening to curlews at dusk and tawny owls calling across Woodfidley all night. Sometimes we even ventured into it at dusk to watch the bats. We awoke to the song of woodlarks. In December of that year a psychopathic great grey shrike arrived and terrorized all the other birds, and a flock of forty pied wagtails 'whitened the road' near the station. The Tomes note that the shrike, our English butcher bird, had 'white underpants'.

Magnificent raft spiders, *Dolomedes fimbriatus*, lived in 'great numbers' in Second Bog, and we observed how they would sub-merge, when alarmed by us, clasping little air-bubble diving bells like bright pearls for as much as twenty minutes at a time. We timed their dives with nerdish precision. The sight of a schoolboy, intent on the second hand of his H. Samuel 'Everite' watch, was an obvious challenge. Under a bridge there, ten-spined sticklebacks hovered in the golden peaty water. We kept a pair in an aquarium in our laboratory and saw with what loving care they built their nest of twigs. Out with Barry Goater watching tiny flies struggling in the clutches of the science-fiction sundew plants on Dyke Heath, we also clocked two new birds to add to the ninety species already listed in the log: a pair of hobbies, the male perched on a stump, and a spotted flycatcher.

On the morning of 14 September 1956, a boy called John Rose, out wandering in Gentian Valley, saw the first adder at Beaulieu Road. We often saw grass snakes, particularly in the alder woods along the Matley Stream or on the railway embankment when we went to fetch water from the spring, but the Tomes only list adders as 'occasional'. Common lizards scuttled about everywhere in the dunes of gravel-diggings by the camp and on the heaths. Slow-worms, on the other hand, are recorded as 'rarely seen'.

The relatively low snake count, at least in the adder department, came as something of a surprise after all the stories of 'Brusher' Mills, the legendary New Forest snake-catcher of the late nineteenth century, who lived in the woods in a charcoal-burner's turf-roofed lean-to of sticks and drank in the old Railway Inn at Brockenhurst. There were photographs of him in there in his pudding-bowl hat, bearded, with a forked stick, the tool of his trade, dangling a snake by its tail, standing proudly before the entrance of his bothy. He was an object of some fascination to us. We noticed he wore tall boots, at least two leather waistcoats under his jacket and sturdy corduroys, possibly several pairs. He was said to have caught many thousands of live snakes in his lifetime and put most of them on the London train to the Zoo, where they were fed to the birds of prey. There were also local rumours of a roaring trade in homoeopathic unguents, somehow based on essence of adder. There were times when we wondered if old Brusher might, perhaps, have caught *all* the snakes in the New Forest.

Two days into my first camp, on 26 April 1959, we heard the first cuckoo and entered it in the Tomes. Under the strong influence of Robert Frost, I was moved to write a beginner's poem about it, later published in the school magazine, a lament for the ousted fledglings, 'Who'll never fidget, squeak or yawn / Beneath the breast that is your pawn'. I remember feeling whining poetry was somehow subversive of the objective, scientific approach Goater encouraged us to adopt. Yet he himself was always so full of enthusiasm and passion for nature he could never hide his own strong emotional attachment to Beaulieu Road and its natural history. Later more of my Beaulieu scribblings appeared in the magazine, a Wordsworthian effort occasioned by my first encounter with a marsh gentian in the eponymous valley. Not one of us was immune to the poetry of the place. One boy, Greystoke, who had only ever stayed in luxury hotels before, took to camping with all the zeal of the new convert and never missed an opportunity to rediscover his inner backwoodsman at Beaulieu. It was only much later that I realized the whole point about Beaulieu was that in teaching me to make connections, it was revealing the intimate kinship of ecology and poetry.

A comma lands on my pencil-jar and flexes its wings in the morning sun. Butterflies keep drifting in and out at the open door. They fly right through the study and out into the deeper green of the mulberry tree on the other side of the house. Four thousand mulberry leaves, green windows to the filtered sun, pale green and lovely. A big blue anax dragonfly hangs vertically from a twig. Dead still, it must be sleeping, although it can never close the 25,000 eyes in the clear bubble of its head. A tetchy squirrel squawks and rasps in the hedge on the other side of the moat. I reach for a pencil and start a list: things that have changed around here. Things there are more of. Things there are less of. Two columns. Things there are more of. Women speed-walking alone along the common. Dog-walkers. Dogs, on or off leads. The electric whine of strimmers at weekends, even Sundays. Four-wheel-drives. Orange security lights drowning out the stars.

Things there are less of. Stars. Walking for its own sake. Lapwings on the common. Skylarks on the common. Snipe drumming in springtime. Cuckoo flowers. Old boys or girls on bicycles. Allotments. Goats. Geese in the yard. Farm sales. Hedges. Signal boxes. Glowworms along the railway.

Now and again you discover the perfect pen and carry it everywhere until one day you lose it. But nothing is so universally dependable, or comes so naturally to hand as a pencil. What could be simpler? For much of my life, I have lived with one behind my ear: either to mark out saw cuts or mortices for carpentry or to scribble marginalia or underlines when reading. I often write with a pencil. It suits my tentative nature. It allows me literally to sketch out ideas before proceeding to the greater definition of ink. It was the first tool I used to write or to draw, and still suggests the close relationship between the two activities. I know I shall never outgrow pencils. They are my first, most natural means of expression on paper. It is comforting and liberating to know that you can always rub out what is pencilled. It is the other end of the spectrum from carving in stone. The pencil whispers across the page and is never dogmatic.

For all the same reasons, I like a soft pencil better than a hard one. It is gentler on the paper, as a soft voice is easier on the ear. Its low definition draws in the reader's eye, which must sometimes peer through the graphite mist of a smudge where the page of an old notebook has been thumbed. Rub your finger long enough on a soft-pencilled phrase and it will evaporate into a pale-grey cloud. In this way, pencil is close to watercolour painting.

A pencil is an intimate, elemental conjunction of graphite and wood, like a grey-marrowed bone. The graphite is mined from deep inside a Cumbrian hillside in Borrowdale, eight miles south of Keswick. Fired in a kiln to 1,000°C to make the slender pencil cores, ranging in hardness from H to 9H and in softness from B to 9B, it is laid in a groove in one of the split halves of the wooden casing which are then glued together invisibly, clasping the lead tightly. But examine the cross-section of grain at one end, and you will notice it runs two different ways. In Tasmania there are trees they call pencil pines, but only because of the way they look. The fine-grained, slow-grown mother of all pencils is incense cedar from the forests of Oregon, where a single tree may grow 140 feet high, with a trunk five feet across, enough cedar wood to make 150,000 pencils. It is the incense cedar that infuses pencils with the nutty aroma I remember as I opened my pencil-box. In a scooped-out hollow in my Oregon pine work table in front of me lies a smooth, round pebble from the Hebrides. It sits snugly in the wood, like the pencil between finger and thumb, and like the hidden vein of graphite, poised inside the cedar to spin itself into words like gossamer from the spider.

A fragment of the Newland oak stands on the windowsill before my desk. I rescued it out of a cowpat in the meadow at Spout Farm in the Forest of Dean where the great tree, forty-four feet eight inches in girth, stood until it fell in a storm one night in May 1955. Weighing just two and a half ounces, my relic is roughly triangular and measures three and a quarter inches on two sides by an inch and a half thick. It is shaped like the figurehead on the prow of a ship, with the streaming, full head of hair such a goddess or ancient Celtic queen would proudly wear. It always seems feminine to me and has a powerful presence. Sometimes I decide it is Diana in full cry with her hounds at her heels, racing after the quarry, her graceful arm drawing the bow, golden tresses blowing in the slipstream. The flowing lines I see as hair are the complicated, liquid, playful contours of the grain. What I have here is part of the surface of the trunk, however tiny by comparison with the immense full hide of the tree. I have stood in its ruins and do not doubt the measurement, or Alan Mitchell's estimate that it was 750 years old when it fell. Now it is no more than a stubborn atoll of dead wood, a nuisance to the farmer, a nest of nettles, a rubbing post for cattle, assailed by the elements, an extinct volcano sinking into the grass.

The grain of my figurine is intricately wrinkled, full of little waves like the kinks in my mother's hair where the Kirby grips pinned it. The surface is polished perfectly smooth where the cattle have rubbed against it, and crazed or minutely fissured where the sun has dried or shrunk it. It is lighter in colour than a chestnut and a little darker than a donkey but with the same dun-brown softness. Yet tannin and iron salts have reacted together over time to harden the wood into something approaching rock: the inside surface has the look and feel of it, and is even still raw from being broken off. Turning the piece over in my hand, I notice for the first time that two flecks of cow dung still cling to the wood, and there's even a single gleaming splint of straw no longer than an ant embedded in the grain, like quartz or a hint of gold. Towards the base, the wood is of a darker hue, with a microscopic bird's-eye pattern you might expect to find on the veneer of a harpsichord. But the uneven surface of the whole – its sutures, pingoes, potholes and tiny tumuli – throws a hundred miniature shadows across it. The longer I gaze at it, the more interesting this toenail clipping of a giant becomes. It is an exquisite thing in shape and texture and in the infinite complexity and refinement of its grain.

On the web outside my window this morning, sixty concentric threads, just strong enough to catch a fly and entangle it. The morning sun catches the silk and backlights each thread in burning white. A spider's web follows the same pattern as a tree-trunk. Each concentric ring represents a patient circuit by the engineer, and the radial threads represent the medullary rays of wood, along which a trunk will sometimes split as it dries.

Three weeks ago by night, I steered a sailing boat out of the Solent and into the Beaulieu, following the narrow channel by lining up certain houses and trees on shore with the port and starboard posts and lights that stood eerily out of the high tide. We moored up at Buckler's Hard for the night. Sitting on deck, listening to the curlews, I resolved to return to the New Forest, the source of the Beaulieu and of my own understanding of nature. In the pine top of my work table, the dark knots are boulders standing up in the river of grain, sending eddies and ripples spinning downstream, delivering the driftwood thought of a new journey to be taken, through trees.

PART TWO

Sapwood

The Bluebell Picnic

I drive south across the county to the valley of the Stour on the borders of Essex where my friend Ronald Blythe lives in the old farmhouse he inherited from his friends John and Christine Nash. He has invited me to join him and a group of friends at their bluebell picnic. Each year, on the last Sunday in April, they gather in Tiger Wood, a mile or two up the valley, to raise teacups and glasses to spring, as announced by bluebells.

Few people think of Suffolk as rolling country, but here I am, floating along a ridge high above the Stour Valley, turning off the road and diving along Ronald's familiar bumpy track down a green tunnel of hazel in the deep holloway that follows the contours of a hill to the farmhouse, first down, then up and round past a sprinting rabbit or two, then down again and around one final twist to arrive beneath a row of oaks by an old boarded garage-cum-garden-shed that hasn't actually housed a motor car for decades. The doors, twin compasses on their sinking hinges, have etched a pair of arcs in the ground, where layers of autumn leaves, ploughed in by earthworms, have raised it to meet them over the years. The undulating holloway, which has itself sunk through the steady erosion of cartwheels and hooves up to fifteen feet beneath the hillside, translates you from the present into an earlier era when

John Nash carved out his woodcuts in English boxwood at the kitchen table under a single lamp-bulb and cultivated the half-wild garden. Like his friend Cedric Morris further down the valley, Nash called himself an artist plantsman, and both men put the creation of their gardens on a par with their art. The tall horsetails Nash liked so much waltz up the track to greet me: chimney brushes on gartered stems. In the deep shade of the arching hazels on the track, I have a brief premonition of bluebells and the pink blush of red campions.

A brick path wanders through the garden to the front door, past Japanese knotweed and gunnera, an English jungle John Nash introduced around the margins to spice up the poplar, oak and hazel. Nash's stagecraft was to float little glades of lawn here and there among the long grass, rose beds, old orchard trees and wild trees, so garden and woodland are all one. The inspiring sound of water trickles through the open door: the springs in the hillside, which also supply the house, send a little stream running under a path and splashing past a ferny brick wall that leans precariously like the tangled crack willows on the way down to the horse pond where Nash would sometimes bathe.

Ronald is always busy about the garden, scything, filling a barrow with plums, pegging out washing on a line between orchard trees. He has taken on the mantle of the artist plantsman from Nash. A couple of years ago, he was the only other man I knew in Suffolk without central heating, until his friends at last persuaded him to relent. But a stack of oak logs, neatly split by his maul, still fills a recess to one side of the hearth, and there's always a winter fire. He has just had his study painted out in white and is working downstairs at his typewriter on John Nash's paints table.

In Tiger Wood we are welcomed by Veronica and Rosemary, the sisters who look after what is now a nature reserve of some thirty-four acres. The wood itself covers about twelve acres, and takes its name from the sabre-toothed tiger whose curved canine was unearthed there like a murder weapon some years ago. Our hostesses' mother, Dr Grace Griffiths, cared for the consumptives at a sanatorium on the hillside founded by Elizabeth Garrett Anderson. She was the local GP, liked and respected by everyone, and her six children were Ronnie's childhood friends. He thinks she probably delivered him into the world. She could never remember names, he says, so in every household people were 'mother' or 'father', and the children were all 'dear ones'. But Dr Grace knew all the names of the flowers and birds and taught them to Ronald and his friends. She also became deeply attached to the woods, retreating into them to escape the pressures of the sanatorium on the hill. Eventually, she began buying the woods and the surrounding meadows bit by bit as a way of preserving them in their wild state, and had an elegant wooden shed from Boulton & Paul's joinery in Norwich erected next door to the brickmaker's cottage where Veronica and Rosemary now come to stay. It is still there, painted green, with a cool cream interior.

Rosemary, who is a considerable botanist, has just returned from North Carolina, where one of her sisters lives in a self-built cabin in woods of giant dogwood, all in full spring blossom. We join a dozen of Rosemary and Veronica's old friends, mostly botanists from Cambridge, round the picnic rugs on the brick-cottage lawn looking down into the intense mauve-blue haze of bluebells in the wood. Rosemary says they thrive here because the bracken is always being beaten down by the many badgers that emerge after dark from two different setts in the wood. The browsing and grazing of deer, muntjac and rabbits also help to keep the woodland floor open.

In the upper wood, Rosemary leads us down narrow paths through the dense blue seabed to a 500-year-old oak, pronounced dead by Oliver Rackham [the renowned biological historian] after a prolonged drought two years earlier. However, a new spring has just appeared a few dozen yards away, and Rosemary thinks it likely the tree died simply because its water supply had moved in the London clay beneath the valley. The clay suits the unusual Tiger Wood variety of pale-pink dead nettle, and there are stinging nettles and small-leaved limes the sisters have planted at Dr Rackham's suggestion. Higher up the sides of the valley the ground changes to sandy gravel; the entire wood was once a medieval warren. Further along the path, the giant trunk of an oak lies where it was felled in 1936, now grooved and furrowed by time like the flank of a blue whale. A timber merchant was let loose in the wood by the Assington Estate that year to take whatever he wanted, and left the debris where it still lies.

Since then the wood has recovered and reshaped itself through a succession of crises spanning the lives of Dr Grace's daughters. Each of the trees we encounter has its own story to tell. An unexpected horse chestnut among the oak and hazel is the 'myxomatosis tree', because it dates from 1953, the year the plague really struck, so the sudden absence of rabbits allowed the sapling to thrive. The cherry plum creeping away from just outside the cottage garden grew from some delicious fruit whose stones ended up in the compost and sprouted from wherever it was spread. A greengage and a pair of walnuts have all been planted by Dr Grace, but 'too close to the house', says Rosemary. Walnuts grow canopies thirty feet across or more, so need plenty of space. The abandoned trunks and limbs of oak all date from 1936, the year the timber merchant felled them. The drought year 1975 was when the elms succumbed to disease and began to die, and a good many of the 'victims' of the 1987 storm now thrive as horizontal trees like candelabra. Now the elms have suckered up from their wandering roots in circular thickets where the nightingales sing. Blackthorns and sallows have been left alone to grow into groves of graceful, sinuous trunks: trees in their own right, no longer to be insulted as 'scrub'. 'We could be walking in the eighteenth century,' says Ronald, who thinks the bluebells 'jazzy, in a way': too blue and intense for his taste. He and Rosemary remember how, in less botanically correct times, people regarded it as almost a duty to pick as many as you could. I remember the trail of trodden, slippery stalks that used to litter the paths back to suburban Watford through Cassiobury Park from the wild Whippendell Woods each spring.

How does a moth experience the swooning scent of so many

bluebells? In the soft light of the wood they glow like phosphor-escent waters, casting a misty blue penumbra like the moon's at a change in the weather. It blurs the blue meniscus lapping at the trees, obscuring the ground, floating them. Geoffrey Grigson thinks that the loveliness of the bluebell is not so much an individual beauty but the striking impression of many plants growing together, splashing a big area with their own uniform colour. Poppies can also be spectacular in this way. During the 1880s so many people crowded on to trains from London to see the hotly blushing hill-tops above the cliffs from Cromer to Overstrand that the resort was successfully promoted as 'Poppyland'. Snowdrops, wood anem-ones, primroses, foxgloves and ramsons can all infuse woods with colour through sheer force of numbers. Yet the individual flower of the bluebell has a special pre-Raphaelite beauty, hanging upside down from the stem, bending it into a shepherd's crook.

What he calls the 'countlessness' of bluebells never fails to delight Gerard Manley Hopkins. Alone in Powder Hill Wood near Oxford on 4 May 1866, he writes in his journal: 'I reckon the spring is at least a fortnight later than last year for on Shakespeare's birthday, April 21, it being the tercentenary, Ilbert [a fellow undergraduate at Balliol] crowned the bust of Shakespeare with bluebells and put it in his window, and they are not plentiful yet.' Hopkins is always trying to define the special essence of the bluebell's beauty. In a little wood near Balliol College, he observes that 'they came in falls of sky-colour washing the brows and slacks of the land with vein-blue.' Perhaps, for him, they bring the heavens to earth. A journal entry for 18 May 1870 reads:

One day when the bluebells were in bloom I wrote the following. I do not think I have ever seen anything more beautiful than the bluebell I have been looking at. I know the beauty of our Lord by it. It[s inscape] is [mixed of] strength and grace, like an ash [tree]. The head is strongly drawn over [backwards] and arched down like a cutwater [drawing itself back from the line of the keel].

Hopkins continues, almost as though he is patiently dissecting the flowers, noticing the 'cockled petal-ends', the 'square splay' of the mouth and the 'square-in-rounding turns of the petals', whose jauntiness always reminds me of a jester's cap. The comparison with the ash, whose strength and supple grace preoccupy Hopkins, is interesting. He seems attracted to flowers and trees that hang their heads, as Christ hangs his head on the cross in medieval paintings: catkins, ash keys, bluebells. They all arch down 'like a cutwater'. Elsewhere in the journal, he sees the 'overhung necks' of bluebells 'like the waves riding through a whip that is being smacked' and concludes 'they have an air of the knights at chess.'

Although the taxonomists have rechristened the plant *Hyacinthoides*, I still prefer the old name we grew up calling it: *Endymion non-scriptus*. The shepherd Endymion, son of Zeus and the nymph Calyce, was lying asleep in a cave on Mount Latmus one night when Selene, the moon, first saw him, fell in love with him and kissed his closed eyes. He is said to have fathered fifty of Selene's daughters and returned to the cave, where he fell into a dreamless sleep, never growing old but preserving his youth for ever. These are the bones of the story, as retold by Robert Graves. Keats, writing to his young sister Fanny from Oxford in 1817, where he was working on his poem *Endymion*, tells it like this:

Perhaps you would like to know what I am writing about – I will tell you – Many Years ago there was a young handsome Shepherd who fed his flocks on a Mountain's Side called Latmus – he was a very contemplative sort of a Person and lived solit[a]ry among the trees and Plains little thinking – that such a beautiful Creature as the Moon was growing mad in Love with him – However so it was; and when he was asleep on the Grass, she used to come down from heaven and admire him excessively from a long time; and at last could not refrain from car[r]ying him away in her arms to the top of that high Mountain Latmus while he was a dreaming . . .

The dreamy lake of bluebells in Tiger Wood, some still in bud, like the snake's heads Hopkins saw, and the hanging mist of their scent plausibly suggest the eternal sleep of Endymion. And each arched shepherd's crook of a flower stem certainly belongs to him.

Quite why so many woodland plants are poisonous is an interesting question, but the bluebell is one of them. The sleep of Endymion is for ever. As a wood engraver, John Nash's botanical triumph is the celebrated *Poisonous Plants, Deadly, Dangerous and Suspect*, published in 1927. In a review of an edition of Nash woodcuts in *Hortus* in 1988, Ronald Blythe writes:

His garden was always plentifully supplied with henbane, hemlock, monk's hood, foxglove, meadow saffron, spurge laurel, datura, caper spurge, herb Paris, Helleborus foetidus and other such species which he had often been found staring at, much as one might at a murderer. He was proud, not only of their robust growth, but of their capabilities, and I have often watched him cast a wary eye over the gaunt reaches of the henbane. Gardens were not entirely benign places to him; they contained their darker moments.

Ronald and I had walked through Tiger Wood in the snow the winter before. The day was brilliant, the trees sparkling and frilled with frost. A white line of snow was pencilled up the north-east side of each tree. John Nash loved woods, particularly in winter, when their architecture is revealed. The lines of the nude trees are so much stronger. The bones of the landscape stand out. He loved the ruins of woods: dead trees fallen over one another, fungi and brittle twigs. He hated woods to be tidied, and the fashion for management that rubbed out all evidence of past inhabitants, all natural continuity of living denizens. As a war artist in the First World War, he painted the shattered woods on the battlefields of France. They came to stand for the dead and maimed of both sides. Some of the action took place in or around woods, which afforded cover for troops or tanks, until they were blown to pieces. Their skeletons might be the only landmarks left on the trenched and cratered waste land. Nash writes of 'the trees torn to shreds, often reeking with poison gas'. He went out to France as a member of the Artists' Rifles, taking only a copy of George Borrow's *The Bible in Spain*. In the winter of 1917 he found himself in the front line at Marcoing near Cambrai, and on 30 December was ordered to advance from the front-line trenches across open ground with eighty fellow soldiers. Nash returned with just eleven of his comrades and painted *Over the Top* to commemorate the experience. Bayonets mounted, the men clamber out of a trench and advance into a mist across a bleak expanse of snow. Some already lie dead; some have even been thrown back into the trench. Trees, snapped off by shells, their limbs amputated, appear in most of Nash's war paintings, and woods often provide their titles: *Oppy Wood, 1917, Evening*, for example.

The trenches consumed vast quantities of wood, since they had to be floored and connected with miles of duckboarding over the mud and water, and often reinforced with wooden stakes to prevent a collapse of their walls. And the stretchers, thousands of them, were of canvas between a pair of ash spars with turned handles. In his great war poem *In Parenthesis*, a first-hand evocation of life and death on the Western Front in prose and verse, David Jones writes of the 'muffled hammerings of wood on wood' he heard continuously as trenches up ahead were dug and timbered, and wood piling driven in. Jones was an infantryman in the London Welsh Battalion of the Royal Welch Fusiliers on the Western Front in the winter of 1915/16. Part 4 of the long poem contains the dramatic account of the death and wounding of the poet's comrades and enemies in close combat in Biez Copse. Those who planned the campaigns were so deeply divorced from any sense of nature or history that the French woods were all given codes. Like John Nash, Jones, who was himself an artist as well as a poet and Catholic scholar, often describes war in terms of wounded nature and the disfiguring of trees and woods:

Very slowly the dissipating mist reveals saturate green-grey flats, and dark up-jutting things; and pollard boles by more than timely wood-craftsman's cunning pruning dockt, – these weeping willows shorn.

And the limber-wheel, whose fractured spokes search upward vainly for the rent-off mortised rim.

In David Jones's poem, as in the paintings of John Nash, the ravaging of nature, the dishonouring of woods, comes to represent the unnatural perversity of the war. The limber-wheel's broken spokes detached from their mortised rim suggests Hamlet's 'The time is out of joint, O cursèd spite / That ever I was born to set it right.'

Shakespeare is ever-present in the undertones of the poem. Both artists are acutely aware that the woods being desecrated are one with the forest of Arden, or the ancient mythology of Sir James Frazer's *The Golden Bough*. They are the province of Oberon and Titania. 'No one, I suppose, however much not given to association, could see infantry in tin hats with ground-sheets over their shoulders, with sharpened pine-stakes in their hands, and not recall ". . . or we may cram, / Within this wooden O . . ."' writes Jones in his preface. Later he describes an old timber barn where the soldiers were given lectures on the very wet days, 'with its great roof, sprung, unpreaching, humane, and redolent of a vanished order'. The woods represent human culture as well as wild nature. And the 'woodsman's cunning pruning', one of the staples of rural life, has also fallen victim to the barbarity of war. The flowers, trees and birds are the only vestiges of anything familiar left in the waste land of the trenches, and they themselves are as vulnerable as the soldiers:

And now the gradient runs more flatly toward the separate scared saplings, where they make fringe for the interior thicket and you take notice.

There between the thinning uprights at the margin straggle tangled oak and flayed sheeny beech-bole, and fragile birch whose silvery queenery is draggled and ungraced and June shoots lopt and fresh stalks bled runs the Jerry trench. And cork-screw stapled trip-wire to snare among the briars and iron warp with bramble weft with meadow-sweet and lady-smock for a fair camouflage.

The perversion of traditional greenwood values by the war, and the natural kinship between human beings and woods, between sap and blood, pruning and amputation, are constant themes throughout *In Parenthesis*. The irony is that in this strange land, he is in two woods at once. The old, self-renewing, playful, benign greenwood with its unicorns and may queens has given way to a vision of hell: a dying and deadly wood, an ambush, abandoned by its animals and birds, its magic suppressed.

The keepers in this wood set their traps for men, driving out unicorns as well as birds and foxes. War drives out poetry from the woods, its natural habitat, and Jones, as steeped in Shakespeare and the classical world of myth as Keats, laments 'the pity of it'. He knows that woods were always places of sacrifice and ritual death as well as merry-making, freedom and romance.

As Ronald and I walked through Tiger Wood that winter's day, following a stream along the valley, he spoke of the woods as havens for intimacy in the past. All country children, he said, were conceived in woods, because the cottages were simply too full of other people. Children, grandparents and others lived hugger-mugger in the cramped rooms, so couples adjourned to the woods for privacy. David Jones is intensely aware of the irony that his war-racked woods in France once stood for continuity and pro-creation: 'To groves always men come both to their joys and their undoing. Come lightfoot and heart's-ease and school-free; walk on a leafy holiday with kindred and kind; come perplexedly with first loves – to tread the tangle frustrated, striking – bruising the green.'

We walked over the dormant bluebells of Tiger Wood that winter, flicking at the snow with sticks selected from a sheaf Ronald keeps near his door. His was a bird's-claw stave of blackthorn that had belonged to John Nash, topped by a palm-smoothed egg of hard, dark wood clutched by a scaly foot. Mine was a thumb-stick of hazel, originally carved and owned by John Masefield. As a means to boost morale and keep the soldiers under his command from losing their wits as they sat in the trenches, he taught them to cut coppice sticks from the woods and whittle them into walking sticks. Masefield had given this stick to his Oxford friend Dr 'Bird' Partridge, who eventually handed it on to Ronald Blythe. Asked by Robert Frost why he had enlisted to fight in the war, Edward Thomas famously scooped up a handful of English soil and offered it as his reply. Perhaps the hazel wand I held, carved by a soldier-poet who had survived the war, would have been part of *his* answer, a green baton to pass on.

The Rookery

At dusk I crossed a hilltop Essex meadow towards the swelling
tump of a wood, Slough Grove. The General, who used to live in
Little Horkesley Hall down in the valley, always pronounced it
'Slow Grove', with two rounded 'o's. There's a spring and a damp,
ferny place in the middle halfway down the hill, so perhaps that's
the slough. Venus shone from above the trees in an inky-blue sky,
and the wood was a black castle, its roundness echoing the greater
roundness of the hill itself.

The last of the rooks had hoisted home and settled in their dark
constellation of nests to roost. They raised a chorus of alarm and
flew up as I approached, scattering into the sky as if I had a gun,
then circled off downhill to the lower part of the wood, slipping
sideways to lose height. No stars yet, only Venus, and a fragment
of a vapour trail from a jet leaving Stansted forty miles away.
Strange how beautiful such sky-litter can be. I entered the wood
through a farm gate that clanked, went downhill along a ride, then
turned left on another that traversed the hillside. In the softening
dusk, the wide wood floor glowed with bluebells, the kind of
pensive blue Les Murray invokes when he says, 'Shade makes
colours loom and be thoughtful.'

I wanted a front-row seat at the rookery and headed towards the very tallest of the slender ashes reaching up to top the canopy. It is a mixed bluebell wood of hazel, ash, sweet chestnut, oak and cherry, with a good deal of elder in its under-storey, and interesting things like wild redcurrants. The elms that once dominated the top of the hill and would have housed the rookery are beginning to grow back. Rooks always seem to favour elms, provided they are tall enough. Some of the other trees, mostly cherries, lean at odd angles, monuments to past storms. These are called widow-makers by lumberjacks because of the explosive energy in the sprung trunk, coiled to kick back and fling the saw in your face or just knock you flat. Beyond an old hunched sweet chestnut, I came to a glade directly beneath a group of nests and pitched the bivouac pup tent facing east on to the ride. Pink campions and tousled goosegrass rose on either side, camouflaging it nicely. Nettles were splashed white. I turned in early and lay on my back in my sleeping bag with my head out of the tent, studying the noisy neighbours upstairs. Gilbert White writes of a little girl he knew who, as she was going to bed, with the rooks chorusing outside the village, used to remark that they were saying their prayers. The parent birds had all returned from their foraging and sat about the nests with their young, now almost fledged. Every now and again, as if blown by a gust of wind, they would all take off and flap about above the wood, cawing loudly, then settle back one by one.

At ten o'clock it was dark and they still hadn't settled down, but their treetop conversation was more spasmodic, their cries more tentative: an odd sort of lullaby for a solitary camper. Then, nest by nest, they fell silent, until all I heard was the shaking out of wing feathers or the click of preening bills. The night was so still, and sound carried so clearly in the humidity of the wood, that I could even hear the fledglings as they shifted position in the nest. I wriggled about in my own nest, drawing up the sleeping bag to lie face to face with the stars, head and shoulders out of the tent in the warm May night.

Twilight, the gradual softening of the day into darkness, is surely the gentlest, most natural way to prepare for sleep. And yet it is a pleasure we deny ourselves with the switch on the bedside lamp. Even the guttering of a candle or the afterglow of a paraffin lantern is less abrupt. A couple of generations ago most country people went to bed when it was dark, at least in summertime. And so we miss the time of darkling shades in which our pupils can dilate by slow degrees and dreams drift in as, wide-eyed, we enter the rook-black night.

Trevor, Vicky and their children Thea and Luke, who own and care for this wood, said they often encounter badgers and foxes, muntjac and roe-deer in it. Whenever I see a muntjac, with its neat brown coat and apparently docked tail, my first thought is always that I am seeing someone's stray dog. I lay half expecting to see one skipping innocently along, taking the occasional nibble at a plant-top, sampling the wood. Unfortunately, they have a preference for hazel, as roe-deer do, and can prevent the regeneration of coppice hazel by nibbling the young shoots. All grazing animals have their own favourite leaves, and others they find distasteful. Oak is not generally much liked because it is full of tannin. Holly and ivy are popular, and fallow deer enjoy ash. Most deer, according to Oliver Rackham, hate aspen and chestnut, and all love elm and hawthorn. The special food fad of muntjac, he says, is to eat the flowers of oxlips.

The sky can seem very pale in summer once you've grown accustomed to the darkness. I could make out the silhouettes of trees, but the rooks and their nests melted into the general blackness. In the wood, complete silence but for the occasional minor rustling further off. Starlight filtered down, strained through the black leaves. Then I heard a tawny owl enter and traverse the wood calling to other, more distant owls, which called back. Even the cuckoo was singing in the dark for a while. As I began to drift in and out of sleep, drugged by bluebells, I felt doubly submerged, a long way beneath the surface on the sea floor of the wood. Once I was woken with a jolt by a sudden mad commotion in the rookery caused, I suppose, by a bad bird dream: a pouncing fox in the skull of a rook that sent a wave of alarm through the canopy. Some rooks took flight and circled briefly in the dark before they settled back. Do birds fly in their sleep? I heard the whisper of wood-pigeon wings as a pair slipped away into the darkness.

Hours later, while the sun was still in the horizon, I drifted back into consciousness to the most raucous of dawn choruses. It was still only ten past four. Rooks are early risers, but not as early as crows, which are often already on the wing above my meadows in the hour before dawn. From my rabbit's perspective I was aware that in the birdsong, as in the physical zoning of the wood, there was an under-storey. The sweetness of robins and chiffchaffs descanted subtly from hazel or elder beneath the harsh, relentless chorus of the rooks in the ash-tops. Blackbirds arrowed silently through the shadows. Mist swam into the deep green of my glade through the waving seaweed of nettles, goosegrass, pink campion, bluebells, grasses and ferns. In the foreground, burdock, ground ivy, self-heal and bugle. Further off, layers of vapour hung in the new shoots of the hazel coppice. In Suffolk, when a misty wood like this is called 'rooky', as in Macbeth's 'the rooky wood', it has nothing to do with rooks. I turned and lay on my back, sliding myself like a caddis grub out of the mouth of my tent to gaze up the skirts of the wood, following the long, smooth limbs of ash to their golden tops where the rooks' nests are. They say rooks nest high like this when the summer will be fine. Young rooks will always return and try to nest in the parent rookery, but may have to settle for nest sites on an outlying tree somewhere on the margins. Settling my head back into the mossy pillow, I exulted in the luxury of waking in a rookery in full cry.

By the time I swam into full consciousness, most of the young rooks were out of their nests, perched among the topmost twigs. They basked in the first rays of the sun that turned the green to gold around them, their black feathers gleaming blue, green, purple and bronze, and absorbing the warmth. No doubt the blackness of rooks, crows and ravens has always made them suspect to country people. Occasionally, white rooks have been recorded. Gilbert White mentions a pair near Selborne, stupidly killed by a carter and nailed to the end of a barn, their legs and beaks as white as their feathers. Writing about John Bunyan and his native parish of Elstow, near Bedford, my friend Ronald Blythe discovered another mention of white rooks in some parish records. In 1625, when the author of *Pilgrim's Progress* would have been a child of three, the vicar of a neighbouring parish mentions some other member of the family: 'one Bunyan of Elstow, climbing of rooks' nests in the Berry Wood, found three rooks in a nest, all as white as milk, not a black feather in them.'

Rooks build their untidy-looking nests of twigs in a series of strata on top of the previous year's structure, as storks do. (Look at any archaeological dig in, say, the City of London, and you'll realize we do just the same.) They choose live, pliable twigs and must weave them well to stand up to the winter storms, lining the nest with leaves, grass, even some clay, hair or wool. With twigs, as with food, rooks are prone to envy, and not above stealing from one another, as people do from building sites. After five or six years of layering, the structure grows top-heavy and may at last tumble down in a gale, a useful find for a cottager in need of dry kindling. I counted eighteen nests in the clump of ashes above me, but I know an oak tree near where I live with over thirty nests in it.

The parent birds soared off in sallies of flight accompanied by crescendos of cawing, returning with breakfast for the fledglings, who expressed their satisfaction in half-choked high-pitched mewling. Each time they landed, the rooks fanned their tails in greeting: gesture is an important part of their language. A good deal of the rooks' circling, gliding flight seemed to be nothing other than joyful orisons with no apparent destination in the fields. In February I had watched them here, flinging themselves into a strong wind and somersaulting wildly upward, then diving straight down again towards the wood like bungee jumpers, checking their swoop just in time with a tilt of a wing to glide far away across the valley towards the church on the far hill. Rooks like to fly high, and sometimes, when they arrive directly over the rookery at a great height, they will fold one wing flat against their body and execute a breathtaking perpendicular dive so fast it is audible, twisting at the last moment to land in the tree. This is called 'shooting the rook'. Gazing straight up through the fish-bone ash leaves, I watched the alteration of layers and shades of green turning to gold where the sun caught them. Studying an ash tree on 24 July 1866, Gerard Manley Hopkins writes in his journal of 'a bright blind of leaves drawing and condensing the light' and observes earlier that year in May how the 'pale window-like green' of beech leaves is 'spotted with soft darks by the now and then overlapping of the leaves'. He sees leaves as the windows of the wood, filtering sunlight to a green shade, their ribs the leading of stained-glass windows. Elsewhere, he again writes of 'the green windows of cabbages in the sun'.

As the sun came up over the hilltop meadow and shone through the wood, it began to catch the nettle-tops standing sentinel around the glade in flashes of dewy silver, outlining the saw blade of every translucent leaf. It even illuminated the tracery of veins in the wings of the crane-flies before my tent. The misty sun, rising fast now, broke through an oak in the hazel grove and set the lichened ash-trunks on fire. By now the more melodic music of the other birds had found its rhythm and built into full flow: the soft cooing of wood-pigeons, the lyrical blackcaps and lesser whitethroats, the piping of robins and wrens, chiffchaffs and the confident glissando of the chaffinches.

The more they flew, the more noise the rooks made. Whether you can call it melody is the question I lay pondering. Gilbert White goes so far as to say 'rooks, in the breeding season attempt sometimes, in the gaiety of their hearts, to sing, but with no great success.' Most of the old bird-books attempt some version of 'rude harmony', 'sweet thunder' or 'musical discord', but I prefer to think of their utterances as conversation, or the roughest of folksong. Rooks speak in the strongest of country burrs. They are rasping, leathery, parched, raucous, hoarse, strangled, deep-throated, brawling, plaintive, never reticent and, like all good yokels, incomprehensible. No doubt you could play a dead rook like a bagpipe, all drone and no melody. If you found yourself across the fields from a

Somerset pub late at night at cider-pressing time, you might hear something like a rookery.

There is no doubt that rooks rapidly communicate new locations of discovered food to one another. The alternative, or complement, to the language hypothesis is that other rooks simply observe their well-fed fellows and follow them out to the new feeding grounds. A well-filled restaurant is always popular. It is quite possible to learn Rook as you would learn French, or your own language as a baby, just by listening and watching. If I hear the alarm call of a blackbird or moorhen in my garden, I understand it perfectly. Rooks are highly intelligent birds and can soon learn to recognize individual humans. Living as a tribe benefits them through the greater vigilance of the group's many eyes and ears against predators, but it must also increase their efficiency as foragers.

One of the books that inspired me as a boy was Konrad Lorenz's *King Solomon's Ring*. My favourite chapter, which I used to read over and over again, describes how, beginning in 1927, he raised a whole colony of free-flying jackdaws at his home at Altenberg in Austria, with the object of studying their social and family behaviour. By the time the book was published, I already had a tame crow of my own, so I felt a strong allegiance to Lorenz's work. Jackdaws, the cousins of rooks, also live socially, are highly intelligent and communicate with each other in remarkable ways. Unlike most other birds, jackdaw young have no innate fear of their predators, so each generation must inform the next about what is to be feared. They do this by means of a harsh, aggressive alarm call Lorenz calls 'rattling'. Lorenz also observed that jackdaws form lifelong attachments, as rooks seem to do, and that there is a distinct, well-understood pecking order within the tribe to which all the members adhere without question. Lorenz gradually learnt the Jackdaw vocabulary: 'Zick, Zick' is uttered by the courting male to mean 'Let's nest together' and, once in possession of an actual mate and nest, 'Keep out'. Any act of social delinquency is immediately censured by the other tribe members with a variation of this call, expressed by Lorenz as 'Yip, Yip'. Most interesting of all is

Lorenz's discovery of the subtle distinction between 'Kia' and 'Kiaw'. The first is the cry uttered in flight by the dominant jackdaws to urge the whole flock outward to new feeding grounds. The second is to urge them home. Thus, 'Kiaw' plays a vital role in maintaining the integrity of the flock when one meets another.

Most birds seem to keep their song quite separate from their language. The staccato alarm cry of a wren or blackbird is quite distinct from its sweet song. Jackdaws, however, incorporate their words into their songs to create, as Lorenz puts it, something more like a ballad, in which they can re-create past adventures or directly express emotions. Not only this, but the singer accompanies the different cries with the corresponding gestures, quivering or threatening like the lustiest performer passionately enacting a song. In a way, the jackdaw is mimicking itself, as a solitary jackdaw kept in a cage will come to mimic human speech, but it may also, Lorenz thinks, be expressing emotion. When a marten broke into the roosting aviary at Altenberg and killed all but one of his jackdaw flock, the lone survivor sat all day on the weathervane and sang. The dominant theme of her song, repeated over and over, was 'Kiaw', 'Come back, oh, come back'. It was a song of heartbreak.

Intruding on the privacy of rooks from a small tent on the wood floor was never meant to be at all scientific, but it was plain to me that the birds have quite as rich a language as Konrad Lorenz's jackdaws. From where I lay, I sometimes heard a private, muted, muttering note, uttered into the depths of the nest behind net curtains, strictly for the ears of the family. Also pitched in a lowered voice was a kind of squeaking that sounded like contentment. The rooks didn't seem to mind my presence at all. It even occurred to me that having roosted a whole night under the same ash-leaf roof, I had somehow been accepted into their company by some ancient law of hospitality. Rooks are, after all, the most sociable of birds and seem to like to build their nests close to people's houses.

I have also noticed more and more rookeries close to roads; apparently the more congested the better. Driving together up the A1 to the Lake District earlier in the spring, Richard Mabey and

I began noticing rookeries on roundabouts planted with oaks or hybrid poplars thirty years ago. Even after we turned off at Scotch Corner on to the undulating A66 to Penrith, the rooks still showed a marked preference for nesting by the roadside, ignoring the splendid giant sycamores that command the limestone hills. We whiled away the long car journey speculating on the reasons why. Richard observed that rooks like to range over a wide area, flying in straight lines. Could a major road, he wondered, help them with their bearings? I suggested that road verges are a scavenger's delight, with discarded sandwiches and early-morning roadkill. Or was there some more subtle attraction such as the combined warmth of sun-soaking tarmac and combustion engines? In the end, we decided the simple sociability of the rook towards our species might just as well be the cause.

Any rookery confers a special atmosphere on a place, but rooks have always been controversial. Even today, there are those who persist in the belief that rooks are an enemy. At one of our local Suffolk rookeries at Homersfield on the River Waveney, the farmer still enters the copse each spring and shoots into the nests from below to kill the fledglings. This would have been unpopular among our villagers in the past, not out of any sentiment for the rooks, but because they partly depended on them for food. Rook pie was one of the staple dishes of cottagers everywhere, and very nearly the equal of pigeon pie. Like rabbits and pigeons, rooks were part of the unofficial commonage of the parish.

The early-nineteenth-century naturalist and pioneer conservationist Charles Waterton was the rooks' first great champion. In one of his two essays on rooks, he tells how he had once been anxious to divert a troublesome footpath on his estate. The local farmers said they would agree to this on condition Waterton destroyed a large rookery in one of his estate woods. The villagers, however, protested that the proposed destruction would deprive them of their annual supply of about 2,000 young rooks. Waterton seems to have stood by his rooks, and the villagers. One of his essays is about the rook's bill, and the origin of the characteristic bald patch at its base, the popular belief at the time being that the birds rubbed off the feathers by digging in their search for worms and grubs. By observing the development of young rooks, Waterton shows that the baldness is purely natural and unconnected with their feeding habits.

Waterton did most of his birdwatching from inside trees, living the life of a tree-climber very like Cosimo in Italo Calvino's *The Baron in the Trees*, who vows at the age of twelve to live his entire life in the branches and never again to set foot on the ground. I have always preferred the succinct original title of the novel: *Barone Rampante*. Like Cosimo, Waterton was well born and squire of his own considerable estate at Walton Hall near Wakefield. He was also an English Catholic and therefore an outlaw. As is usual in our society for anyone who chooses to think and act for himself, Waterton was branded an eccentric until eventually rescued by Julia Blackburn in her marvellous biography. It was entirely through Julia Blackburn's love of Waterton that I was first introduced to him, and it was she who first guided me around his lovely wooded estate. It was full of thousands of ancient trees, which Waterton nurtured and protected, even retaining dead, hollow or rotten ones for the sake of the owls, jackdaws and woodpeckers. To protect this paradise on earth from poachers, he spent four years and £9,000 building a massive stone wall up to sixteen feet high and three miles long around Walton Park. Much of it remains, part ruined and covered in ivy and ragged robin: a snail heaven.

All his life, even into his eighties, Waterton followed the habits of his early life travelling and exploring in the forests of South America. He went barefoot about the park and climbed the trees barefoot, reclining for hours in the boughs of the old oaks, reading books or watching owls or foxes. Waterton stood six feet tall, all but half an inch, wore his silver hair in a brush cut, slept on a bare elm floor with a hollowed oak block for a pillow all his life and was double-jointed until his death. He often wore an archaic tailcoat like a nineteenth-century Sergeant Pepper. At the age of fifty-five, he writes of himself: 'I am quite free from all rheumatic pains; and am so supple in the joints that I can climb a tree with the utmost facility.' Thus he was able to write quite casually, in his essay 'The Rook': 'Last spring I paid a visit, once a day, to a carrion crow's nest on the top of a fir tree. In the course of the morning in which she laid her fifth egg, I took all the eggs out of the nest, and in their place I put two rook's eggs, which were within six days of being hatched. The carrion crow attended on the stranger eggs, just as though they had been her own, and she raised the young of them with parental care.' He then abducted the fledgling rooks and had his incredulous gamekeeper befriend and tame them in a similar project to that of Konrad Lorenz with the jackdaws a hundred years later. Unfortunately, the rooks were all so tame they met untimely ends, including one that was drowned by an aggressive chicken. Waterton's defence of the rooks is that for ten months of the year they eat nothing but insects, especially wireworms and leather-jackets, to the great benefit of the farmer. For just two months they eat his grain too, at seed-time or harvest, or during a hard frost, but Waterton points out that these are low wages for the farmer to pay for their work in the organic pest-control department during the great majority of the year.

Waterton befriended all the members of the crow tribe, as well as all the hawks. He called his neighbour Sir Thomas Pilkington a scoundrel when he showed him the fresh corpse of the last raven in Yorkshire, and he protected the much persecuted magpie with greater care than any other bird 'on account of its having nobody to stand up for it'. The popular hatred of magpies was and still is more probably fear, based in the many folk beliefs about their occult powers over our fortunes. Charles Waterton calls the magpie 'the English bird of paradise' and made his astonished keeper encourage and protect the birds. Waterton proudly records magpies as other landowners logged pheasants: 34 nests at Walton Hall one season, and 238 birds successfully reared. 'I love in my heart to see a magpie,' he writes, 'for it always puts me in mind of the tropics. There is such a rich glow of colour, and such a metallic splendour of plumage in this bird, that one would almost be apt to imagine it had found its way here from the blazing latitudes of the south.' His observations of jackdaws led him to anticipate Konrad Lorenz in the conclusion that they mate for life. He thinks the loveliness of the blue, the black and the white in the bastard wing and greater covert feathers of the jay unsurpassed anywhere in the world. 'Nothing can possibly be conceived more charming. No other known bird in the creation possesses such a rich exhibition of colouring . . .' This is high praise from the naturalist who wrote *Wanderings in South America.*

Watching rooks strutting about my meadows among the mole-hills, I often think how like people they are. And in autumn and on winter evenings, I watch amazing numbers of them rowing through the heavens high and straight above my house to congregate noisily in the woods along the Waveney between Wortham Ling and Redgrave Fen. This is a parliament of rooks, several thousand of them, and it has been in session every year as long as anyone round here can remember. The notion that the voluble birds may be engaged in some sort of discourse is natural enough in view of the manifest intelligence of the entire crow tribe. My first encounter with the most distinguished corvid in the history of cinema came one snowy afternoon in the exciting Paris of 1968. I sat with a friend for hours keeping warm in the Cinémathèque watching Pier Paolo Pasolini's *Uccellacci e Uccellini* (literally: *Big Birds and Little Birds*), made two years earlier in 1966. It is a most engaging film and was Pasolini's own personal favourite: a surreal, picaresque tale of a father and son taking to the road across Italy from Rome. They are played by the veteran Italian comic actor Totò, and Ninetto Davoli, and are soon joined by a talking crow: a left-wing intellectual crow who poses moral and political questions, delivers ponderous diatribes about Italian politics and society, and tells the story of the medieval brothers Ciccillo and Ninetto, sent by St Francis to preach God's message of love to the hawks and the sparrows. The crow transposes the pair of pilgrims into the Middle Ages, turning them into the two Franciscans, complete with sackcloth. After long efforts, the brothers somehow learn the language of birds and preach universal love, first to the sparrows and then to the hawks. It makes no difference: the hawks just carry on killing the sparrows, and eventually, driven mad by the moralizing crow, the brothers unceremoniously kill and eat it. If it sounds an odd story, that's exactly what it is. Pasolini called it an 'ideo-comedy'. My friend Gilbert and I watched it over and over again, trying to make sense of it, only to realize that the whole point was the very banality of the fable. The film was an elaborate, comic shrug to the old questions about the meaning of life. Feeling that I had a claim to a special relationship with the crows, I was deeply impressed, and the memory of this odd road movie and the slushy snow outside the Cinémathèque on the way home has stayed with me.

As I rolled up the bivouac tent and my sleeping bag in the rookery, nine-year-old Luke came down the path through the wood to join me. We walked back up the hill to the house for breakfast along a woodland path white-lined by the splash of rook shit on nettle leaves. He asked me what was my favourite feather. I said the small blue wing feather of a jay. His was a sparrowhawk's he had found in the wood.

The Moth Wood

The others were already there as I approached the shadow island of the grove in the dusk. Out in the meadow near the wood's edge, in a little pool of pure white light, four men and a girl knelt in the grass around an outspread white sheet and a powerful mercury vapour lamp. In their intense concentration on the little arena inside the halo of light, there was the unmistakable air of theatre. Clearly, they were at their devotions before some blinding vision, some deity. Closer up, as my eyes adjusted to the brilliance, I perceived that the dazzling aura was filled with the fluttering of a dozen or more moths, most of them small, with insubstantial papery wings. I took my place in the circle quietly, and we introduced ourselves.

I had been invited back to the wood where I camped under the rookery at Little Horkesley to join a small party from the Essex Moth Group, including its chairman, Joe Firmin, for a night's moth-hunting. My friend Trevor Thorogood was there with his daughter Kiri, whose keen naturalist's eye was to impress us all that night. Joe is something of a legend in the moth world: an elder of the tribe who, in Essex parlance, tested positive for *respect*. His friends Ian and Philip constantly consulted him on the finer points of identification. Perhaps, in unconscious imitation of the moths, all three appeared vaguely camouflaged and sported the floppy cotton hats I associate with the jungle.

I should explain that moths are now generally hunted humanely: gone are the days when they were etherized upon a table or transfixed with pins. Instead, their names are entered in a kind of visitors' book, and they are gently sent on their way.

Stacked around the foot of the stem of the mercury lamp was a jumble of egg boxes, forming a miniature cave system into whose shadows the moths crept once they had flown in towards the white light and circled it a few times. Moths are attracted to the blue end of the light spectrum just as bees and butterflies like buddleia and other blue plants. The ultraviolet blue light from the mercury lamp attracts but also dazzles the moths, so they seek out the shelter of the shadowy papier-mâché egg-tray hollows and come to rest.

Joe said nobody understands quite why moths are drawn to the light. Migrating moths seem to navigate by the moon and stars. There have been theories that the wings nearest the darkness beat faster, while those closest to the light react to it by slowing down, with the contradictory result that the moth slews off course and wheels in curving flight towards the light. But the truth is that nobody knows. Moths, in any case, live in a world of smells, as wild mammals do. It is smells that draw them to the female, or to the flower. They have eyes and can see, but sight is less important. They also have tympanal organs, sensitive to sound, situated on the thorax or abdomen. The moth 'hears' vibrations.

It was a warm night, and the lamp's brightness had the effect of blackening the night around us. Moths were emerging in a steady stream from the wood, and, as they approached the trap, Joe, Ian or Philip could often identify them on the wing. We were all intent on them and alert for the slightest movement coming out of the darkness. It was like angling, and the total concentration on the fishing float: the way everything else just lifts away and you are left with a kind of meditation.

Over the summer, I had found myself growing more and more fascinated by the moths I encountered in woods, or flying in through my study window or door at night. Their names alone, as Joe and his colleagues added them to their growing list, were a kind of poetry: the willow beauty, the dingy footman, the clouded silver, the flame shoulder, the smoky angle shades, the dew moth. The moth we most desired that night was the white-spotted pinion, *Cosmia diffinis*. It emerges from the pupa from late July to mid September, and its larva feeds on elm leaves. Since Slough Grove is rich in resurrected elms, there was good reason to hope for the moth. A few days earlier the Essex Moth Group had set traps in the not-so-distant Chalkeney Wood and caught no fewer than eight white-spotted pinions, now scarce because of the effects of Dutch elm disease. If the white-spotted didn't deign to appear, we would gladly have settled for the lesser-spotted pinion.

Neither moth showed up, but there was no lack of excitement to punctuate the calm of the evening. Every now and again an onlooker from the shadows would have seen our little circle erupt into activity. A net might be waved about in the darkness, or some innocent new winged visitor pounced upon and imprisoned for a short while in a small Perspex pillbox in which it could be minutely examined and identified. Positive ID often involved a good deal of discussion, and reference to two key books by the lamplight. 'Let's see what the Bible has to say about this,' Joe would say as they all peered at a tricky specimen in the jar, or 'Goater should settle this one for us.' The sudden reference to Goater alerted me to take a closer look at one of the books, *British Pyralid Moths*. It was by Barry Goater, a teacher I hadn't seen for years. The other was *The Colour Identification Guide to the Moths of the British Isles* by Bernard Skinner. 'Barry Goater taught me botany at school, and most of the natural history I know,' I said. The Essex Moth Group were visibly impressed.

Barry Goater was by far the greatest influence and inspiration to me in my passion for all things natural. People say everyone should be lucky enough to encounter a great teacher just once in their lives, and that is just what he was. To my shame, I had lost touch with him, but had been thinking that I must somehow make efforts to contact him, not least because I wanted to return to the New Forest. Who better as a companion than my original mentor, a native of the Forest himself? Joe promised to send me his address.

The first moth to fly in after I arrived was a sturdy little creature with dark-brown striated forewings. It settled on the sheet, quivering all over the way moths do, and Philip said 'uncertain'. Joe wrote a note in his book, and I assumed they weren't sure what it was, until they explained this actually was its name: the uncertain, a member of the *Noctuidae*, like its relation, the anomalous. I asked Joe which moth he dreamt of seeing one fine night, and he chose the alchymist, a woodland denizen that feeds on oak and elm. Only fifteen have ever been recorded in Britain, including a solitary Essex sighting down the road in Colchester on 9 June 1875. He also mentioned a butterfly, the elusive white letter hairstreak, whose food plant is elm. He kept hoping it would turn up where the trees are regenerating, as in woods like Slough Grove. Joe had a list of the two to three hundred species we might reasonably hope to encounter at this time of year in Essex. On an average night's moth-hunting in the summer, he would expect to see as many as eighty or a hundred of them. But some of his hunting grounds were particularly rich. At Stour Wood on the Wrabness shore of the Stour Estuary, an old chestnut and oak wood, Joe said he and others had captured 260 species in a single night in June.

Just then there was a sudden flurry of arrivals: a common wainscot, several green carpets, a straw underwing, and two or three scorched carpets, which would most likely have been feeding as caterpillars on the spindle trees in the wood. The maple prominent that came in next would likewise have been feeding on the maple coppice. Kiri nimbly captured the moths, one at a time, in the little Perspex pillbox. Many moths are christened only in Latin, but the lovely vernacular names, Joe said, date from the seventeenth century: one species that flocked to our trap that night was the relatively common setaceous hebrew character, so named to denote the hieroglyphic on its forewing. 'Setaceous' is simply one of those specialist words used in the trade to mean 'bristly', just as 'lunate' means crescent-shaped and 'ocellate' means eye-like. The late, bearded lepidopterist Baron Charles de Worms was always known affectionately to his friends by the same name as the moth. As our nocturnal callers arrived, the lepidopterists announced them like major-domos at a ball: 'Large yellow underwing, iron prominent, lesser cream wave, brimstone moth, lime-speck pug.'

There is always rivalry between the various county moth groups. Ian told the story of a recent joint field meeting of the Essex and Suffolk moth societies on opposite banks of the River Stour, which forms the county boundary. A magnificent convolvulus hawk moth was spotted by the Suffolk lepidopterists gliding in downriver along their bank. At the last minute it changed its mind, crossed the water and, to a great cheer from the Essex party, landed on the sheet beneath their lamp.

We kept hoping for a hawk moth: privet and poplar hawk moths were both still flying, but none appeared. Some moths, once they have emerged from the pupa, will fly for as long as a month, but most live only a few days, or even a day, their brief lives dedicated to marriage and procreation. I reflected on the minutes ticking by as the moths languished in the shadowy honeycomb of the egg boxes: an hour of our time might be ten years of theirs. Death is never far away for them. No wonder the Greeks called moths by the same name as the soul: *psyche*. It is also the name of one of the most eminent journals of lepidoptery. One of the many aspects of moths and butterflies that fascinated Vladimir Nabokov, as famous for his entomology as his writing, was the 'immemorial link' between overcoming gravity and transcending death. The earthbound caterpillar coffins itself in the chrysalis where it lies all winter, apparently lifeless, then emerges into the heavens as a moth and flies into the night.

Bats, out hunting moths with deadlier intentions than ours, swerved about above the trees, swooping over us. Some species of moth can actually hear the radar squeak of the bat and instantly close their wings in flight, dropping to the ground like stones. Down on hands and knees admiring the subtlety of the moths that sat quivering in their beauty like nervous ballerinas, or marched and sprang about on impulse, unhinged by the sudden glare, I began to realize what a rich field of study they present: over 1,600 species of the larger British moths, and over 200 species of the smaller pyralids. Moths are the small print of natural history, something you come to in good time. They are essentially private beings, more mysterious than butterflies. I love the trustful way a moth will cling to my hand or walk about on it. A friend who used to spend her summers in a little whitewashed stone goat house in the Dordogne remembers how the moths and crickets used to enter it at night and arrange themselves about the wall 'like brooches'. Details of the anatomy can be spectacular in their sculptural intricacy: the male drinker, a summer moth of woodland rides which at first looks like a teddy bear with a handlebar moustache, wears its antennae branched into delicate combs, like the cow-catchers on old American steam locomotives.

Moths are exquisite in their symmetry, all the more so because so many of them are miniatures, perfect in every detail and far finer than any human art. Seen under a microscope, the wing markings are composed of tiny scales, which appear as powder on your fingers if you try to grasp a moth by the wing. Often moths will lightly touch you as you sleep by an open window. Imprison one in your cupped hand, and you will feel its defiant energy as it struggles to escape. Moths wear the colours of lichens, of the bark of trees or of leaves, painting themselves to the point of invisibility. In *The Unquiet Grave*, Cyril Connolly wonders, 'Why do soles and turbots borrow the colours and even the contours of the sea bottom? Out of self-protection? No, out of self-disgust.' This can't be true of moths, whose lives are predicated on desire. So intimate is the moth's relationship with the tree, feeding on it as a caterpillar, living on it and hiding in it, that its coloration is a badge of loyalty. The pale-green small emerald melts unobtrusively into the leaves and flowers of the traveller's joy it frequents on hedgerows and along the edge of woods. The september thorn could be an autumn leaf.

The stirrings of moth-passion I felt that night were in truth a reawakening: I have to confess to having been a boy lepidopterist of the old school. I was a raw hunter-gatherer, with a killing bottle and a setting board. From the age of nine or ten I never went anywhere without my butterfly net. It was no bamboo-and-curtain-net affair but a serious professional model with collapsible aluminium frame. At some point I hit on the bright idea of pinning my entire collection of moths and butterflies on my boarded bedroom ceiling. I could lie in bed and gaze up into the clouds of trophies. But the real living things knocked spots off my fading collection: the way the moths seemed to come up like bubbles at dusk as the colour drowned out of the flower beds in our back garden and the night-scented phlox or buddleia began to glow with pale wings. My mother was a great gardener, creating with her endless harmonies of flowers a giant, benign moth-trap and a butterfly Eden in which I flapped my net about like a lepidopteron myself. I have always thought of the moths and butterflies as a bonus to the flowers, as though Nature were admiring her own work. The royal visit of a hummingbird hawk moth passing from rose to rose heightens and makes memorable everything in the garden. It is entirely logical to pass from gardening or botanizing to a study of butterflies and moths. All caterpillars have close relationships with particular food plants, as every gardener knows. The wings of moths have the delicacy of petals, and their antennae are as slender as stamens. And in their mimicry of other insects, some moths are almost obsessive about the detail. Bee hawk moths have acquired transparent wings and, unlike the other hawk moths, fly by day alongside the bumble-bees they pretend to be. The insect is both artist and trickster. 'The mysteries of mimicry had a special attraction for me,' writes Vladimir Nabokov. 'When a certain moth resembled a certain wasp in shape and colour, it also walked and moved its antennae in a waspish, unmothlike way.' Nabokov observes how often the moth's protective devices are 'carried to a point of mimetic subtlety far in excess of the predator's power of appreciation'. He sees in moth mimicry a form of magic, 'a game of intricate enchantment and deception', and concludes, 'I discovered in nature the non-utilitarian delights that I sought in art.'

In the very first line of *Lolita*, 'Lolita, light of my life', Humbert Humbert mimics the moth in the intensity of its desire for the light. There is the symmetry of the moth's wings in Humbert's name, in the beginning and ending of the novel with the name of Lolita, and even in such playful details as the name of another character, Avis Byrd, *avis* meaning 'bird' in Latin. Such details are the stuff of Lolita, and of Nabokov the trickster. It was perhaps partly this love of detail that led him to lepidoptery in the first place, and would eventually result in his spending six years as semiofficial curator of Lepidoptera at the Harvard Museum of Comparative Zoology, often working fourteen hours a day.

Nabokov became as famous as a lepidopterist as he already was as a writer. 'Few things have I known in the way of emotion or appetite, ambition or achievement that could surpass in richness and strength the excitement of entomological exploration,' he writes in his autobiography *Speak, Memory*. His mother and father shared and encouraged his interest, and he relates how he would return home late to their Russian country house after a successful moth-hunt shouting triumphantly about his catches to his father through the open lighted windows: '*Catocala adultera!*' Nabokov was able to summon all his potency as a writer to express his refined, intimate appreciation of moths like no one else. He describes the handsome black larva of a hummingbird hawk moth as 'resembling a diminutive cobra when it puffed out its ocellated front segments'. 'My pleasures', he writes, 'are the most intense known to man: writing and butterfly hunting.' By the age of six he was already leafing avidly through his parents' butterfly and moth books. Wandering the woods alone aged twelve, searching for moths, he longed to be the first to discover a species new to science and would allow his imagination to savour the reports: '. . . the only specimen known of *Eupithecia petropolitanata* was taken by a Russian schoolboy . . .'

Thirty years later Nabokov was to succeed. On 7 June 1941, en route by car from New York to Stanford, he found a butterfly he recognized as new and named it *Neonympha dorothea* in honour of the student who happened to be driving the author and his wife at the time. Again, in 1943, at the alpine lodge of his American publisher, James Laughlin, above Sandy, Utah, he captured a moth now known as *Eupithecia nabokovi*. Butterflies, moths, naturalists and lepidopterists not only wove through much of his literary work but inspired it. Nabokov was well aware of the absurdity of the public image of the lepidopterist wielding a butterfly net, but nobody has succeeded like him in evoking the ethereal magic of moths and butterflies.

A little snout moth paraded up and down before us on the sheet, skipping into flight now and then. The night was cooling, and dew was beginning to fall. A barn owl cried out in the wood and was answered by some muttering among the rooks. A clouded border fluttered in, then another moth with pale underwings and forewings shaded in tawny contours, two copies of the same map. 'Isn't this a dark spinach, Joe?' asked Philip. Joe peered at it closely and pronounced that it was, only an unusually dark shade. All moths have a tendency to vary their shades, and the subtle gradations of the dark spinach illustrated in one of Joe's colour reference books enchanted me in their sheer artistry. From a delicate pale green to dark, the species can vary from one place to another. Hot weather can trigger the minor mutations that control these colour changes. Melanism is sometimes the result, as in the famous case of the peppered moth, *Biston betularia*, whose melanistic form, the black peppered moth, evolved during the Industrial Revolution from the original white-with-dark-brown-peppering to the all-black form known, somewhat like the spaghetti dish, as *carbonaria* in the blackened industrial regions of northern England, where it still forms the total population. 'Not a bad moth, the dark spinach,' said Phil, half to himself, as he released the creature and it ran for cover in the labyrinths of the egg-box system. We sat quietly in our circle watching it like a movement on a Ouija board. After a while Ian seemed to come out of a reverie. 'Not bad at all,' he sighed. The dark spinach had made quite an impression. 'We haven't had another footman,' said Philip. It was getting late. At 11.30 p.m. a green carpet landed on Kiri's leg, followed by a spectacle, identified by Philip: 'If we get two of these we'll have what we call a pair of specs.' 'There's a red twin-spot carpet floating about here somewhere,' Ian remarked absently as he took up the net and hunted about on his own in the gloomy hinterland outside our halo. Joe was telling Trevor about Dewick's plusia, a rare Essex speciality named after Bob Dewick of Bradwell-on-Sea, a member of the Essex Moth Group who maintains the world's biggest moth-trap, built of brick, with a fan to suck the moths in. It is an immigrant, and only thirty-three specimens have ever been recorded in Britain. Kiri, meanwhile, had captured a light emerald in the pillbox, and we had been joined by a meadow grasshopper and a giant cranefly, the biggest of its tribe I have ever seen, with big patterned wings like clear church windows: the daddy of all daddy-long-legs. Joe pronounced the lesser cream wave, a late arrival, 'a bit worn' and computed that in the course of the evening we had been visited by forty-seven different species. It was nearly midnight, and the foxes were barking in the wood. We emptied the egg trays, tapping them to dislodge the moths clinging on inside and checking for any we might have missed. By now moths were all over us, in our hair, on our jackets, even walking all over their own pictures in the two Bibles lying open on the sheet. The lamp was dismantled and loaded with the nets into the back of a car I confidently identified as a Volvo Estate. Ian and Trevor gently shook out the sheet, and the last lingering moths fluttered off into the night. As our friends drove away, we caught a snippet of their conversation through the open window of the passing Volvo: 'Not a bad moth, the dark spinach, not bad at all.'

Living in the Woods

My friends rowed across the river from their island to meet me, and we unloaded the bundles of hazel from the open back of the truck. The shorter rods and the tools went into the boat, and Mike and Mana rowed them across. I had set out early from Suffolk and crossed the Thames at Walton Bridge by mid morning. The longer poles were twenty-five feet long, green and whippy, overhanging the back with a white handkerchief flapping in the slipstream. We floated them out into the river off a landing stage outside Walton Rowing Club. Lashing them together in a raft, we towed them sixty yards across the Thames to Tumbling Bay Island, leaning hard on the oars and heading well up into the current.

Tumbling Bay originated as an island swimming club in the nineteenth century. It is one of those little independent republics you find hidden away up and down the Thames, full of brightly painted hutments among the willows and pampas grass with their names tacked up on boards. Swimmers would come upriver in skiffs with tents for weekends or even holidays, cooking on a camp fire and living the life of *Three Men in a Boat*. The islanders always entered two rowing eights in the Walton Regatta, and its swimmers competed in races and galas up and down the Thames. There is still an annual Tumbling Bay Ball and Dinner in May, and a cricket match on the island in which it is traditional to lose the ball almost every time you hit it for six, or even for one. In last year's match the river claimed eight cricket balls. During the war, so many tents were pitched on the island that the Germans thought it must be a military camp and bombed it, killing two campers in their tents.

Over the years a towel and a picnic spread out on the bank, with perhaps a tent or two, had grown into a colony of picket-fenced demesnes dotted about the island. 'No Name', the yellow wooden shack on the plot my friends Mike and Mana had recently taken over, was built in 1898 and inhabited for years by Graham Eliot, a clerk who rode a bicycle to work at the bank in Twickenham every day until he retired. At eighty he married for the first time and continued living in the shack for two more years until his bride protested. Although its back room, the bedroom, is built on stilts, the shack still had an irritating habit of floating away during floods and had to be retrieved more than once.

My friends' idea was that when the river rose in winter spate, a bender would simply let the water flow through it, so long as it was stripped back to its skeleton in the autumn. It would also be a suitably diffident structure, blending with its wooded surroundings. Ideally, we would have got our bender wood locally, but none was available, so I had better admit that we cut the rods from my hedges in Suffolk, and from the rookery wood at Little Horkesley, and drove them over to Walton in the back of a truck.

We hauled the hazel from the river and began laying out the bundles in order of length. Then we strode about like geomancers, debating the most propitious site. Eventually we resolved on a spot near the river bank looking south, close to the landing stage to one side of the shack. A shout from over the water, and the first of the construction team had arrived. Mike rowed across to collect them and soon there were ten of us: far too many, but we made light work of it and enjoyed ourselves.

The dimensions of the structure decided themselves with a logic of their own, according to the length of the hazel poles. With the longest ones we began to create a basic frame. By laying out two poles on the ground and bending their tops together so they overlapped, we calculated that the width of the bender should be 200 inches, or 17 feet. Then we drove in holes with a steel stake and set the poles in them at opposite sides of the circle, wedging them firmly with offcuts of hazel. We had attached ropes to the tops, which we used to bend them down into an even curve and hold them fast while a third person lashed the top few feet together with sturdy garden twine. We had begun with a knot lesson, with me as scoutmaster, and everybody practising slip-knots, clove hitches and lashing. Of course, we should have made nettle rope, or used twisted bark of the small-leaved lime in the traditional Neolithic way, but we compromised with brown twine. We readjusted this first arch several times, standing back to look at it, or walking about underneath, until we were satisfied with the shape of the curve and its height. It became the template for the frame, and we raised a second arch to bisect it, lashing them together at the apex. It was eight feet high, giving plenty of headroom over a wide space inside. We now began bisecting the angles of our four-legged structure to give it eight legs and then sixteen, except that we left out the sixteenth pole to make a doorway and lashed a lintel in place crosswise above head height between the first and fifteenth pole. The idea was that the lintel, once reinforced, would eventually support a porch entrance to keep the interior well sheltered from the weather, along the same lines as an igloo.

We reinforced the skeleton with diagonals, choosing long, flexible poles and anchoring them in the ground, then weaving them in and out of the uprights and lashing some of the intersections. As we wove more and more horizontal or diagonal wands of hazel into our frame, treating it as an inverted basket, it became more and more rigid. We reached into the roof on stepladders, and it wasn't long before the frame would easily support our weight, hanging from the roof. There is a freshness and innocence about green coppice wood that inspired everyone to a kind of free-form building that would not have been possible with the straight lines of conventional building timber. There were no architectural drawings, and no carpenters' conventions to observe, so no inhibitions. We were making it up as we went along, as a tree seems to do. By the time we stopped work for a picnic lunch the bender was more or less complete, and we imagined various ways to make our bothy weatherproof. Canvas tenting or sailcloth would be the best, we thought, traditionally dyed red-brown in the tannin of oak bark, with insulating blankets underneath. The bender at this stage was at its most abstract. As an object of beauty it seemed an end in itself. It even seemed sad to cover it up, although it wouldn't last long if exposed to the elements. Kept dry and protected from the sun, the greenwood frame would last several years. At the end of its natural life, it would leave not a trace on the island.

The project had been sparked a few weeks before, when Mike and I had met by chance in a London restaurant. He and Mana had just taken over their plot on the island and wanted to put up a simple shelter that would withstand floods, blend into its surroundings and serve as an occasional summer house: an English dacha. A parliament of the islanders had decreed that their structures should be temporary, or 'low impact'. My friends dreamt of a bender, and wondered if I would help them build it. I agreed on the spot, and two weeks later Mike and I were off on a research trip to Somerset to meet the encamped woodland community at Tinker's Bubble, near Yeovil.

The name of the place arises from the spring in a glade at the bottom of a wooded hill. Streams fan out through the woods, then join up again lower down. Here we met the dozen woodlanders and four children who live as a cooperative in tented benders, growing organic food, milling their own timber from the woods, generating their own electricity and harnessing the hydraulic energy of the stream in a ram pump to raise their water uphill from the spring. Tinker's Bubble is a social and ecological experiment in a tradition that stretches back to Winstanley's Diggers at St George's Hill in Surrey in 1649. It is a self-sufficient community farm on forty acres of woodland, orchards, arable land and meadows originally purchased by the various shareholders in the project. When Tinker's

Bubble was founded in 1994, few imagined it would last more than a summer. It is hard not to hear an echo of the South Sea Bubble in its name. But, in spite of the difficulties it has faced, from the planners to the initial suspicion and hostility of the local villagers, it has survived. It has even secured five-year planning permission for a hamlet hidden in the woods on the strict conditions the residents had already set themselves: that there should be no more than twelve adult residents, and that the houses they build should tread so lightly on the land that, were they eventually to be dismantled, nobody would notice they had ever been there.

The first thing we saw when we arrived was the enormous vintage Britannia steam engine the community uses to drive a sawmill with a twenty-foot bench housed in a barn they have insulated for sound with dozens of mattresses in the roof and straw-bales for walls. Half the woodland was planted with Douglas fir and larch in 1960, so the milling of the harvested timber into planks and other building wood provides an important resource and a significant part of the group's annual income. They never fell any trees until there is a market or a clearly defined use for them. The shareholders of the group decided from the beginning that they would use neither internal combustion engines nor mains electricity. They run the steam engine on sawmill offcuts and the cherry laurel they are gradually clearing from the underwood. It must be well dried, however, because burning green laurel would release poisonous hydrogen cyanide from the prussic acid contained in the sap. The other component of their motive power is a shire horse called Samson, which hauls the logs out of the woods, pulls a cart and ploughs the land for the longstraw they grow for thatching.

We followed a path past the spring and stream uphill through the woods towards an aroma of woodsmoke and the communal roundhouse, thatched with home-grown longstraw over Douglas fir planking and other timbers from the mill. Here we met Simon Fairlie, leading light of the experiment from the beginning, eloquent veteran of the Twyford Down road protest, sometime Associate

Editor of the *Ecologist* and once a stonemason at Salisbury Cathedral. He is also a considerable expert on planning as a result of his experiences at Tinker's Bubble, and author of a well-respected book, *Low Impact Development*, setting out the case for a rethinking of our planning laws that might allow people to work independently on the land and live in houses whose effect on their surroundings would be so unobtrusive as to be negligible. Simon was deep in conference on planning questions that very afternoon, sitting round a central hearth with some of the other residents, one of whom, Michael Zair, invited us to tea in his bender home. Part of the policy at Tinker's Bubble is that, in addition to the communal space of the roundhouse, the kitchen, the orchard cider house, the washhouse and the various workshops, everyone has their own individual home.

Michael's bender, sited high among the trees, looked out downhill through a big window set in one end. We entered through a tented porch of canvas and stepped on to a wooden floor on two levels, emerging into a warm space some twenty feet long. A wood-stove welded from an old Calor-gas bottle sent thin smoke up a ribbed pipe that twisted out through a fireproof metal plate fixed into the tenting. A table stood before the window with books and papers on it. Bookshelves lined the bender walls of hazel, which were well insulated beneath the canvas with blankets. We sat on straw bales, and Michael explained the importance of the drainage system of scooped channels to divert rainwater away from each bender. I noticed the small moats that ran around the walls and realized that keeping dry, as well as warm, must be a major preoccupation among the bender dwellers.

Michael took us out visiting. We met Gary and Bonnie with their three young children in a domed bender beautifully warmed by a wood-stove. There was always a porch, a liminal space between outside and in, essential to conserve heat, and a floor of rugs and carpets. No two benders could ever be quite the same, and we encountered ingenuity everywhere. Mary was living in a perfect miniature geodesic dome of hazel rods joined at the intersections of the hexagons by starfish of copper plumbing pipe flattened at the centre and held together by a thumbscrew nut and bolt. Each hazel rod had been whittled to fit snugly inside its sleeve of copper. Becca's bender was domed and canvas-clad with a polythene roof-light, the canvas roped and pegged into the ground against the wind. It was walled at one end with cob, and it too was moated with little drainage channels. All the shelters made use of salvaged windows, and several were attached or guyed to trees. They were collages of different materials: ash and hazel coppice from the wood for ridge poles and framing, tarpaulins and rope from farm sales, windows and doors from salvage yards. Rope was clearly of the highest importance, wrapping the benders in tarpaulin like fragile parcels, secured to trees or wooden tent pegs. A yurt was under construction, and at a discreet distance in the wood stood a compost toilet. All the woodlanders were cheerfully tolerant of our intrusion, and of the fact that we had arrived incongruously by motor car.

It was sobering to encounter people living out their ecological politics without a hint of compromise. If they were fundamentalists, they were the most peaceful and liberal imaginable, and surely we should all be treating the fundamentals of our existence with equal seriousness. All they wanted was to live the woodland life as simply as possible, working hard and mostly doing without things they couldn't make or grow themselves, or which might be ecologically damaging. But far more important was their practical demon-stration that there is another way to live, on terms of greater intimacy with the woods and land – slower, more deliberate and benign: a quiet assertion of greenwood values.

The New Forest Revisited

Having lost touch since schooldays, I had written to Barry Goater from the farm of the Essex lepidopterists, by the wood at Little Horkesley. I had immediately received an invitation to come down and stay in the New Forest and revisit our old haunts around Beaulieu. Barry is now in his seventies and has retired from teaching to concentrate on his entomological work and his writing, living with his wife Jane in the house where he grew up on the edge of the New Forest in Chandler's Ford.

Barry reintroduced me to the Beaulieu Tomes, the record of our ecological labours. He now keeps them in his study, which is lined with the classic wooden entomology cabinets made by Hill & Company. Behind the glass-panelled doors are tiers of drawers full of mounted specimens of his beloved pyralid moths, and others. Barry brought out the two books, and we looked through them. Tome One chronicles our botanizing, and Tome Two records our zoological adventures. Each loose-leaf volume is bound in brown cardboard canvas-backed covers in an ingenious stationery contraption called 'The Loxonian Binder', in which two bootlaces passing through the holes in the lined paper are drawn tight and cleated under a pair of snail-shaped springs in the front, as though you were in a dinghy and had just gone about.

*

As Barry, Jane and I walked up the track across the heath to our old campsite, we passed Gentian Valley, and, reassuringly, the deep blue marsh gentians were still there, in flower, half hidden in the heather. But gorse had taken over the campsite hollow, so there was no clue it had ever been there. We crossed the wooden bridge over the railway cutting and turned downhill past the Scots pines on Black Down, following the path to the spring. It was still there and flowing well enough, but fenced off by the railway company and inaccessible.

As we headed towards the pony corrals, I asked Barry why we never seemed to find many adders in such an ideal habitat for them. He said all the snakes in the New Forest had declined, even grass snakes and the smooth snake, which was always rare, because people persecute them like wasps or hornets. We found the pony pens rebuilt in smart new wood and gravelled over. There was not a trace of *Myosurus minimus*. Down at Shatterford Bottom, on the other hand, the rare unsexed cuckoo flower colony was doing well, having apparently disappeared for years in the meantime when Railtrack built a fence there. A bit of it must have survived to bring it through the crisis and multiply.

When we reached First Bog, we lay flat on the wooden bridge and searched the peaty water for the aquatic lesser bladderwort, another of the local insectivorous plants. It was still there, and so was the bog myrtle. But at the next bridge, over Second Bog, the water looked black and oily where it had once been golden clear. The rare intermediate bladderwort had disappeared, and so had the splendid ten-spine sticklebacks. 'I love Hampshire and the New Forest,' said Barry, 'but I grieve for what is happening here.' Through mismanagement by the Forestry Commission, the forest upstream of the bog, and the bog itself, had been extensively drained and the streams dredged in an attempt to gain more grazing. This has caused the local extinction of the sticklebacks. Later, realizing their mistake, they dammed it and reflooded it, blocking the essential flow that had always kept the water clear and oxygenated. The raft spiders had also disappeared.

Our spirits rose again, however, when we discovered the native wild gladioli, still growing where the Tomes say they should, concealed under bracken near the Bishop's Dyke. Circling into Woodfidley, we made for an old oak stretching out impossibly long horizontal branches, surrounded by birches. In late spring we used to search its creviced bark for the caterpillars of the *merveille du jour* moth. And in August, Barry sometimes used to take the lepidopterists digging under the tree for the buried chrysalises of the moth. Over Crater Pond we saw an emperor dragonfly, and further on, among the old oaks and holly under-storey of Wood-fidley, we came upon an ancient stag-headed oak in a cloud of hornets, hoverflies and butterflies. Sap dribbled and cascaded from pencil-sized boreholes all over its trunk, darkening it with glistening syrup that was plainly irresistible to the insects. The tree was still living, but its massive old frame was clearly weakened, and it seemed to be slowly bleeding to death. It was like an elderly bull elephant being eaten by ants.

It seemed amazing that so much succulence could spring from such dry ground. I thought of the prostrate lion on the Tate & Lyle golden syrup tin, alive with bees, and the motto: 'Out of the strong came forth sweetness'. Close up, we watched dozens of tipsy hornets, red admirals, speckled woods, commas and peacocks staggering about the carcass of the old tree, sipping for all they were worth at this Happy Hour. This, explained Barry, was a goat moth tree, host to the big wood-boring larvae; these live in galleries inside the sapwood for four years before pupating and emerging as adult moths. Generations of goat moth larvae had stag-headed and deformed the oak. We stood and watched the hornets, marvelling at the striped beauty of these much misunderstood insects. I have never found them aggressive, although one should treat their nests with respect. As artists in papier mâché, they are unrivalled, chewing up wood to a fine pale grey pulp and creating great insect architecture in their nests. Compare the flowing, exuberant design of a hornets' nest to the work of Frank Gehry, and it is hard to escape the conclusion that buildings like the Bilbao Guggenheim may have been inspired, however unconsciously, by the humble hornet.

Going through the woods, we were never far from the song of grasshopper warblers, our Hampshire cicadas, in the sallows of the bogs and marshes. Turning north into Denny Wood, we trod the soft floor of golden-brown beech leaves and noticed how open and empty of new growth the forest was. We had passed through a little grove of free-standing hollies, much nibbled by deer and ponies, possibly the remains of an ancient holly holm, the characteristic holly thicket of the New Forest. The constant browsing had deformed the trees into wonderfully complex, contorted, outlandish shapes.

We noticed the conspicuous absence of natural regeneration within the woods, whose canopy was dominated by the tall beeches, long ago coppiced but now grown to a good sixty feet. A clear browse line some six feet off the ground was a sign that plenty of deer were still browsing in the forest from which they were officially banned by an Act of Parliament: the Deer Removal Act of 1851. At that time, according to Colin Tubbs in his ecological history of the New Forest, there were probably seven or eight thousand deer in the forest, mostly fallow deer, with three or four hundred red deer. These are about the same figures as for 1670, when the first census was conducted in the forest. Such a large population needed to be fed artificially with hay, especially during hard winters. At least 6,000 deer were officially killed after the 1851 Act, and many more unofficially, but some inevitably remained, and the population seems to have risen gradually to about 2,000. Up to 800 a year are still culled. Roe-deer may have become extinct in England in the fourteenth century but were reintroduced from the nineteenth century on, and there are now probably some 300 of them in the New Forest, as well as muntjac and sika.

When he rides through the New Forest in October 1826, William Cobbett asks, in his usual practical, sceptical way,

What are these deer *for*? Who are to *eat* them? Are they for the Royal Family? Why, there are more deer bred in *Richmond Park alone* . . . than would feed all the branches of the Royal Family and all their households *all the year round*, if every soul of them ate as hearty as a ploughman, and if they *never touched a morsel of any kind of meat but venison!* For what, and FOR WHOM, then, are deer kept in the New Forest?

Cobbett sees the keeping of deer as simply 'another deep bite into us by the long and sharp-fanged Aristocracy'. Pointing out that the New Forest is a piece of public property, a common, and that 'there is no man, however poor, who has not a right in it', he questions why any man may be transported if he goes out by night to catch any of the game. Cobbett thinks it absurd that the public purse should pay the Commissioners of Woods and Forests to farm hay and feed it to the deer, and at the same time pay them to plant young trees which the same deer would eat. Twenty-five years later, the 1851 Deer Removal Act was designed to address that very question.

Deer, ponies and cattle are fond of eating saplings in the woods. When experimental enclosures have been fenced off inside the beech woods, many more young trees have grown, but the majority have been the shade-tolerant beeches. The greatest inhibitor of regeneration within Denny Wood is the shade cast by its own canopy of beeches, which will eventually come down, either naturally or felled, letting in light and sparking a new cycle of mixed woodland regeneration. George Peterken, our schoolboy fern-surveyor, later returned here as a graduate to begin the work on the conservation of natural woodlands for which he is now famous.

Every so often we passed dead beeches standing in ruins, much perforated by the woodpeckers we heard calling, questing for insects and larvae. Barry described how ingeniously a woodpecker is adapted to go vertically up trees. To keep its body braced close to the trunk, the keel of its breastbone is unusually shallow, the legs short, the feet and claws splayed, with sharp hooked toes pointing back in the opposite direction. The bird even insures itself against falling backwards by digging in its short, stiff tail feathers against the bark. The tongue of a woodpecker is long and barbed at the tip, with filaments that will hook larvae out of their galleries in the wood and into its Black & Decker bill.

As we crossed the Station Heath on our way back, I checked the damp peat for sundew plants, and they too were still there, leaves unfurled so an unwary insect might trigger their honeyed, deliquescent tentacles. Purely in the interests of science, I used to keep two or three of them, filched from Beaulieu, in flowerpots on our kitchen windowsill. My mother gamely tolerated them, along with the odd praying mantis on the net curtains, smuggled home on the Train Bleu from Menton, where my French pen-friend, Jean-François, lived. I loved the bright-green mantises, part plant, part insect, with a swivelling triangular head and eyes like the Mekon in the *Eagle* comic. I suppose, as entertainment, the gladiatorial struggles of the flies on the kitchen window stood in for horror films at the time. But nowadays, when they film this sort of thing and call it 'natural history' on television, I find it cheap and loathsome. Beaulieu and the New Forest affected me now, as in my schooldays, all the more profoundly by being so intimately known and, at least partly, understood. We were a kind of tribe, this stretch of wild country was our dreaming, and Barry our sage and chieftain. We even spoke a secret Linnaean language with its own poetry: *Drosera rotundifolia, Impatiens nolitangere, Myosurus minimus, Dolomedes fimbriatus*. Even 'insectivorous' rolled nicely off the tongue. But privately I knew nothing could be more evocative than 'sundew'. Like the layers of springy sphagnum moss that grew in the peat bogs, the Tomes grew by gradual accretions into something of lasting value. Between us, we set down some of Beaulieu's stories, charted them on a map of our own making that each of us still carries in his head and learnt some of the New Forest's distinctive language: what Keats calls 'the poetry of earth'.

On his way over to Beaulieu village from Lyndhurst on Tuesday, 17 October 1826, Cobbett rode across our Campsite Heath and Black Down, skirting the bogs with Woodfidley over to his right, and then through Tantany Wood two miles further on. The foragers he most often encountered that day were not cattle, ponies or deer but pigs.

A little before we came to the village of Beaulieu (which, observe, the people call *Bewley*), we went through a wood, chiefly of beech, and that beech seemingly destined to grow food for pigs, of which we saw, during this day, many, many thousands. I should think we saw at least a hundred hogs to one deer. I stopped, at one time, and counted the hogs and pigs just round about me and they amounted to 140, all within 50 or 60 yards of my horse.

Commoners were allowed to turn out their pigs in the forest during two months of the autumn to feed on the beech mast and acorns. These rights of pannage still exist. It was a way of sweeping the forest of the early green acorns of October that might otherwise have poisoned the cattle or deer.

Barry and I went the same way as Cobbett next morning, following the river past the big pond in Beaulieu village and past Buckler's Hard, where the navy built and launched its warships from New Forest oaks. We arrived close to the sea, as Cobbett did, at a farm by the ruins of St Leonard's Chapel and a huge tithe barn. He had, in fact, been misdirected there by a man in the village, but he was delighted by the views of the Solent, the Beaulieu River and the Isle of Wight, pronouncing this to be a far more beautiful place than so-called Beaulieu itself and therefore the original *beau lieu*. He also proceeded to give the farmer, a Mr John Biel, the benefit of a short lecture on the Norman etymology of 'Bewley'.

We followed a lane south and crossed fields to the sea past cowering, wind-blown hedges of oak and blackthorn that looked out of place on this calm, glorious morning. There was no one else on the beach, no sign of human life except the tops of sails just visible sliding in and out of the Beaulieu River, and the driftwood along the tideline. Squinting against the morning sun across the flat calm Solent, we made out the silhouettes of dozens of yachts off Cowes: a distant forest of masts and sails that not long ago would have been wooden, crafted from straight-grained spruce, but were probably almost all aluminium or carbon fibre.

This being a remote and more or less private beach, its flotsam had escaped being tidied. It is part of Lord Montagu's estate, a nature reserve, and most of its visitors are birdwatchers. Every now and again we encountered their improvised encampments of driftwood benches, places to munch sandwiches, unscrew thermos flasks and exchange intelligence of the latest arrivals. Driftwood and the rich bird life along this shore are closely connected. Flotsam gives shelter to sandflies and other food for the small flocks of wading birds that kept wheeling in like a single organism, landing or taking off on the instant in perfect unison: sandlings, ringed plover, gadwall and dunlin. All were feeding along the shore, keeping a wary eye on a peregrine at rest on a post in the river mouth.

The lonely spit of shingle runs out a mile or so between the saltmarsh and the sea to the mouth of the Beaulieu River. We made our way along it, Barry shouldering a telescope and tripod, which he set down now and again for us to observe the birds. Across the sparkling Solent, the undulating landscape of the Isle of Wight with its wooded hills, fields and hedgerows looked far too homely and inviting ever to have been the prison it was to my great-uncle Joe.

The wonderful thing about driftwood is the way the action of the sea etches the softer wood between the lines of grain, revealing the sinews, bleaching it to a pale grey, smoothing it, rounding all edges and corners. You want to pick it up and handle it. Responding to just this impulse, I lifted one side of a handsome slab of pine twice the size of a loaf, with beautifully sea-rounded corners. Given time, the sea would probably sculpt it into an oval. Beneath it in a hollow was a long-tailed field mouse and her nest. She stood her ground beside it as two or three of her young, half grown already, did just the right thing, escaping efficiently into the cover of the next-door clump of samphire. Embarrassed to have disturbed the family in so remote a spot, I gently returned their roof into position, wishing there were some way of reassuring them that this was a genuine mistake and they were quite safe. The look of hurt, uncertainty and puzzlement in the mouse's face has stayed with me. So has her courage in standing by the nest, decoying us from her young. It is salutary to be reminded of the extent of your own power and your potential for accidental brutality.

Halfway along the spit a makeshift flagpole flying the French flag at half-mast announced a driftwood den like a bowerbird's nest. All sorts of flotsam had been gathered and assembled into a surrealist installation. A wigwam of driftwood spars lashed to the central totem pole was encircled by a pattern of grey sticks laid out like basketwork and punctuated by such objects as the flip-flop sandals and trainers that seem perpetually to ride the waves, Coke cans, garish cork or plastic lobster-pot buoys and the armoured white carapaces of spider crabs that abound on this beach. This was the work, Barry thought, of 'the Cottage Pies': these were the weekenders who appeared every Friday night in a row of estate cottages the other side of the marsh, and who came under observation through the birders' telescopes during their idle moments.

Driftwood being free, like sand and sea, the temptation to play with it is strong. As with sandcastles, it seems to bring out an Aboriginal architectural urge in people, as well as a need to leave behind a signature on the beach, however ephemeral. Driftwood fires are unusually beautiful, especially at dusk, because the salt in the wood burns green and blue.

Almost every seashore plant seemed to be here: bright-yellow long-horned sea poppies were still in flower and so was the pale-pink sea rocket. Sea holly, sea beet, sea campion, cliff samphire, sea spurge and the sea kale, which Lord Montagu is said to eat, all clambered about the shingle, sheltered in little driftwood alcoves, their colours accentuated against the pale silver of the pickled wood. On the marsh behind the shingle bank, mauve beds of sea lavender and the deep crimson foliage of the burnet rose, while across the water at the very mouth of the river the peregrine continued to sit sentinel on his post.

Oak Apple Day

At nightfall I walked a mile uphill through cornfields out of Great Wishford towards the greater darkness of Grovely Wood stretched along the sleeping ridge. It was a perfect starlit night, nearly a new moon, and the chalky track, lined with cow-parsley, shone luminously in the darkness. A dozen yards inside the wood, in the long grass of a bank above the track, I found the perfect camping nest. It commanded a view of the cart-way descending to the village, yet, once inside the bivouac bag, I was hidden by the steepness of the bank. I roosted in that instinctive blend of weariness and vigilance familiar to the unofficial camper. Badgers soon began squabbling noisily in the wood, joined now and again by the hoarse bark of a fox. But when all fell still and I lay gazing at the stars, the dew was audible as it fell softly on the oak leaves around me, and on my face, and I drifted towards sleep.

It was the eve of Oak Apple Day, and the annual reassertion of rights to collect wood in the Royal Forest of Grovely by the villagers of Great Wishford in accordance with a charter granted to them in 1603. The charter affirms that their rights to the wood have existed 'since time immemorial', usually taken to mean since well before Domesday. In all seriousness, it requires the whole village to 'go in a dance' to Salisbury Cathedral six miles away once a year in May and claim their rights and customs in the forest with 'The Shout' of the words 'Grovely! Grovely! Grovely! and all Grovely!' The villagers' right to take away as much 'deade snappinge woode boughs and stickes' as can be carried or hauled in a hand cart was still exercised by some of the older parishioners until recently. But what seems to be the most ancient *rite*, with clear pagan undertones, is to cut green boughs of oak on Oak Apple Day, carry them into the village and decorate the doorway of each house and the church tower. The custom is to begin the rite early, hence my presence in the night wood.

At this stage I knew little more about Grovely Wood than what the map had told me. I knew it lay high above the fork of the rivers Nadder and Wylye three miles from their confluence at Wilton before meeting the Avon at Salisbury, and that there were 2,000 shadowy acres of it, draped east–west along the top of the chalk ridge. Its nearest edge, where I was ensconced, is just under a mile outside Wishford. I also knew that I was encamped on a minuscule percentage of the property of the Earl of Pembroke and Mont-gomery, Lord of the Manor and Ranger of the Forest, whose ancestors had from time to time attempted to deprive the villagers of their right to firewood.

In the middle of the night I was woken by footfalls on the track below. Someone walked right by me in the dark and disappeared into the wood. It was twenty to four and I was too comfortable to stir. A poacher? Rustic insomniac? At ten to four the first light began to glimmer, and a few rooks left the wood through a dense mist. The bats were still flying as the first skylarks rose above the fields below. I lay listening to the cuckoo. Then, at five minutes to four, the rough band struck up in the village below: a cacophony of everything noisy that would serve to wake the citizenry. It was not a pretty sound that rose up the hill through the mist. Bass drum, hunting horn, saucepan lids, football rattles and the old church bell on a trolley were all trundled in ragged procession from house to house and vigorously sounded until the lights came on. It was all trick and no treat.

Blackbirds and thrushes were by now in full voice in the woods, and by four o'clock I was up and gazing across the deep sea of mist that hung across the valley of the Wylye. I turned round to witness a green figure, half-tree, half-stag, striding towards me down the track out of the wood fully enveloped in antlers of leafy oak boughs. This wodwo wished me a cheery, almost casual 'Good morning' and passed on. I caught him up and discovered he was bearing two choice boughs: one for his house and another, the 'Marriage Bough', to be hoisted up the outside of the church tower and hung out to bless the season's marriages with fertility. He explained, from somewhere inside the leaves, that no bough thicker than a man's arm may be cut.

By the time we reached the village the rough band was returning to the Town End Tree at the far end from the church, now an oak but reputedly an ancient elm in earlier times. It marks the starting point for the Oak Apple Day procession in the afternoon. Lights were going on in the windows, sending beams out on the mist, and wood-pigeons still slept on the telegraph wires. The church bells peeled, and people armed with billhooks and bowsaws began to appear under the bunting in West Street, heading for the woods.

I went with them, hiking back up the hill with Chris Lock, who writes educational books from his home in the village. Higher up, we emerged from the mist into the early sunshine lighting up the fringes of the wood and entered a wood pasture of oaks with a browse line that was probably the result of centuries of Oak Apple pruning as much as the browsing of cattle. Chris and I joined other villagers already busy claiming their oak boughs. Chris chose his carefully, explaining the finer points of the art to me. Later in the day, the boughs would be judged and prizes awarded by a committee of the Oak Apple Club, founded in 1892 to stand up for the wood rights and perpetuate the May celebrations. A prize-winning bough would be branched like a stag's antlers, abundantly leaved, symmetrical and, ideally, studded with oak apples, the curious rich brown spherical galls grown by the tree in response to the larvae of the gall wasp.

Instances of such relics of tree worship as this are well documented all over the world. In Cornwall people decked their doors on the first of May with boughs of sycamore or hawthorn, and in the county of Westmeath in Ireland a whole bush was set before the door on May Eve and decorated with spring flowers from the fields. The maypoles set up in villages to dance around would originally have been live new trees brought in from the woods each year. In *The Golden Bough*, Sir James Frazer quotes the North Bavarians, who still bring in a fresh fir tree from the forest every few years, stripping its branches but carefully leaving a bunch of green foliage at the top 'as a memento that in it we have to do, not with a dead pole, but with a living tree from the greenwood'. Ceremonies such as the Grovely rite were originally performed with the most serious possible intent: to promote the general fertility of every living thing in the parish for the whole of the coming season. People really believed there was a sanctity in the living bough: that it contained the invisible god of growth. It was a kind of sacrament that might bless the house and all who went in and out, and, by being carried in procession round the village farmyards and into the fields at the high point of spring, might impart its power of regeneration and growth to everything it encountered.

The once sacred wood was by now alive with people and talk. Two women posed for a photograph, holding boughs like big bouquets, looking down at the valley: 'Just look at the mist – we could be in Switzerland.' 'I'd rather be in Wilts.'

Most of the oaks, holly and hazels showed signs of the pollarding or coppicing that would have maintained a plentiful supply of underwood, autumn nutting and perhaps holly fodder when the wood was worked and harvested. I went deeper in among the oaks, admiring open glades full of herb Robert, wood avens, the intense blue of bugle and the dusting of yellow pollen on dog's mercury. The heavy dew and mist had brought out snails in their dozens, riding the chalk, active and questing like little knights in armour. As I followed the flinty track to the very top of the ridge inside the wood, I found more and more holly, ash and mossy old beeches. One giant beech seemed to have collapsed under the weight of its own branches into a clearing in a plantation of larch. It had peeled and split its trunk, as top-heavy mushrooms, half rotten and saturated with water, outgrew their stems. As the sun came up, its beams, embodied by the mist, slanted through the larches on to the bluebell-wood floor. Roe-deer bounded off down a ride, and I found a naturally spiral oak. Another had grafted itself to a hazel in a mock hybrid that seemed to grow as a single tree with two sets of roots.

I was back in Great Wishford at half past eight by the church clock, as the bells pealed and they hoisted the marriage bough up the outside of the tower to hang it off the top like a flag. I joined the neo-pagans in the pub. Having worked up a healthy appetite decking out their houses in oak boughs, they too had adjourned to the Royal Oak for breakfast before piling into coaches to travel the six miles to Salisbury.

At the cathedral, four women in the rural costume as worn by Wishford women in 1825, holding bundles of hazel and oak sticks above their heads, danced a stately measure to the music of a squeeze-box on the lawn of the close. They performed in a square marked by garlands of oak, watched by the Oak Apple Club, assembled beside a large banner proclaiming 'Unity is Strength'. We all crowded into the cathedral, and the shout went up before the priest at the altar: 'Grovely! Grovely! Grovely! and all Grovely!' Asked years ago why the wood is always named three times, an ancient villager is said to have replied, 'We d'want jist three thirds o't and noo less.' But I noticed they didn't shout the bit about Unity and Strength.

Everyone trooped back for a huge sit-down lunch with toasts, yards of trestle tables and dozens of speeches by local dignitaries in a marquee in the Oak Apple Field. I met my friends Sue and Angela for a picnic on the grass under a blazing sun. Back in 1970, the seventeenth Earl of Pembroke, by now an honoured guest instead of the enemy, stood up at the lunch and told the village, 'Oak Apple must go on.' Perhaps the lunch had been rather too good, but the applause must have been deafening. Still not sated with all this ritual and ceremony, the company, now numbering well over a thousand, assembled at the Town End Tree for a post-prandial beating of the bounds in a procession led by a brass band and the four stick-dancers followed by the Oak Apple Club banner, a May Queen, villagers carrying their oak boughs, farmers with painted wheelbarrows and the Bourne River Morris Men. They went all round the village and across the water meadows as far as the parish boundary at the Stoford River Bridge and back. Then the Morris men danced, and there were games and a fête on the Oak Apple Field.

By tea-time I was feeling distinctly weary, not least with the effort of keeping up with the constant challenge of the day's ambiguities. First, an obviously pagan fertility bough was installed, without protest from the vicar, on the tower of the parish church. More pagan rites were then performed at Salisbury Cathedral, including fertility dances, under the appreciative eye of various local Salisbury dignitaries. A fair cross-section of a constituency that regularly returns a Conservative MP with a comfortable majority then sat down to lunch together and later went in procession wearing oak-leaf buttonholes and carrying green oak boughs under a royalist banner emblazoned with the unmistakably Old Labour slogan: 'Unity is Strength'. Just to confuse matters further, the day chosen to celebrate the distinctly republican stance taken by the village on the question of Grovely Wood was 29 May. It is known as Oak Apple Day all over the country because it is the anniversary of the Restoration to the throne of King Charles II in 1660, after hiding in an oak at Boscobel in Shropshire. In the original charter, the oak boughs were meant to be cut between May Day and Whit Tuesday, so it seems likely that the feast was deliberately moved in honour of the Restoration.

Puzzling over these ambiguities, I unravelled some of the Grovely story through history. First there was the historical question of the origins of the charter itself. It was drawn up at a meeting of a manorial court held in Grovely Forest in 1603, presumably because the villagers' rights to collect wood and to cut boughs in May were under some threat. There is evidence of several earlier attempts by the Forest Ranger, in 1292, 1318 and 1332, to prevent the exercise of these rights. On each occasion the villagers fought off the challenge in court. In 1603 the manor and forest had recently been bought by Sir Richard Grobham, an enthusiastic hunter who was to slay the last wild boar in England in 1624. It seems likely that he too was keen to have Grovely Wood to himself.

But surely securing the right to collect merely dead wood, and only as much as could be carried away on foot, was no more than a pyrrhic victory? It was a poor second to what must almost certainly have been the commoners' original right and custom: to coppice and pollard the living under-wood. This was the 'lop and top' that traditionally fired the bread ovens and cottage fires of ordinary villagers up and down the country. The right to dead wood amounts to little more than crumbs from the rich man's table. As every woodlander knows, dead wood is bulky but light: it makes good kindling and can be useful for the rapid heat burst you need in a bread oven, but has already been half consumed by fungi, bacteria, woodlice and insects. The obligation to 'go in a dance' for six miles to Salisbury, although a charming idea in fantasy, carries more than a hint of 'Let them sing for their supper.'

Whatever the private feelings expressed inside the Great Wishford cottages by tiny dead-wood fires in midwinter, things then seem to have settled down until 1807, when the Earl of Pembroke bought the Manor of Wishford and the forest, and promptly brought an Act of Enclosure upon it to Parliament in 1809. In 1825 there was another attempt to extinguish the rights, by the eleventh Earl of Pembroke, but he was challenged by a young woman of eighteen, Grace Reed, and three others who went as usual to gather wood in Grovely. All four were arrested and taken into custody. Too poor to pay their fines, they were committed to Salisbury Prison, but later released after a popular outcry and the intervention of a lawyer. Again the villagers' rights were upheld in court, but more disputes followed all through the years of agricultural depression and acute rural poverty, when firewood from Grovely would have been an absolute essential for the cottagers of Great Wishford to bake bread and warm themselves through winter. The disputes over Grovely Wood between the villagers and the Earls of Pembroke were deadly serious and would have dominated the lives of people in Great Wishford during the whole of the nineteenth century. The four women dancing with sticks on the Cathedral Close now came to represent Grace Reed and the Grovely Four who stood up against the Earl of Pembroke.

In his play about John Clare, *The Fool*, Edward Bond evokes the anxiety of Clare and his fellow villagers around 1815 at the Acts of Enclosure by the big landowners that were robbing them of their rights of commonage, including their rights in woods and forests:

PATTY (*nervously*). They saw chaps gooin' round the fields this morning with chains an' writin' books. Thass how it all come out. Wrote the river down in the books.

DARKIE An' the forest.

CLARE *You* heard a this gall? (*she nods*) How'd you git rid of a river – (*laughs*) turn the river off!

PATTY Dam her up an' pump her out boy!

CLARE Can't – thass our's as much as his. An' the fens. An' the trees. What's it mean boy? We'll lose our fishin' – our wood – cows on the fen common. How'll we live? Not on the few bob they pay us for workin' their land. We need us own bit a land.

DARKIE They take all the land they'll hev t'pay us proper wages.

But the landowners did not pay proper wages. In August 1826, the year after Grace Reed and her friends were imprisoned for gathering wood in Grovely, William Cobbett set out from Salisbury and rode up the valley of the Wylye through Great Wishford and was shocked by the ruin and poverty he encountered everywhere. He had lived three miles away at Steeple Langford for a while as a boy and had glorious memories of the valley. So he was bitterly disappointed to find the ordinary people so unhappy. When he reached Heytesbury, further up the valley, he met some 'very ragged' men and boys at the inn who had come all the way from Bradford-on-Avon, some twelve miles, to gather nuts in the woods. They were unemployed cloth workers, turned out of their factory. Cobbett saved his supper and fasted in the morning so he could 'give these chaps a breakfast for once in their lives'. 'There were eight of them, six men and two boys; and I gave them two quartern loaves, two pounds of cheese, and eight pints of strong beer.' Cobbett is unequivocal about what he saw in the Wylye Valley:

I really am ashamed to ride a fat horse, to have a full belly, and to have a clean shirt upon my back, while I look at these wretched countrymen of mine; while I actually see them reeling with weakness; when I see their poor faces present me nothing but skin and bone, while they are toiling to get the wheat and the meat ready to be carried away to be devoured by the tax-eaters. I am ashamed to look at these poor souls and to reflect that they are my countrymen.

Defying the will of an earl was a dangerous thing to do in 1825. Grace Reed and her friends must have been desperate.

More disputes over the Grovely rights ensued, and by 1892 the situation was so dire that seventy-four Wishford parishioners formed the Oak Apple Club, adopting the motto 'Unity is Strength'. There was such an upsurge of collectivist political ideas during this period that it is hard to imagine that both the choice of the motto and the formation of the club itself were not directly inspired by some of the many socialist and anarchist thinkers and writers of the time: William Morris, Bernard Shaw, Edward Carpenter, John Ruskin and many others writing in a flood of pamphlets and weekly papers such as *Justice* and Morris's *The Commonweal*. The Fabian Society had been founded in 1884 and the Democratic Federation, whose membership card William Morris designed, in 1882. Its motif was an oak tree, rich with foliage and acorns, in which hung banners with the motto 'Educate, Agitate, Organize' beneath the words

'Liberty, Equality, Fraternity'. The carrying of banners such as the Oak Apple Club's in procession was, by 1892, a well-established tradition among the trades unions.

Disputes continued over Grovely, with more trouble in 1931 and 1933, but things must have been resolved by 1987, when Lieutenant Colonel C. C. G. Ross published a short history of Oak Apple Day in Great Wishford. Its foreword was contributed by a certain Earl of Pembroke: 'At a time when so much is changing for the worse in the English countryside,' writes the Earl, 'it is heartening to know that Oak Apple Day in Wishford remains unchanged and as solid as it has been for many hundreds of years. The rights which are held by the people of Wishford are still zealously guarded and the near pagan ceremonial which takes place in Salisbury Cathedral is surely unique. I believe Oak Apple Day plays a very important part in the history of English village life and sincerely hope it will continue for "time out of mind".'

This would surely have brought a smile to the face of Grace Reed and her three friends, not to mention Cobbett. By the end of the day I could no longer tell if I was pagan or Christian, Tory or Old Labour, royalist or republican. But after another visit to the beer tent on the Oak Apple Field, I decided it must be best to be all of them at once, like everyone else in Great Wishford. 'There must be a lot of wood-burning stoves in Great Wishford,' I said to the woman next to me as we queued at the bar. 'Too much like hard work,' she said; 'we all have central heating.'

Willow

The day I go over to talk willow with Brian White on his withy beds at Kingsbury Episcopi, a mad westerly wind is blowing across the Levels. I drive down out of Castle Cary, where the evening before had been calm, and I had witnessed a posse of badgers sauntering nonchalantly along the street beneath Lodge Hill, knocking the tops off dustbins like teenagers and rifling them, even pausing to tip over the ice-cream sign outside the newsagents. Emerging early from the snouting dingles of the town at dusk, they went their rounds with impatient efficiency, jogging from house to house like council workers on some lucrative bonus scheme.

Dropping down into the southern Levels off the ridge at Somerton, I pause at Muchelney Church to see the angels in its ceiling, painted in the early 1600s around a plump carved oak, gold-leafed sun. As the church guide primly explains: 'The angels are wearing Tudor costumes, and, unusually, some are very feminine.' They are, in a word, topless, and at this time of year one can't help seeing the ripeness and rosiness of the massed angelic bosoms reflected in the laden apple orchards outside. Why don't vicars plant orchards in their churchyards? As a symbol of renewal and sweet pleasure in life, what better tree could there be to rise from the dead? I ask two stonemasons descending from the scaffolding on the church tower if they know of the Green Man anywhere round here. 'Sorry, sir, can't help you there,' they reply warily. In fact, as I learnt later, the work on the tower had uncovered an entire bestiary of hitherto unnoticed gargoyles and punkies; half-human, half-animal wood-land beings carved in stone, and I suppose the men wanted to keep them to themselves. Reveal them to a stranger, and their magic might evaporate.

All the way to the next village, Thorney, the hedges, generally of elm around the Levels, really are full of thorn. In Kingsbury Episcopi churchyard, up Orchard Lane, the topsy-turvy gravestones reveal the constant shifting of the damp ground. Windfalls tumble about the storm-tossed graves. I am early, so I go a mile up the road and ascend the storybook Burrow Hill, topped with a single sycamore and a wooden swing. It hoists you a few feet above the summit. You sway gently in it, surveying cider orchards and meandering lines of willows or poplars showing the silver backs of their leaves to the wind. Withy beds are laid out between the reedy drainage channels, and tiny cattle lie about the meadows. The still water of a lode stretches off to the east, a buzzard mews, and someone bumps slowly round the orchard molehills below on an old motorbike, inspecting the sheep. My sycamore perch, I notice, has been carved up, skinned and the wound in the bark, about two feet square, painted pale blue, perhaps to repel insects. Flies, especially, are said to have an aversion to pale blue, and it is a traditional colour for farmhouse kitchens. I observe a goat moth caterpillar climb the trunk and skirt along the rim of scabbed bark, duly veering off the blue. It trudges on eight feet to the crown as I watch.

Down in the village, Brian White and Brian Lock are among the last of the willow growers on the Levels. Bundles of osier rods stand in a shed ready to be sent away, bound with willow bark, knotted in the traditional rose pattern. In a big open-fronted hangar, the year's crop is stacked criss-cross, twenty feet high. Brian White meets me in the yard with his black-and-white dog and we head out towards the withy beds on West Moor. Brian says the moor was once planted like this from end to end. Everybody in the village worked with willow, one way or another. Ten years ago there were still ten serious growers on the moor. Now the industry is dying out: there are only four big growers left in the Levels, and a lot of small ones with beds of a few acres each. This year another of the local willow men, Mr Male, reached seventy-five and retired. There is no one to take his place.

The two Brians work twenty-six acres of withies segregated into lesser beds of three or four acres. The willows grow in rows two feet apart, planted every fourteen inches in the rows: about five or six hundred to the acre. The wind makes a chaos of their red-brown stems, dishevelling them as if to test their pliability, in spite of a protective hedge around each bed, of dogwood, maple, elm or ash. We walk out along a cart track raised above deep rhynes: the drainage ditches connecting with the larger dykes. They keep the water level just high enough to moisten the willow roots. *Rhyne* rhymes with 'seen' and comes from the same old Germanic stem as the River Rhine. Meadowsweet, comfrey and reeds line the banks.

Brian points out the different varieties of willow. Black maul and Flanders red were always the most popular on West Moor, he says, and they still grow plenty of both. Next best for baskets after the pliable black maul is Holton's black, and they also grow the French noir de Verlaine and orange-stemmed golden willow. In the next bed, a swaying jungle of the exceptionally vigorous bow's hybrid is already well on the way to the eight or nine feet it will grow in a single season. The other withies are little more than half as tall. Brian says there are 1,200 varieties of willow at the agricultural research station at Long Ashton, and some sixty hybrids and culti-vars of *Salix viminalis*, the osier principally grown for basket-making.

The willow men begin cutting in mid November once the leaves have dropped and the sap is sunk. Everyone used to harvest with billhooks. 'We used sickle hooks, and they glided through the stems. You had to stick at it all day,' says Brian. 'It took a week or two to cut an acre by hand. That's four or five hundred stools, and it ripped your wellingtons to bits. But hand cutting is best. Years ago we had beds seventy or eighty years old. Stools only last twenty years with machine cutting, but with the machine and the tractor we harvest three acres a day, and it gathers the rods and ties them in bundles for us.'

Replanting the beds is hard winter work, with the foot-long butts of stout rods as cuttings. Brian says you wear a kind of mitten made of an old boot on your planting hand, using the sole to shove down the sticks into the earth. A bed takes three years to establish, cutting back the new growth each winter to stimulate more, weeding the rows, and controlling fungal and insect pests. The willow's natural habit of spontaneous self-setting from cuttings is embodied in its name, *Salix*, which stems from the Latin verb *salire*, to leap. It literally springs into life. The verb to sally, meaning to go forth boldly, comes from the same root. It is all too easy to plant willow inadvertently by, for instance, driving in a willow fence post or just leaving a green log of willow lying on damp ground. All willows abound in life and vigour, and their pliable wands give them grace.

'Willow takes a lot of handling,' says Brian, back in the yard. The cut rods must be laid out all summer to dry. They need a year for seasoning, though eighteen months or even two years will improve them. Some are stood up in baths and kept alive from Christmas until April, then stripped of their bark to make white willow. Others are boiled continuously for eight hours in a sixteen-foot-long tank like a cattle trough, heated by a brick coal-fired boiler beneath it. Tannin dissolves out of the bark and stains the wood golden-brown. The tank is black with it. The rods are fed into a bark-stripping machine – a revolving brake like a threshing drum – and they emerge as the *buffs* that make fishing creels or bicycle baskets. Ten years ago, says Brian, buffs were most in demand, but now people want brown willow: the more rustic-looking rods with the bark left on. They even buy bolts of them to stand in the church aisle at weddings, but the growers now sell more to individual women making basketwork as a hobby than to wholesalers or manufacturers. They also supply the makers of hot-air balloon baskets, for which willow's resilience and strength is ideal, or the weavers of willow coffins.

Plastic carrier bags and supermarkets have put an end to most of the basket industry, although a few of the old trades survive. A man in Norfolk still makes the wicker frames of guardsmen's bearskins, and down in Hampshire on the River Test someone is still making eel-traps. At Longstock, a mile upstream from Stockbridge, you turn down a little street called 'The Bunny' to the river, where a dozen eel-traps of willow basketwork, looking like beehives, are strung across the river from a wooden plank bridge beside the river-keeper's thatched, conical-roofed bothy.

Not very long ago working with willow could support a modest living. Writing in 1938, H. J. Massingham describes his visit to an ordinary English village basket-maker. 'If business is good,' says Massingham, 'the basket-maker will use as many as 8,000 bundles a year.' For nearly forty years this man had been making coal and flint baskets, fruit hampers, five-bushel chaff baskets, feeding baskets, 'and those in common use by butchers' boys and green-grocers'. Earlier in his career he had regularly made eel, lobster and 'hoddie pots': wicker pots baited with snails to trap sparrows. He also made a speciality of the 'butter plat': 'a basket with a lid designed to hold either three dozen pounds of butter, three pecks of fruit or from eight to twelve Aylesbury ducks'. The diversity of uses for willow was enormous, and the dexterity of the craftspeople naturally inherited down the generations. 'In two hours – we took half the time talking – I watched a bundle of rods wave and bend and twist until they had reached a final end in which the art and use were one, an architectural experience I am not likely to forget,' writes Massingham. At the height of his powers, this man could make a dozen baskets in a day. The spidery beginnings of various baskets hang up in odd corners of my own workshop. My stumbling beginner's attempts have taught me how much strength and skill the craft demands. Basketwork is often described as 'slow' or 'contemplative'. So it may be for some, but when you see a professional at work, it is all speed and fluency.

According to Brian White, the Environment Agency has shown little enthusiasm for the continuance of the withy-growing tradition on the Levels. They have even bought cheap willow from Poland to maintain the river banks, undercutting and ignoring the local growers. Several summers back, when the West Moor withy beds were flooded with stagnant river water full of sewage and dead fish after heavy rains, not a single person from the Environment Agency would come out to inspect the ailing willows. The stagnant, poisonous water ruined the entire crop that year, causing Mr Lock and Mr White to incur losses of £30,000. They were never compensated. A good many naturalists and walkers come to West Moor and appreciate the culture as well as the nature of the withy beds, yet Brian says the Environment Agency has plans to flood the place permanently. It would mean the end of the local willow and basket industry.

The following week I set off for Essex, to one of the holy places of the cricketing world, in search of the cricket bat willow. In the wood yard of J. S. Wright & Sons, Willow Merchants, at Great Leighs near Chelmsford, I find willow clefts, roughly sawn to the size and shape of cricket bat blades, stacked high on pallets, drying naturally in the air and looking like pale, creamy loaves fresh from the oven. More cricket bats begin life at J. S. Wright's than anywhere else in the world, and forty or fifty examples of the craft, all by different makers, are ranged around the office walls of the man I have come to see, Chris Price, the only director of the firm who isn't a member of the Wright family. Any remaining wall space not festooned with bats displays photographic archives of the hundred-year history of the firm: famous cricketers, or men in waistcoats and shirtsleeves standing on ditch banks beside felled willows.

One of the many curious things about our national game is that you can make a decent bat only from the wood of the cricket bat willow, and the trees will grow really well only in England, preferably in Essex or Suffolk. People manage to grow them with moderate success in Kashmir and Australia, somewhere to the north of Melbourne, but the poor willows aren't really happy so far from home. The climate isn't quite right. As a result, the Kashmir willow is too heavy for anything other than beginners' bats, and the Australian is often strangely coloured, because it must be artificially watered. Naturally, it remains a source of deep frustration to Australian cricketers that to obtain a top-quality bat, they must still import the willow from England.

Of all the hundreds of different species and varieties of willow, it is a particular variety of the white willow, *Salix alba coerulea*, that yields the ideal material for a cricket bat. It seems to have appeared first about 1780 in Suffolk and is fond of water. Durham is about as far north as it will grow, and Devon as far west. It is best grown along banks beside the waters of lazy streams and dykes in rich, dark, damp soil. The essential for the even growth of the very best willow is consistent rainfall over most of the year. The cricket bat willow grows at a prodigious rate. During June, July and August a tree can put on four inches in girth. It is capable of reaching sixty feet, and a circumference of four-foot eight inches, in fifteen or twenty years. This is the moment to fell it. Traditionally, J. S. Wright & Sons would have sent out a team of four men with a big cross-cut saw that was almost as fast as a chainsaw with two men on each handle. They cut the felled bole into twenty-eight-inch rolls and carried them off the field on their shoulders to load into a lorry. You never put in a throat, or notch, when you fell one of these willows. Instead, you drive in a wedge behind the saw. Today, J. S. Wright & Sons use chainsaws, travelling about the country, felling twenty-five or thirty trees a day and bringing them back to the yard in Essex. A standing tree may be worth £150, according to quality, and they are spaced about thirty-five feet apart along a ditch bank, or planted out at thirty to the acre. Chris Price says the company always aims to plant three times as many trees as it fells. Some farmers, like the Goodwin family in the Blackwater Valley, have a tradition of growing cricket bat willows, and may now be on their fourth or fifth crop. It can be profitable, but the trees must be highly manicured as they grow.

Just after the war, the Stationery Office published a book entitled

The Cultivation of the Cricket Bat Willow. It is one of those titles you think is going to be about something else altogether, like *Zen and the Art of Motorcycle Maintenance*, but, unless I've missed something, this seems to be the story it tells. Each sapling begins life in the nursery as a *set*, a cutting from a *tod*, a four-foot pollard mother tree cultivated from stock of the noblest pedigree. When your young willow has achieved twelve and a half feet of straight, unbranched stem, you plant it out in the field to a depth of at least thirty inches. This leaves nine or ten feet, the height of three or four cricket bats, to grow into a tree-trunk. For the next five or six years, you must, like King Herod, cut off any infant lateral shoots almost the moment they appear. This means two or three annual prunings until the tree is more mature, when you can relax and shave it only once or twice a year. The pruning knife is set on the end of a pole, so you can reach up and push it against the buds or shoots to amputate them, always working upwards with the grain. Such meticulous care ensures that the wood will be free of knots, with a straight and even grain.

These days the felled boles are transported in one piece to the yard, where they are sawn into traditional twenty-eight-inch lengths: the rolls. The next job is to cleave each one along the grain into eight, using wedges and the back of an axe. The sawyer then studies the clefts, decides which side will look best as the face of the bat and saws them to the rough shape of a blade. They are dipped in wax at both ends to prevent them splitting as they dry out naturally in the air for three to twelve months.

Each cleft at J. S. Wright's is inspected and graded on a scale of one to four. Only the top grade will make a bat for a Test cricketer. Chris picks one of the clefts off a stack in the yard and thumps the face with a ball hammer. It dents easily. 'At this stage, the willow is a soft wood, but once the face and edges of the bat have been compressed in a roller, it becomes a hardwood. Balls come down the pitch at 90 mph. The bat would soon pulp if it weren't compressed, and it wouldn't drive back the ball.' Chris says they once experimented with poplar, but it wouldn't retain its compression.

What is it about this particular willow that suits it so uniquely to making bats? It is light, strong, fibrous wood that won't snap. It is also very consistent in its density, and, counter-intuitively, the wider the grain, the longer the bat is likely to last. A good bat should last a thousand runs, but it may have as few as three or four grains in its face. A closer-grained bat with up to ten or more grains in the face may be a hard hitter, but might last only two hundred runs. The bat Don Bradman used for his record score of 334 against England in the third Test at Leeds in 1930 had ten grains, but might not have lasted much longer than the innings. This is because the wider-grained wood is younger and more resilient. In fact, Bradman was known for his nonchalant attitude towards bats, sometimes even borrowing one on the spot for a match. W. G. Grace, on the other hand, was so particular that he used to employ several junior batsmen to play in a selection of bats for him.

There are strict rules about the dimensions of bats, but individual bat-makers are free to exercise their own preferences as to shape, balance and 'feel'. Rules have evolved pragmatically. Ever since 23 September 1741, when Mr Shock White of the Ryegate First XI advanced to the crease with a bat as wide as the wicket itself in a match against Hambledon, there has been a rule, proposed by the miffed Hambledon team, that the bat 'shall not exceed four-and-a-quarter inches in width'. And, in the wake of Dennis Lillee's attempt to introduce an aluminium bat in 1979, there came the commandment: 'The bat shall be made solely of wood.'

A certain mystique has always surrounded cricket bats: the smell of raw linseed oil rubbed in ritually with the fingers, and the supposed extra potency of a blade signed by a famous cricketer. Persuading one of the big names to dedicate his signature to a maker will cost at least £40,000 a year. 'Knocking in' a new bat is still an essential rite of passage: tapping and toughening its oiled face with a rounded wooden mallet for ten or fifteen spells of ten minutes. Selecting the right bat requires skill and experience on the part of the cricketer. Every one is unique, its qualities dependent on the original character of timber, tree, soil and weather.

Bat-making is still a craft industry, and you don't need much in the way of machinery or tools to get started. Blades are shaped with draw-knives, spokeshaves and wooden block planes, their shoulders blended into the rubber-sprung Sarawak split cane handles with a thin blade. The best makers still polish their bats with a horse's shinbone to render a really smooth finish, and that most characteristic of English music: the sound of leather on willow.

I grow common or garden willows myself and hold them in great affection. A giant pollard crack willow stands close to the farm gate at the edge of the common. Some of its over-long boughs split off during the October gale of 1987 and barricaded me in, and the postman out, for a day or so until I could saw my way out. The old tree soon sprang back into life and contains in its crown a thriving miniature wood of elder, bramble, ivy, ash, nettles and goosegrass, as well as a whole city of woodlice, earwigs and beetles. Before its shipwreck, it even sported a tree house, admittedly low on maintenance, its former inhabitants having departed into adolescence. I like the goat willows in the hedges for their yellow duster of pollen, droning with early bees in spring. Flowering as early as March, willows are a valuable source of food for hungry bumblebee queens emerging from hibernation. Sometimes they will grow along the sides of a green lane, weaving their roots into a living raft beneath the track, reinforcing it and helping to drain it. Willow makes good firewood too, provided it is thoroughly seasoned. I saw it into logs and stack them end out against the woodshed wall to face the sun all summer. A pollard willow grows at one end of the moat, sending up green-barked new poles so fast in spring you can almost hear the cells dividing. It is a fountain of sap, evaporating hundreds of gallons into the summer air.

Shelter

My friends the Randall-Pages have lent me their oak cabin in an old oak wood in the valley of the Teign near Drewsteignton. With a rucksack full of food I hike in past a pair of hedgerow wych elms, down a plunging field, into the flickering oak woods that line the river gorge along a charcoal-burners' path cut into the hillside. Every now and again there's one of their wide, level platforms beside the path, an area of blackened stones, often dark purple at closer inspection, many of them shattered by the slow heat. Until about eighty years ago the whole oakwood had always been coppiced for the charcoal the tin smelters needed on Dartmoor. Some of the charcoal was also exported off the moor by wagon to the south coast, where it was loaded on to sailing barges at places like Devonport and shipped to London for sale. Now the oaks have grown up from shoots on the coppice stools into an open wood of tall, slender, relatively straight-trunked oaks. The Dartmoor National Park Authority have been at work among the trees *singling* the oaks: reducing the number of limbs growing from any rootstock to one, which will eventually grow into a bigger, stronger standard tree. They are also engaged in something of a purge, cutting out any other species than oak, ash or hazel. Trunks of oak and sycamore lie about on the wood's floor. Birch logs are stacked to dry beside the path.

So well does the cabin blend into the wood that I hardly notice it as I approach. Trees and cabin are all of a piece. It is built on one of the old charcoal-burners' platforms, the wood falling away steeply below. From the plank veranda before the door I can see the river hundreds of feet below, racing over rocks. It has been sunny and very warm all day. Now, in the dusk, robins are singing all down the valley. One gives me a personal recital from an oak bough a few feet away.

The cabin is eleven feet wide and eighteen feet long, with a ridged, oak-shingled roof. It is built entirely in green oak cut in the wood here. Each shingle is cleft from a foot-long oak log and is five inches wide by half an inch thick. All the beams of the oak-framed hut have been morticed and pegged together by Cameron, who built it. The floor is of wide chestnut boards and the place is warmed by a wood-stove. I've been cooking on this too: kettles for tea, a tin of tomato soup heated to boiling point and ladled out with an oak spoon I made because there seems to be no cutlery. I spent a happy hour whittling it from a piece of firewood with my Opinel knife from the Dordogne. By luck, it just fitted inside my mug, so I could ladle the soup into it. I write at the kitchen table by the light of a paraffin lamp and a candle in a wine-bottle candlestick. They cast an orange glow on the oak table.

The walls of the cabin are of upright oak boards nine inches or a foot wide, with vertical weather strips fixed over the joints between the boards outside. Apart from the oak pegs in the mortices, all the fixings are forged iron nails. They bleed black stains of tannic acid where they have wounded the living oak, still half full of sap when the cabin was built. All the traditional oak-framed houses you see in English villages were originally built in green oak. The wood is much easier to cut and work, before it hardens into something more like iron with the action of its own tannin. As they season in the building, the beams flex and twist themselves into new shapes, and this is one of the things that gives timber-framed houses their organic character. People repairing oak-framed houses or extending them often make the mistake of building in dead straight lines, instead of letting the line of a roof undulate gently, so that the tiles rise and fall and rearrange themselves with the passage of time like the scales on a fish.

Above the table I'm sitting at is a sleeping gallery reached by a vertical oak ladder. There is a single stable door to the low-roofed veranda outside and a window either side of it facing across the steep valley to more woods and cliffs, and the river. Opposite the door on the back wall is a wood-burner, crackling and bumping gently now and then, and glowing deliciously when I open it for refuelling. In one corner is the axe I have been using this afternoon, splitting logs of birch and oak for the stove. They are so dry, I only needed to let the axe fall with its own weight and the shivered wood leapt apart.

Fashioning the rudimentary spoon felt a suitably Robinson Crusoe sort of activity. Creative in the most primitive sense, it purged my mind of all other thoughts but the here and now of this beautiful wood. Sitting here as night falls, all I hear is the river rushing over the boulders and stones below. The steady sound could be rain, or it could be wind in the trees. No doubt when all these come at once, they harmonize into a single chord.

The night before, sleeping in the yellow spare bedroom just under the thatch at Peter and Charlotte's cob-built farmhouse, I had lain listening to the stream that flows within a foot or two of one end of their house. Over dinner, we had sat beside a fig tree, under the burgeoning new growth of a vine, pruned back hard last year. The sky was clear and starry. Peter brought out some oblong offcuts of Kilkenny limestone from his studio and pushed them together to frame a fire. He cooked mackerel and squid over a barbecue powered by an antique foot-treadle bellows that once supplied air to naval divers. Peter had taped a spout of iron piping to the rubber tube, which he plunged into the charcoal and oak, then pumped to fan the fire into instant red heat. We sat by the fig tree for a long time, savouring the first outdoor evening of the summer. 'I love being outdoors,' said Peter. 'I would live outdoors all the time if I could.'

The cabin falls into shadow at sunset, so I move thirty yards up the hillside to sit on a golden clifftop overlooking the Teign and its wooded valley. The low sun renders all the foxglove flowers translucent pink, and the hillside bracken shines like the river. Back in the cabin, I keep the stove going, light candles, open some wine and sit out on the veranda, watching the bats go by and listening to the river as darkness falls. When it is truly dark, owls begin hooting in the wood, and fireworks boom in the distance at Teignton Fair, on the other side of the hill in Drewsteignton.

I wake up early, feeling at one with the roosting birds in the wood, perched as I am in the loft. During the night I heard only the steady song of the river, full of subtle variations played on the rocks, and the occasional bump somewhere deep inside the stove as it cooled and contracted its stove-pipe. Surveying an aerial view of the inside of the cabin from my bed, I admire the minimal furniture of the place. It is more or less the same as Thoreau's in his cabin at Walden Pond: a table and two chairs, one for himself and another for a guest.

The wood-burner does the heating and the cooking, and there's a high beam to sling the bedding over to air, well away from the mice, which I imagine will come out to play like the Borrowers the minute I leave. All I have brought, including food and drink, fits easily in a rucksack. This is one of those places where everything, even a single baked bean, tastes so good that you don't need much to eat anyway, and each cup of tea is a major ritual. This was especially true of the first of the day, which necessitated lighting the stove to boil the kettle.

The deck of the veranda feels warm to my bare feet when I climb downstairs. Blackbirds are singing all over the wood, a greater spotted woodpecker flies along the bottom of the valley, and a pair of buzzards ambles past, flying at the same level as my breakfast table. The sun lights up the leaves like stained glass, dancing on the mossy trunks of oaks, reflecting highlights off the river. In a wicker chair beside the door, I notice every living thing that comes past. Bees on their way to a clump of foxgloves to my right. A dor beetle that keeps turning up, clambering over shivers of oak where the wood is chopped. A red admiral sails past. A yellow brimstone. As soon as the wind gets up, the insects disperse into the wide clearing of bracken, bluebells, stitchwort, foxgloves and saplings of silver birch before the cabin. A squirrel comes close to the door, quite bold, looking for crumbs.

Later, as I sit reading in the afternoon sun, a pearl-bordered fritillary comes and settles on my book, enjoying the reflected sunlight. Insects are often attracted to the brightness of books. At home in my garden, dragonflies and damselflies often settle on the page, and will stay there for some time. Such moments are leisure for them as well as for me. What else could they be doing but resting and sunbathing, perhaps even catching up on some lost sleep? I can never decide whether insects and small animals are profligate with their energy or highly economical. A fly will apparently buzz about far more than it really needs to, but a spider will sit still in its web for hours on end, only stirring itself to race out and capture a snagged fly, or to flee some danger. Spiders will build communal webs across whole fields, covering them in dazzling lakes of early-morning dew: as massive an expense in work and materials as when Christo wrapped up the Reichstag.

The Sacred Groves of Devon

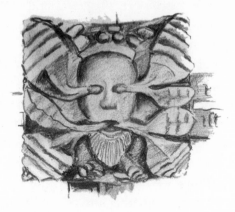

At King's Nympton I had an appointment with the Green Man in the church, up a path near the village pub, the Grove. He is a reticent figure, always half hidden in the woodwork or carved stone like a wren in a hedge. Inside the church I lay on my back along the seat of a pew, peering up into the half-light of the timbered barrel-arched nave roof. Each of the cross-joints in the gingham of beams was adorned with a carved oak boss about a foot square: an ornamental device to create an illusion of seamless timbering. Adjusting to the dimness, I began to make out the leaf-masked face of the Green Man looking back at me in half a dozen different shapes. With him, concealment is everything. He hides high in the church roof, or crouches in carved misericords beneath the seats of choir stalls, where choirboys stuff their sweet wrappers. In King's Nympton Church, with my head crammed against its thousand-year-old north wall, I knew I was being watched.

It must have been strange for a fifteenth-century craftsman to find the Green Man taking shape like Pinocchio under his chisels and gouges, to see him staring back from the workbench with the leaves bursting forth from his mouth, ears, nostrils, even sometimes his eyes. The leaves flow from him like poems or songs. He himself is a kind of folksong. Everyone knows it, but each singer has a different, personal version, a variation on the theme. 'I am not elderly,' says the Green Man in one of Jane Gardam's enchanting stories about him; 'I am the Green Man.' He is the spirit of the rebirth of nature. He is the chucked pebble that ripples out into every tree ring. He is a green outlaw and he is everywhere, like a Che Guevara poster.

The eight oak columns of the fan-vaulted rood screen stretched into out-curving branches crowned in a rich, leafy forest canopy, with here and there a face in the leaves. At the back of the church stood a massive twenty-foot rustic ladder made from a single oak cleft in two, leading up into the belfry, and, in the porch outside the giant oak door, I gazed in astonishment at thirty-six foliate roof bosses in yet another extravagant display of the skills of the King's Nympton carpenters and wood-carvers of the fifteenth century. Each individual boss was, as children say, 'the same only different', and the structure must have contained ten or twenty times more oak than was practically necessary to support the modest lead roof. The worn stem of a fallen Celtic cross that forms the threshold would once have marked this spot as sacred years before the church stood here. The holiness was surely bound up with trees, oak in particular, as the glory of the porch roof alone made plain. Even the hinges of the box pews were forged into acorns, and there was evidence that the Green Man had marched to the Great War with the King's Nympton men in the Devonshire Regiment. In the roll of the dead was the name of Private Sylvanus Hill.

All round North Tawton, along the valleys of the Taw and the Yeo, I had freckled my map with pencil rings and underlinings to highlight a remarkable concentration of two things: churches containing masks of the chameleon Green Man, and places called Nymet, Nympton or Nymph, of which there are at least thirteen. Never quite shaking off the field mouse feeling of being watched, I circled through Nympton St George and Nymet Rowland, then went a few miles south to the populous churchyard of Sampford Courtenay. Stepping into the church was like entering a grove of oak, its arched, wagon roof was so exuberantly timbered. 'Look at the strength of our faith,' it said. I found seven faces of the Green Man, including a magnificent one in the chancel almost directly above the altar, bearded and saintly-looking, and another with a fishtail for a beard. The rest were, as Jane Gardam says, 'all wrapped up in leaves like a Greek dinner'. Elsewhere in the roof, a sow suckled her litter, and on two of the bosses a trio of hares chased each other in a circle. In a neat illusory device worthy of Escher, they shared between them only three ears, which formed a triangle at the centre of the design, yet each animal seemed to have two. The same *trompe L'œil* motif appears in seventeen churches across Devon. Because it was the final animal to bolt from the standing corn as the reapers approached the last of it at the centre of the field, the hare was identified by the old country people as a version of Ceres, the corn goddess, escaping in disguise. In Galloway, according to Sir James Frazer, the reaping of the last standing corn was still called 'cutting the hare' when he published the 1922 edition of *The Golden Bough*. And hares are well known to go mad, lunatic, in March at the swelling of the moon when the corn seed must be sown. Chasing each other in a moon-circle on the roof boss, the trinity of animals suggests the three phases of the moon: waxing, full and waning. Like the pig and her piglets, they are another manifestation of the life and fertility the good folk of Sampford Courtenay wished to invoke and perpetuate in the fields through the oak carvings in their church. Some of the carpenters along these Devon river valleys would acquire reputations for their skill in fashioning wood and travel more widely. Close to my home in Suffolk, in villages like Huntingfield and Wingfield, the flamboyant de la Pole family made angel roofs of oak in the churches of their manors, and even took Suffolk carpenters to Ewelme in Oxfordshire to make one there.

I found more hares, and a haunting, bearded, deathly pale Green Man wearing a Dionysiac crown of grapes, gagged and blindfolded by the giant leaves springing from his eyes and mouth, in the church at Spreyton. At South Tawton, the Green Man gurned down from every other roof boss just above rows of lyrical carved angels along the leafy oak roof plate. Nowadays such an inspired conjunction would be called 'multiculturalism', but, as Ronald Blythe says, 'the Green Man is no enemy to Christ.' In his dazzling chapter 'The Nature of Gothic' in *The Stones of Venice*, John Ruskin celebrates the freedom and independence enjoyed by every workman in the Medieval Gothic 'system of ornament', contrasting it to the state of slavery of the workman on the building sites of the Greeks, Assyrians or Egyptians. The approach of the Christian church- and cathedral-builders was, by contrast, liberal and relaxed, 'Christianity having recognized, in small things as well as great, the individual value of every soul'. It was consistent with the true, humble spirit of Christianity freely to acknowledge human frailty and unworthiness by encouraging its expression in the shaping of stone or wood. 'And it is, perhaps, the principal admirableness of the Gothic schools of architecture', says Ruskin, 'that they thus receive the results of the labour of inferior minds; and out of fragments full of imperfection, and betraying that imperfection in every touch, indulgently raise up a stately and unaccusable whole.' In praising the Gothic, Ruskin is arguing for a return to the dignity of labour. He sees the new industrial mechanization of his nineteenth century enslaving the very souls of its people, workers and consumers alike, by shackling their self-expression. 'Look round this English room of yours,' he exhorts his readers, 'about which you have been proud so often . . . Examine again all those accurate mouldings and perfect polishings, and unerring adjustments of the seasoned wood and tempered steel . . . Alas! If you read rightly, these perfectnesses are signs of a slavery in our England a thousand times more bitter and more degrading than that of the scourged African or helot Greek.'

What makes Ruskin's writing on the Gothic so electrifying is that he interprets it politically, seeing it as a positively revolutionary force just where we least expect to find one, in our medieval churches and cathedrals:

And on the other hand, go forth again to gaze upon the old cathedral front, where you have smiled so often at the fantastic ignorance of the old sculptors: examine once more those ugly goblins, and formless monsters, and stern statues, anatomiless and rigid; but do not mock at them, for they are signs of the life and liberty of every workman who struck the stone; a freedom of thought, and rank in scale of being, such as no laws, no charters, no charities can secure; but which it must be the first aim of all Europe at this day to regain for her children.

Listing six defining characteristics of the Gothic, Ruskin begins with 'Savageness or Rudeness' and includes the love of natural objects and the 'disturbed imagination' that leads to the grotesque. Ruskin suggests that the best of the grotesque, which he calls 'that magnificent condition of fantastical imagination', is almost always composed of two elements, 'one ludicrous, the other fearful'. Like the two masks of Dionysos that still represent the modern theatre, the Green Man is both playful and terrible. He is at the same time comic and tragic, or, as Ruskin puts it: 'the grotesque falls into two branches, sportive grotesque and terrible grotesque', pointing out that 'there are hardly any examples which do not in some degree combine both elements.'

In the lava-flow of leaves that gushes from him, the Green Man is clearly uttering something. But what is the meaning of his green speech-bubble? It sounds very like the call of the wild. And yet he often seems more anguished than joyful. This is not the open face of Robin Hood lifting his horn to his lips: more like Edvard Munch's *The Scream*. The spirit and energy of the grotesque is essentially satirical, and lives on in our time in the work of Gerald Scarfe or Ralph Steadman. And if the Green Man often looks deathly at the same time as overflowing with life, that is because paradox is his very nature. Since he is life itself, the thing he utters, or 'outers', is the living green of the woods in spring. He carries the spirit of Dionysos himself, whose haunts are woods and wild places, and who is never seen except as a mask left hanging in a tree.

Many of the carpenters who carved the North Devon Green Men must have known each other; may even have been related. The carvings all date from the fourteenth and fifteenth centuries.

As contemporaries from different parishes, the craftsmen would have compared notes, and 'The Green Man' or 'The Three Hares' would have been handed down as a kind of repertoire from father to son. You see hints of some of their own Devon looks, or those of their neighbours: faces you could still see in the old farming community that survived, more or less intact round here, into the early 1970s. These are the faces that loom out of Ted Hughes's *Moortown Diary* in 'She has come to pass', a poem about a livestock sale:

> A whole day
> Leaning on the sale-room gates
> Among the peninsula's living gargoyles,
> The weathered visors
> Of the labourers at earth's furnace
> Of the soil's glow and the wind . . .

In his notes to the poem, Hughes, who lived and farmed at North Tawton in the heart of this Green Man/Nymet country, describes the ancient lineage of the North Devon farmers who were his neighbours: 'Buried in their deep valleys, in undateable cob-walled farms hidden not only from the rest of England but even from each other, connected by the inexplicable, Devonshire, high-banked, deep-cut lanes that are more like a defence-maze of burrows, these old Devonians lived in a time of their own.' 'Devonians' takes us back 360 million years, to the geological era when the first forests began to appear. The pun evokes the ancient, fossil feel of this country. A mere 2,000 years ago, the old inhabitants of this introverted country north of Dartmoor around the River Taw and its tributaries were the Celtic race known to the Romans as the Dumnonii: 'the people of the deep valleys'. They are the clue to the cluster of Nymet or Nympton names here. These places were almost certainly named after the local sacred rivers. The River Mole, known to the ancient Celts as the Nemet, rises and runs close to the Nymptons. Nymet or Nimet is also the old name of the River

Yeo, whose source is at Nymph, close to the modern East Nymph Farm, and which takes a course past at least six places named after it: Nymet Tracey, Broadnymet, Nichols Nimet, Nymet Rowland, Nymetwood, Nymphayes. Sources and springs are always specially numinous places. These present-day Nymet, Nymph and Nympton names share a Celtic origin, the Gaulish *nemeton*, Old Welsh *nimet*, Old Saxon *nimid* and Celtic *nemeto-* or *nemitis* all meaning 'a sacred grove'. The local villages of Morchard Bishop and Cruwys Morchard take their names from the Celtic *mawr coed*, 'big wood', and another dozen places in the area called Beer, Bear or Beere are all modern versions of the Old English *bearu*, whose meaning is close to the Celtic *nemeton*.

Nemetotacio is the name recorded for the fort the Romans built a mile or two away on the banks of the Taw at North Tawton, close to the Roman road from Exeter. It is an amalgamation of the Celtic *nemeton* and the Latin *stationis*, meaning 'road station' or 'outpost': 'The Road Station of the Sacred Groves'. Designed to accommodate a cohort of 500, it was flanked by two more forts near by, at Okehampton and Bury Barton, as well as a marching camp less than half a mile off, big enough for half a legion: a force of 2,500 men. Such a concentration of military power in the area suggests the Romans encountered determined resistance from the native Dumnonii people, refusing to surrender their sacred woods and the holy rivers Nimet and Nemet.

Flying over this part of Devon in the summer of 1984, the archaeologist Frances Griffith made a remarkable discovery through her aerial photographs of crop marks. Half a mile to the west of the village of Bow, close to a bend in the Yeo, she recognized, towards one corner of a cornfield, the dark outline of a prehistoric wood henge: a circular space up to 148 feet in diameter enclosed by a substantial ditch with openings to the east and west. Within the enclosure was an oval of nineteen pits, most probably post holes, each originally supporting a substantial timber. This was the first wood henge discovered in Devon. It has been carefully surveyed, and probably dates to the third millennium BC like others of its kind. The name of Bow has contracted over the last seven centuries from Nymetbowe and Nymetboghe. Its root is the Old English *boga*, a curve, describing the wide bend in the River Yeo near by.

Just outside Bow, I climbed the gentle slope of a stubble field from the road and stood in the top corner looking down towards the rolling valley of the Nymet River, hidden in the fold of land between a dozen neat hedgerows. I could just detect the levelling of the ground within the invisible ring of the ditch. Its bank had long ago been ploughed out. I wandered about, scanning the balding stubble optimistically for signs of flint or bone, making a mental picture of the wooden circle as it might have looked, with deep ditches and steep banks, and the stark drama of timbers against the sky.

Frances Griffith's discovery of this timber circle echoed that of Woodhenge sixty years earlier by Gilbert Insall, a distinguished First World War pilot and one of the pioneers of aerial photography in archaeology. In December 1925, flying over Stonehenge at 2,000 feet in his single-seater Sopwith Snipe, he had spotted something in the corner of a field a couple of miles away: a large circle with oval rings of white spots in the centre. Leaning out of the open cockpit, he photographed it. By the following July, when the corn was up, he was able to take more photographs revealing the outline of six concentric ovals of pale spots. They were later revealed by Maud Cunnington, in her excavation of the site promptly begun in 1926, to be no fewer than 168 post holes, each holding a timber post, possibly of oak. She estimated that one of the largest posts would have been at least thirty feet tall, standing nearly twenty-five feet above ground and almost three feet in diameter. They would have been whole tree-trunks, grown tall and straight in dense woodland with a high canopy. The layout of Woodhenge appeared remarkably similar to that of Stonehenge a short way to the south, and in the central space, towards the back of the oval of posts, was the grave of a young child. Clearly the place had a ceremonial or ritual role.

It was not too long before other wooden henges began to be discovered. In 1929 Gilbert Insall spotted and photographed one at Arminghall near Norwich with an oval of eight massive post holes up to three feet across. The following year Maud Cunnington found, and excavated, the Sanctuary, on the downs to the west of the great Avebury stone circle; smaller than Woodhenge, it had ninety-three post holes arranged in six concentric rings, with evidence of standing stones in the inner circle.

The most dramatic discovery came in 1967, with Geoffrey Wainwright's excavation of Durrington Walls, the biggest known henge enclosure in Britain, four miles from Stonehenge and close to the River Avon. It has now emerged as an integral part of a single interconnected system of monuments that seems to have included Stonehenge, its avenue, the lines of cursus ditch banks, the river and the hundreds of barrows on the downs. It is slightly bigger than Avebury and once enclosed circles of timber rather than stone. Woodhenge lies immediately to its south, apparently part of the same complex. Wainwright uncovered the remains of two timber circles within Durrington Walls. The larger one was over 120 feet wide, with a confusing mass of at least 200 closely spaced post holes. Opinion was divided at the time between those who thought the timber circles were open, free-standing wooden versions of Stonehenge, and those, like Wainwright, who thought the posts once supported a vast roof, probably open at the centre along the lines of a building like the Globe Theatre. But there was no evidence of the ground erosion copious volumes of rainwater would have caused in tumbling off such a mighty roof. Patterns of thought change all the time in archaeology, and the free-standers seem to have prevailed.

The archaeologist and writer Mark Edmonds is interested in the way people experienced places like timber and stone circles in relation to their day-to-day lives and their own individual lifespans. He believes free-standing posts, which would have looked and felt as dense as any copse, may have allowed for the arrangement of people for ceremony. It is easy to underestimate, he says, the extraordinary numbers of people who would have congregated around the area of Durrington Walls at certain times of the year for feasting, exchange of goods and the immense communal work-effort that went into the long-term building of the monuments in the area. Great middens containing the bones of pigs and other animals have been found there. Huge numbers of the Late Neolithic people who made Durrington Walls and its timber henges would have come together from some distance out of small, scattered groups at particular times of the year, and Edmonds thinks the feeling of being part of something bigger would have been of great importance in their lives. Participation in the building of monumental henges, as well as feasting together, would have helped cement the bonds of kinship among the scattered Neolithic people.

As Barbara Bender points out in her book *Stonehenge: Making Space*, the work was prodigious: an estimated 11,000 hours of work to position the southern timber circle at Durrington Walls and another 500,000 working hours to dig the perimeter ditch with antler picks. The felling of so many trees to furnish the henge posts would also have opened up tracts of the surrounding woodland. The archaeologists Aubrey Burl, Richard Bradley and others have estimated that the creation of Silbury Hill to the north of Stonehenge would have required 35 million basket loads of chalk and soil, or 18 million hours of work. Participating in the work itself must surely have been a highly important part of all the ceremonies and gatherings that went on around the monuments under construction.

Why is Stonehenge, or any henge circle, where it is? In the Stonehenge car park, three white spots mark where the post holes that once held three massive pine poles have been concreted over. Aligned with them is a hole that may show where a big tree once stood. Radiocarbon dates from the post holes have revealed that they are very, very old: as old as the eighth millennium BC, when the last Ice Age was still receding from Scotland, and Salisbury Plain was still covered in pine forest. That the huge posts were of pine, not oak, is another sign of their vintage. The archaeologist Tim

Darvill has woven a kind of creation myth in which the big tree would have given the place significance, and might have been the first landmark at the place we now call Stonehenge (or, at least, its car park) at a time when hunter-gatherers wandered the land. Some may have placed the timbers in line with the living tree to dramatize its importance to them as a place of remembrance and myth.

No further marking of the place has, so far, been found for several thousand years until around 3100 BC, with the excavation of the parallel chalk banks and ditches of the cursus, and then, some 150 years later, the chalky, dazzling moon-milk-white of the circular bank and ditch enclosure of Stonehenge. From about this time, 2900 BC, timbers began to be raised, first at Stonehenge and later, from 2500 BC, across to the east near the River Avon at Durrington Walls and Woodhenge. So Stonehenge was first of all timbered, and even as stone gradually replaced wood from the Late Neolithic into the Bronze Age, it seems to have overlapped in time with wooden posts in the henge circle itself, and with the great timber henge at Durrington Walls. As Barbara Bender points out, at Stonehenge the stones were shaped and jointed using woodworking techniques: mortise and tenon, tongue and groove. The famous bluestones from the Presceli Mountains in Wales show signs of tenons and mortice holes that have been chipped away.

The notion that Stonehenge and Durrington Walls were built as a single complex of complementary wooden and stone circles linked by the River Avon is the subject of the 2003–4 investigation of the area led by Mike Parker Pearson. It was inspired by an observation of his colleague, the Malagasy archaeologist Ramilisonina, that Stonehenge 'was not built for the transitory living but for the ancestors whose permanence was materialized in stone'. Henges are often linked to rivers, and Stonehenge is no exception, linked to the Avon by an earthwork avenue. The south-eastern entrance of Durrington Walls opens on to the same river a little further upstream, and Parker Pearson and a team of over seventy have discovered a Late Neolithic flint-cobbled avenue leading from the Avon to the henge's east entrance; sixty-five feet wide, including its banks, it is precisely aligned with the midsummer sunset. The avenue that leads from the river to Stonehenge is, conversely, aligned with the midwinter sunset. Parker Pearson is investigating the possibility that this might have been a funerary and processional route in the Late Neolithic. If stone commemorated the dead at Stonehenge, wood could have been the province of the living at Durrington Walls. To people who were prepared to lug bluestones 240 miles from Wales, spend thousands of hours quarrying chalk with antler picks or raise tree-trunks three feet thick in henges, natural materials were obviously of the greatest symbolic significance. Barbara Bender traces an elemental progression over time in the building of the monuments, from ditch banks of earth to chalk, to wood, and then to stone: both the relatively local sarsen and the bluestone from far away. Beyond these are the elements of sky, or air, and water in the alignments with the sun and moon, and the ways to and from the river, which led to other worlds, as well as geographical places.

As the place of the dead, Stonehenge seems to have been left in peace much of the time. By contrast, Durrington Walls, whose element was wood, was full of life and activity. The flint cobbles of its road to the river are worn smooth along the middle by walkers, and it is clear from the trodden, compacted pathways on the ground that large numbers of people moved through the timber circle guided on a fixed itinerary by posts, corridors and screens that controlled sight lines and gave access to the centre. The cattle and pig bones heaped in the middens indicate feasting, yet at the same time people were placing offerings in formal, set patterns around the timber posts of the henge.

In his influential *An Archaeology of Natural Places*, Richard Bradley argues that 'It is quite clear that ritual permeates every part of [Neolithic] social life and that it can take place in a settlement just as it does in a shrine.' He also believes that the Neolithic monuments of Wessex 'have a quite specific structure, and this can be understood in terms of the movements of the people who went there.' Radiocarbon dating has revealed that bones or artefacts placed as offerings beside the timber posts were sometimes already of some age. Others, such as axes, may have come from distant places: quarries high up in Langdale in the Lakes, or in the Presceli Mountains of Wales. Materials from distant places or distant times would have been symbolically charged in their new, formal, architectural context. Bradley goes on to make a vital recognition: 'By bringing together elements that were otherwise deposited in quite different kinds of locations, these earthworks, and the buildings within them, eventually became a microcosm of the landscape as a whole.' At the same time Bradley noticed that the formally ordered sequence of materials that would be seen on the guided way towards the centre of a timber circle amounted to a presentation of the history and evolution of the Neolithic people in Wessex. In the timber circle at West Kennet, the simpler, undecorated pottery vessels were placed in the entrance, and those with the most elaborate designs deep inside. In a variety of different circles, the general pattern of the sequence moves from the wild to the domestic. If rituals are a way of enacting a story, suggests Bradley, the narrative of the Neolithic monuments of Wessex is about history, origins and people's place in the world. The story may well have been a creation myth, a singing up of the songlines of the land.

The wood circle at Bow was once again a place of remembrance. Frances Griffith had put it back on the map. Until then, the antiquarian charts of Devon had shown plenty of ancient stone monuments all over the higher ground of Dartmoor, where granite was the natural material, but only a white space centred around the lower arable land of Bow and the Nymets. Sited in the *Nymetbowe* – the bend in the holy river – the henge was associated with the Yeo as Durrington Walls was with the Avon. In further work on the area, Griffith discovered a huge cluster of barrows and ring ditches surrounding Bow. She is convinced it was a major focus of ceremonial activity comparable with others up on Dartmoor, or further east on Salisbury Plain.

A mile to the west at Broadnymet, at the end of a long track,

Phil and Rachael led the way out of their farmyard through an orchard and a vegetable garden to the abandoned chapel of St Martin. It had once been a parish church, and for years it had been used to store old furniture. Now ivy spread veins across the stone gable wall and it stood empty, overhung by a tall beech and ash trees. Phil said there were two long barrows in the next-door field, scarcely visible now: ploughed out, and all the old hedges pulled up. The nymet places are perched on a slender lick of new red sandstone that runs out west from Exeter to Okehampton. It turns the fertile soil, and the cob walls of the barns and farmhouses, bright rusty-red with the occasional hint of pink at sunset. Dig, and you hit the sandstone a foot down. Trees spring up everywhere. 'Oaks come up here just for fun,' said Phil.

Green light filtered into the little wagon-roofed church through the surrounding trees. The elaborately timbered roof contrasted with the fissured plaster tumbling off the walls. On the dusty stone floor lay the mummy of a barn owl beneath a nesting box in the rafters. It was a young one, fully fledged. 'It died two days after the bloke from the wildlife came and climbed a ladder to the nest and ringed it,' said Phil. He had lost his whole healthy herd during the foot-and-mouth through 'contiguous culling'. The farms either side had the disease, so his cows were doomed too. Then Rentokil descended on the farm and poisoned all the rats and mice. That was the first time the barn owls died. A pigeon clattered out of the roof beams and disappeared through a shaft of light under the ridge tiles.

Broadnymet's name persists as a clue that it may have been particularly sacred to the early Devonians. 'Broad', descended from the Old English adjective *brade*, is still in modern usage to give emphasis, as in 'broad daylight' or 'broad Yorkshire'. As an enthusiastic fourth-century converter of pagan shrines into churches, Martin of Tours would have been an apt choice as the parish saint. The stubborn survival of the Nymet names suggests a remarkable propensity for the old beliefs among generations of free-thinking Devonians. They have been leading double lives here for centuries.

Going south towards the moor, I stopped to explore Cocktree Throat, a darkling lane with a ford at the bottom of a valley in a dense oak wood. At Taw Mill, the Cocktree Throat stream enters the Taw. Others arise and wind through boggy woodland in directions that defy my understanding. Some even seem to flow uphill. Beyond East Nymph and West Nymph I followed an oak wood called Trundlebeer: it flanks one of the source streams that will soon become mid Devon's Ganges: the nymet-river Yeo.

The car climbed south on to Dartmoor through the high-banked lanes, past the remote North Moor Arms to Gidleigh. At Scorhill, I struck out across the moor to the stone circle and its processional avenue of menhirs, the Stone Rows, then downhill for a mile over uneven gorse-topped tinners' spoil-heaps in furrows of yellow, heathery purple and green, towards the thread of the Teign and the solitary, flat-topped may tree that marks the river pool at Teign-turn. There's an old buzzards' nest of woven heather twigs and wool in the thorn's wind-bent tangle. Its twisted trunk, lichened in the crevices, is a rubbing post polished by sheep and ponies. Such lone trees are landmarks on Dartmoor, saviours in a winter mist, like the *ur*-tree at Stonehenge. The nearby hamlet of Thorn, in the parish of Chagford, grew up around such a tree. Richard Thorn, the great-great-grandfather of the famous landscape historian W. G. Hoskins, farmed the thirty-two acres there from which his ancestors had taken their name. First the old tree gave its name to the farm, then the farm gave its name to the first owners (Thorns had lived there since Robert atte Thorn in 1332). Richard Thorn was Parish Clerk of Chagford from 1800 to the end of his life, and was succeeded by his son, the village saddler and postmaster. The pair served for a continuous eighty-two years. Hoskins writes: 'These things delight me when I come across them. This is the immemorial, provincial England, stable, rooted deep in the soil, unmoving, contented and sane. Those are my forebears, who have made me what I am whether I like it or not . . .' The pool in the Teign was peaty, clear and cold, entered from a perfectly level grassy bank between clumps of reeds. Seen from water level, the thorn at the bend in the river filled the sky.

I went up to Thorn that evening to look for descendants of the original tree. In its old hedges I found holly, furse, hazel, oak, ash: everything but thorn. In the fading light, a farmer stood calling his cat home across the lane.

The Forest of Dean and the Wye

Crossing over the Severn, even at Gloucester, still feels to me like going abroad, as crossing the Tamar into Cornwall does. I was on my way to the very rim of England, the wooded border country along the valley of the Wye, to meet the man who has done more than almost anybody else for woodland conservation in Britain: my old school friend George Peterken, author of *Natural Woodland*. I slipped along the far banks under the high woods of the Dean, past the mudflats off Lydney, where the elvers that swim up the Severn each year from the Sargasso have mysteriously diminished recently from hundreds of millions to mere millions, like the sperm count of Western man. Apple and pear orchards crowded up the steep meadows beneath the forest: immense, unruly trees of rosy-cheeked Robin pears, blushing teardrops, left unpicked by the pony or pet-sanctuary people who have moved in along here. Half-hidden winding roads climbed through the woods, and the houses and garden walls were soft dark-crimson sandstone. However you approach it, the forest feels fortified and secretive, exactly as in all the Dennis Potter plays. It has always had an uneasy relationship with the outside world, and there are still people in the villages who have never ventured even the twenty miles to Gloucester. Hoisting myself into the forest, I saw everything in crayon colours:

a bright-blue British Legion hut, orange bracken, bright-red leaves of gean in the woods, the black shadows of yew. The road tunnelled through beeches, past Furnace Cottages, past diving squirrels and an old man on his knees raking acorns into a bag with the crook of his walking stick. Deeper into the forest it got darker, like a mineshaft.

As befits a woodland magus, George Peterken lives deep in some of the oldest, most interesting woods in Britain, down the bewildering lanes that run about St Briavel's Common like the veins on the back of your hand. St Briavel's lies on the high ground three miles to the west of the forest far above the wooded Wye Valley. The last time I saw George was at one of the last of the Beaulieu Road camps, when I was still at school and he was already at university but had come back to rejoin us. He was always deeply attached to the New Forest, regarding parts of it as the wildwood of his youth, and returned again later to do his doctorate field research there on the regeneration of holly in the woods. For George, as for me and others, Barry Goater is still the original inspiration for a life's commitment to ecology and conservation.

George came out to meet me down the garden, medium tall, gangling and skinny in an athletic way. Bespectacled, with the loping stride of the seasoned walker, he was quite obviously a creature of the woods. Like anyone accustomed to trees, he used his arms a lot, swinging himself up stone walls by their overhanging branches, vaulting farm gates with an easy action, grappling his way up or down steep woodland slopes hand over hand, sapling by coppice, shoot by branch by rock. He wore the favourite dark-blue fleece he had found hanging from a branch in a wood and claimed like Excalibur.

Like true woodlanders, George and his wife Sue live perched 800 feet above the treetops of the ancient small-leaved lime woods that cover the south-facing bank of the Wye Gorge upstream from Tintern Abbey. Across the river on the other bank is Wales. We began with a tour of the Peterken domain: an astonishing maze of miniature enclosures separated by long piles of pudding stone, the conglomerate rocks the Ice Age left littered all over the hillside here and on St Briavel's Common. Until about 1800 this was wood pasture where commoners of the forest grazed their animals and coppiced or pollarded the small-leaved limes, oak, beech, hazel and holly. Towards the end of the eighteenth century, squatters had begun to settle on St Briavel's Common on the edge of the forest. There had been squatters before. In the previous century Cromwell had expelled nearly 400 households who had settled in cabins on the forest's commons, and by 1680 another thirty cabins had sprung up, with enclosures, and were demolished. But the coal miners, charcoal-burners and iron-smelters had to live somewhere, and industry was booming in the Forest of Dean.

As in the New Forest, there is a long history of conflict between the Crown and the native commoners of the Forest of Dean, the foresters. But the presence of iron ore and coal made things different here. To become a free miner of the forest a man had to have been born within the Hundred of St Briavel's and to have worked for a year and a day in an iron or coal mine in the Hundred. Strong traditions of independence have persisted among the free miners and foresters. From 1800 to 1820 there was something of a population explosion around St Briavel's Common, and a large part of it was enclosed by squatters. George said he thought the cause was some sort of administrative breakdown, but this steep, remote boulder-strewn obstacle course would hardly have been of much interest for either farming or forestry. In just twenty years the landscape changed completely. Working cooperatively, the poor people of St Briavel's decided they would take over this equally poor but beautiful stretch of land. With astonishing speed and determination, they cleared it of boulders, dragging them about by hand or with horses into giant lines of heaped rocks some three or four feet high with flat tops wide enough to drive a tractor along: medium-scale versions of Hadrian's Wall. In fact they were not generally intended as walls, although many of them were faced with dry-stonework to create a haphazard-looking system of little paddocks, some no bigger than a modest back garden. The effect was of wandering from room to room through the ruins of some bosky castle or Mayan ruins in a jungle. George likened it to parts of Highgate Cemetery, where you stumble through a dense wood to find ruined graves or mausoleums now and again. The pudding stones have been piled on top of, or around, huge old coppice stools of small-leaved limes, oak or hazel. They were also stacked against the trunks of pollards. The result is that trees over 200 years old are growing up out of the ferny rocks from coppice stools that were already well on in years in 1800.

Small-leaved limes have a tendency to layer their outstretched lower branches when they touch the ground. As if weary of resisting gravity, they stoop to nuzzle the earth and hunker down, soon burying themselves in enough leaf mould and scuffed soil to sprout roots and send up new shoots. Thus the tree spreads and creeps along through the stones of the rocky bank or wall. But what may eventually come to look like a row of independent trees is really still a single organism. George showed me how to look at the distinctive habit and shape of each tree, even the exact shade of its leaves, and to recognize how different each one is from its neighbours of the same species. So the limes that towered above us as we went were often single beings that had reproduced themselves repeatedly as clones over 200 years of layering, shifting along many yards of the bank like the walking wood in *Macbeth*. The surreptitious way these trees had crept across St Briavel's Common, gaining new land for themselves by slow degrees, exactly mirrored what the squatters did. In *Cotters and Squatters*, Colin Ward describes how the commoners and squatters of the New Forest would enlarge their holdings by an organic and cunning process that almost exactly mimics the small-leaved limes of St Briavel's: 'The inside of the hedge was cut, and the briars and stuff thrown outside. These shot out and formed a sort of rolling fence, and so the would-be squatters kept trimming the inside and adding to the outside.'

I kept thinking of Colin Ward and William Cobbett as George unveiled this small-scale people's landscape created by a combination of hard work, mutual support, and the stubborn, often courageous assertion of the rights of the foresters and commoners to shelter and a share in the land. In his books about allotments, squatters, and the Essex and Sussex plotlanders of *Arcadia for All*, Ward has always championed the virtues and productivity of the self-sufficient cottager for whom Cobbett originally wrote *Cottage Economy*, with its insistence on the possibility of the riches of happiness and independent well-being for the labourers who had always been degraded as 'the poor'. Cobbett was a rural idealist, but he was a practical one, and his little book, published in 1821 at exactly the moment when the squatters of St Briavel's Common were asserting themselves as free woodlanders, is full of 'Information relative to the *brewing* of BEER, making of BREAD, keeping of COWS, PIGS, BEES, EWES, GOATS, POULTRY, AND RABBITS, and relative to other matters deemed useful in the conducting of the affairs of a Labourer's Family'. Cobbett's aims in writing this practical, polemical book are at heart political: 'It is *abundant living* amongst the people at large, which is the great test of good government, and surest basis of national greatness and security.' In his chapter on pigs, Cobbett might have had St Briavel's in mind when he writes: 'much must depend on the situation of the cottage; because all pigs will graze; and therefore, on the skirts of forests or commons, a couple or three pigs may be kept, if the family be considerable.' In an aside a paragraph further on, Cobbett is careful to let his readers know whose side he is on:

I once, when I lived at Botley, proposed to the copy-holders and other farmers in my neighbourhood, that we should petition the Bishop of Winchester, who was lord of the manors thereabouts, to grant titles to all the numerous persons called trespassers on the wastes; and also to give titles to others of the poor parishioners who were willing to make, on the skirts of the wastes, enclosures not exceeding an acre each. This I am convinced would have done a great deal towards relieving the parishes, then greatly burdened by men out of work . . . Not a single man would agree to my proposal!

When Cobbett has the good sense to ask, as he rides through the New Forest, 'What are these deer *for*?', the answer to his implied question, 'What are these forests *for*?', is consistent in its support of the commoners and squatters:

The only good purpose that these forests answer is that of furnishing a place of being to labourers' families on their skirts; and here their cottages are very neat, and the people are hearty and well, just as they do round the forest of Hampshire. Every cottage has a pig or two. These graze in the forest, and, in the fall, eat acorns and beech-nuts and the seed of the ash; for, these last, as well as the others, are very full of oil, and a pig that is put to his shifts will pick the seed very nicely out from the husks. Some of these foresters keep cows, and all of them have bits of ground, cribbed, of course, at different times, from the forest, and to what better use can the ground be put?

The Ordnance Survey map of St Briavel's Common looks very like the 'newtake' land around villages like Chagford and Throwleigh on the north-eastern fringe of Dartmoor: land reclaimed in the past by small farmers and commoners an acre or less at a time from the open moor and enclosed, so the farms grow by cell division. The tiny fields at St Briavel's appear like the creases round an old lady's mouth: tiny enclosures of a quarter to half an acre at most, with a hay meadow here, a grazing paddock there, a pightle, or just a stone pigpen. George showed me a walled enclosure on his land no bigger than a couple of average living rooms, possibly a place for enclosing free-grazing pigs at night or even a tiny hay meadow. Going from room to room like this in a landscape evolved on a modest, human scale could logically be called 'homely'. The containment of this landscape in miniature creates endless surprises, invites you at every turn to settle down in some mossy corner or beckons you to discover more of its secrets. I thought of the 'hornbeam rooms' planted by eighteenth-century gardeners, little hedged enclosures for quiet repose.

The way George put it, we were walking through a 200-year-old landscape superimposed on a much older one, that of an ancient woodland, a wood pasture common for cattle, sheep and pigs. We scrambled steeply downhill through the woods, parachuting down on low branches as far as a clear line about 700 feet above the River Wye, defined by a wall beyond which the land had been neither squatted nor cleared. Beyond, all the way down to the river, was a steep woodland common where foresters ran pigs and grazed cattle and sheep. The Badgers, the landless itinerant shepherds who still lived in the forest, also exercised their right to graze their animals where they pleased.

Elm, ash, gean, the wild cherry, and the rare native large-leaved lime, *Tilia platyphyllos*, also grow in these woods, and stripes of alder wood follow the swampy seepage from springs and wells higher up. There was plenty of water in the stone dip wells we encountered, and George said they never seem to dry up. Most of them lie on the course of winter-bournes like the one that runs through his garden and invariably floods his swimming pool. Uniquely, the small-leaved limes of the Wye Valley are relatively gregarious. Lime woods are normally unmixed with other species. In many other parts of Britain they vanished a thousand years ago with the Romans from former strongholds they dominated like Epping Forest and the New Forest.

Deeper into the woods, we followed part of the network of old tracks and came to one of the square stone-walled enclosures they link together. These are the assarts, where sheep could be penned for the night, often in barns. Near by was 'Laurel Cottage', a ruined squatters' dwelling, cloaked in dense ivy, jungled in the laurel that once stood tame and trimmed before it, with an oak lintel supporting the upstairs stone wall and a pigpen at the back. The place was so overgrown it was almost invisible to us as we approached. Some of these isolated houses along the side of the valley were used by the boatmen who used to navigate the Wye, carrying goods in and out of the forest. George said there are so many footpaths all over St Briavel's Common, it would take at least a day to walk them all. We followed one uphill to the top meadow George and Sue have reconstituted, fencing it off, clearing the encroaching hedge back to its original line and grazing it with sheep. Stone walls and hedge had become a single organism. Blackthorn, hazel and holly grew out of the crevices, armoured against the browsing animals. An oak had seeded itself on top of the wall, and in two wet, boggy patches George had planted black poplar cuttings from one of the original trees beside the bridge over the Usk at Crickhowell. There were now so many badgers in the woods, said George, that he and Sue had woken up one morning to find the entire field ploughed up.

The high woods along the Wye are ribboned with ancient green lanes. In the Coxbury and Wyegate Lane above the river at Lower Redbrook, George, Sue and I tramped uphill along a deep holloway scoured out by winter floods dashing down in torrents, washing away the earth year after year from the smooth limestone boulders. We walked between hedge banks of pollard limes and holly in a green tunnel. The lane runs south-east to St Briavel's Castle, the medieval court and administrative centre for the forest, and continues all the way to the banks of the Severn via Hewelsfield, with its thousand-year-old churchyard yew. St Briavel's Castle was also an arms factory and munitions store, where iron mined from the forest was made into huge numbers of arrowheads and cross-bolts, with shafts of yew or seasoned ash for the royal armies. These would have been carried by pack horse and pannier up and down the lane to boats on the Wye.

After a mile or so, we turned off the lane and climbed steeply to our left through the old limes of Highbury Woods, towards the great limestone bank of Offa's Dyke running along the top of the hill. At the core of the wood here, an area of secondary woodland had regenerated out of the earthworks of the dyke bank and a string of limestone quarries. Huge old yews grew along the dyke, their roots exposed in the cliff walls of the lime quarries immediately beneath it. In the artificial limestone pavement of the quarries, native whitebeam had sprung up, and we found a lime kiln hidden in the trees. The far older primary woodland of limes and holly surrounded the more recent woods, so the effect, as

George saw it, was of a monk who had allowed his tonsure to grow back.

Lime grew fast here on the limestone and conglomerate rock, and a good many of the old pollards were top-heavy. We came across a gigantic triple-branching pollard like a wine glass that was about to crack and split itself in two. George estimated that the base, although monumental, was no more than 200 to 250 years old, with another eighty or ninety years' growth on top. He said there had never been so many trees in the Wye Valley. Coppicing and pollarding were now things of the past, and the trees were constantly spreading, recolonizing old meadows and grazing enclosures. Much of the land along the valley is owned by the Woodland Trust, which is sensibly maintaining some of these meadows as grazing, as well as allowing others to run to woodland. Another pollard lime, collapsed on a bank, had already sent down roots into its own detritus and was growing vigorous new shoots. Having come to know this place intimately, George said that what struck him was its mutability: a flower you knew was there one year wasn't there the next, but something new was there instead. The dynamic ways of nature impressed him more and more.

Apart from the occasional statuesque old pollard, ash seemed relatively scarce in Highbury Woods, but high up near the lime quarries we found an ash and a birch that had grafted themselves together, joined at the trunk, locked in an arboreal embrace. Deep in the heart of the woods we found an unusually tall hollow oak and the scorch mark of a small fire before it. This was quite likely a sign, we decided, of some Beltane fire-leaping ceremony before the oak. On my way over, I had received an account of the light-hearted rituals of the Cheltenham Pagan Gourmet Witches, a group of eight or nine self-confessed 'lardy women of a certain age', whose custom it is to go out into the woods and countryside of Gloucestershire and celebrate the old seasonal festivals, always provisioning themselves with a generous picnic of the choicest delicacies and fine wines. They are, of course, careful not to cause any damage, and do their Beltane fire-leaping, I was told, over a

modest fire in a cake tin. George said he had occasionally encountered women in these woods during his nature rambles, sitting
under trees playing flutes or recorders. According to my informant,
these gatherings of the Cheltenham Ladies are entirely good-
humoured occasions full of hilarity and not in the least secretive.
She described a recent outing to the tall, creaking pines on May
Hill outside the town, where the Gourmets danced to a recorded
tape before arranging themselves into the shape of a star and lying
together under the trees gazing up at the emerging night sky, keenly
observed from the long grass of the ridge by an ill-concealed group
of Borstal boys from the nearby institution.

I asked George what he thought of the assertion I had heard
from a forester in Oxford a day or two earlier that none of our
native trees would be able to survive in Britain by the end of the
century because of the effects of climate change. The notion had
also found its way into the *Independent* as the basis for a feature, the
idea being that, far from planting our local varieties of trees, we
had better start importing cultivars from the countries of Eastern
Europe, where the trees are used to hot, dry summers and cold
winters, or more southern versions of the oak or beech. George
considered the whole notion complete nonsense. It ignored, he
thought, the resilience of our trees and the past fluctuations in our
climate they have successfully withstood.

Looking down towards the Wye, George talked about the way
trees have influenced the course and history of rivers. Fallen trees
form dams or riffles. Gravel and detritus accumulate around them
to create shoals or pools, increasing the diversity of habitat in the
river. Beavers used to do the same sort of work, but they were last
recorded on the River Teifi in 1188 by Giraldus Cambrensis, and in
Scotland, according to George. Dead or dying wood is a vital
component of woodland ecology often missing in contemporary
woods that are managed and cleared. There is simply too much
management and not enough informed neglect. Of all the many
species our natural woodland can potentially support, George
thought about a fifth originally depended on dead or slowly dying

wood or on the fungi that live in trees and dead wood: the beetles, woodlice, spiders, larvae and other invertebrates collectively termed saproxylics. Woodland ecologists now talk a great deal about the need for more of what they call Coarse Woody Debris. Francis Kilvert, writing his diary upriver at Clyro in April 1876, calls it 'fallow wood': 'We came tumbling and plunging down the steep hillside of Moccas Park, slipping, tearing and sliding through oak and birch and fallow wood of which there seemed to be underfoot an accumulation of several feet, the gathering ruin and decay, probably of centuries.' This kind of vintage rot, and the kind that spreads gradually into old living pollards, hollowing their trunks and crowns to the point where they are what Kilvert calls 'dottards', is particularly rich and valuable in a wood, because it contains older woodland species of wood-feeders, many of which have been rendered locally extinct by being literally tidied out of existence. Unlike birds or moths, these are animals which cannot easily spread from one wood to another, so once lost in a particular wood they cannot recolonize it and are gone for ever. This is yet another reason for the need for retaining and valuing ageing and ancient trees. Most healthy trees have dead branches by the time they reach 150, and by the time they reach 250 to 300 years of age it is perfectly normal for them to have developed the hollow trunks, boles and dead branches that are home to a rich world of fungi and invertebrate life.

In *Natural Woodland*, George Peterken has documented the extraordinary diversity of species that can be living in a forest or wood. The Bialowieza Forest in Poland is reported, he says, to contain 11,000 animal species, including 8,500 insects, 206 spiders and 226 species of birds. Animals greatly outnumber plants, but there are still 900 species of flowering plants, 254 mosses, 200 lichens and an estimated 1,000 species of the higher fungi. By comparison, the far smaller Monks Wood Nature Reserve in Huntingdonshire still contained, in 1973, 372 flowering plants, 97 mosses, 34 lichens and 337 fungi. Its 2,842 animal species, all but 149 of them invertebrates, also outnumbered the plants. These can only be approximate figures, because woodland conditions are changing all the time. So too is the understanding of fungi as more and more are identified, but their crucial role in the lives of woods and trees has yet to be fully revealed. Leaving trees to lie where they fall should they blow over is the least that foresters can do to help conserve a more natural balance and diversity of life in the woods.

As we scrambled downhill again, braking our descent by briefly hugging the trunk of each tree in our path, George talked about the year he and Sue spent in New England, and the Massachusetts woods of Thoreau. Everywhere in the woods there, they would come across ruined farmsteads and old stone field walls hidden in ivy and encrusted with moss. St Briavel's Common, said George, is the only landscape like it in Britain, concealing everywhere within its woodland the signs of the old agricultural landscape.

In Hewelsfield churchyard further down the green lane, I squeezed inside the hollow of the thousand-year-old yew and looked up into the lantern of its twisted trunk, illuminated like the inside of a dovecot through the perforations where long-dead boughs once emerged. Yet the tree was in full foliage and blackbirds were sampling the first of its ripe pink berries.

Among Jaguars

It might have been a library, and the studious-looking people in white coats librarians or archivists moving bundles of old manuscripts about very carefully, leafing through them, or settling to pore over them at well-lit desks. At the Jaguar factory in Coventry, 160 cabinet-makers were at work in two shifts, day and night, selecting and cutting out the shapes of delicate walnut veneer for the dashboards and door panels of the higher animals – 'cars' seems too mundane a word – that have all evolved from the feral SS Jaguar 100 sports model of 1936, with its sweeping wings, wire wheels, knock-on chrome hubs and immense, dashing bonnet louvred like a cheese grater, a seemingly endless perspective, viewed from the driver's cockpit.

These days the cars are full of plump upholstery and chubbier, like the well-fed executives or politicians who drive, or are driven, in them. Each new model advances gracefully along the production line like Tarzan in a suit and tie. Modern Jaguars still belong to what Roland Barthes calls 'the bestiary of power', but they have evolved from a primitive to a classical form, a process first described in Barthes's essay on the new Citroën DS, written when it made its first dramatic appearance at the Paris Motor Show in 1955. He believes that modern cars are the exact equivalent of the great

Gothic cathedrals: 'the supreme creation of an era, conceived with passion by unknown artists, and consumed in image if not in usage by a whole population which appropriates them as a purely magical object'. Barthes sees that mythology is the key to understanding the world of cars: that, considered as objects, they are 'messengers of a world above nature'. The new Jaguars on the production line were infinitely smoother and more luxurious than their ancestors in the company's museum next door. The XJ120, introduced in 1948, brilliantly emulated the graceful wave-motion of the leaping *Panthera onca* in the forests of the Amazon. The impression it created was primarily animal, and yet, like its feline mentor, it luxuriated in the possession of surplus reserves and the effortless elegance that went with them. Just to have been passed by one in the street as a schoolboy conferred a kind of benediction and a temporary rise in one's status in the class. 'I saw an XJ.' 'Golly! What colour? Can I sit next to you?'

In our less adventurous times, the appeal of a new Jaguar is more homely. 'Inside the welcoming cabin of the XJ,' says the brochure, 'you're cocooned in a heady mix of luxurious leather and polished walnut veneer', and in the 3-litre XJ6 model and the XJ8, 'Burr walnut veneer fascia and door trims are matched with the walnut and leather steering wheel and walnut gearknob.'

Why is 'walnut' such a potent word in the copywriter's vocabu-lary? Its roots lie in the Old English *Walhhnutu* and the Old German *Walhoz*. That first syllable, *wal*, is related to the Old English *wale*, which evolved into *weal*, as in *commonweal*, and then became *wealth*, in the sense of well-being as much as possession. No doubt the well-being, in both body and pocket, referred originally to the benefits of the nuts. But walnut inside a car still denotes wealth. It also stands for a tradition of craftsmanship and, by extension, engineering. It looks back to the very best English cabinet-makers. Until the eighteenth century, walnut was the most prized of woods, sought for its hardness, its rich shades of brown and its intricate grain patterns, but during the early 1700s a run of bitterly cold winters spread across Europe, culminating in the winter of 1709, when temperatures sank below −20°C and walnut trees every-where froze to death. Walnut timber had become so scarce by 1720 that the French banned all exports to conserve their depleted stocks. Faced with the crisis, the English furniture-makers turned to mahogany from the tropical colonies, and were so delighted with its fine grain, strength and resistance to decay that it soon caught on as the new fashion.

Walnut, however, remains the more beautiful wood, and the relative rarity of burr veneer also imparts a sense of individuality to the Jaguar owner. Burrs are found only on large, old trees, perhaps one in a thousand. They are like pearls in oysters. The veneer used in Jaguars comes from the old walnut orchards of the valley of the Sacramento River in California. The trees are Persian, or English walnuts, *Juglans regia*, grafted on to black walnut stock, *Juglans nigra*. A burr, if it grows, will tend to develop around the graft at the crown of the root and in the base of the trunk, swelling it like a sprained ankle. Walnuts have huge tap roots, and their confluence with other roots at the meeting with the trunk is like a tide line, where things change and struggle, and leave the signs. Trees with burrs at least sixty to seventy years old are uprooted, not felled, because the best of the burr, its finest, most intricately figured grain, is in the crown of the root where it becomes the trunk. Burrs will grow higher up the trunks of old trees too, like pot bellies. I had seen the scars left by the English burr-poachers who came to the Ferghana Valley in Kyrgyzstan in the 1930s. Like any trade in things of great value, the walnut-burr business is no stranger to skulduggery. Burrs, which are sold by weight, are sometimes covertly soaked in water to raise their apparent value. They vary so much that there are no standard prices. Each one must be haggled over, sometimes with great passion, often in remote places. Dave Condon and Brian Pearce, who showed me round the Veneer Manufacturing Centre at Jaguar, told me that in the past, buyers from Jaguar searching out burrs in California have had the occasional gun pulled on them in the course of their work.

Once uprooted, the burr log is scraped clean and weighed like the vegetable it is. Then it is boiled to prevent it splitting, rotated on a machine like a pencil-sharpener, and veneer half a millimetre thick comes peeling off the blade. The veneer is sliced off the burr, not sawn. Leaves of veneer three or four feet long and two or more wide are bound together in bundles of twenty-four in the same sequence as they were cut. Each one is barcoded in number order, so the grain can be exactly 'mirror-matched' inside each new car. In its raw state each leaf of veneer feels like suede, and the symmetry of the grain in the sequence in which they are 'bookleaved', as they say in the trade, is very striking.

In Oxford, Dr Peter Savill, who works on walnut in the Plant Sciences Department, had told me that a well-established firm of fine furniture-makers in Ipswich had recently bought a large walnut tree from the Queen's Sandringham estate for £5,000. By the time it had been converted to veneer, the tree's total value had increased to £50,000. It is not unusual for the uncut root boles of walnuts to change hands for anything up to £10,000. They can be enormous. One specimen, garnered in California in 1980, is reputed to have weighed 4,000 pounds and produced 12,000 square feet of veneer. Once cut, the leaves of veneer must be kept damp to prevent them cracking. As they move through the factory, you see people gently spraying them, like hairdressers, with purified water to keep them in condition.

The burr is an excrescence of would-be buds rising from somewhere deep inside the tree like a spring. When cut across the grain by the giant pencil-sharpener as the buds bubble towards the bark of the tree, their turbulence is displayed, with every little eddy and vortex held perfectly still. A burr may arise as a reaction to some itch in the tree, a kind of benign wood tumour. There is an outburst of mad cell division, and elephantiasis sets in. What begins as a disfigurement ends life as an opulent adornment. A frog is revealed as a princess. Cutting the light a thousand ways in its eyes and prisms, the veneer is a celebration of the tree's pent-up energy in a whirling wood-dance.

The Jaguar veneer-cutters all sat under bright lights calculating, with the help of computers, how to make the most economical use of each leaf of veneer and match it with the grain of its twin, the next one in the bundle, to create a perfectly symmetrical pattern on the dashboard or the entire central console of a sports Jaguar. Watching these skilled people at work, I couldn't help feeling that the mother tree had somehow given up a secret. I was witnessing a form of taxidermy. Whatever secret anguish had created the burr was now on display, coopted as a sign of the genius that created the car, part of the stage-set for some future performance of, say, the Monteverdi *Vespers* on the in-car stereo at 120 mph on the Autostrada.

Each car consumed six and a half square feet of the precious burr veneer. I watched as the car-shapes of walnut were bedded gently on foundations of three strata of poplar veneer, each laid with its grain at right angles to its neighbour. The wooden sandwiches were cunningly moulded under pressure to the metal contours of the dashboard, door panel or gear console in a press, and cooked at 140°C for five minutes. Grinling Gibbons, the great woodcarver of the seventeenth century, would have been astonished. Now the veneered components were sanded, polished, varnished, sanded smooth again and fine-polished twice. 'It is well known', says Roland Barthes, 'that smoothness is always an attribute of perfection because its opposite reveals a technical and typically human operation of assembling: Christ's robe was seamless, just as the airships of science fiction are made of unbroken metal.'

'My brother Esau is an hairy man, but I am a smooth man.' I fought down the insistent thought of Alan Bennett's lines in the sermon in *Beyond the Fringe* as I stood in the cathedral hush of the Jaguar assembly lines during the morning tea-break. Everything about these cars was the essence of smooth. Walnut is so close grained that it takes a high polish better than any other wood, imparting to the Jaguar cockpit the rich glow of a classic violin. There is even something nut-like about the neat way the doors open to admit the driver into a soundbox in which the roar of the engine has also been smoothed to a subtle purr. Deeply burnished, the dark-brown swirling smoke patterns of the veneer's grain suggested an old master. I sat grandly in the cockpit, and was aware of more than a hint of walnut: it was a fashion statement. The expanse of it extending in perfect symmetry across the dashboard, with its bewildering array of dials, clocks and controls, and echoing in the turned walnut gear knob, and the walnut-and-leather steering wheel, reminded me of something subliminal I couldn't quite pinpoint at the time.

Later, in the middle lane of the M42, it came to me. It was the neat rows of sporting guns on parade in the sombre mahogany-panelled hush of James Purdy & Sons' shop in South Audley Street. Walnut has always been the favoured wood for gunstocks. It is lightweight, flexible, doesn't shrink or expand when wet, and is particularly shock-proof. It can be machined to very fine tolerances, so makes a good seating for metal parts. Gunsmiths favour it for all these reasons, and because of its intrinsic beauty. Purdy's prefer Turkish walnut, others choose English or French, or even black. Walk into any gunsmith's and you'll encounter the unmistakable walnut vibe. It is mildly ironic that a tree whose nuts are celebrated as an elixir of long life should find itself reincarnated in guns, and that wars should always have increased demand for the wood. The role of walnut is to mediate between the machine and its owner. Like the wooden handle of my bread knife, or any other tool handle, it cushions the cold energy of the steel and is warm, comfortable and smooth to the touch. In the Jaguar factory, one of the cabinet-makers had improvised a screwdriver handle from a walnut gear knob.

Another result of walnut's long-standing affair with engineering, craft and design is the laminated Lucifer propeller hub that sits on my desk. Most European manufacturers used walnut for their propellers, for its strength and even grain. Lamination increased strength and stability, made more economical use of the timber in the tree, and made cutting, drying and shaping easier. A good many of these propellers and wood-framed aircraft were made at

Tibbenham's Aircraft Company in Ipswich. During the First World War over a hundred women worked at the factory, and ninety men, experienced cabinet-makers, whose skills were most valued at home. In the propeller shop, rows of women in long overalls with their hair pinned into caps drew the paper patterns. The men, in waistcoats, white aprons, cloth caps and collars and ties, cut out the shapes of the blades on bandsaws from three-quarter-inch planks. Then they splayed them in decks of ten, like playing cards, and glued and clamped them into the laminated outlines of propellers. Working in teams on ten propellers at a time, the joiners planed and smoothed them into shape, using metal templates as guides. Then, in a long, airy upper room lit by skylights, the hand-fashioned blades were sandpapered smooth by women in long skirts, with spats over their heeled shoes. Hung up on the walls on a row of pegs, the eight-foot propellers dwarfed the workers. Meanwhile, both men and women bustled about a huge factory floor under wooden beams, jointing, assembling, gluing and fixing the wooden aircraft wings together on trestles. Finally, the propeller blades and tips were sheathed in doped fabric, varnished, packed in long wooden cases, and sent away on wagons driven by draymen in tweeds, waistcoats, caps and boots, drawn by Suffolk horses with names like Pegasus. Others, the timber-haulers and sawyers, delivered a constant supply of seasoned sawn English walnut trunks, stacked carefully in the yard in big concertinas, sticks separating every plank to keep the air flowing. Biggles and Algy called their planes 'crates' because that is more or less what they were. Almost every aeroplane of the Lucifer generation was constructed of wood, normally ash, covered in a taut skin of stiffened fabric, with one or more wooden propellers. Even by 1930 only five per cent of airframes were metal, and as late as the Second World War one of the most successful fast bombers, the De Havilland Mosquito, was built of spruce, birch plywood and balsa wood. It was introduced in 1938, and nearly 8,000 Mosquitoes went into action in the war. Even Reginald Mitchell's revolutionary Spitfire had a wooden propeller.

A good many cars, and the cabs of lorries, were also wood framed. The original SS Jaguars were no exception. They were built by bolting an ash frame on to a steel chassis and panelling it with metal, just as Morgan sports cars are still made today. Ash is light and strong, with enough flexibility to absorb the stresses of driving, or flying. The Jaguar company's original name, SS, seems, in retrospect, an odd choice for the thirties, but denoted nothing more sinister than 'Swallow Sidecars'. William Lyons had founded his company to make motorcycle sidecars, also timber framed, and cars were a new departure. When the advertising agency suggested the name 'Jaguar' for the new SS sports car in 1936, Lyons accepted it only with great reluctance. But it wasn't to be long before he was grateful to drop the 'SS' discreetly from the company name. Now thoroughly assimilated into English, the word 'jaguar' is borrowed from Tupi or Língua Geral, a language once spoken by millions all over Portuguese Brazil and now probably destined to disappear, since no more than a few hundred speakers remain. Literally translated, *jaguara* means 'predatory beast'. 'Piranha' comes from the same language, and is still available, as far as I know, to the motor industry. Nobody knows quite how many jaguars remain in this world, but the wild rivers and forests essential to their lives are disappearing every day from the map of South America. The same forces that are creating global warming are bringing about the accelerating extinction of the wild jaguar. Most of these superb animals, the third largest of the big cats, now inhabit the Amazon basin, with only a few hundred left in what was once a stronghold: Central America. Loss of habitat is the main factor, but it hasn't helped that throughout the 1960s some 15,000 jaguars a year were trapped for their fur, and many are still hunted. What is certain is that the great majority of them now exist in chrome effigy on the bonnets of fast cars.

It cannot have escaped the executives in the Jaguar board room that they might soon be presiding over a company named after an extinct mammal. This would not go down well with the advertising agency. Shell, we notice, quietly dropped their 'Put a tiger in your tank' campaign some years ago. Over at the Reliant factory in Tamworth, they have no such problem: the robin is still one of the most successful birds in Britain. So if Jaguar has recently got into the habit of winning prizes for its outstanding green credentials as a manufacturer, and is at pains to promote a caring nature-loving image, who can blame it? No company has greater reason to work towards a greener planet, less destruction of forests and the consequent resurgence of its beleaguered totem animal. It has stopped using mercury and cadmium, turned off unnecessary lights and taps, recycled its office paper, purified and recycled the water it uses to wash new cars, and formed its own Environmental Strategy Committee as long ago as 1992 'to look at ways of making its cars more eco-friendly'. As a maker of high-performance cars with hefty engines, Jaguar knows it is under scrutiny by the environmental movement. Its brother company, Land-Rover, another member of the Ford Motors group not known for the sparing use of fuel, has recently had a taste of direct action from Greenpeace.

Even the burr walnut trees from the old Californian orchards are getting harder to find. Jaguar's public response has been to fund the creation of a two-hundred-acre stretch of walnut woodland in Staffordshire: the Jaguar Walnut Forest. Planted in 2001 on arable farmland at Lount, near Ashby-de-la-Zouch south of Derby, as part of the new National Forest, it contains 13,000 walnuts and 70,000 other trees. This is, of course, meant as a gesture and not to assure future supplies of veneered dashboards, gear handles or steering wheels.

Robin Bircham grows walnuts in Suffolk and supplied 6,000 of the saplings for the new Jaguar wood. I went over to see him at Boxted Hall Farm, where he tends 180 trees in a seven-and-a-half-acre orchard. Many of them were planted in 1935, and the main variety is Bardwell, which may be the same as the French Bijou, so called because women sometimes keep jewellery in the big shells. We walked between rows of well-spaced trees sixty or seventy feet tall, spreading into an unbroken canopy. Blight, said Robin, was often a problem in damp Suffolk, diminishing the yield of sound nuts, but he used no chemical sprays. Once the canopy of an orchard has closed, the trees themselves, which hate competition, secrete their own organic weedkiller, juglone, from their leaves. Squirrels, crows and humans also steal from the orchard, and a late frost can ruin a whole year's crop. In a good year Robin harvests up to three and a half tons.

At first Robin and his wife used to pick up the fallen nuts in October and November, sending them to Covent Garden, where most were simply left to rot, unsold, so instead they decided to specialize in fresh, wet walnuts, and began supplying them to Harrods, Fortnum & Mason and Buckingham Palace. They wash the nuts and grade them by size. The bigger ones go to London, and the smaller nuts are sold to local shops and delicatessens. There are hundreds of different walnut varieties, just as there are apples or plums to suit different tastes and growing conditions. All produce nuts of different shapes and sizes with distinctive flavours and textures, and some are easier to crack than others. The reigning varieties in France are Franquette, Marbot, Ronde de Montignac, Lara, Fernor, Fernette, Chandler, Serr, Tulare and Broadview. Lara, says Robin, can yield over a ton of nuts per acre.

Walnut grown for its nuts in an orchard is less likely to make useful timber, because for fruiting you want plenty of low horizontal branches. A good timber tree, on the other hand, is straight, with as few branches as possible. In the Dordogne around Périgueux, one of the centres of walnut growing, the French orchardists will choose one or two of their trees for pruning as timber from an early age to create a twelve-foot straight bole, and will prune all their nutting trees to make butts of seven or eight feet, taller than the four or five feet usual for an orchard walnut in England. Walnuts are best grown directly from seed, since they dislike being transplanted, even when young. The seedlings send down a prodigious tap root very quickly, and it is easily damaged.

Robin Bircham introduced me to the Walnut Club, a select band of about a hundred enthusiasts for the tree who would like to see

a revival of its popularity in Britain. I went to my first meeting one
late-summer morning at the Northmoor Trust near Oxford, in the
lee of Wittenham Clumps, the Iron Age hilltop fort made famous
by Paul Nash, who painted the hill and the beeches at its summit
endlessly. Ronald Blythe had told me how Paul and his artist brother
John used to go and stay at Sinodun House, Wallingford, with
their Aunt Gussie, who had been engaged to Edward Lear. Paul
discovered in the Clumps the element of timelessness and mystery
that elevated them beyond their purely physical presence in the
wide, otherwise level landscape. He wrote that they 'eclipsed
the impression of all the early landscapes I knew . . . They were the
pyramids of my small world.'

Against this deeply English backdrop, two dozen of us took a
morning walk in a twenty-acre plantation of young walnuts that
have sprung up from seed brought over from Kyrgyzstan in 1997
by Dr Gabriel Hemery, whose aim is to select and propagate new
varieties of *Juglans regia* most suitable for timber from this unique
source of genetic diversity. We were looking at the progeny of 375
promising-looking trees selected in the wild walnut forests of the
Ferghana Valley by Dr Hemery. We are ten degrees further north
than Kyrgyzstan, but the parent trees grow at 7,000 feet and have
to withstand the bitter Central Asian winters of the Tien Shan
Mountains, so Dr Hemery's reasoning is that they should easily be
hardy enough for our climate. He grew the walnuts in plastic tubes
because he soon discovered that the seedlings do far better in their
shelter, humidity and higher temperature. The local hares, as he
also soon learnt, have a tendency to chew off the terminal buds if
they are left unprotected.

By now up to eight feet, the saplings had been seeded directly
sixteen feet apart to allow them to spread into ample domed
crowns. In relation to its height, the walnut develops a bigger crown
than any other tree in Britain. Dr Hemery and his team had
conducted some ingenious experiments with nurse trees. Reasoning
that walnuts appreciate humidity and nitrogen, they planted a shrub
native to Asia, *Elaeagnus umbellata*, on either side of each young

walnut. *Elaeagnus* has nitrogen-fixing roots, which may possibly nourish the walnut, and grows to a height of sixteen feet, creating both humidity and shelter for the young tree, concentrating its growth upwards rather than outwards and suppressing weeds. They had done the same thing using Italian alder, hazel or elder as nurse trees, with promising results.

There was much talk of developing tall, fast-growing trees with straight trunks for timber, whereas it seemed to me and several other Walnut Club members that the singular virtue of the tree is best appreciated by the French, who compromise by growing a rather shorter bole and harvesting the nuts for sixty to seventy years before eventually uprooting it for timber or veneer. I know several joiners who think, like me, that the grain of an old fruit tree, complete with knots and burrs, is far more attractive than the relatively bland, uniformly straight grain of a commercially grown timber tree. I fell into step with Sebastian, who has fifty Franquette trees in the Lot in France, and Clare and Matthew, who planted an orchard of Broadview trees in Norfolk and are now harvesting plentiful nuts, when they can beat the crows to them.

The walnut research at the Northmoor Trust is sponsored by Jaguar, who seem only too eager, like their parent company Ford, to prove their environmental concern. You can hardly blame them, when even their own shareholders are pressing for far more radical changes in the design and manufacture of cars in response to global warming. In April 2005 William Clay Ford Junior, Ford's Chairman in America, announced that the company would soon be issuing 'a comprehensive report . . . that will examine the business implications of reducing greenhouse gas emissions from Ford vehicles'. The Connecticut State Treasurer, Denise L. Nappier, a long-term shareholder, was delighted. 'I congratulate Bill Ford', she said, 'for his recognition that planning for climate change is not *merely* an environmental issue, but a key business issue.' The italics are mine, since 'merely' appears to privilege 'the business implications' above the future of the Earth. The question is, how serious is this concern, really? How far are Ford, with their English offspring Land-Rover and Jaguar, prepared to go to put an end to the damaging emissions of large, powerful cars with big engines?

Anticipating some of what Roland Barthes was to write sixteen years later in his 1955 essay on the Citroën DS, Antoine de Saint-Exupéry says, in *Terre des Hommes*, 'The more perfect machines become, the more they are invisible behind their function . . . It seems that perfection is attained not when there is nothing more to add, but when there is nothing more to take away. At the climax of its evolution, the machine conceals itself entirely.'

Watching one of the big Jaguars inching along the assembly lines, it occurred to me that one way for this machine to 'conceal itself entirely' would be if, like the true wild animal when it takes to water, it were to leave no sign of its passing, no carbon vapour trail, no damage at all to the Earth. Take all these away, and it would attain perfection. And there would be no more need to plant walnuts.

David Nash

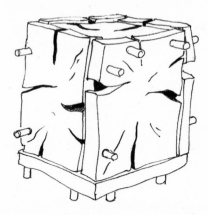

Approaching Blaenau Ffestiniog, I feel I have landed in a black-and-white film. Everywhere I look, the monochrome of slate fills the screen. Yet somewhere within it, like the glow inside a coal fire in the grate, I know David Nash is there, inside his chapel studio filled to the rafters with his works of wood: a furnace of imagination and adventure in a sombre world. Gigantic spoil-heaps of slate, angular molehills thrown up by the mines, rise away steeply in silhouette, dwarfing the sombre terraced houses and their gleaming roofs. The steep paths of the quarrymen zigzag up, or ramp in diagonals across the gloomy, unstable screes that loom everywhere above the town. A ruined viaduct leans out into a void. Tramways and railway tracks run to the cliff edges of the heaps, buffered by air. After the soft wooded valleys you wind through on your way up, it is a treeless world, except for the odd rhododendron clinging to the slate, or hugging the wall of a roofless winding-house. There is something architectural about the zigzags, diagonals and monochrome waste-tips of broken slates, discarded like loose change because only those few that split cleanly could be used to roof houses.

Blaenau Ffestiniog hunkers down at the head of a valley in the mountains of north Wales ten miles from the Irish Sea. An odd place for an artist whose name is synonymous with wood to choose to be, but this is the country of Nash's youth, where he and his brother spent all their holidays exploring the Vale of Ffestiniog and the banks of the Dwyryd River from their grandfather's house. He has been walking its lanes for fifty years. The irony is that Nash came here after art school to escape a grey world: the suits and money culture of London in the mid sixties. This is a place of deliberate self-exile, in the working landscape of a Celtic country where they still speak another language. Coming here to see David Nash feels as I imagine it did to journey to remote Cornwall in the 1930s to visit Ben Nicholson and Barbara Hepworth at their studios in the fishing community of St Ives.

Capel Rhiw, the Victorian Methodist chapel where David Nash lives and works, stands almost grandly in a row of slate miners' cottages on the outskirts of the town. There were once 18,000 people and twenty-six chapels in this Welsh Machu Picchu. The chapels were so crowded on Sundays that the congregations overflowed and sang in the streets outside. Nash and his wife, the painter Claire Langdown, live in the schoolhouse they have converted behind the chapel, which is both studio and a store for all the works that are in transit, waiting to be dispatched to some new exhibition overseas or retained because they're old friends Nash isn't inclined to let go.

I step inside to a surprising burst of pagan colour: the warm glow of wood. It is a beautiful, uplifting building with little nuggets of primary colour in the stained-glass friezes of its high windows that beam down blue, yellow and red. I shall not forget the sheer drama of the exuberant throng of Nash's work that fills the tiered space literally to the lofty ceiling. Moving through the chapel, I mingle with the wooden multitude, 'the congregation', as Nash calls it. It is like meeting the family, an unusually big one, exciting and daunting at the same time: impossible to remember all their names, only a general impression that you want to get to know them much better one by one in due course. I catch a hint of the impression I often had as a teacher entering a classroom: that the moment before I came in, they had all been deep in conversation.

We leave our boots at the kitchen door and sit down to tea. The Nash cat sleeps in an ingenious cantilevered basket that hooks over a radiator. It is such a vociferous creature, says Nash, you can play it like bagpipes. The one-inch copper water pipes leading from the cooking range meander like euphoniums on their way up to the ceiling. This is surrealist plumbing but typically practical, because it acts as a radiator as well as being gently comical. The kitchen worktops too are characteristically bold, practical and larger than life: four inches of thick-sliced sycamore. This is the wood tradition-ally used to make milk-pails, says Nash, because it imparts no taste. A series of early carvings on offcuts of Canadian cherry by Claire depicts in relief a curtain blowing through the top of an open sash window, like Marilyn Monroe's billowing skirt in *The Seven Year Itch*. Wind translated into wood. Outside the window, slate and more slate. Two men barrow slabs of it about the garden.

Later on Nash drives us up a hill above the town, and we climb over a low fence on to a sheep-grazed mound, ascending over what appear to be cinders, until my companion stoops and holds up a singed fragment of leather and I realize we are standing on the charred remains of a gigantic pyre of ancient army boots. It is like a scenario from the *Goon Show*. All that remains intact is metal: the clicking heel studs, the little bootlace eyes, and a million hobnails, tacks and studs. Nash loves this dark tumulus: another burial mound of an extinct industry. The boot factory had been established to supply the army during the war. Then, when both came to an end, they built a boot-mountain and set fire to it. As an accidental installation, there could be no more telling expression of the history of Blaenau Ffestiniog, no better war memorial for all the unemployed slate miners who marched off to war.

Back at the chapel, I recognize many of the individual pieces of work: the soaring, high-backed, spoon-shaped *Throne*, the various *Ladders*, stairways to heaven made by cleaving the inverted tree in two and joining the opposed halves with carved staves, and *Vessels*, symbolic boats carved from a single trunk. There is an Alice-in-Wonderland feeling about wandering among all these bowls, spoons, chairs, vessels, stoves and tables: versions of human arte-facts plucked from their domestic scale and context, often larger than life, reminders of the ubiquity of wood in our daily lives.

Some of the work I had seen before, in galleries and exhibitions, but encountering it off duty in the workmanlike surroundings of the chapel, a long way from the urban world of culture and the arts, is a quite different experience. Nash now works in a separate workshop and yard up the road where his chainsaws won't disturb anyone, so the chapel and its contents have become, quite con-sciously, an installation. There is soon to be another international exhibition, this time in Orléans, and several works are being wrapped up and packaged ready for their journey to France, here and at the new workshop. Some are already in packing cases, wood within wood, and stand like suitcases in the hall on the eve of a holiday. Waiting to be wrapped up is a pair of *Ubus*, named after the outsized King and Queen in Alfred Jarry's Absurdist play *Ubu Roi*. The wandering, priapic, outward-leaning, etiolated dinosaur necks of these creatures reach upwards from the contrasting solidity of their squat bodies like the branches of the tree they actually are. Nash keeps on returning to this form. Like Nash's various ladders, trees have traditionally connected the earth and sky, and the natural vertical axis, the direction the wood grain takes the eye, runs through all his work. 'The problem with wood is it's already beautiful,' says Nash. 'How do you make it more beautiful?'

I find myself drawn to one work in particular: the *Cracking Box* of oak. As if entering the wild life of the wood, or at least taking its side, Nash has put as many difficulties in his way in the making of the box as he can. He may work with the skills of the forester, hedge-layer or carpenter but firmly rejects any notion of craft and indeed declined, for years, the open offer of a Crafts Council exhibition. You can feel that resistance, dramatized in his wilful transgression of the rules of carpentry in the construction of the box. Five of its six oaken walls are sawn, perversely, across the end grain of the tree, anchored to a single wall conventionally machined along the grain. Nash bored out the peg holes with a two-inch hand augur and carved oak pegs, which he drove in to join up the box. The anarchic work thumbs its nose at the basic rules of woodwork, triumphantly so, because it holds together in spite of the wriggling of the wood as it warps and cracks. The more the wood struggles, the tighter the grip of the oak pegs in their augured sockets. As Nash points out, hand-carved oak pegs make the best joints because their uneven surfaces create greater friction as they are driven in. This is what he calls an 'outside in' work. He made it from green oak outdoors, where the feeling is quite different from working inside the studio, then brought it inside to crack and warp. Things look bigger when they come inside and smaller when they go outside, by a factor of about one third, says Nash.

Nash works in the same tradition of the artist as artisan as Constantin Brancusi, an acknowledged influence since his earliest days, who was a trained carpenter as well as sculptor and also lived at his studio, which he kept peopled with his best works. These days Nash works principally with the chainsaw, transformed in his hands into a tool of great delicacy as well as one of power and scope. He says he is a sprinter by nature, too impatient to see results to work more slowly with hand tools as he used to do until 1977, when he stopped sawing firewood with a bowsaw and discovered a tool that suited his nature. The chainsaw liberates him to work in bold strokes. It is perhaps the equivalent of the charcoal with which Nash likes to draw, also working fast: he loves its fluidity. The chainsaw lends itself to big, ambitious ideas, enabling him to work on a large scale, quarrying the wood from the tree. He makes no distinction between 'wood' and 'tree' because the green wood in which he works still has a dynamic, organic life of its own and will continue to shift, warp and reshape itself as a living sculpture. Nash prefers his work unadorned, leaving the marks of the tool on the wood. The chainsaw leaves circular marks, often blackened. The axe leaves roughness and torn slivers. Polished or finished surfaces resist your gaze, distracting it from the essential form. Instead, Nash's grainy, cracked, warped, sawn, fissured, charred, scarred and hollowed works absorb light, involve the viewer, like the bold charcoal drawings that precede them and sometimes accompany them on a gallery wall as a two-dimensional counterpoint to the sculpture's three.

Nash always begins with an idea: it is ideas that excite him and drive the work along. On a blackboard in the little converted shop across the street he uses as his drawing studio, and for seminars and workshops with the groups of art students who sometimes make the journey here, he has chalked up the trajectory of a putative project that begins with *Idea*. He likes the dynamic implications of the word, its forward-tending energy and movement. On the blackboard, arrowed chalk lines lead off in all directions like comet-tails to possible interpretations. There too are chalked the names of some fellow artists of his generation whose work and ideas are akin to his: Richard Long, Hamish Fulton and Roger Ackling. *Family Tree*, drawn in pastel in 1995, traces the evolution of consistent ideas and themes in Nash's work from the *First Tower* he built in 1967 on a hillside in Blaenau Ffestiniog. Appraising a life's work to date as a formal tree, Nash represents himself branching out from those early beginnings into the range and scope of his more recent projects, all related in a single living system of thought. There is more than a hint of Platonic ways of thought in all this, and Nash is a strong believer in the notion of ideal forms, returning again and again to the sphere, the pyramid and the cube. Wood often suggests the past, memory and something fixed, so to work as freely with it as Nash does can create fertile tensions. We are accustomed to spheres, pyramids and cubes as sculptural objects in stone, not wood.

Nash chose early on in his career to work in wood, in preference to stone. For him, it offers just the right degree of resistance. Stone has too much and clay too little. Chiselling oak, he feels a balancing strength coming back up his arm. Carving lime, he senses its receptivity, the smoothness of movement through it. He is interested in the past life of the tree, in its relationship with time and the diary it keeps of its life in the annual rings. A tree may live eighty or a hundred years, or for several hundred years, but even then its life is not so very much longer than a human span when you compare it with stone. Our ability to identify our human lives and history with trees influenced Nash's choice of wood as his sculptural medium. Wood, unlike stone, lives and dies on a human scale. This idea is expressed in the old English folk-saying based on the ancient notion of the Seven Ages, quoted by Robert Graves in *The White Goddess*:

> The lives of three wattles, the life of a hound;
> The lives of three hounds, the life of a steed;
> The lives of three steeds, the life of a man;
> The lives of three men, the life of an eagle;
> The lives of three eagles, the life of a yew;
> The life of a yew, the length of an age;
> Seven ages, from Creation to Doom.

A wattle or hurdle of willow will last for three years, so on this reckoning a yew lives for 729 years, a modest but reasonable estimate.

Time and the living forces of the elements within green wood continue to shape the *Crack and Warp Columns* long after the artist has finished work on them. Nash has made a series of them over the years out of a variety of woods from birch to tulip to beech. Lime often creates the best effects, with its energetic warping. Working his chainsaw with extraordinary deftness, he executes a series of toothcomb incisions that may exceed a hundred into a column of green wood. The impression is of a tall sheaf of papers, all gently levitating, joined together by a solid backbone at the core. Nash says he goes into a sort of trance as he makes the repeated saw cuts, allowing the rhythm of the work to take over. At any point he might cut through that bit too much and lose the piece altogether. It is like a jazz solo: it has a beginning and an ending and a formal structure but a free, open, anarchic feeling. It is daring and risky. These crack-and-warp columns are quintessential Nash in that they tend upwards like trees, involve a virtuoso chainsaw solo and continue changing shape long after the work is apparently complete, cracking, warping and splitting at random as the element of air enters the sculpture and water evaporates from the un-seasoned wood to mingle back into ourselves through the air we breathe. These are, says Nash, air sculptures, where others might belong to earth, water or fire. There is an air of fragility about them that suggests the sculpture itself might easily evaporate.

Like any other congregation, the sculptures in the chapel are constantly shifting, stretching and discreetly yawning as the wood silently groans and twists into subtly changed shapes. The crack and warp of green wood is nature at work, continuing where Nash has left off. *Running Table* and *Three Dandy Scuttlers*, sculptures that appear to be making a run for it or dancing on their legs of inverted branches, dramatize the dynamics at the heart of everything Nash makes. His aim, he says, is to 'resurrect the tree in a different form'. There is a kind of collaboration between the artist and the living wood that continues well beyond the original hewing.

We drive out to the wooded valley at Cae'n-y-Coed near Maen-twrog, the next village, where Nash owns a four-acre plot of mixed woodland inherited from his father. This is where he literally plants and grows his living sculptural work. He began work on one of his best-known outdoor sculptures, *Ash Dome*, in 1977 when he planted twenty-two ash saplings in a ring thirty feet in diameter on a level eminence on the hillside in the Ffestiniog Valley. It was conceived as an act of hope during the dark days of the cold war. Nash had already made drawings of a lattice of living ash that would enclose a dome-shaped space. He was trying to find a way to make a large-scale outdoor sculpture that genuinely belonged in its location and would embrace and engage the elements instead of resisting them, as so much outdoor sculpture seemed to do. Inspired by hedges and their half-natural, half-husbanded forms, he was looking for a way of actively collaborating with nature.

From long familiarity with the local hedges, often drawing or photographing the sinuous forms of the laid trees, Nash knew that ash was the most resilient to constant shaping, would lean furthest from its roots and naturally grow into sinuous, idiosyncratic forms. Nash likens the way he is guiding the trees to the way the ancient Chinese potters kept their minds on the invisible volume of space inside the pot and worked up the clay around its shape. He was also attracted by the gradual, long-term nature of the project: its long reach forward and its continuity.

His first ring of saplings was eaten by sheep, so he put up a fence and planted another. He also put in birches as a windbreak, and to stimulate the ashes to compete with them in growth. Then he began to apply some of the techniques of the hedger, pruning and shaping the trees as they grew, grafting on side shoots, working on the shape every winter, up ladders and even a wooden scaffold as the dome grew taller. At one stage an elaborate system of guy ropes and tent pegs urged the lead growth of the *Ash Dome* towards the centre. He shows me how, in 1983, he made the first bends in the trunks, leaning the trees anticlockwise by making a series of saw cuts nearly all the way through the growing trunk on the insides of the bends to allow for compression, binding the wounds with damp cloth under plastic until the cambium layer had healed, guiding and supporting the trees on stakes. Thus he has kinked the trees several times over the years into their wild and graceful dance on the hillside.

As in any collaboration, the trees have their own ideas, and Nash must continually work his hedgerow skills to influence them as the sculptor, or choreographer. He admires and enjoys the sense of purpose in each tree, its stroppiness. Again it is a question of resistance, of arm-wrestling the muscular trees. 'The tree has a purpose, and it will always keep trying to fulfil its purpose whatever happens,' says Nash. I notice that at each place where an ash has been bent or cut it has grown stronger, swelling into a callous like a human knee or puckering into a bump of scar tissue round the little star-cracked crater of each amputated branch. Every one of these details represents a decision, a little setback for the tree to which it responds with redoubled vigour that is certainly defiance and might even be anger, but only adds to the dramatic sense of muscularity and movement in the whole. But Nash has no desire for rigid control: it is the unpredictability of growth that interests him, and he has charted the life of this sculpture by drawing it over and over again, from year to year, through the seasons, even setting up a drawing table on the spot. His drawings of the *Ash Dome* are, he says, 'its fruit'. This is by no means a figure of speech. Sculptors have to make a living just like the rest of us, and the next morning I help Nash to carry a harvest of a dozen or so ash-framed drawings of *Ash Dome* out of his drawing studio to be packed and sent off to a gallery.

In its rootedness, the *Dome* expresses Nash's commitment to a settled life in one place, and a deep rapport with the landscape in which he lives. In hedgerows, sheep will often bite off leading shoots of trees and shape them with their browsing, or branches will fuse together through close contact. As linear woods, hedges have a naturally sculptural quality that is reflected in the dome of ash. But the space enclosed by the trees also suggests to Nash the great hidden, hollowed dome of the slate mine inside Manod Mawr, one of the mountains across the valley. All the leaning trees are *Ubus* of a kind. The curious swaying, zigzagging habit of the trees in *Ash Dome* is like the tentative, tangential progress of a hare down a lane, reminiscent of Ted Hughes's line in 'The Warm and the Cold': 'The hare strays down the highway like a root going deeper.'

There is a strong sense of the serious business of play about working with trees like this. You bend them down, they spring back. You cut them down, they spring back again. You lay them down and they send new shoots growing straight up. It is worth noting that Nash dedicated one of his books to his brother Chris, 'who took playing seriously and let me join in'. A short walk away across the hillside we encounter *Sabre Growth Larches* swirling elaborately upwards like Isadora Duncan, and the striking *Celtic Hedge*, a deliberately contrary version of a sixty-foot sycamore hedge, planted in 1989. Nash fused the branches of this wild trellis by peeling off the bark to expose the living cambium layer at the point of contact, then drilling and screwing them tightly together, removing the screw once the wooden joint had grown and the trees were one: a streamlined version of the way a scion would traditionally be bound and grafted on to the rootstock of an orchard fruit tree.

Higher up on the hillside, with a tall grove and a holly bush at its back, Nash has constructed a shelter like a coracle, a hazel bender sprung on a foundation cruck frame of a bow of oak made from a single limb sawn lengthwise in four, with a matt-black canvas skin stretched over the woven wood, a small stove and an ingenious beak-like chimney, like the spout of a jug. It is open fronted, like the Aboriginal shells of the Sydney Opera House, rimmed inside with a curved wooden bench that looks over the woods and valley. We sit and talk of beavers and their natural sculptures of chewed cottonwood stumps outside Chicago, and the rhomboid of seven rows of seven white Himalayan birches Nash planted seven feet apart just down the hill, hoping they would grow precisely forty-nine feet high. Looking at them, I realize it was probably David Nash who quietly influenced the planting of the elegant, close-set miniature forest of birches that grows outside the Tate Modern.

From Cae'n-y-Coed we drive down the Ffestiniog Valley to a lane beside the Dwyryd River and a small bridge over a tributary stream. Sheep pause in their grazing and watch us go by, chewing in their nervous way. One of the features of the Welsh countryside David Nash appreciates and enjoys is what he calls 'sheep spaces': the hollows the animals wear and harden into the ground in their own image over generations. Such unassuming shelters are often among the roots of trees, which the sheep polish and impregnate with the lanolin of their fleeces. Nash has often drawn them in charcoal or pastel, and even created them in situ, *gratis* for the sheep, carving out containing walls of wood. They are signs of settling, of the intimate, long-term connection with the earth that is Nash's own way of life too. In that sense they are of a piece with

Ash Dome, which is also a containing, protective form, now well rooted at Cae'n-y-Coed, with similar squatters' rights.

If *Ash Dome* is about putting down roots, *Wooden Boulder* is an equally radical work about letting go. It is adventurous in every sense, a great gesture of liberation in which Nash has surrendered his work to nature and the elements and set no limits. In the summer of 1978, he heard of a great oak that had recently been felled directly uphill from where we were now standing by the stream, and that was available to him. Its owners had feared it might fall on their cottage. Working the tree where it lay over a two-year period, Nash carved a dozen or more sculptures from it. The first of these, a giant oak ball three feet in diameter, was originally intended to go into the studio and dry out. When the moment came to sever the half-carved sphere from the main trunk and roll it to continue carving the underneath, Nash had the idea of using the nearby stream and water slide to carry the half-ton sphere down to a pool below, then haul it on to a track where it could be rolled along to the road and trundled off to the studio. This is what would have happened, except that the wooden ball jammed itself halfway down the water slide and wouldn't budge. At first it looked like a problem until, thinking it over in a Zen frame of mind, Nash realized it was an opportunity, a happy accident that would transform the work by enabling him to release it back into nature: to shed it like a leaf. He would let it go its own way and be a rock in a stream, with water playing about it, freezing to it, papering it with autumn leaves. From that moment on, it became *Wooden Boulder*, a new kind of work with its own independent life, its own story and the sculptor as its biographer.

By the following year, the deciduous sculpture had shifted position during the winter spate and settled into the pool beneath the waterfall. Nash had already begun recording its progress in photographs and drawings, and helped it, like a scarab beetle, into the shallows to be washed down into another waterfall and the next pool in August 1980. Here it stayed for the next eight years, darkening by the action of the water into the colour of the other stones in the stream. The boulder had taken on an independent life of its own, and Nash drew and photographed its changing moods and fortunes through frosty or snowy days, engulfed in raging foam during storms, or jammed with leaves and sticks. It shifted downstream three more times, until, following a massive storm in 1994, it hid itself completely, wedged under a bridge. A scarab once again, it was winched out by Nash and rolled back into the stream the other side, where it sat on the stony bed under some trees close to the confluence with the River Dwyryd for eight years until November 2002, when a strong enough flood eventually carried it into the main river. It travelled three miles towards the sea on the tides and beached itself on a sandbank in the estuary.

In the new setting of wide horizons and reflected sky, the sculpture stood out heroically and, like a Celtic saint, began to wander the waters of the estuary, mysteriously disappearing up creeks, endlessly doubling back on itself in the ebb and flow, moving with each new tide, responding to the moon. By now utterly obsessed, Nash went searching for it in a boat and lost it altogether for a while. 'Capricious' is how he describes its behaviour. He even put out 'Wanted' posters around the estuary. During those chilly winter days of hide-and-seek he studied the tides and pored over charts, mapping the uncertain voyage. Then one January day the great oak apple reappeared on a saltmarsh and seemed almost settled for a moment until the Equinox tide of 19 March 2003 floated it free. Nash watched from a boat, and, as the heavy sphere floated 'like a seal', most of its body submerged, rolling slightly as it rode the tide, bumping the bottom, its rough-carved angles smoothed and rounded by so much passage over stone or sand. He had charted its progress whenever he could with his camera as well as on paper. It was just a far-off dot when he last saw it on 30 March. Somebody sighted *Wooden Boulder* floating close to the estuary's mouth a few days later, but it vanished in April 2003. The 'Wanted' posters went up again, to no avail. Nash is still sceptical about the idea that the sculpture is out there in the Irish Sea, perhaps even gone for ever, a message in a bottle. He keeps on searching the beaches and creeks of the estuary, quartering it endlessly on board a boat, as he did before. In contrast to *Ash Dome*, which Nash describes as a 'coming', or 'becoming' sculpture, *Wooden Boulder* is a 'going' sculpture.

The very notion of a wooden boulder is a metaphysical conceit, just as the first stone pillar was in ancient Greece. Until the original Doric column was conceived and built, all temple pillars had been trees, and the fluted stone, with its foliate embellishment below the roof, audaciously mimicked them. Like Dylan Thomas's 'Dogs in the wetnosed yards' in *Under Milk Wood*, it surprises and delights by fusing two hitherto separate elements. In one of his early notebooks, Gerard Manley Hopkins makes a sketch of a lasher, a steep, fast-flowing overflow channel on the canal at Wolvercote near Oxford, and describes the racing water as 'running like a wind'. The sudden translation of water into a different element is, again, striking and extraordinary.

We stand on the bridge over the stream where the boulder jammed itself, looking out downriver towards the estuary beyond as Nash tells its story. It is low tide, otherwise we might be out in the boat. I have the impression that the searching will go on a long time, whatever the results: it has become part of the work, almost a habit. Claire said later, 'I have never seen a man so happy as when David was out in the boat sighting the boulder far out in the estuary.' We go back in the car and follow the old droving road past the house where Inigo Jones was born, crossing the Dwyryd by the lovely triple-arched stone bridge he built, with seats of slate set in the triangular pedestrian refuges where people sit and watch the oak-fringed river on summer evenings. Along the way, we have to run the gauntlet of a farmyard where two sheepdogs savage the car, as Nash predicted they would, biting at the bumpers as we wind up the windows. He and his brother used to walk this lane as boys, and always hid a pair of stout sticks in the wall to seize as they approached the farm, for beating off the dogs.

I sense that perhaps *Wooden Boulder* has become an alter ego for Nash: its unfolding story part of his life, the restless thing itself an embodiment of his soul. Something about it reminds me of the

Irish story of Sweeney Astray as told by Seamus Heaney. Sweeney, a poet king, is exiled, naked, into the wild, turned into a bird, flies about Ireland, lives in trees and roosts in the ivy, eating watercress and drinking from the rivers. There is a mythic feel to the story of *Wooden Boulder*. An artist turns a tree into a boulder, which miraculously floats and swims its way over many years towards the sea, where it rolls over like a seal and seems to disappear. The work is close in spirit to the journeys of Richard Long: Nash entering and exploring the landscape, and experiencing the raw life of 'the elements', in particular the element of water, through the medium of the wandering oak ball. Nash himself is an artist deeply rooted in his own place but also an adventurer, like many other sculptors, who loves to travel to work in new landscapes with new materials: California redwood or madrone, Tasmanian eucalypts or palm trees in Barcelona. He points out appreciatively the wavy compression grain in one of his redwood sculptures from California, the sheer weight of the tree buckling the wood lower in the trunk and stippling its grain. Trees and wood vary greatly across the world, even within the same genus or even species. Birch is little regarded in Britain except as a useful nurse tree to shelter and encourage saplings, and its wood is almost ignored. Yet in Finland or Japan the tree is revered and its wood highly valued. Birch is a different wood in different parts of the world. When Nash first put his chainsaw into it in Japan, he thought there was something wrong, that the saw needed sharpening, but it was only that the wood was slower grown, therefore much harder than in Britain. The elements themselves, Nash finds, are different wherever he travels. The air may be sharper or more humid. In Australia the sky is more penetrating, more extreme a thing than here. In Japan the water behaves quite differently: it is brighter, more vigorous, even boisterous, and it is more solid. The waves are different too. On a lake in Hokkaido, Nash saw waves slapping against each other just as they do in Hokusai prints, running at each other, colliding head on and spouting upwards like trees. Waves, he says, never do that here.

Over dinner, Nash describes the pleasure of his first visit to Japan, and the island of Hokkaido. Because of the scale and nature of his work, he always needs assistants, whom he recruits locally. He describes the special pleasure of getting to know people by working alongside them in their own place. It is the best kind of introduction, he finds, to people and place, and through it he soon finds his way to the idea: the right thing to make in that particular place. In Barcelona he explained to the gallery his need for whole trees and his reluctance to cut any down, and so was led to the city's tree hospital, where sick and ailing trees, uprooted by gentle diggers, are taken in tree ambulances to be nursed back to health in huge trenches of fresh earth. About forty per cent of them recover, but among those that had succumbed, Nash found palms and Australian pines, neither of which he had ever carved before. He resurrected them as sculpture and created his show of columns after the manner of Gaudí.

Next morning, in the covered carving shed at Llwingell, down the road from the chapel where Nash has expanded to accommodate the heavy-duty tools and materials of his trade, his assistant Roland is at work with a gas blowtorch, carefully charring a new work carved from yew. All around him, the whole trunks of hardwood trees lie or are stood up in the shed or outside in the yard. Nash has good practical reasons for charring wood in some of his sculptures. Blackening the edges, for example, will make the shape stand out more clearly, especially against the white walls of a gallery. Crazed, black-charred wood surfaces absorb light and seem to alter the sense of the size of a sculpture so it feels further away, although Nash isn't sure whether it makes it bigger or smaller. He says that when he sees a sculpture made of wood, the first thing he sees is the wood, and then he sees the form. But Nash's fundamental instinct to apply fire seems to arise from somewhere deeper: an underlying awareness of time and the elements that consistently informs his imagination. Talking to Nash about why he chars wood only confirms what a metaphysical artist he is. Like the drenching and immersion of *Wooden Boulder* in water, one of the four elements that sustain the lives of trees, charring drenches the wood in fire, symbolic of the warmth and light of the sun. As the ancient Chinese fifth element, wood is an amalgam of earth, air, fire, in the form of sunlight, and water. Fire alters the fundamental nature of the surface of wood from vegetable to mineral to become carbon. This brings it a step closer to stone. Charring, says Nash, erases the almost human intricacies of the grain, which suggest the tree's life story and a lifespan not so different from our own. Charring his sculptures, he feels, enables him to transcend the finite timescale of living wood and alter the sense of time in the viewer.

Like Brancusi, Nash is always acutely aware of the importance of the setting and presentation of his work in a gallery or outside space. By setting the charred *Pyramid, Sphere and Cube* he made in elm in Japan in 1993 against a white wall with two-dimensional charcoal images taken directly from the sculptures framed on white as a background, Nash deliberately enhanced its dramatic impact. He had done something similar in 1987, in *Nature to Nature*. He also raised interesting questions about our different ways of seeing two- and three-dimensional images. We read the size of three-dimensional images in relation to our own body scale, Nash thinks, and we experience them far more physically. A two-dimensional image is read more purely by the imagination. Juxtaposing both kinds of representation sets up interesting tensions that enhance both images. Nash believes yet another level of internal struggle arises between the visual and tactile apprehension of his charred sculptures. The eye is drawn imaginatively towards the blackness of carbon, but emotionally the sense of touch knows carbon sets your teeth on edge, and distances it.

Nash will often char a sculpture such as his tall, spoon-shaped *Throne* by encasing it in a sleeve of scrap wood and setting fire to it. Just as in the use of the chainsaw to carve, there is a sense of drama and controlled power to the pyre. There is also more than a hint of ritual, of cremation: even the idea that the work might be sacrificed as an offering to the woodland deities. When in 1990

I first saw the famous image of the charring of the base of *Comet Ball* by means of a small kindling-wood fire beneath it, my first thought was that the event itself dramatized the fiery comet crashing to earth. Charring also has a wonderful way of black-holing the containing interior of some of the hollowed cylinders, like *Charred Column*, reminiscent of the way lightning so often strikes ancient trees and burns out their hollows. This happens to gum trees in Australia, and Nash was inspired by the dramatic sight of such burnt-out cases, often standing starkly alone in the midst of open country in Tasmania. In a lightning strike, according to Nash, the tree is cooked at 15,000°C. The sap boils instantly and explodes. The splintered tree-shrapnel can be devastating.

I ask Nash about his other use of charcoal in so much of his two-dimensional work on paper. What wood, I wonder, makes the best charcoal for drawing? Willow is his favourite. It has long fibres, which hold together even when charcoaled, and it has a softness he likes. He has tried drawing with all sorts of charcoaled woods. Oak is too scratchy, but alder can be good. For a dense black, Nash uses compressed charcoal, which has first been powdered and then reconstituted.

Inside one of the workshops across the yard a nest of chainsaws lines up neatly in pairs; these range in size from 21-inch blades to nearly three feet. They are all red Stihls. Nash sometimes even borrows a four-footer from a friend in Sussex, where his favourite English oaks come from. I have a chainsaw myself, and mention the fear as well as the awe it stirs in me whenever I start it up. Does Nash feel the same? He admits to a healthy modicum of fear informing his respect for these machines. Owning a pit-bull terrier must feel much the same. Keeping the saws sharp is an art in itself. Nash and Roland spend a lot of time lovingly filing the dozens of little curved teeth on each chain by hand. Trees and big timbers often present technical problems. Working in the Bialowieza Forest in north-eastern Poland, Nash discovered that many of the trees contained shrapnel from the war, disastrous to chainsaws. He had recently taken delivery of twenty massive oak trees, chosen from

300 used as sea defences at Eastbourne and renewed by the town council. They had withstood, he calculated, 18,000 tides over twenty-five years, but were so ingrained with sand that it was impossible to use a chainsaw on them without instantly blunting it. He turned them into charred columns instead. Nash loves these life histories of wood and trees, and speaks of the timber that comes from standard lots in a sawmill as 'dumb', because it holds no stories.

One particular tree history with a strong appeal to Nash's keen nose for signs of human collaboration with nature is embodied in the Powis Castle yew trees. Many of the trees date back 300 years, and they made a deep impression on him when he first saw them. They are huge, up to forty feet high, and their apparently random free-flowing shapes have led to the local name *twmps*, an abbreviation of the welsh *twmpath*, meaning a 'mound' or 'pile' with an Anglicized plural tacked on. The yews have grown into their outlandish shapes because for fifty years or so from about 1800 they were neglected and left uncut. Then, when cutting resumed, the gardeners were enlightened enough simply to follow the surreal organic forms that had mushroomed around the castle gardens, climbing 52-foot wooden ladders and cutting the yews single-handed with slashers, for fear of letting go of the rungs at such a height to use shears. By Nash's reckoning, the trees have outlived twelve generations of gardeners, whose human intervention has created sculptural forms quite different from the natural yews of the same age that grow in the lower part of Powis Garden. Characteristically, it is the touch of humour these 'great comic beasts' bring to the garden that Nash enjoys. He sees them as dark green clouds, floating about the garden, enveloping the stone walls. In his charcoal-and-pastel drawings of the *twmps*, Nash has explored the interplay between their black, skeletal interiors and the intricacy of the lacework of twigs and growing tips that create the green undulating exterior. The heart of darkness inside the yew is irresistible to Nash, and in his dreamlike drawings of the *twmps* they seem to loom greenly out of a charcoal mist.

Nash has often challenged the idea that trees are anything but moving things by giving them legs, sometimes literally so. The idea is there in all the living, dancing trees on the hillside at Cae'n-y-Coed, in *Running Table* and all the sculptures where the tree is upturned and the branches become gangling legs. Nash's very first sculpture at the age of four was a bundle of Virginia creeper stalks bound together and stood up, bent out like legs. Fortunately, it was praised by the family's two artist neighbours when he took it next door for them to see. The 'Birnam Wood effect' is there too in the 'wheelies' Nash once sold for three pounds each at an early show at the Arnolfini Gallery in Bristol, natural shapes of wood wheeled at the heavy end so you could wheelbarrow them about. People still own these small sculptures, which actually dare suggest that you might play with them.

As with *Ash Dome*, such a collaboration between humans and nature as created the *twmps* over 300 years is, for Nash, a potent symbol of a much wider ideal for our relations with nature, involving work and love. His sculpture has resurrected fallen trees into meaning as well as beauty. Describing the strength and assurance of the work of one of his mentors, the sculptor David Smith, Nash once said 'he speaks metal.' Nash has discovered an equivalent language of wood. He speaks of 'the fact of sculpture', which, like theatre, lives in the same three dimensions as we do.

The idea that Nash is engaged in a lifelong act of faith in the face of a poor prognosis for nature is irresistible when, surrounded by the assembled 'congregation' in the Capel Rhiw, you look up to the inscription still there in Welsh above the central east window: *Sancteiddrwydd a weddai i'th dŷ* ('Sanctify this house with prayer'). With characteristic modesty, Nash puts it another way, speaking wood: 'A dormant faith is revived in the new growth on old wood.'

East Anglian Coast

Just where the Peddars Way may be said to begin is an interesting question. You can pick up its beginnings on Bridgham Heath just to the north of the Thet where the river flows west from East Harling through Bridgham into a land of twisted Scots pines and sandy woods full of pingoes like the bunkers of long-deserted golf links. Then it heads off more or less north through the Brecks, past Wretham and Blackrabbit Warren, until it seems to fizzle out a mile beyond a little wood called Shaker's Furze among a cluster of tumuli on Sparrow Hill, only to pick up its thread after miles of dull arable fields in a broken line running past Swaffham to the west. Like the intermittent conversations people have on long walks, it comes and goes across Norfolk, past the busy Catholic shrine at Walsingham, all the way to the edge of the known world at Holme-next-the-Sea.

It is barely dawn and high tide when Harry Cory Wright, Adam Nicolson and I set out from nearby Brancaster Staithe with John Brown, the Scolt Head Nature Warden, in his open wooden motor boat, heading up the channel through Brancaster Marshes towards Scolt Head and the open sea. We have intelligence that 50,000 pink-footed geese have arrived and are roosting on the island, and we are on our way to see them. The island's shores are grey with the birds, and already they are taking off, rising in undulating tresses and ribbons, trailing like kite tails through the sky, skimming the water, or veeing high above the rising mist. We chug across the clear grey, perfectly calm water, sliding over sandbars as the sky fills with patterned skeins of geese. Their plaintive honking echoes across Brancaster Harbour as they head inland towards their feeding grounds on stubble fields. Someone mentions that a circle of ancient wood has begun to emerge in a very slow-motion striptease out of the sands and peat banks on Holme beach below the high-water line. The braiding geese overhead might be pointing towards it as they fly off in their chevrons to their grazing fields. John knows the hows and whys of these snaking channels and marshes, and steers along them: the Gush, Whin Creek, Felters Bay. We steer between two sticks bearing pennants that hang limply in the fine drizzle, land on a sandbar, and follow a sandy path through the low scrub of sea lavender up to the warden's oak-framed hut, originally built in 1928 for visiting naturalists.

John brews up tea on a gas stove, and we sit round a table flicking through some of the books on the shelf, which include *Scolt Head House* by J. A. Steer, published the same year as the hut was built. There's a fading photo on the wall of a group of naturalists who came here in the late 1920s. John says the little boy in shorts squatting at the front of the group was later killed in the war. Two ancient conical red fire extinguishers sit, half rusted, in a corner. Their brass plungers have never been used, and probably wouldn't work by now anyway. The brick fireplace and flint chimney, an elegant, tapering cone, both have the stamp of the Arts and Crafts movement, of Lutyens and Gertrude Jekyll. So do the patterned bricks and flints in the yard before the hut, and the pair of slender, weathered, carved oak pillars that support the porch roof.

Leading off the main room, with its elevated views inland over the marsh to flint churches and glittering creeks, are three pine doors, dark stained, with artificial grain stippled in. We open them and go exploring. All three lead to narrow bedrooms like cabins, or monks' cells, with just a minimal bed or bunk and a mattress barely wide enough to balance on. They are made up with the pale-blue blankets and cellular coverlets I remember from visits to aunts in the 1950s.

The biggest, or least tiny, of the bedrooms contains a double bunk and a single bed. They're more like elongated cots, and turning over in one's sleep might be hazardous. Each of the other two cells has a single bed. The one I choose looks out west along the north shore of the island towards Hunstanton and the Wash. On a clear day, you can see all the way to Skegness, if that is your choice. The greyness of the sea and the narrowness of the beds give the hut a distinctly bachelor, not to say monkish, atmosphere. But every inch inside is boarded with graceful tanned and seasoned pine, whose resin has somehow pickled it into a lovely amber that accentuates the knots and emphasizes the grain. I think the look and aroma of the pine improves the hut's potential for cosiness no end, and even begin to fantasize about long winter nights curled up under the blue blankets with a book, until I remember curling up is out of the question.

John Brown says he thinks the hut feels spooky; somehow haunted, and not an easy, comfortable place to be. Adam, Harry and I take a heartier, more down-to-earth approach and say it's just a bit damp and needs a good airing. 'Light a fire in here,' we say, 'and dry out those blankets and sponge-rubber mattresses. Then cook some bacon and eggs, or sardines on a spade in the embers, open a bottle of whisky, and you'll soon feel differently about the place.'

With Professor Steers's book on the island spread out on the table, and more tea, we are already beginning to steam up the windows and generally settle in to the hut. The book contains a remarkable series of line drawings demonstrating how the island has shifted its shape and position over the years. A fixed line drawn east–west from A to B kept on intersecting different parts of the restless island from year to year in response to the longshore drift and other currents, freighted with pebbles, tugging at the island this way and that. Adam says this is just the kind of book he would like to write: the product of months and months of staying in the same place, concentrating on the details of its geology and natural history, doing some proper research into a phenomenon such as the life of this island. I think this is just the sort of hut I would like to inhabit for a spell, with a good stack of dry firewood and the North Sea raging outside across the dunes.

Outside again in the fine, drizzling rain, we climb to the highest point on the island just behind the hut and gaze down over the marshes and the long beach across the sea to the northern horizon the pink-footed geese have so recently crossed in their migration. Descending to the beach, we follow it to a place where a crashed and long-buried Lancaster bomber has recently begun to reappear, washed out by the eroding sea. Harry finds part of a gun turret. I kick away the sand and reveal the cellular structure of a wing. Adam follows it, scraping away more sand, and finds a copper cable encrusted with green and blue leading to a wing-tip light. We find we are standing on a buried fuel tank. I think of the dead pilot and crew, and feel a curious *Lord of the Flies* shiver about our discovery. At the far northern end of the beach we come across a dead fulmar and marvel at the size and ferocity of its beak.

We now adjourn to the other warden's hut on the island, where Neil, whose job it is to watch over the island, lives from May until October, keeping an eye on the terns that nest in the shingle beach. Hardly a soul comes here, even on the warmest summer days, so Neil's life is not a hard one. He has just left to winter in India, migrating every year to watch birds in his favourite haunts. This is a much smaller, simpler wooden hut with only a bedroom and a living space. John tidies it and brews more tea. Neil collects rainwater off the roof in a water butt, and solar panels provide power for lights, TV and radio. He hardly ever leaves the island all summer, depending on John to bring over supplies from the mainland when he brings over the boat to go cockling at low tide. So there is always shellfish too. This hut has an altogether different, lived-in feeling. It is relatively dry and full of odds and ends that suggest a less Spartan way of life: a small TV, a double bed, even a fridge.

The tide is dropping dramatically and we have to slide the boat down over the mud into the ebbing channel. With just enough depth to get over the sandbar, we reach open water and make for the Staithe.

Back home at North Creake, Harry cooked us all a huge breakfast and declared that we must visit John Lorrimer, the original dis-coverer in 1998 of the controversial 'Seahenge'– a vast ancient wood circle on the inter-tidal zone of Holme beach.

Further south, at Aldeburgh, I go down to the black-tarred pine fishermen's huts on the beach to buy fish and find a living counter-part to the trees at Holme. On a radio somewhere inside a voice gives out the weather forecast and wishes everyone good fishing. I buy a pound of sprats to cook on a shovel in the fire later on. The fisherman, his tattooed forearms silver with fish scales, wraps them in newspaper. I walk north up the beach towards Thorpeness and Maggie Hambling's controversially sited giant bronze oyster shell. 'Hear those voices that will not be drowned,' she has written in bronze across the shell, quoting from *Peter Grimes*. Sure enough, quite a few voices have been raised in Aldeburgh against the siting of Hambling's sculpture in so commanding a position, and will not be drowned.

In the dunes behind the big shell there's an unobtrusive natural memorial to all the drowned fishermen of this coast, just keeping its head above the shingle, surviving against all odds. In its quiet way, it is more spectacular than *The Oyster*. It is an apple tree, growing miraculously out of the barren-looking pebbles in a low crown only three to four feet high but seven yards in diameter and thirty in circumference. The tree is something of an iceberg: most of it is invisible, overwhelmed by the invading dunes. It is only the topmost branches you see in leaf.

I keep puzzling about that tree, buried up to its neck in the shingle beach like a daddy. It can't quite see the sea. If it grew another ten feet, it could peep over the top of the long ridge of shingle that sweeps from Aldeburgh to Thorpeness. It grows in the shelter of a bunker, a hollow in the dunes of shingle and sand that protects it from the winds of the Ural Mountains that whip across the muddy North Sea. The sheer withering intensity of the wind must prune the budding twigs relentlessly, so the tree takes the one course of survival open to it: it creeps ever outwards, crouching low and close to the shingle, creating a pincushion of densely branched fruiting spurs. I have met people gathering apples from it in summer, a little too early and too green, so as to beat the competition and ripen them in the fruit bowl. I want to pick an apple to identify but am too late, beaten by the eager Aldeburgh scrumpers. Outside the seasons of its blossom and fruit, most people would pass by the tree, mistaking it for a scrubby goat willow like those on the marsh that backs the dunes. George Crabbe used to go there and botanize, and lick the wounds inflicted by the scornful, bullying fishermen of Aldeburgh, who, having known him as a boy, scrubbing out barrels in the town, despised him, first as a doctor and later as their curate. He seriously thought about throwing himself in the marsh, but decided instead to go to London, where he received the generous patronage of Edmund Burke and began to make his way in life.

No doubt the salt spray of winter gales must provide the tree with an anti-fungal dusting to help keep it healthy. A hundred yards inland, looking over the marshes just the other side of the road to Thorpeness, is the derelict cottage whose orchard, once much further inland, may originally have contained this tree. As the North Sea has eroded more and more of this coast, it has edged the shingle bank further and further inland, burying the orchard and stifling all the trees but this one. Somewhere down below, where the shingle sits on the chalk, the roots are finding fresh water, perhaps from a spring. It must count as one of the hardiest apple trees in Britain, and grafts should be propagated. And even if Crabbe lived too long ago to have known this particular tree, he must surely have known the orchard. The Crabbe Apple deserves official recognition by the town.

★

Back at Holme, where this part of the East Anglian coast seems always to have been a numinous other-world, half in and half out of the North Sea. You still find trees under the sea, and their hulks are washed up in storms. Eight thousand years ago a great forest stretched all the way from here to Holland and Germany. Even from inside a car, a week later, approaching it feels like a pilgrimage. It is the threshold of big skies and intense reflected light as well as water: when you eventually stand on the beach facing north, there is nothing but sea and ice all the way to the North Pole.

John Lorrimer had caused an archaeological sensation when he at last persuaded the county archaeologists to come and look at the circle of oak timbers surrounding the up-ended two-ton stump of an oak he had first noticed as he walked on Holme beach at low tide on 17 August 1998. The timbers were emerging from the peat beds created by an ancient wood, now gradually exposed by the sea's erosion. They appeared very tentatively at first, like men peering over the rim of a trench after a gunfight. Twelve months earlier, John had found an exquisite Bronze Age axe-head and several bronze buttons at the same spot and felt a strong hunch there was something very special about this particular patch of the enormous beach. Yet it took him over a year to convince anyone that the wooden ring that began to seize his imagination as it took more and more shape from tide to tide was anything other than the wishful thinking of an amateur archaeologist.

John and I drive up to Holme through heavy rain, bumping along the track behind the sand dunes to the nature reserve, past thorns bent nearly horizontal by the on-shore wind. We park by the warden's house and climb into full waterproof kit before venturing on to the beach along a path that winds through a squat forest of buckthorn. The savagery of the tides here has all but washed away some recent breakwaters built of coppiced hazel and woven hurdles, a brave attempt to defend the retreating dunes.

The receding tide is already revealing banks of peat and rows of posts standing up a foot out of the mud; they run a hundred yards or more in great V-shapes to form the open mouths of funnels facing inland. These were Saxon fish-traps that would catch the shoals as they swam out with the tide. We can even make out delicate fragments of the wattle of hazel that was woven between the posts, which had the orange glow of alder.

Holme beach is so littered with shrapnel from the wartime gunnery range, miscellaneous wrecks, and the crashed hulks of Heinkels and Hurricanes that metal detectors are quite useless, even dangerous. The only way to find things is to walk the vast beach over and over again, seeing what each new tide reveals.

Passing close to Grime's Graves, the Peddars Way would have been a natural route to take if you were a trader or pedlar carrying knapped flint tools to the coast. As a pilgrimage way, it is one of our English answers to the rather hillier route across southern France and Spain to Santiago de Compostela. I still can't help feeling like a pilgrim whenever I go up to the luminous Norfolk coast, even by car.

Mary Newcomb

Every now and again if you're lucky, exploring a wood, sitting by a river or looking out of a train, you may experience what a friend of mine calls 'a Mary moment'. Such minor epiphanies, often apparently unremarkable in themselves, will lodge in your memory and may be recalled in their essentials long afterwards. They are the distinctive subjects of the Suffolk painter Mary Newcomb: a flock of goldfinches dispersing, a magpie flying up from a wet road, a football match seen through a hole in an oak leaf eaten by a caterpillar. These are all actual titles of paintings by Mary Newcomb. Such poetical vignettes are essential to the particular effect of these deceptively modest pictures.

Mary Newcomb belongs firmly in the greenwood tradition, peering unnoticed from behind leaves like the Green Man at things that are very often half hidden themselves. In the Newcomb world, people and plants sometimes surreally hybridize, as in *Girl at the Garden Centre in the Rain*, in which a woman, mostly hidden beneath an outsized green-and-black striped umbrella, has grown into an umbellifer. And in *Lady with a Bunch of Sweet Williams*, a woman standing in an exuberantly flowering meadow, hidden from the waist up by her giant posy, seems to have burst into full bloom in sympathy. Such chameleon impulses in many of the paintings come close to a visual expression of Andrew Marvell's lines in 'The Garden': 'Annihilating all that's made/To a green thought in a green shade'. They have a notable affinity with poetry. Mary is an admirer of John Clare, whose words 'I found my poems in the fields and only wrote down what I saw' describe very well how she paints, and the connections she notices between, say, pylons and cobwebs, or butterflies and bits of torn paper. Indeed, the notes in her diaries are very often written without punctuation in a style that strongly suggests that of Clare as well as the stream of consciousness she wants to express.

I appreciate Mary's pictures in a way that must be informed and biased by my affection for the part of the world where we have both lived through the poignant closing years of what might be called the old rural Suffolk: the northern stretch of the county broadly defined by the valley of the River Waveney. In her evocation of the natural, mainly rural life of Suffolk, Mary Newcomb is comparable with two other artists of the borderlands, John Nash and Ronald Blythe, whose work is based on their relationship with the Stour Valley along the southern margins of the county. The setting of some of Mary's work in Ronald Blythe's book *Borderland* seems an entirely natural collaboration. She delights in simple, vernacular structures or machines: rowing boats, bicycles, weather-vanes, telegraph poles, bird boxes, lighthouses, windmills, church towers. 'They serve a purpose. They have a point,' she writes in her diary. She also loves to travel, in the old, unhurried way on trains, steamers or on foot, and records her excursions in paint.

When Mary and Godfrey first came to Suffolk, they lived at Needham so close to the Waveney that one night two dog otters fought each other right under their window. 'They were on their back legs, teeth in each other's necks, and balanced by their tails,' Mary wrote to me in a letter. 'In the morning I saw their bloody trails in the dew on the marsh, going in different directions.' They farmed in a small way along a stretch of river bank with goats, hens and cows. Mary would get up early and paint from five until seven and then do farm work for the rest of the day, scrubbing eggs clean with cold water or milking goats. Now they had moved to Peasenhall, a few miles inland from Walberswick, where they also lived for a while, and I have driven over with the East Anglian painter Jayne Ivimey, an old friend of Mary and Godfrey, for tea.

The house is at one end of the village, with a walled garden and a homemade wooden aeroplane on a pole as a weather vane. The first thing that strikes you about Mary is the calm depth and steadiness of her clear blue eyes. She walks and stands stoutly, with definite steps and great certainty about everything she does, looking remarkably young for a woman in her eightieth year. She wears her rich dark-brown hair, which has never turned grey, neatly cropped. Mary Newcomb bears the air of someone who has worked hard, and to some purpose, all her life. Everything about the house suffuses it with a lively spirit of curiosity and inquiry. There is something of or by Mary in every room of the house except Godfrey's, which houses his beloved Philip Suttons. Godfrey, says Jayne, is a man of sudden strong enthusiasms: the saxophone, the penny whistle, the spinning wheel.

Mary has been painting rooks. 'A Brooding Rook in its Heaven' is the working title of her new work in progress. On the floor beside the canvas are half a dozen of the birds drawn in charcoal on sheets of paper, and on the wall is another one, standing confidently, bald beak raised aloft, about to caw. The poetical titles always come first. They are like haiku. And there is something Japanese about the clarity and profound simplicity of Mary's work. This has not come about through any deliberate study of such things. Mary has simply arrived quite independently at similar conclusions through her own original route. Every so often, as we have our tea, a live inhabitant of the rookery beside her garden comes down and pecks about on the lawn.

Mary generally places her paintings on the floor and sits on a low stool, bending over them to work. This accounts for the close focus. Sometimes the picture is propped against the wall, and she uses a small step that enables her almost to walk right into the work. At one point in the diary, she describes herself as 'so tired

I almost fell into the canvas'. Unlike most artists, Mary keeps not a sketchbook but a notebook or diary. She fills it with handwritten thoughts and observations that often find their way into the work verbatim. 'Be sure to put it down,' she writes in one diary entry, 'be it squirrel in a woodpile, men with white-toed boots working on a mountain railway, caterpillars hanging stiffly and staring from a laurel bush, the magnitude of the stars – there is no end.' That reference to the stars inevitably suggests one of the best-known Newcomb pictures, the beautiful watercolour *Ewes Watching Shooting Stars*: three ewes on a clear, cold night, invite you to identify with the animals inside their warm coats. The painting reminds me of Ted Hughes's poem 'The Warm and the Cold', an evocation of the animal world on a freezing, starry night in terms of the particular form of shelter each one takes, including, by contrast, the 'sweating farmers' who 'Turn in their sleep/Like oxen on spits'. Newcomb and Hughes share an acute awareness of the minutiae of life in the wild, and a deep, affectionate understanding of the lives of farm animals and all creatures. In another picture, *Very Cold Birds Where One has Flown Away it Knocked the Raindrops Off*, the raindrops are drawn very nearly as big as the birds on a tree, so the three drops in mid fall suggest the absent bird. Proportion is very often skewed like this in a way reminiscent of children's art or 'naive' painting, in order to represent the thing that looms large in the artist's mind at a particular moment.

Years before she eventually began to write in a series of red-bound diaries from W. H. Smith's, Mary instinctively preferred writing or drawing on separate sheets of a favourite A5 paper, torn from a book and carefully kept in the folder she carried with her. She was well aware that this was the medium that best suited her mode of thought and sudden, crystalline perceptions. To write in a notebook or diary implies a burden of narrative, of things unfolding in sequence through time, which Mary was temperamentally reluctant to take on. Entering one of her paintings, like entering a wood, alters your sense of time. The act of drawing, as John Berger points out in a recent interview, 'is a way of learning to leave the present, or rather, of gathering the past, the future and the present into one'.

At the head of a jotted list of projected ideas, Mary writes, 'The lady in her landscape, her rightness, her industry, her involvement, respect and pride.' It has the ring of a self-portrait. There is a certainty about Mary Newcomb that includes an absolute belief in the importance of the clear-sighted moments that engender her paintings. The impression you often have, looking at one of her paintings, is that 'Suddenly there it was, and Mary painted it.' But, in fact, each painting evolves slowly in the studio. Mary paints a first version, blocking out the main elements, then stands it against the wall. Over a period of weeks or months she will then begin to tear out bits of colour or texture that catch her eye in magazines and arrange them on the floor beside each picture. As we move through the house we step carefully around these pools of colour.

At the end of each day's work Mary also paints out all her brushes on to pieces of hardboard and stands them near the painting in progress. 'Just now I'm still stuck on green,' she says. A particular colour will preoccupy her for weeks, and the painting out of the brushes is much more than 'a good way to use up spare paint', as she deceptively claims. It is the gradual preparation of the underpainting that gives the pictures such depth and mystery, and often pushes them to the edge of abstraction. Turner did something similar in his 'colour beginnings'. It is the most profoundly uncon-scious part of the painting: the music of the song. I notice a predominantly blue work from an earlier phase, a back view of two figures sitting in the garden. Mary often paints people from behind, perhaps shyly, in a way that suggests that they too are lost in their own private worlds. Another example hangs across the room: three female figures leaning over the railings of Southwold Pier, looking out across a sparkling sea with a pair of distant sailing ships on the horizon. One wears a black-and-white harlequin-patterned dress. Wind catches her hair.

The people in these paintings seem to be part of the landscape. They do not dominate it, but take their place in it like any other being. Mary's *Man Cycling Madly Down a Hill* seems airborne on his bicycle in an abstract 'green shade', his arms and elbows akimbo over the handlebars like wings, cloth-capped head leaning forward like a bird's. Mary's men often appear in the cloth caps worn by Suffolk farm labourers or fishermen until recently: a badge of belonging to the land or sea. These anonymous figures are in some ways Green Men, emerging through deep layers of foliage. The just-visible *Lady in an Unsprayed Field Seen in Passing*, an after-image, might be a corn spirit. Mary Newcomb seems attracted to paint what is half hidden, invisible even. In *The Last Bird Home*, the small figure of the bird, in a slight halo of warm amber dusk light, descends into a long smudge of dark-grey hedge we know is crowded with concealed birds, all singing. 'After a long wet evening,' Mary wrote while she was working on this picture, 'the birds *must* sing. They have to get it out and shout insistently.' Birds are everywhere in the work, yet they are often half concealed, hard to spot, as in a wood or a hedge. A cock pheasant in a field is actually a half pheasant submerged in grass, and in the diary there is a reference to 'half men' as subjects for pictures: 'half men in hollows, in fields, in dips in the road, in long grass'. This is how it is in the fields, hedges and woods: things heard but unseen, or glimpsed, partly hidden. Seen collectively as hedgerow or wood, trees are abstracted by nature into a mass of colour and texture. The experience is distinct from the architectural look of a single tree. And this is what you see in a Newcomb painting.

Driftwood

The three of us – Margaret Mellis, her son Telfer Stokes and I – have climbed two flights of steep, bare pine stairs to Margaret's top-floor studio. Catching our breath, we peer out through a pair of sash windows into the dullness of an afternoon sea mist at Southwold. Borne on the coastal currents of the North Sea, where Margaret used to swim every day until well into her eighties, fresh shoals of flotsam are homing towards the beach. In the room, a scree of driftwood tumbles down from the picture rail at one corner. Margaret, diminutive and always notably young-looking, is in her nineties. She often used to sleep in the studio and now sits on the single bed, contemplating the flotsam tide that advances across the paint-spattered hardboard floor. In another corner, her various tools are laid out: hand drill, electric drill, screwdrivers, hammers and pliers. Jam jars of brushes, screws and nails, boxes of oil paints and sketchbooks cover a table.

Margaret's driftwood constructions are hung on nails and screws artlessly driven into the walls: collages or 'assemblages' of assorted shapes and fragments, bleached, pickled, painted, battered or frayed by the action of the waves and shingle. These are the disembodied components of things – chairs, boats, tables, herring boxes – reassembled into abstract forms. They lie somewhere between painting and sculpture, between two dimensions and three. Driftwood is full of the tonal colour and depth of years of flaked or peeling paint, half revealing a deep strata of soft pigments from generations of painters and decorators. Dozens of unknown craftsmen and artisans have unwittingly contributed to these works. They are collections of silent stories. Each piece of driftwood carries its own secret history that begins with the seed of the unknown tree it came from, continues with its life as part of something made and nears its end with a voyage across the sea, perhaps halfway round the world over many years. All this information is compressed into each assemblage, the more potent for being a complete mystery. Every fragment of driftwood carries the history of a past life, so there is inevitably an element of rescue about Mellis's work. She takes what is 'washed up', disjointed, apparently finished, and resurrects it.

Although essentially abstract, there is often a hint of the figurative about a composition like *Marsh Music*, hung halfway down the stairs, an accidental rudder shape that might be a bittern's upstretched neck and beak among the reeds, or the last of a skeletal wherry stranded and half sunk in mud. *Jungle Paradise*, at the end of the corridor outside the kitchen, ripples out like the grain of a tree in a series of tall, thin wooden strips, each one a different shade of red or rust. At its centre is a deeply grained, half-charred oblong of Columbian pine suggestive of a human figure crowned with torn shreds of blue and yellow plywood like feathers. The playful spirit of Picasso and his own early assemblages presides over much of Mellis's work. On the landing, she has set the sprung-open back of a bentwood chair upside-down to represent the horns on a bull's head.

Most of the constructions are more purely abstract, and Mellis has sometimes applied paint here and there herself, as in the palette-like *Sea*, in which a whole range of different blues is set against patches of red and the grain of natural wood. The patina, the visual feel of the wood, varies all over this work. Often, the found wood is selected for the figure of its grain, as in *Fisherman*, in which a slender crescent of sea-bleached pine suggests moving water or waves. The strength of the work is its ingenious composition of colour, texture and form, all improvised in a lively, playful spirit. It is wood jazz.

There are no carpets in the house, and the white-painted floorboards, worn bare in all the most-trodden places, communicate exactly the same feeling of human use and habit over time as animal tracks, a footpath, a dished doorstep, a child's painted wooden bricks or the driftwood on the walls. Margaret has made the whole house an installation. As you go through the front door, a dado rail on the left of the hall and corridor leads you to the kitchen with an unbroken line of beach pebbles along its ledge. On the kitchen wall a large homemade calendar says 'Today is Monday' and gives the date. Ironically, in this house adrift on lost memories, Alzheimer's has come to live with Margaret Mellis too, and she now needs constant care.

Everyone in Southwold used to bring the driftwood harvest of their beach walks to Margaret's doorstep, leaving it in the front garden for her. The best of it would find its way upstairs to the studio, where Margaret separated the painted from the natural wood, the former bleached and muted by the sun, the latter chamfered, flayed or shattered by the sea. As one accustomed to living by the sea, Margaret Mellis had always been in the habit of collecting driftwood for the fire. One winter's night, about to place another spar in the flames, she hesitated, recognizing its individual beauty, and set it to one side. The moment of reprieve was the seed of her work with driftwood.

Telfer, himself an artist and sculptor, is the son of Adrian Stokes, whom Margaret Mellis met at a Cézanne exhibition in Paris in 1936 when she was twenty-two. They married two years later. She had studied at the Edinburgh School of Art. Stokes, who was twelve years older, had already established himself as an influential art critic and writer, and was now turning to painting. When war broke out, he and Mellis moved to Cornwall to live on Carbis Bay near St Ives, close to their friends Ben Nicholson and Barbara Hepworth. Naum Gabo and Peter Lanyon soon joined them, and so did

Christopher Wood and a stream of visitors who included Graham
Sutherland, Victor Pasmore and William Coldstream. Ben Nicholson encouraged Mellis to make her early abstract compositions,
although she had already begun to make small-scale 'constructivist'
collages, perhaps influenced by Gabo. But it was in St Ives that she
met an artist who was to leave a deep impression on them all:
Alfred Wallis, the local fisherman she and the Nicholsons discovered
painting seascapes and boats on odd pieces of cardboard at his
cottage.

After the war, the marriage broke up, and in 1948 Mellis married
the painter Francis Davison. They moved to the South of France,
where they lived for three years in a half-ruined château at Cap
D'Antibes before returning to live in Suffolk at the beginning of the
1950s. A fine collage by Davison hangs above the mantelpiece in
Margaret's living room, and another on the kitchen wall, surrounded by pink artificial flowers, beside a dark-blue Aga. It wasn't
until 1978 that Margaret Mellis began making her driftwood reliefs,
at least partly influenced by Francis Davison and his collages. But
from the mid fifties she made a series of over seventy coloured
pastel drawings of flowers on opened-out envelopes. The envelope
drawings prefigure the driftwood assemblages: letters, like driftwood and ideas, arrive out of the blue. They are gifts. The envelopes, like the driftwood, had a former life, and would generally be
discarded. Mellis gives them new status and a function. Ingeniously
reusing an envelope, or driftwood, to make a picture is, in the
context of environmental politics, a deliberately frugal act. Both
were once trees, and what would otherwise have been wasted is
turned to good use.

To say all this is to suggest that there is something strongly
conceptual about Margaret Mellis's work. It would be perverse to
ignore her choice of such deliberately unconventional materials as
envelopes and driftwood. Damien Hirst noticed this when he met
Margaret Mellis early in his career, even before art school. He had
been impressed by an exhibition of Francis Davison's collages at
the Hayward Gallery and wrote to her as his widow to find out

more about him. Her own show at the Redfern Gallery then inspired him so much he ended up on a train to Southwold, where he stayed the weekend with Mellis, swam in the sea with her and admired more of her work.

As a sea creature herself, in that she was a regular swimmer, Margaret Mellis felt a natural affinity with driftwood. She took part in its life and knew what it was to float in the tidal currents off the Suffolk coast. Over time, water imparts an abstract quality to wood by sculpting away its inessential, softer parts, emphasizing the sinews of grain until the knots stand out like inset pebbles. Driftwood maps the movement of water around it in its own grain.

You find driftwood in rivers as well as in the sea. The spar of slender oak heartwood that now hangs on the beam above my fireplace comes from the Rhinnog Mountains of Wales above Harlech. I found it cast into a stream, which had combed and etched its grain into relief, bleaching it pale grey. It is like the sloughed skin of a snake. Perhaps it was a stake riven by the hedger's billhook. I imagine the knee of a hollowed knot halfway along it deflecting the current, making an eddy, a little aquatic sheep-space in which a miller's thumb might hunker down, all gills and pectoral fins and wide, ugly mouth. This fragment of stream flotsam, elevated to the status of a modest totem above the hearth, is a kind of story-stick. I can only guess at the first half of its life. The hollow knot tells me that a fair-sized branch once grew away from the tree. Somebody coppiced it. Its cleaving implies long service in a hedge or fence, and its bleached erosion says it lay for several years wedged in the gravel bed of the stream until the day I noticed it. Hot from an uphill hike one sunny morning after rain, I bathed in a tiny pool and threaded the wet sliver of wood through the flap of my rucksack like a yoke, carrying it all day and the next until I returned to my car and laid it on the back seat like a sleeping child.

More of this half-dissolved wood lives beside me on my desk. One talisman is a ring of olive like a wreath, a tough hollowed knot carved to fine filigree inside by sea creatures. I found it on a beach in Lesbos. Another is a pine Japanese prayer sandal washed up on a beach on Hokkaido with dozens of others, where all the wooden prayer sandals of Japan seem to drift eventually. There is a custom among the monks on a certain island in Japan of an initiation in which the novice lies in a wooden box made specially for the purpose and is launched on the tidal rips. The currents may take him out to sea and he will never be seen again, or they may carry him on a circular voyage that will bring him back to the shore. So the box may be a boat or a coffin, a way towards a new life or straight to death by exposure or drowning. The novice consents to be human driftwood. The sandal on my desk might have belonged to such an initiate, stepping out of it on the beach as he embarked on his uncertain voyage, but its true story will always be a mystery. It is carved from a single piece of pine, with three drilled eyes that once held the thongs, and a pair of ridged platforms to raise the foot above the mud. Sea and sand have worn the sole to little more than the thickness of a book cover, reducing it to an abstract embodiment of Japanese simplicity.

I hear the story of the monk over dinner with Roger Ackling and his wife Sylvia, who live a mile or two inland from the coast of north Norfolk. Roger has often worked with driftwood. The sandal was a present from Sylvia, who mounted an exhibition of flotsam temple shoes on Hokkaido a few years ago. Until the encroaching North Sea drove them out, the Acklings lived yards away from it in the old coastguard station at Weybourne. The sea brought the flotsam and jetsam straight to the studio, although Ackling makes his work out of doors. He draws by focusing the sun's rays through a magnifying glass and burning lines on the surface of a small piece of wood or card. He works from left to right across the surface of the piece, with the sun always at his shoulder. The work is photographic in the truest sense: each mark or dot is a small black sun, registered on the wood instead of on photographic paper. It records the moment of arrival on earth of rays that left the sun light years ago, coinciding with another journey's end for the driftwood after a voyage of unknown length in days and sea-miles.

Each line is a repeat pattern of burnt-sun images, scaled down many millions of times. It is an act of meditation, a ritual of some rigour that requires the artist to empty his mind and be very still. He began working with a magnifying glass during his lunch-breaks as a gardener. 'All I need', he says, 'is a pair of standard magnifying glasses from Boots.' He points out that they mustn't be too powerful in case they set the wood on fire. Patience and slowness are the essence of Ackling's art. Every work is a faithful representation of the weather as it really was during the hours it took to make it. He will often work for six or seven hours at a time. If a cloud passes over and obscures the sun, or even if a bird passes, its presence is registered as blank space or 'shadow' in the picture because Ackling is moving the glass very slowly and evenly, from left to right along bands of successive lines from top to bottom. He is a camera. Sylvia says she can tell when Ackling has been at work from the pleasant aroma of woodsmoke that lingers in his beard.

Ackling would often walk the beach from Weybourne to Blakeney Point and back in a day, looking for driftwood. Then he took to using only what was delivered by the sea to the door of the coastguard cottage studio. Now, he says, driftwood is becoming scarcer. Sheringham Town Council clear their beaches in quest of awards for civic tidiness, and sea anglers make fires of it at night. At one point he was even reduced to picking up lolly sticks. He tells the story of finding a hand-printed message in a bottle from a schoolgirl in Holland who had thrown it from an oilrig on a school outing. He posted a reply to the address given, printing it because his handwriting is so hard to read. The letter she wrote back, full of questions like 'Have you got a rabbit?' and 'How old is it?', clearly showed she thought she was writing to a child.

The most dramatic driftwood Ackling has seen was on a trip with Hamish Fulton to a northern corner of Iceland that took two days to reach. There they found a man living alone in a bunker constructed entirely of the driftwood that floated up from Russia. His only possessions appeared to be a chainsaw and a wealth of driftwood. Hamish Fulton and Richard Long, Roger Ackling's contemporaries at St Martin's in the 1960s, continue to be important influences, along with Dada, Carl Andre, and the sixteenth-century Japanese sculptor and Buddhist monk, Enku, who dedicated his life to walking from temple to temple all over Japan in a quest to carve 120,000 Buddhas. Ackling has often worked and exhibited in Japan, and the house is full of little wooden Shinto shrines of the household gods: tiny four-inch-tall boxes with a sliding front wall and a hole like a bird box for the god to go in and out, bought in Japanese street markets.

Driftwood makes a vital contribution to the sea's ecology. It is as important to the oceans as dead and rotting trees are to terrestrial forests, but its mode of decomposition is quite different. Whereas in a living wood it is fungi that do most of the work, floating driftwood in the sea is principally eaten by animals. These energetic sculptors fall into two main groups: wood-boring crustaceans and bivalve molluscs. The first of these are the gribbles, responsible for the labyrinthine galleries of tunnels that worm their way through the surface of so much driftwood. The second group, the molluscs, are the shipworms, whose shells are specially adapted to rasp their way into the wood. Between them, they soon soften the outer surfaces of driftwood, making it more vulnerable to the splintering action of waves on rocks, more easily waterlogged, and more accessible to the secondary decay of marine fungi and bacteria.

As they gnaw their way through the outer layers of driftwood, the gribbles and shipworms leave more than half of it undigested, and reduce it to the fine wood powder that sinks into the mud of estuaries as the food known to the marine biologists as micro-detritus. Much of the sediment in the estuaries of great rivers is actually the remains of wood. Deconstructed by gribbles and shipworms, it is a major source of food for marine animals and plants. Tuna and other fish regularly congregate around floating driftwood and logs out at sea. Fishermen in the Pacific routinely look out for driftwood when fishing for skipjack and yellowfin tuna. Dolphins do the same. There are several theories to explain this. The fish may simply be seeking shade, or using the driftwood in the way cattle use rubbing posts, to remove external parasites. But it is likely that a food web grows up, with small fish following the driftwood to feed off the tiny organisms, plankton, eggs and algae, that attach themselves to it. Fish and dolphins will often use floating wood as a reference point in the ocean, ranging up to twelve miles away from it, then returning to it at intervals anywhere between a quarter of an hour and twenty hours. Driftwood, however nomadic, can even serve as the marine equivalent of a cairn.

Thus, through driftwood, the forest and the sea are intimately connected. Natural driftwood probably inspired the construction of the earliest boats, which in turn eventually broke up and provided more driftwood. Rivers rise in forests all over the world, and often run through them on their way to the sea, so the connection extends far inland from the coast. By way of return for its contribution of marine food, the sea waters the forest with rain. Trees growing close to rivers have always been the first to be felled, either naturally by storms and floods, or by foresters because they could be floated downstream easily to sawmills and ports in the estuary. In times of flood, stumps, logs and trees tend to be washed down into estuaries, where they arrest mud and form shoals. Washed up on distant beaches, driftwood forms the core of sand dunes by holding wind-blown sand in much the same way. Drifted trees are often found deep in the base of large dunes when a new cycle of waves erodes the sands. Even a tree, which we think of as a fixed point, rooted as anything can be to a single place on Earth, can be imagined into a drifting nomad, nibbled by fish, wandering the oceans, ending up anywhere from Southwold to a remote beach on Hokkaido.

PART THREE

Driftwood

The Woods and the Water

It is early evening when I pull over above the river at Le Lézard Bleu, the village bar in Vieusson. When I turn off the engine, a wave of nightingale song rolls up out of the valley, riding over the deeper music of the mountain water racing along the winding avenue of a riverside forest. All along the river, invisible nightingales are singing in every bamboo and sandy sallow grove, in the walled cherry orchards on the alluvial soil of the flood plain, beneath every stone village crawling up the hillside. I am heading upstream along the valley towards Olargues, crossing high-arched bridges over this river, the Orb, built to accommodate its spectacular winter floods. From the balcony of the bar, glass in hand, I look down over a quickening bend in the river, a crook of pebbled banks, half obscured by willows. I have never heard so many nightingales. Some may even be heading for Suffolk. I have come to meet them halfway.

I go down a track quietly to the river, lean against the trunk of a poplar to get closer to the birds and listen: the drone of a motorbike coming up through the hairpin bends of the valley, the hollow clatter of water over pebbles, the hissing of bamboos, the slight rattle of poplar leaves overhead and, above all this, the astonishing volume of nightingales at close quarters. Do I imagine it, or are the birds singing faster than in Suffolk? They are masters of the pregnant pause, but seem to be hurrying, as French speech often seems more rapid. Has spring subverted the musical discipline? But it is an illusion, a function of the contrapuntal effect of so many birds singing in a single valley.

The riparian forest is an almost unbroken ribbon of wet-loving trees and shrub that follows the Orb and its tributary, the Jaur, for many miles through the steep hills of the Hérault. Much of the woodland is almost *garrigue*: ash, alder, goat willow, holm oak, strawberry tree, suckering elms, spindle tree, dogwood, elder and white poplar are woven together into a rich limestone scrub by a tangle of wild hops, dog-roses, bramble, traveller's joy and white bryony. Further up on the hillsides, terraced vines, olives and almond groves reach up towards the dark mountain ridge of the Espinouse.

At Olargues, everyone inside the noisy restaurant is watching Barcelona play Real Madrid, while outside, the *rossignol* assails the night air. I throw my hotel windows open and lie in bed listening, far too excited to sleep.

In the clear morning I set out from the hill hamlet of Maroul, taking a path past a graveyard full of heart-shaped white enamel memorial plaques that flash in the sun. To my left hand, tiny terraced cherry orchards stand along the head-high bank above the path. To my right, blinding yellow thickets of the broom they once used for thatch round here, lichened rock and, somewhere below, the sound of a rushing stream. I ask a little girl in a cottage garden: 'Is this the right path out of the village?' 'Yes, this is where there is a pool in the river, and fish, yes, this is the *sentier*.' The child's clear gaze and the succinct detail of her reply enchant the place for me.

At the river pool I sit on a boulder and test the water. It is cold but bearable, and I decide to defer the pleasure of bathing and explore a little. Green lizards dart away into old terrace walls that contain chestnuts and walnuts above the pool. On the other bank, meadow brown and yellow brimstone butterflies waft about a tiny meadow, naturally walled by boulders. The sudden blue of jonquil jumps out of the trees, against pure white strata of stitchwort. I push on through more broom, clambering about derelict chestnut terracing of limestone crisp with dead leaves, until I find myself on a path well trodden by the hooves of wild boar. An orange-tip butterfly goes by, riding the thermal that rises off the edge of a terrace to one side.

Back at the bathing hole I am made painfully aware of the first holly I have encountered. A little whirlpool of beech mast endlessly rearranges its pattern of seeds and tiny fragments of twig. I slide in off the big smooth limestone rock and float like a trout, facing into the current. Sun glows through the leaves of chestnut, walnut, rowan, ash, maple and a solitary cherry. The tracks of wild boar are all round the shallows between clumps of yellow-green euphorbia and herb Robert. The pool is needle-cold and soon washes away the long journey here. I notice something I have seen before: a cloud of gnats gathering over the water, attracted, perhaps, by the warmth of my body. It is easy to see how a gnat-cloud might be seen as a dancing naiad, a water sprite.

I dry off in the sun on a warm, grey boulder that seems to melt into the roots of two old friends from home, an overhanging walnut and a hazel. It takes time to bring these wild walnuts into focus. It dawns on me that they are all along the river banks, self-seeded in the black alluvial soil from nuts washed down in the winter floods, lodging in rock fissures. Walnut seedlings sprout enormous tap roots that will dive in and anchor them almost anywhere. The trees don't declare themselves immediately; they mingle with the ashes, whose pinnate leaves and grey bark can look so alike, especially in their early years. A bright-green caterpillar swings out over the water from the walnut on a long strand of cobweb. I float out a walnut boat, wondering if one of the fish will appear. Perhaps they are trout.

Filling my water bottle at a tributary spring near by reminds me of Gérard Depardieu in *Jean de Florette*. The capriciousness of natural water supplies in hill country like this, and access to them, can dominate entire lives and village relationships. I notice that lizards lie in wait beside the spring-puddle, waiting to pounce on flies when they alight to drink. It's the same on the paths: wherever even a trickle of water crosses them, a lizard will be waiting for an unwary fly or butterfly.

Leaving the pool, I follow what must be a pack-horse or droving track four feet wide through the old chestnut terraces, between drystone walls called *calades*. Old chestnut trees overarch it from the terraces, and its floor, thick with their dried, toasty leaves, is littered with the hedgehog shells of chestnuts. Every few yards the fresh, damp excavations of the leaf mould suggest foraging wild boar: the original pork scratchings. Some of the tracks leading up into the mountains are very old. Those known locally as *drailles*, just wide enough for a pack horse or a trickle of sheep, were for transhumance: leading the animals to the summer pastures high on the mountain, and back to the shelter of the valleys for winter. The further I go, the more ruinous the track. It must have fallen out of use years ago. Further on, a small ruined cottage or shed stands among the chestnuts, so camouflaged in ivy I scarcely notice it. Its roofless walls are of limestone, and what is left of the floor is chestnut. There's a stone chimney at the back and a fireplace in the cellar-like lower storey, beneath a single upstairs floor supported by heavy chestnut beams. This is, I realize, the chestnut-harvesting equivalent of a Kentish oast house: a miniature chestnut-drying house, a *secadou*. In fact, the chestnut harvesters would light a deliberately smoky fire downstairs to dry and smoke the chestnuts, piled into the upper floor, at the same time. Most of the hillsides of the valley of the River Jaur around Olargues were planted with terraces of chestnuts, which was the main source of the flour that was ground from the nuts. I have chestnut bread with me in my rucksack, bought at the bakery in Olargues, and very good it is too.

The chestnut leaves are so dry and tough they seem not to decay very much, and it is easy to stumble into deep drifts of them in the hollows, mixed with the spiky husks. Some of the coppiced chestnuts are enormous: sinuous and half ruined by now, they spiralled as they twisted towards the light in their youth. And there are giant stumps and boles five feet across. As I gain higher ground, still following the track along a ridge above the stream, chestnut gives way to beech, and lovely hangars bearing clouds of bright-green new foliage rise out of the ginger biscuit-brown of the steep hillside forest floor.

In a deserted *mas*, a simple farmhouse halfway up the mountain, I catch sight of a pigtailed man in his mid thirties splitting firewood 200 yards away across the valley of a small stream. I pause beside the log pile I assume is his to eat my sandwich, wondering if it would be too intrusive to go to talk to him. I am curious about his life here and the wild life of the woods, but, like him, I am also happy with my own company. He has a rainbow-painted house-truck full of cats, with a tarpaulin bivouac pitched over the back doors. It is parked beside an old white Renault Four on the track where I have stopped. From the underpants and khaki shorts on his washing line, I deduce there is no woman in residence. He has chainsawed the chestnut logs into professional-looking cord lengths and secured the stack with stakes. He has also dammed the stream into a pleasant-looking pool above the footbridge to the house. He must have seen me, and disappears inside, so I too move on quietly.

Most of the chestnut trees went into decline years ago, infected with the fungal ink disease, or with canker, and there has been a mass retreat from the old mixed farms of the mountains and hills, leaving ruined houses as well as trees. The half-rotten, dying trees hold on to life stubbornly, adapting, sending up new shoots from the base: becoming coppice trees. Higher up, the beech-trunks are all pale silver, like the rocks, and I meet a bright metallic dor beetle on the path. It is iridescent blue, black and green all at once, like the smart new cars in Montpellier. Higher still, the beechwood floor is blue with jonquils, and tobacco-brown with leaves and beech-mast husks. The boar have been stripping bark off the stubby, sturdy little mountain beeches, but still they cling on.

Looking down at the woodland from the ridge, I see the beech woods stand out bright green against the soft mauve of the chestnuts. On the way down again to Maroul, I do all the things lone walkers do: race myself and stride out to rhythmical chants of 'John Brown's Body' or the sort of nonsense doggerel that arises from the thought that a snake might be sunning itself on the path: 'What could be badder/Than the zigger-zagger/ On the back of an adder?' It was perhaps just as well that I hadn't met a soul all day.

Pyrenees

Autumn comes late to the wooded southerly slopes of the Spanish Pyrenees. The mountains are a natural climatic boundary between the rest of Europe to the north and the African Sahara to the south. My friend Andrew Sanders and I have climbed through the leafy fireworks of mixed beech, oak, maple, chestnut and hazel woods in a bright-blue morning up a steep track from Cantalops, an agricultural village in the foothills, to Requescens, a hamlet that is really a long farmhouse, extended down the generations, with a small bar-cum-restaurant, the Cantina, in one end.

Coming in sight of the place, we enter the circle of a hillside wood pasture of cork oaks. A dozen white geese graze outside a two-storey wooden shed with a worn staircase visible inside. Some of the oaks are deep ox-blood red where the sock of cork has recently been peeled, the year's last two digits painted white on the tree as a reminder of its next date, in just under a decade, with the cork-harvesters. The grass is well trodden and manured with crusty cowpats. This is the home pasture for the cattle now out browsing in the woods. Entering the level farmyard, we are greeted by four dogs. An old mongrel bitch ambles over gently. The others, barking half heartedly, are chained beneath a big horse chestnut. A pointer slinks away back into the shadow of a firewood store under the house. One half of the old stone building is a magnificent ruin like a monastery, in the shade of a giant plane tree and a small lawn above the rocky ramparts looking south for miles across the hazy Catalan hills all the way to the sea.

Inside, the Cantina is all dark-brown woodwork and cream walls. The woodwork still bears the brush-stippled imitation grain once fashionable in the thirties. The corner cupboard, door and window frames, skirting boards and beams have all had the same ambivalent treatment, as though wood itself were simply too crude to leave unadorned. Cats lie outside the door and two woodmen sit talking in an even darker inner bar. We warm ourselves with coffee and press on.

It takes us three more hours to reach the top of the Puig Neulos, via a ridge from the Puig des Trois Thermes, along tracks through mixed deciduous woodland in a state of autumn carnival. For as far as we can see, the southern slopes are clothed in the rusty hues of hippy pullovers. Up high in the snow, ridges stretch away to east, west and south in a bloom of rosy-purple light glowing behind the pencilled outlines of the hills and mountains. To the west, Canigou and the higher mountain-tops are swimming in mist. Hollies, browsed over the years by cattle to domes or cones, hunker down either side of the ridge. Bonsai hawthorns no more than waist high crouch against the winds and snow. The small pale fawn or brindled cows are stocky and long-bodied, with half-moon horns. They clank about the glades mostly unseen, wearing bells on leather collars. These rare animals are Alberes, the local semi-feral breed of the Albera Massif, the Catalonian Eastern Pyrenees. There are no more than 900 of them in six herds, three of which live in the woods around Requescens. They divide into two tribes: the fawn Fagina Alberes and the Black Alberes. Only 350 Fagina Alberes and 100 Black Alberes are considered pure-bred animals, with the sire bulls reduced to six: four Fagina and two Black. This is, officially, an endangered breed. The cattle live half wild and raise their own calves in the woods. They are hardy and long-lived, and so essential to the ecology of the slopes, helping prevent forest fires by browsing and clearing the undergrowth, that the Catalan national park authority sponsors their husbandry. Andrew says this is his idea of the classical wood pasture of Virgil's *Georgics*. The place feels timeless enough, but the reality is that, as with most hill and mountain farming today, running a herd of Fagina Alberes makes little economic sense. They say the breed has never recovered from a disastrous epidemic of foot-and-mouth disease in Spain in 1774, and it is something of a miracle that any Alberes at all exist today.

It has taken no more than a fortnight for the entire mountainside to change colour. Near the ridge, the pale, frosty grey of hawthorn softens into mist or whitens into pockets of snow, flecked dark green by stubby pines or holly. Lower down, seams of blood-red maple and dogwood shoot through the strata of golden beech, pale yellow poplar, elm and hazel, and the violin-browns of chestnut and oak. With the shortening of the days, the mountain is displaying its geology through the minerals in its leaves. Each species flags its terrain in a subsiding flourish of its colours.

The chameleon leaves are litmus to the chemical changes going on inside them. The tree senses a particular moment when the balance between day and night has altered. It appears to measure the hours and minutes with some precision, and shorter days trigger the development of a suicidal hormone in each leaf. It creeps down the leaf stem to the joint with the woody twig, where it stimulates the growth of a sphincter of brittle, hard tissue that gradually closes on itself, cutting off the supply of sap. Thus deprived of water, the chlorophyll in the leaf disintegrates. Chlorophyll makes leaves look green by absorbing the blue-and-red light of the sun and masking other pigments. As it breaks down, the leaf reveals the colours of its other underlying chemical constituents. Then it dries still more, the stem joint snaps, and it goes floating off to the woodland floor to settle in pools of yellow, orange or soft chestnut-browns matched by the Alberes cows in the glades. The leaves of different species contain distinctive pigments: the yellow carotenoids of willow, poplar or hazel; the red anthocyanins of maple or dogwood (the same pigment you encounter on the rosy side of the apple where it faced the sun); or the earthy tannins of oak leaves. The evaporation of the sap concentrates the leaf pigments so that they show up more vividly. The questing roots of one species will take up more molecules of phosphorus, magnesium, sodium or iron than another. The sap of one will be more acidic or alkaline, or contain more tannin, than another. This is the natural chemistry that paints the woodland colours.

The process leading to leaf-fall is not affected by Indian summers or unusually cold weather. Photo-periodism is strictly about light and darkness, and the shortening of the days. The total surface area of leaves on a single mature deciduous tree is astonishing. The tower of the trunk and the cantilevered branches rise up and present as many leaves as possible to the sun, whose rising, circling and setting around the tree during the course of the day are answered in its essentially domed shape. Individual leaves have also evolved to present as much surface area as possible to the heavens, so a single big tree, with its foliage running into the hundreds of thousands, may easily amount to a half-acre of solar-collecting chlorophyll surface. The economy and cunning of the architecture is analogous to the means by which the labyrinthine alveoli of the human lungs extend their oxygen-absorbing surface to the area of a tennis court. Summer leaves are heavy with water. Their desiccation and fall in autumn lighten the load on the woods as a whole by many tons before the stresses of winter storms and snow. All across the Pyrenees, the broad-leaved trees are preparing themselves quite deliberately like this for the next stage in their lives.

Wandering the mountain above Requescens feels like the beginning of Yeats's 'The Wild Swans at Coole': 'The trees are in their autumn beauty,/The woodland paths are dry.'

We collect sweet, fresh chestnuts, easing them from their hedgehog husks. Following a steep-sided holloway veined with the exposed roots of beech, holly, hazel, chestnut, maple, ash and oak, we drink from the woodland springs. As noon approaches, crickets begin singing hesitantly, and young lizards venture on to the sunny track. The curious thing is that we often encounter solitary trees: a single elder by the track, a spindle tree and its bright pink berries, a lone rope of traveller's joy hoisted over a hazel bush. Why have they never spread elsewhere? Our only clue to this Noah's Ark effect is that the whole mountainside here was once an aristocratic estate, and the trees, like the single horse chestnut outside the Cantina and its farmhouse, may have been planted as collector's specimens.

Back in the Cantina for a late lunch, Andrew and I demolish a large tureen of bean stew followed by a curious, tasty *fruits secs* pudding with almonds, cobnuts and walnuts soaked in a sweet muscatel wine decanted from a carafe like a little watering can. Outside, leaves waft down now and then from the plane tree by the lawn. The afternoon is cooling, and the cats have moved inside closer to the stove. The patron brings in more logs as we leave, and as we swing downhill to Cantalops, the cowbells in the woods fall silent.

Wild Horses

I have never seen so many people up trees as I did that afternoon in Lesbos. The entire population of the hill town of Aghia Paraskevi seemed to have climbed them, shinning up to every available perch in the branches of the long-suffering olives and pines along the dusty, crowded street to get a better view of the horse races. The town was alive with its horse festival, and nervy with the wild, unpredictable energy of the animals, as they clattered uphill over the cobbled streets towards the racetrack. Down every lane, in every yard, men were busy decking out their horses in ceremonial harness, all silver medallions, embroidery and brightly coloured braid. Groups of older women gathered on their front steps, or on rush-seated chairs in the street. In the shade of a spreading oriental plane and an ancient wisteria that roofed an entire street, extra tables and chairs spilled out of the bars and tavernas. All along the main street stalls sold baubles, sweets and toys, and balloon women strolled about. Each time a new horse was ridden or led up the street, the onlookers all retreated into the doorways, wary of the wild rearing and kicking.

Half the townspeople, and most of the riders, had obviously been drinking pretty seriously. Even the horses, they said, were given ouzo to make them wilder and more fiercely competitive. All over

Lesbos, where everyone is horse-mad, men save up all year for this event, and drink, they say, for three days and nights. I made my way to the starting grid, a professional-looking bright-yellow steel contraption with sprung starting gates that had been wheeled in specially. The racetrack was just another street, running between two stone walls. It was hard and dusty. At the finish, a half-mile dash up the hill, a big crowd had swarmed all over a lorry and an olive tree. Every tree along the course was alive with spectators, who also lined the stone walls and crowded the roof of every shed. Spectators actually shinned up the grid itself and nobody seemed to mind. Even quite portly middle-aged men had climbed the poplar tree beside it, and punters sat in every branch. Everyone was shouting, arguing, laughing. Bare-chested youths in bandanas, crew-cuts and sturdy workboots led up their horses with evident pride.

A striking man in his forties with a mane of greased black hair, tight jeans, black shirt with white buttons open halfway down his chest, heeled cowboy boots and silver-buckled belt walked up a giant charcoal-grey stallion that seemed barely under control. The animal steamed with scarcely contained passion. Every few minutes it asserted its power with a snorting whinny, rearing straight up and lunging towards one of the mares. Black shirt checked him with a rope and a sharp blow with the crop, but the stallion would not be ruled and caused a huge, contagious commotion of rearing and whinnying horses. The crowd scattered before the battery of flailing hooves. More shouting, worse oaths. Everyone wanted black shirt to take himself and his horse away. Man and stallion, now united like a centaur, stood their ground furiously. Both flared their nostrils. Black shirt shouted and snorted, stamped his foot and gestured wildly. So did his horse. Circling and kicking, the stallion cleared a wide circle at the dusty crossroads. Everyone backed off. Man and horse then went into a kind of clinch, he resting his head against his steed's neck, burying his face in the ample, silver mane. The crowd subsided into a respectful silence, then, with some dignity, the hot-headed pair walked quietly away.

It was all a long way from an English point-to-point, or Newmar-ket races. The nearest comparison I could make was with some of the travellers' gatherings: the Bungay May Horse Fair in Suffolk in the mid seventies, Appleby Fair or Stow-on-the-Wold. It was more gypsy than C&W, but with a strong dash of something primeval, such as bull-running in Minoan Crete. Money was changing hands, for sure, but, whatever the betting system, its ways were as obscure as the organization of the races themselves. Men kept coming and going out of a shed halfway along the course, and here and there tight knots of others dug into their trouser pockets and flicked off notes from wads with fingers greased with the sweat of horses. Each race was a two-horse dash in clouds of dust along the dirt road, level at first, then uphill to the finish, the jockeys hanging on somehow. Ambulances stood by to rush those who took a tumble to hospital. They had a busy afternoon.

The proceedings had begun with the entrance to Paraskevi of a procession carrying an icon of the Black Virgin from a shrine outside the town, said to be ancient and possibly Dionysian, to bless the horses. It was carried by a small boy, accompanied by the mayor, the priest, and a three-piece town band of trumpet, clarinet and gourd hand-drum. It seemed half the island sat down to dinner on the streets of Paraskevi that night. I dined with my friends Tony and Jane in the taverna of their friend Perikles. Thin, long-legged cats of many colours threaded between the chairs, and even a hedgehog appeared, busy on its rounds, almost bumping into the table leg before it turned and hurried away into the shadows.

At least eleven million olive trees grow on Lesbos. They stretch in terraces high up into the mountains, and they reach down to the edge of the sea. Higher up, the stone-walled plots are built like individual fortresses for single trees, so their silver leaves wave in the breeze like flags. In a great frost, after a very mild spell had deceived the trees into coming into spring buds in January 1850, the temperature plummeted to −13°C. Nearly every tree on the island died back to the ground that night. The old ones fared best, sending up new shoots from the base the following year and gradually recovering. As emblems of longevity and historical continuity, olives on Lesbos play a role similar to that of oaks in Britain. They are the longest-lived of the cultivated plants, but it is often hard to count their annual rings. Many of the olives in the groves outside Molivos, where Tony and I took an evening stroll next day, looked extremely old. Some grew in the shape of an hourglass, hollowed years ago, their boughs spread out by the weight of their fruit. Others spiralled out of the ground like springs. The shallow furrows where a farmer had ploughed beneath the trees to kill off the weeds seemed to continue up the ridged tendons in the ankles of each trunk. We began under two olives outside the church at the top of the hill and threaded our way downhill among the groves along stone-walled donkey lanes. Dead hedges of olive prunings were woven along the tops of the walls, and self-sown figs grew from between the stones. We passed a half-built house full of hobbled goats. They struggled upstairs on to window balconies and gazed down at us intently, slit-eyes missing nothing. We offered them buddleia over the wall and they devoured it in seconds. Two dogs on chains came clanking out of a pair of oil-drum kennels.

Tucked into the boughs or trunk of each olive tree was a roll of black netting the farmers would spread beneath it at harvest-time in October or November, to collect the fruit. The netting hardly showed up against the black, lizard-skin bark. Olives fruit well every other year, with only a moderate harvest in between. They may be laboriously hand-picked, or you can spread the net and wait for them to ripen and drop of their own accord. But the quality of the oil is better if the olives are harvested green, and for this the tree must be shaken hard, often with a long pole. There are even machines to do the job now, but fortunately they can be used only in the lowland groves. Since olives must be pressed within twenty-four hours of being harvested, every little town and many larger villages have a wooden olive press and an oil-making works, but most are now derelict, as the olives all go by lorry to modern pressing plants. Greece, and the islands in particular, benefited from the same dire frost of 1709 that killed the walnuts in France and Italy. It caused a sudden demand for olive oil in those countries, and the Greek olive farmers obligingly expanded their output to seize the new markets.

I awoke early for an expedition with Heinz Horn, who has lived in Molivos for years. Heinz used to buy and sell carpets from Isfahan and lived in Kabul for a time during the sixties. When he was thirty-seven, he set out to walk from Istanbul to Damascus. When he reached the Syrian border, he experienced a breakdown and was taken to the hospital in Aleppo. There, he encountered a kind doctor who sent him to the hospital in Beirut; he had a wonderful time and stayed on for months in the city.

Heinz had suggested we try to reach the deserted mountain village of Clavados, on the slopes of Horeftra, a 2,000-foot mountain immediately to the west of the Lepetymnos Mountains, up a very rough track above the village of Lafionas. Clavados was the scene, in 1912, of the last battle to liberate Lesbos from its 450-year domination by the Turks. It must have been a bloody affair, because no one has lived there since.

Except for their roofs, the stone houses were, surprisingly, still intact, and parts of them had even been covered with tin and used as shelters for grazing sheep. Brambles ramped everywhere. Beside the track, we found a spring in the mountainside and the substantial remains of a stone-built hammam to one side of the spring-cave. Clear water trickled into a water trough full of tadpoles. Frogs sunbathing on a ledge plopped into the water.

We made our way down a path, past a half-ruined farmhouse with the wooden front door and shutters still on their hinges. Someone had been repairing its stone walls. Further down the sheep track we entered an orchard of sharp-tasting, almost-ripe damsons. The trees were bent down with them, and, amid masses of blackberries, three walnut trees and several almonds had somehow survived. The shepherds still bring their flocks up here in spring, but it is too hot and parched in summer. At what must have been the village centre, the living remains of an enormous oriental plane stood. Its massive trunk was hollow and had broken off ten feet above the ground, perhaps as a result of a lightning bolt. It was charred inside and burnt out, yet fresh living boughs were again springing from a tree that must once have shaded the spring and the steam bath.

In the middle of the island, at Karini, I had seen another of these great trees, also hollow, in which the noted naive artist Theophilus lived beside a series of superb springs and pools. Someone had opened a bar near by in his memory, and its owner proudly pointed out to me a pair of four-inch nails protruding from the inner wall of the tree. On these, I was assured, the great man would hang his clothes when he retired to bed. So capacious was the trunk that there was indeed just about room enough for a bed, and perhaps a small table and a couple of chairs to complete the Walden Pond effect.

When we drove up the hills to Argenos that evening for a drink, and wandered up through the village, we found a square dominated by yet another huge oriental plane tree at its centre, much carved with lovers' initials and much climbed. The tree seemed to dribble out of its branches like candlewax, and solidify into the spreading trunk and gorged roots. Over to one side was a sacred grove of pines and poplars surrounding a little shrine and a spring. The place had a pagan feeling. Goats and horses stood in a paddock beside it, sheep bells tinkled somewhere in the evening, and five old men sat in a row under the tree.

What is it about these oriental planes, apart from their stature and great shade, that makes places so special? I know one in the Fellows' Garden at Emmanuel College, Cambridge, that stands near the fellows' bathing pond, the oldest swimming pool in the country, in use since at least 1690, with a lovely thatched Victorian changing hut built in 1855. The plane tree was planted in 1802 and is now immense. It is the backdrop of green you see in summer from the bus station, beyond the stone garden wall of the college. The Spanish/Mexican poet Luis Cernuda wrote a poem about it called simply 'El Árbol': 'The Tree'. It is a very different tree from the London plane. It is like a flock of rooks flying home to roost across a windy evening sky. They tumble and dive, glide and soar, ecstatic in the sheer pleasure of flying, confident in their mastery, flinging themselves about the sky in great arcs. This is what this oriental plane does with its branches. They dance in a wild, slow-motion orgy, defying gravity, swooping and soaring, reaching up high, then diving all the way to the ground to take roots as a new tree. So it is that this old mother tree with an apronful of children is forever growing down to the lawns and propagating young, so that when she eventually dies they will already have grown up and become a spinney. But by growing down, the tree is also buttressing itself, creating a support system for its ageing trunk. That trunk will eventually become hollow, just like the one Theophilus inhabited, and, because a cylinder is a lighter and more stable structure, all the stronger too.

The Bieszczady Woods

Prague railway station, like the rest of the night city, appears to be lit by a single forty-watt bulb. It may help create atmosphere, but not when you're struggling to read a railway ticket with your reservation details on it in Czech. Prolonged scrutiny with the tiny Maglite I have learnt to carry when in Eastern Europe reveals our sleeping car is Number 315, and we clamber up the steep iron steps and tumble into our home for the next twenty-four hours clutching a bottle of Mikulovsky Muller Bohemian white wine bought on the platform. We stow away our picnic of apples, oranges, bread and Prague ham in a cupboard above the tiny dining table that is also our desk, which is in turn the hinged cover to the washbasin. Life in a sleeping car is a miniature, tightly organized affair, like caravanning, or sailing.

Our Ukrainian steward welcomes us aboard. Well, he nods briefly as he checks the tickets, anyway. He is a suave, taciturn character with his own den and a stash of Pilsner at the far end of the carriage. We have a compartment to ourselves, and explore it much as you would try out a new Swiss army knife. Everything folds or slides away, and, yes, you can get two people into one bunk, but it's a squeeze. We draw the net curtains, turn on the bedside reading lamps and pour out the wine. As we slip out of dimly lit Prague, I half wish I had brought slippers and a dressing gown, perhaps even a cigarette holder. We spread out the picnic dinner and trundle through the blackness towards Slovakia and the Carpathian Mountains.

Later, lying on our backs like knights in effigy, we drift into sleep. To sleep on a train is to be teased endlessly, lulled insensible by the rhythmic mantra of wheels and rail joints, then, just as the dream is getting nicely into its stride, jolted awake by a sudden lurch to the left and the banging of bogeys directly beneath as we sway wildly round sharp bends or squeeze through tunnels, climbing steadily into the Tatra Mountains. We could tell we were in the mountains by the wheeze and screech of steel on steel as we wound upwards.

Next morning at eight fifteen we are woken by a gentler, more respectful tapping. It is our steward, bringing breakfast of tea, rolls, ham and cheese, and the news that we will soon be reaching the Ukrainian border at Tchop. Tchop Station looks remarkably like a lot of other places in the Ukraine: it is oblong and concrete, and far bigger than it really needs to be, like the giant frying-pan caps worn by the Ukrainian customs police. If they ever smile, it must be behind closed doors.

We journey out of Tchop across the Ukrainian countryside towards Lviv, past acres of goods yards full of rusting wagons, sets of spare iron wheels, empty grey carriages, and a trainspotter's dream of wooden guard's vans and elephantine locomotives, some with snowplough noses, others even complete with resting drivers, feet up on the dashboard, as though they too have been retired with their machines and left waiting in the goods yard until further notice. In the far distance beyond the plain rise the snowy peaks of the Carpathian Mountains. Enormous hedgeless fields slide by, half flooded by the recent rains and in poor heart, the flatness relieved only by rusting dumps of derelict machinery and the hulks of abandoned factories, their windows so diligently smashed by some local Cromwell that hardly a whole pane survives.

The landscape is eerily empty: we seem to be crossing an

immense plain of set-aside land. There aren't even any birds except an occasional hooded crow picking about in a rubbish heap, and hardly a human figure except for one or two old ladies bent over a cottage potato field. The land looks utterly spent, and rubbish blows about like tumbleweed almost everywhere. Little piles of charred cans and half-melted plastic bottles turn up in the middle of forests or line the banks of grey, lifeless reed beds. The only landmarks in this brown set-aside prairie of ravished earth are occasional empty concrete silos or electricity pylons. Here and there are pathetic patches of grass, parched, starved and stunted, and not a farm animal in sight: no sheep, no cows or pigs, only the heaps of their dung mucked out from the tin-roofed farmers' sheds, and miniature lollypop haystacks balanced on poles outside every cottage to feed them. Later, there are rivers, swollen and brown with meltwater from the mountains, and poplars full of mistletoe. Every cottage garden has its own miniature orchard: a dozen trees set out in two rows with the lower trunks whitewashed like bobby socks to keep the insects at bay. We debate this whitewashing of the tree-trunks. My travelling companion, Annette, thinks it might be to make them show up at night and help people avoid them as they return home, legless with vodka. My theory is that no streetwise insect would dream of exposing itself to predatory birds by crossing a band of whitewash.

The Ukrainians take their railways seriously, and as we pass each geranium-filled signalbox its occupant stands at attention outside the open door holding a small flag aloft. By early afternoon we are climbing out of the plain into the Bieszczady Mountains, winding up wooded valleys past wooden farmhouses, once thatched but now roofed in tin, set in steep meadows dotted about with the lollypop haystacks and neat piles of drying beech or hazel coppice wood. The thick woods of beech, hazel, oak and sometimes pine reach right down to the fast-running, shallow, rocky rivers. A group of youths loll on the embankment, their bicycles tossed down beside them. A horse and cart go by. Two boys push a trolley loaded with firewood ready for stacking outside the wall, sawn ends making a random pattern. Long before it is burnt on the fire, the second wall of stacked wood helps keep the house warm by insulating it.

Each bridge we cross over the mountain rivers is guarded by a lone soldier in a sentry box, and as we speed through the forest we pass timber yards stacked high with the trunks of beeches, and the bull-nosed lorries of foresters in smoky clearings. Every so often in a hillside town, the metal-clad domed roofs of an Orthodox church glint across a valley. Then a long downhill run and a halt in a village station while a wheel-tapper works his way patiently along the train with his hammer, tapping and feeling the wheels for the heat of a jammed brake. He listens to the note of each wheel like a piano-tuner. 'Now that's the job for me,' I think.

It is dark by the time we arrive in the city of Lviv and step into the big central hall of its imposing antique station, packed with waiting Ukrainians all lined up on benches, hugging huge red-and-white plastic bags tied up with string. Before the last war, Lviv was part of Poland and known as Lvov, and during the eighteenth and nineteenth centuries, as part of the Austro-Hungarian Empire, it was known as Lemberg: 'Lion Mountain'. Everywhere you go in Lviv you are watched by lions: lion faces carved in stone, grinning from the balconies of the old sixteenth-century houses in the splendid Italianate Rynok Square, silently roaring outside the opera house, rampant on every other shopfront. We stay at the George Hotel at one end of Mickiewicz Square and dine on borsch and huge casseroles of baked carp at a suave little café-restaurant near by. They have made a brave attempt at translating the menu, which offers such delicacies as 'meadows fried on butter' or 'frog tights coated'.

Next morning outside the hotel two ancient sisters in long overcoats, one tall, one short, stand on the pavement singing folk-songs in a cappella harmony. They sing simply with profound passion and sadness, and the tall one proffers a tiny plastic cup that she hastily empties into a coat pocket the moment she hears a coin fall in, for both sisters are blind. Further down the street a solitary four-year-old girl sits begging. Everyone seems desperate for a few hryvnia in a blank-faced, resigned way. A few coins or wrinkled notes is all they need to keep them going, but in some countries people seem able to be cheerfully poor, or at least to seem to be. Here they are just desperate, grim, miserable: resigned and worn out by years of it. Things, their faces say, are long past a joke. Rynok Square, the old market, slopes uphill and is lined with the tall, slender façades of houses that date back to 1530, when they were all restored after a fire. Behind the stucco façades they have timber frames. You sense echoes of the old prosperity here and in the bulky pale-green opera house with its cracked walls. Now the market overflows into all the nearby streets, a tide of country people offering pitifully small bunches of carrots or onions, tiny bags of potatoes or a row of spindly horseradish roots.

It is Sunday morning, and we take Tram No. 2 through the outskirts to the museum of wooden buildings in Schevchenkivsky Gay, Lviv's equivalent to Hampstead Heath.

It is trying to snow as we plod up Machnikova Street past well-tended allotment gardens full of miniature greenhouses improvised from plastic bottles upturned over almost every plant. We pick our way over cobbles between huge brown puddles. A variety of uninhabited wooden farmhouses, barns, even a wooden church with a spire are half hidden among the trees. The solid, single-storey farmhouses are built of massive baulks of pine, each one a tree-trunk squared off with the adze. They have tall, steeply pitched thatched roofs overhanging the walls of the house by three or four feet, to shelter a veranda that runs continuously round the front three walls. The exterior doorways are elaborately decorated with carved pine in the kind of symmetrical flower or leaf patterns we would draw on the backs of our geometry exercise books at school with the aid of compasses. The verandas are generally walled with wood and entered up wooden steps via a sliding gate of carved pine. The dog kennel, set on the veranda round the corner of the house nearest the front door, is the upturned half of a large hollow log. The farmyards are fenced with an ingenious addition to conventional post and rail. Hazel wands are woven vertically between three horizontal rails to create a wattle fence that must be proof against poultry or dogs and probably pigs too. I particularly liked the hollow-log dog kennel, versions of which we were to see all over this part of the world. I resolved to try to make one myself some day, rationalizing my impulse to plagiarism by remembering that this is how ideas and motifs in crafts and woodwork have spread across the world throughout history.

We take the afternoon train to the Polish border at Premysil. It is a commonplace to say that corruption permeates every corner of Ukrainian society. This is a country whose president, Leonid Kuchma, was actually tape-recorded ordering the contract killing of a journalist who dared to criticize him. Later, the body of the journalist was found in a wood, minus his head. Even the selling of railway tickets is questionable. At a travel agency in town we were asked 54 hryvnia each for tickets to Premysil. We decided to take our chance at the station ticket office, where we paid 22 hryvnia to a woman in a flowered frock who glared at us silently throughout the transaction, ignoring anything we said. Everyone on Lviv Station was highly trained in the art of being really unhelpful. Being in the Ukraine felt like being softened up for an interrogation. One minute they treated you like dirt, the next they were all smiles. So it is on Train 75, in Carriage 14, that our conductress plies us with cups of chai or Nescafé as we perch on our Rexene banquettes gazing at passing fields full of wind-blown rubbish, molehills the size of nuclear bunkers, and nuclear bunkers like molehills, only with tell-tale stove-pipes protruding through their turf roofs. If this is farmland, it is in a pitiful state. There is barely a tree in sight.

The San River, turbid and brown, runs along the Ukrainian border. Someone had been felling the poplars that lay along its banks, perhaps to afford a clearer view from the watchtower that overlooks it. Along the double border fences topped off with rolled barbed wire there are mute loudspeakers and barking guard dogs. We pull up by a wide platform and the outsized Ukrainian customs hall. We wait, watching the only three figures on the platform: a dog, a crow and a blonde customs woman in black stockings and high-heeled black cowboy boots. Suddenly, once we are in Poland, there are rooks. There were no rooks in the Ukraine, only hooded crows snacking on half-buried rubbish. We will encounter more trees too: rows of pollard willows along the banks of dykes, cottage orchards and even linear apple orchards hedging the fields.

As we walk towards the sad centre of Premysil, the first thing we notice is a solitary weeping ash in a small park. Its trunk, rendered greyer by some kind of pollution, is a mass of scars and calluses where it must have been repeatedly vandalized all its life. The habit of its branches too is unusually contorted where limbs have been torn off or broken. The amazing thing is how it has hunkered down and survived. After dinner we take a bus through the night to Ustriczi and see a pine marten in the headlights as we drive through the forest. Next morning we catch a bus that follows the railway line a few miles out of town to the remote hamlet of Ustianova.

At Ustianova there is nothing but a bar in a wooden hut beside the railway line and a drunk teetering about outside and peeing behind it. It is still only half past eleven. This is the place where Annette's father had got off the train from Lviv during his flight home to rejoin his parents across the border in Poland in his home village of Baligrod at the outbreak of war. He was studying at the Engineering Institute in Lviv and found himself cut off from his family with no passport. At that time, the border with Poland followed the course of the San River, to the south-east of here. Premysil, Ustriczi and Ustianova were all still part of the Ukraine in those days. Abruptly exiled by war, the eighteen-year-old student decided to risk his life by walking home across country, travelling by night to escape detection by patrolling guards from this obscure station close to the border.

Annette's idea is that we should walk the same fifteen miles in her father's footsteps. We climb an embankment and stand on the weedy tracks by the disused station platform looking across country. The station master's house is now just another small holding. I had found a quite detailed old military map of the area in a library and photocopied it but through a misunderstanding, we find we have left it behind. This is such obvious ground for a pointless row that we laugh about it instead, and study the only other, fairly crude one we have, surveying a landscape of wooded foothills and fields rising towards the Bieszczady Mountains.

We set off on our south-easterly course towards Baligrod, along a road between fallow fields for a mile or so, then strike boldly up a track across country. We see no one, but there are signs of recent logging in the surrounding woods, and the track is good. We walk on loamy mud, softened by the melting snows, between hedges of coppiced hazel, alder and willow, diving down steeply banked holloways, which shelter us from the cold of the open fields. It isn't quite raining or snowing, but it is cold. Now and again we pass through the shelter of corridors of felled logs all cut to a standard cord length of four feet and stacked in six-foot walls. Often we are splashing up running streams of meltwater in the ruts of tractors and carts.

Bending close to scrutinize the water streaming down the ruts, we can make out the tiny particles of sand and clay suspended in it, being carried away downhill. This is how a holloway is made. Each time a cart wheel, hoof or boot goes by, it erodes the earth floor of the holloway a shade deeper, then the rains come and carry the dirt surface away downhill particle by particle, year by year, until it is six or fifteen or twenty feet deep. Along one of the holloways we encounter a solitary hedger at work. He has leant his bicycle against the hedge, and tied up his terrier, which growls fiercely. The man bends closer to his work as we approach and doesn't return our greeting, whether out of reticence, fear or hostility it is impossible to tell. All over the bank grow tiny wild daffodils, violets and a species of dwarf lungwort.

Approaching the first houses we have seen, we cross a rivulet and, hearing the farmyard dogs, pause in the hedgerow to cut a pair of stout hazel walking sticks to defend ourselves against their inevitable attentions. Dogs are the one universal annoyance to walkers all over Central and Eastern Europe. The best defence against them is to cut a stick just over four feet long and point it like a magic wand at any animal that threatens you. We pass the farmyard with a minimum of stick-waving. Everything in it is wood or corrugated iron. The barn is timber framed and walled with vertical boards of pine, knotted and weathered grey and orange. Its gently pitched thatched roof, patched with sheets of tin like an old jersey, overhangs a mosaic of cut log ends that wall the whole of the south-facing end. The summer sun will dry out the end grain, drawing out the sap until the wood is pure energy for the fire. A pair of horse carts stand in the yard, one still loaded with fresh green bundles of hazel faggots, their white ends gleaming where they have just been coppiced with a billhook. The whitewashed farmhouse is also thatched, with logs stacked against the walls beneath the overhang of the roof and the usual modest orchard of plums and apples whitewashed to the knee.

The track has now issued into a country road, and at the next hamlet, Lobosew Dolny, we come to a small shop and bar where we buy lunch and sit opposite in the sun on a grassy bank with our backs against a maple tree. In some of the cottage gardens here thatched beehives stand in south-facing rows, and there are rabbits in makeshift hutches. We set off again for the San River, now dammed in a massive hydroelecric scheme to create Lake Solina, crossing the lake along the top of the endless dam wall, looking down to one side where the power station hums, and the San continues on its course hundreds of feet below. We imagine Annette's father crossing the frozen river that winter's night in 1939, sticking to the shadows and somehow evading the Russian patrols, choosing his moment to sprint across the ice. Just as he reached the other side, they spotted him and fired, but missed, and he escaped into Poland. The lake stretches away for miles, with woods of pine or beech running steeply into it on all sides. Apart from a few hooded crows and magpies strutting about the rooftops, Solina is utterly deserted.

We take a path uphill through dense beech woods, then follow the contours of the lake along a ridge. Our idea is to hike as far as Polanczyk by nightfall, stay the night, then set out on the steeper walk over the hills to Baligrod next morning. It is good, springy going on the beech leaves, and a few miles out of Polanczyk a talkative man who is perhaps a forester appears out of the trees and walks along with us, quite unconcerned that we can understand very little of what he says.

Next morning, over a hotel breakfast of 'Potatoes without grease', we worry about the absence of a reliable map of this area. It makes us both uneasy about tackling the next stage of our journey. It is snowing too, as we strike off uphill towards the south. It is at first gentle, even lyrical, floating down through the treetops in big, dreamy flakes. We get lost almost straight away, and it is entirely the fault of my romantic desire to try to find a track across country to the next village, Myczkow, rather than take a short cut along the road. We succeed, but only after wasting time on several wrong turnings in increasingly heavy snow. Myczkow is a village of thatched wooden farmhouses built along the steep banks of a mountain stream. Everyone is inside, hunkered down out of the snow now settling on the thatch. It is the woodsmoke from their stoves that has led us to the village. Each house has the usual modest orchard of a dozen apples and plums and a conical haystack in the yard, hung like a scarecrow's coat on a fish-bone skeleton of hazel. No doubt there are animals inside the outhouses somewhere, but none are visible. The village hides its inner life, as the people do.

We follow the road for a couple of miles through dark woods of spruce as far as Bereska, another huddled, silent village. To say there is a deathly hush about these villages would be literally true. Unspeakable genocidal brutality raged all through the Bieszczady villages during the last war, particularly during the little-known struggle between the Polish and Ukrainian partisans. Tens of thousands of civilians were massacred, and whole villages were exterminated. We heard harrowing accounts of how everyone, including children, would be herded by the SS, Ukrainian partisan or Soviet troops into one of the old thatched barns, the doors locked from outside, and the barn set alight. Everything in these mountain villages was of wood or thatch. There were even wooden pavements along some of the village streets. When the houses, barns and sheds were burnt, all trace of the village would be erased, even its wooden church. All that remained would be heaps of wood ash and charcoal: all that lived on would be the orchards and gardens. Between 1939 and 1945, successive waves of fear swept through south-east Poland, first from the Nazis, in league with the local Ukrainian patriots, then from the Soviet Army when they invaded in 1944, and at last from Poland's new communist government, who ethnically cleansed the entire Bieszczady region by moving everyone, perhaps 200,000 people, at a few hours' notice, into Russia or another part of Poland. Only in the past ten years have some of the sons and daughters of these mountain people begun to move back into their original villages and towns.

Heartened to find that a track marked on our map actually exists, we trudge uphill out of Bereska along a muddy holloway on the droving road that leads through old beech woods towards Baligrod. Woodmen must have been carting timber down this way to the village sawmills for centuries, carving a deep channel overarched with branches. Travellers, woodmen, trees and the land have all evolved in symbiosis here, creating shelter from the storm, a natural haven from the piercing, snow-laden wind that drives across the mountains as we walk on the blessedly soft loam, carpeted by a springy crust of rich brown beech leaves.

Higher up on the same old woodland track, we hear the sudden crack of a twig, and there are fallow deer, white tails bobbing as they bound away through a low underscrub of fine brambles. We have reached a wooded mountain-top at about 2,000 feet, and it is still snowing when we stop for lunch in a clearing on the doorstep of an old wooden hiker's refuge, a half-ruined A-frame of pine boards clad in torn roofing felt. At least it affords some shelter as we sit munching apples and chocolate, watching snowflakes settle on the beech branches.

It is at about this point that we lose our way. Among tall beeches, we follow a wooded ridge towards the south. The woods fall away steeply to our left, and we are going in the general direction of Baligrod. Then the path suddenly veers off the opposite way, and we find ourselves going due north. Instead of remembering we are in mountains and doing the natural thing, which is to trust the path and let it zigzag around the contours of the ridge, we make the mistake of assuming we have missed a turning to our left and strike off downhill through the woods, hurdling fallen trunks. We find no path at all, and eventually reach the stream in the valley bottom. We stumble along following it, lurching under or over the mossy boughs of hazels and beeches. I curse myself for abandoning the hard-won ridge, squandering the height we had gained on a dumb, impulsive hunch.

The problem is that compass and map do not concur. I have since concluded that the map was awry, showing straight lines for paths that actually snaked their way around the mountain contours. Wolves, lynx, bison and bear all live in these Bieszczady woods, but we neither see nor hear a living creature, except for a few robins. There are no more deer, only tracks by the stream here and there as we follow it to a confluence and emerge from the woods to the easier going of open moorland. Our view of the terrain ahead also becomes clearer and we spot a foresters' track that follows a river downhill.

The river is swollen with brown meltwater jumping the rocks, and seems to hurry us along the track, whose wheel ruts and puddles are the first signs of human life we have seen for hours. We pass an untidy collection of recently felled poplars and alders by the riverside, then several neat rows of apple trees or plums show up clearly on the edge of the woods. This is one of the lost villages sought out and destroyed by fire during the war: there is nothing at all left of the houses. Even if parts of them had escaped burning, firewood, bricks and other building materials are such valuable commodities in a poor region like this that they would soon have been salvaged and carried off. The only signs of former habitation are, as so often, botanical. Patches of willowherb suggest the acid soil of places where fire has left behind charcoal and wood ash. Nettles betray the enriched soil of a village midden. The orchard trees remain, still bare branched from winter, and a beekeeper has set out a whole new village of colourful wooden beehives among them. There are perhaps thirty or forty, with pitched felted roofs. Their gaily painted pale blues, terracottas and yellows are probably intended to help the bees in their homing, but they lend a strangely festive air to this solemn, haunted place, so that it is easy to imagine the hibernating bees inside and the fruit blossom that will soon transform the scene.

Further down the track in a clearing we come across a charcoal-burner's hut and kiln, a huge square rusty iron furnace with an eight-foot steel door. Sacks of charcoal stand beside it in a heap, and snow has settled on the beechwood and coppiced hazel that are neatly stacked ready for the next firing. It was impossible to ignore the ghostly overtones of the scene: the massacres, the pogroms, the mass transportations to the work camps in Siberia or Kazakhstan, or to Auschwitz itself, not so many miles away, outside Kraków. The cruelty of the war was so massively traumatic here that it feels as though it had all happened last week, and one might soon come across the still-smoking ruins of a village, or its looted possessions scattered like rags across the fields. A palpable atmosphere of terror permeates this land like soaked blood. The habits of oppression die hard. People here keep within doors, avert their eyes, say as little as possible, regard strangers with alarm.

By now thoroughly disorientated by the twists of the hills, the dark woods and the uniform dullness of the day, we press on along beside the racing river for another mile or more. Out of the approaching dusk emerges the ruined church of Zernica Wysna, perched on a steep bank to our right, surrounded by tall beeches and limes. It is an elegant limestone building with three simple Gothic windows each side and a pitched roof of rusting, pale-grey corrugated iron. The onion minarets of metal over the porch, at each end of the ridge and at the corners of the roof suggest it is

Greek Orthodox. We scramble up the bank, almost a fortification, and look inside through the open oak doors. Inside is still gloomier than outside. The place has a powerful, unsettling atmosphere, as if it has been abandoned like a ship, all at once and in a hurry. Some of the original wall paintings are still discernible in the gloom across the dusty stone floor. In a little stone chapel at one corner is a shrine of flowers in posies and a makeshift wooden cross to St Christopher, his name inscribed on the cracked, cobwebbed plaster wall. There are signs that people have sheltered here before, lighting fires that charred the floor. The temperature outside is now falling, and it occurs to me that if we don't succeed in finding the track to Baligrod before dark, we might have to spend the night in here. I voice the thought to Annette, who shudders and says she couldn't bear to sleep here: she would rather endure the cold and spend the night outside. She is right. The atmosphere inside the church is overwhelmingly desolate. To have merited a church of this size, whose beauty had once been cherished, the village of Zernica Wysna must have been a substantial one, prospering from the timber in the surrounding woods. Now there is no sign of it at all. Walking away past the graveyard, we feel that those who are buried here are the fortunate ones. They lived out their lives at home, and died natural deaths.

After some deliberation over the compass, we decide that a green lane that branches off and fords the river to climb uphill the other side of the valley is our path to Baligrod. The river is so full of melting snow from the mountains that for us to attempt fording it is out of the question. Instead, we find a fallen tree that spans the flood and cross it gingerly, balancing on our bums and shifting ourselves along on our hands inch by inch above the torrent. Our track threads its way along the humped back of a hill in a deeply grooved holloway that might be thousands of years old. Ancient pollard oaks and coppiced hazels line it on either side, very like an English green lane, and higher up there are gorse bushes and heathland off to one side, deep, old woods of oak and beech off to the other. By now we are walking in the dark. Two miles of steady climbing bring us to the ridge and our first view of Baligrod. We stand and watch its few muted lights twinkling weakly in the cold night, eat the last of our chocolate, then plunge downhill and skid down a steep, muddy holloway tunnelling through tall hedges of hazel and wild plum. Approaching the village, the track leads by a farmyard towards the lights we had seen. Watched by the farmer, we stride on into the darkness, straight to the edge of a ford across the hugely swollen river. It is utterly impassable, and the farmer is still there when we retrace our steps, regarding us without a word. We find a wide, wooden planked bridge across the roaring river and arrive in Baligrod at the silent bus station, opposite the Jewish cemetery.

It is late, and we trudge on and on past the darkened houses to the town square and the one bar. We are pathetically grateful to find it still open for its two customers; still more relieved to get a room for the night. Someone even stands us a drink. Crisps and a few Martinis are all we can muster for a celebration dinner, and we are even grateful for these too, retiring to our spartan quarters as if to a palace bedroom. Everything in it is brown but still we love it: the prickly nylon carpet, the limp blankets, even the scorch mark on the lampshade. Shifting the single beds together, we accidentally reveal a gluey mound of desiccated condoms. Pleasure is something you snatch here. It is strange being tourists in a town that hardly knows the meaning of the word. The uneasy feeling might have kept us awake if it hadn't been for the sweet mingling of triumph, relief and fatigue.

We buy breakfast in the baker's and sit eating it on a bench in the chilly square beside an antique tank, its muzzle still aimed squarely at the Ukraine. A multicoloured crocodile of school children clutching balloons on strings and singing a patriotic-sounding song issues from the school and straggles past us on an outing to the grimy old Greek Orthodox church, onion-domed and now dilapidated. We wander the village streets, admiring the single-storey wooden villas with their mustard-yellow walls and pale-grey tin roofs, the bright washing hung out on lines high up between the houses. Each has an overhanging roof and a veranda, often reached by elaborate wooden steps. The orchards in the big front gardens boast several notably splendid old apple trees, grown twisted and unpruned for years. There is an overwhelming silence about the place: such a sense of desolation beneath the apparent normality. People watch us from their windows or doorways, or straighten up from their labours in back yards, but there are no greetings. The roots of their caution go deep.

At the far end of the village we find the sawmill where Annette's father once worked as a student. It is not much more than a big circular saw and a cradle of rollers to conduct the log towards the blade. Planks of pine and beech are stacked to season, and a few old army lorries with cranes mounted behind stand about in the wood yard before a small mountain range of sawdust piles. There is no one about, just another dog on a chain. In a farmyard beside a wall of big-eyed rabbits in wire-netting pens, I find a tractor that must date from before the Soviet era. It comes from the Bronze Age of tractors, a beautiful, cumbersome, elaborate machine, all flywheels and pulleys, with a rude grey bulbous bonnet, a stout chimney of beaten tin and an office typist's chair adapted as the driving seat. Whichever way you look at it, it looms towards you like a telephoto image of itself. It is the one thing of real beauty in Baligrod: testament to its owner's independent spirit. Once he gets it started and wheezed into life, nothing can defeat it, or stand in its way.

As we wait for the bus to take us away to Sanok, we wander through the Jewish cemetery, where hundreds of anonymous Jews from the decimated villages of the Bieszczady Mountains are buried in identical graves, marked only by a star of David. The woods that cover the mountains are forgiving: they have grown over those villages and all but concealed the signs of their former existence. Gradually, the villages, woods and fields are being repopulated. This corner of Poland has achieved a difficult regeneration, from being a place where everything happened, almost all of it brutal and bloody, to a place where hardly anything happens at all. At the post office, Annette sends a postcard to her father in Australia. He is happier living there, as far away as possible from Baligrod and its memories.

Cockatoo

The screeching of a pair of red-tailed cockatoos as they barrelled through the gum trees aroused me from fitful sleep. I had woken more than once in the night, to the call of what sounded like a cuckoo weaving itself into my dream. 'A night cuckoo,' I thought vaguely, and dozed off again. It was the boobook owl, mopoke, a totem being to the Arrernte Aborigines of these arid lands along the Macdonnell Ranges to the west of Alice Springs. I lay on my back and watched the big cockatoos gliding and swooping together, the red feathers in the thick, black tail of the cock bird flashing as it banked and landed in the river red gums that grew along a creek where the land dipped into shadow. I was rolled up inside a canvas swag, sleeping out on Latz's old iron bed frame under a wiltja, a rough open-sided shelter he had thatched with the dried brushwood of mulga bushes supported on four posts. A mosquito net hung from the roof in a wigwam, tucked in and anchored under my swag. I drew aside the net and lay listening to the mad, abandoned cries of flocks of pink-and-grey galahs that raced over me now and again, rolling and tumbling, revelling in their early-morning aerobatics. Some of them alighted briefly in the slender bare white arms of a solitary ghost gum that stood fifty yards from the foot of my bed. Its pale, smooth trunk gleamed pinkly in the morning sun.

The ghost gum is a dancing woman in the Arrernte songs that tell the dreaming stories of the creation of this land. The tree's graceful form was actually created by the gallantry of generations of amorous cock galahs: they would roost in it, break off the terminal shoots of its twigs with their strong parrot beaks and offer them as love-tokens to the hens, which always politely accept them, then discreetly drop them. The constant pruning causes the branches to grow in curves from their lateral shoots and gives the whole tree the fluidity of a dancer. Behind the tree stretched the giant caterpillar dreaming of the Macdonnell Ranges, glowing electric crimson, purple and ochre as the sun came up. A 250-mile-long caterpillar.

There was something homely, even maternal, about this ghost gum that immediately attracted me. It wasn't until a day or two later that I realized it reminded me of the ash tree at home in Suffolk: smooth and pale skinned, with the graceful sinews of a dancer in the wind. The twigs and branches of the ash all make the same embracing gesture, growing obliquely, shyly, towards the sunlight. I notice this circling effect at night when I look through the tree at the moon, and every branch seems woven round it in a halo.

I was travelling the desert parts of central Australia with my friend Ramona Koval, and we had come to stay with the ethno-botanist and conservationist Peter Latz in the bush along the Ilparpa Road outside Alice Springs. Ramona's keen sense of the ridiculous and her unfailing humour in the face of the hardships and uncertainties of desert travel meant that we muddled along in a state of continuous hilarity at the curious outback world around us. We must have seemed a pair of very whitefellas indeed to the Aboriginal people we met, with our pink cheeks and Ramona's blue eyes and striking cascade of curly fair hair.

Her sense of the ridiculous began with me. On our first day 'out bush', she had spontaneously pointed at a flock of budgerigars in a tree and I had patronizingly explained that instead of pointing, which could disturb the birds, she should give a more discreet verbal indication of their whereabouts, preferably out of the corner of the mouth. Thereafter, 'budgerigars at three o'clock' became a private watchword throughout our trip whenever either of us noticed anything interesting.

Alice Springs, in some ways a deeply tragic place, seemed to us like a big desert waiting room. Everywhere you went, Aboriginals sat or stood about as if waiting for something. In the streets the men went about with an expression that said, 'Now where did I put that screwdriver?' or 'Now why did I come into this room?' They scratched their heads, stopped suddenly and turned around, then wandered off in quite another direction. The shocking human dereliction on the streets and in the dusty bed of the Todd River, where Aboriginal families camp out in makeshift wiltjas of blankets and sticks, is related to the grog and the hospital. So many Aboriginal people, women especially, suffer from diabetes or kidney failure that they become dependent on the hospital, which draws them in from desert places far beyond the town for treatment, or to be near a dialysis machine. Others come simply for grog from the supermarket because it is banned from the desert outstations.

Back in town, Ramona and I would sit with our coffee in the Mediterranean Café, headquarters of the large local alternative culture, its windows full of little business cards for therapists of one persuasion or another, from ear candling to primal scream, watching this faraway other world go by. This aspect of the Janus-like Alice was a desert Totnes. Among the window stickers was one for a gardening firm calling itself 'Weeding Wimmin' but these were not the women we saw on the streets, Aboriginal women with one arm in plaster, always the left arm because it is the one they instinctively raise to ward off the blows of their abusive, drunken men. The hospital treats queues of these battered wives every night. 'Alice is tinder just waiting to go up,' a friend told me in Melbourne before we left.

Ramona was still asleep in the house and Latz was already out weeding buffel grass somewhere on his patch. He was obsessed with this rogue plant, an invasive exotic from South Africa that was out-competing the delicate native grasses everywhere, upsetting the fine balance of life among the desert plants he loved. Every morning before the sun rose too high, his first act was to go out and uproot another few square yards of the stuff, a ritual he kept up in a one-man war he knew he might not win. But his work really was making a difference: the grateful native plants were gradually reappearing on Latz's wild acres, and his list had grown to 127 species.

My first impression of Latz the previous afternoon was that of a tall, lanky, bearded figure lying naked in the shade of his bedroom on the telephone to a fellow botanist. He lay under a languid ceiling fan, a muted Beethoven symphony on the hi-fi just at the threshold of audibility. Outside, under the shadow of a hat brim, his ice-blue eyes shone with quiet mischief. Latz is an ethno-botanist and has lived all his life in the Arrernte country of central Australia. He knows more about fire and its traditional use by the Aborigines than just about anyone, and there's hardly a wild plant, bush or tree he doesn't know in the deserts and wild expanses of the centre. *Bushfires and Bushtucker*, the title of his definitive book surveying the use of plants and fire by the Pitjantjatjara, Warlpiri, Arrernte, Pintupi and other central Australian Aboriginal peoples, describes his passions well enough. He ought to know: he grew up as a boy with the western Arrernte people in the Aboriginal community of Hermannsburg, seventy-five miles from Alice Springs, several days by camel in those days. His father worked as the engineer, sinking a bore five miles away and piping in a fresh water supply across country. Latz spoke Aranda and learnt the Aboriginal customs and skills. The red-tailed cockatoo, he said, was his totem animal, his dreaming. It is often associated with fire.

Everybody called him Latz. He lived about twelve miles outside Alice Springs in a house he had built himself after his divorce. He made it small and simple deliberately, so he could spend as much time outdoors as possible: single storey, veranda, corrugated-iron roof, water butt, two bedrooms, bathroom, kitchen and a living room that was also his study. The old caravan he lived in before he built the house was still outside, full of redback and white-tail spiders, scorpions and the odd snake. It was originally meant for guests, but the spiders, which pack an unwelcome bite, took over. A butcher bird sat on the air-con unit outside the kitchen window every day and sang so sweetly you would never guess it was a killer that stabbed and speared its prey, leaving the corpses hanging in a thorn-bush larder. It had even recently tried to assassinate a neighbour's budgie through the bars of its cage. It sounded like a tradesman, whistling as he worked, swooping up and down to the notes like a swannee whistle.

Inside the house, an old cast-iron 'Klondike' pot-bellied stove stood in one corner, and there was a vase full of the red-and-black tail feathers of the male red-tailed black cockatoo. On the walls hung dot-paintings by Latz's Aboriginal friends, painted on bits of card or board. The most impressive of them was by Nosepeg, an old Pintupi man of the western deserts who once met the Queen and introduced himself on equal terms as 'King of the Pintupi'. Nosepeg's dreaming was the mopoke, the boobook owl I had heard in the night. The first white settlers called *Ninox boobook* the cuckoo owl; to the Arrernte, it was the *arkularkua*. This sounded to me so much like the name of our old cub mistress, Akela, that I felt I understood the bird. The painting, on a base of red ochre on an offcut of cardboard two feet by two and a half feet, depicted Nosepeg's dreaming, his mopoke country, in a dreamer's aerial vision of a hill with a waterhole at its peak and ten clefts or valleys running down from the summit like petals. The green dots, Latz said, were mulga bushes, a kind of acacia that grows everywhere on the stony plains, and the smaller white ochre dots all over the bare, inhospitable rock and gravel of the hillside were clumps of spinifex grasses. The bigger earth-brown dots represented the burnt stumps of trees and bushes, and the charred roots of grasses. Areas of mixed green, yellow, white and brown dots showed where there had recently been burning, though the vegetation was growing back. Six dotted circles at the top and bottom of the picture were waterholes, which may have been great distances from the hill, to which Nosepeg and his people would journey. One waterhole, at the bottom right of the picture, obviously different from the others and more delicately painted, may have been more sacred.

I liked the way this picture was unframed, just hung lopsided from a nail in the wall, and I puzzled over it, wondering why Nosepeg would have given away his secrets like this in a painting whitefellas would see. But then perhaps that is exactly what it was: a puzzle, encoded in dots to keep us guessing, or imagining. It was like the Mappa Mundi, a chart and expression of the world of Nosepeg as he saw and experienced it: his home owl-country. What I liked about it was the abstract way it rendered the landscape as a single organism, like the cross-section of a plant stem seen under a microscope, every dot a cell. It made a strange landscape even stranger, and that first night in Latz's house I had been unable to take my eyes off it. It expressed an inner life and a way of seeing so apparently different from my own that the more I looked at it, the more its painted pixels seemed to challenge me, like a riddle or a maze. The way the picture was hung, I realized, was exactly right: it was the Aboriginal way with things. They are not in the habit of attaching much mere money value to objects. That such paintings can fetch high prices on the international art market is said to be a source of private amusement to many of the painters themselves.

On the kitchen wall, next to one of the knitted woollen beanies Latz likes to wear pulled down over his ears in the desert winters, was a permanent list of the things he needed to take with him on his expeditions 'out bush': hat, torch, swag, book, towel, clothes, rucksack, glasses. Film, freezer, camera, shoes, aloe vera, plant-collecting press, diary, map, spare camera and battery, thermos. It had rained heavily in the desert for the first time in several years, and Latz was planning an expedition to see what plants had come up, and which trees and bushes flowered or fruited out there.

Next day we drove into Alice Springs to buy ice and provisions for the journey out west towards Glen Helen Gorge and the Finke River. Back in Latz's yard, we loaded his Toyota truck with our swags, mosquito nets, rucksacks, camping gear and his precious botanical pressing boards. We filled water cans and crammed ice and raw food into the Esky freezer. In the best nomadic traditions of the central deserts, Latz clearly spent most of his time on the road, or rather off it, in a four-wheel-drive: all we had to do with most of the gear was lift it in boxes straight out of a garage shed. There was even a small folding table, and a canvas chair for each of us. The very sight of a four-wheel-drive is usually enough to send me into a green rage, but, as we pulled away, crammed in the cab of the big, dusty ute, moving along the line of rugged hills to the west, fording the great desert rivers – the Hugh, the Ellery and at last the Finke – this suddenly seemed the most natural means of transport in the world.

Near Glen Helen, where the Finke River goes through a gap in the Macdonnell Ranges and heads south towards the Simpson Desert and Lake Eyre, we turned northward upstream and wound along on the rocks and sand of its upper bed, through big river red gums. The Finke is said to be the oldest river in the world. Its course has not changed for a million years, and it was once the size of the Amazon. Since the drying of the centre, it has largely gone underground, yet certain water holes along its course generally retain water, and after heavy rains it will periodically flood. The rains a week or two earlier had brought the Finke to life, and the string of river creeks near where we camped were full of clear, deep water. River red gums always delineate the course of rivers, growing along the banks and in the sandy river beds, where they not only withstand deep floods from time to time but need them. The early explorers of the interior who came this way, men like Thomas Mitchell or Ernest Giles, soon learnt to discern the courses of rivers in the landscape ahead from the river red gums along their banks.

Thirst is a natural condition of life in the desert, and trees have always been used to mark waterholes, or as a source of water themselves. A stone would be placed in a niche in the trunk, a sign carved in the bark, or the trunk painted with ochre. This could mean one of two things: that you could dig for water close by the tree, or that certain trees themselves contained rainwater that would trickle down the branches and collect in the cool tank of a hollow trunk. It would be sucked out through a hollow stem, or squeezed out of a mop made of a ball of grass on the end of a stick and dipped in. As children at Hermannsburg, Latz and his friends never carried water on their wanderings but would know where to dig for it. But there were other ways to get water from trees. In an account of one of his expeditions in the arid lands, Thomas Mitchell writes:

How the natives existed in this parched country was the question. We saw that around many trees the roots had been taken up, and we found them without the bark, and cut into short clubs or billets, but for what purpose we could not then discover . . . I expressed my thirst and want of water. Looking as if they understood me, they hastened to resume their work, and I discovered that they dug up the roots for the sake of drinking the sap. It appeared that they first cut these roots into billets and then stripped off the bark or rind, which they sometimes chew, after which, holding up the billet and applying one end to the mouth, they let the juice drop into it.

A similar technique involves cutting three-foot lengths of root and standing them overnight in a container, always with the cut ends from nearest the trunk facing downwards. In his 1889 classic *The Useful Native Plants of Australia*, J. H. Maiden describes a drink known as *beal* or *bool*, prepared in *tarnuks* (the large wooden bowls 'seen in every camp') by steeping the flowers of banksia or ironwood trees in water.

We camped in the sands of the upper river bank in the shade of a grove of gigantic river red gums, taking care not to place ourselves directly beneath any branches: they have a habit of suddenly dropping off. Until nightfall, the sand was too hot to walk on barefoot, but then it was luxurious: soft and liquid, each grain perfectly rounded by age. We had stopped by a patch of mulga bushes on the way and gathered dead branches for firewood. Plenty of dead wood debris, washed down and left as flotsam by the river, lay about around the camp, but sand fills the pores of the wood and it burns less readily. Mulga burns hard and hot, and leaves good ash for cooking.

Fifty yards across the hot sand of the river bed was a delicious clear, deep waterhole, where we swam. On the opposite bank, in the top of a river red gum, a pair of wedge-tailed eagles were nesting, seizing the advantage of the mass of birds and animals flocking to the river. I floated on my back, gazing up at one of the eagles. We fished too and caught spangled grunters, Australian perch, which had suddenly filled the Finke waterholes since the rains, hatching from dormant eggs and growing at an astonishing speed. Latz said there were ten or eleven different species of fish in the Finke, all of which had the opportunist ability of every desert animal and plant to seize the moment the rains came. They hatched, grew amazingly fast, bred and buried more eggs in the sand to carry their species beyond the next drought.

The trunk of the red gum we chose to shade us was at least six feet across and ragged with torn red bark, hanging off in strips. It was well over sixty feet high and spread quite as wide, its mottled, reddish upper branches twisting and coiling like Baroque carvings into dense foliage. The tree was alive with nesting budgerigars and ring-necked parrots. Each pair of birds had claimed the stub end of its own hollowed branch, a kind of natural didgeridoo tunnelled out by termites attracted by the sugar in the eucalyptus sap. The organ-pipe effect seemed to amplify the massed choirs of a bird I had always known as a rather annoying species of attention-seeking chirpy-chappie pecking a tiny mirror in a cage. It was like camping under an English petshop. Like other parrots, the budgerigars used their beaks as well as claws to climb all over the tree, often upside down. Green gales of them wheeled and dived along the river bed and disappeared into the foliage, chirruping excitedly. They are nomadic, sensing where the rain and food are and flocking enormous distances across Australia to nest and swell their numbers. Latz said the massive roots of these gums will draw up to a ton of water a day through the tree during floods to ensure enough growth to withstand the next inundation. According to J. H. Maiden, red gum was highly valued for its strength and durability, especially for piles and posts in damp ground. 'It is also used', he writes, 'for shipbuilding, railway sleepers, bridges, wharves, and numerous other purposes. This timber is exceedingly hard when dry; this limits its use for furniture.' The tough, sinewy, snaking habit of the tree made its timber particularly useful for the knees and angled joints in wooden boats.

Latz's botanist friend Dave Albrecht and his wife Sarah came and joined us in the camp with their little daughter, Erimea, and we dined on the excellent spangled grunters, grilled over the fire, which we kept going, for illumination as well as a billy of bedtime tea. It also kept away the mosquitoes.

I had rigged a net, borrowed from Latz, from a mulga bush overhanging my swag and reclined in it on my back like a pasha, gazing up at the night sky through the fine gauze with a smug reassurance that the mosquitoes queuing and whining just the other side of it couldn't reach me. Then I focused on the net itself and realized it was riddled with little cigarette burns. I did some hasty rearrangement. Latz confessed next day that he used to lie in his swag smoking before he gave it up and began chewing pituri instead. It is traditionally the Aboriginal stimulant of choice, concocted from the dried leaves of one of four species of the pituri plant, *Nicotiana*, ground up with the ash of at least twelve species of plant or tree, including tea-tree wood. *Nicotiana* is of course the same genus as the commercial tobacco plant, *Nicotiana gossei* being the most prized for pituri, closely followed by *Nicotiana excelsior*. According to Latz, the ash seems to promote the rapid absorption of the nicotine into the bloodstream through the thin tissues of the lips and mouth, and possibly even through the skin behind the ear, where the quid is usually kept when not in use. Pituri was probably the most important item of trade among the Aboriginal people of the desert and was carried over long distances until at least the late 1940s, when Latz remembers a Hermannsburg man, Tamulju, returning from an expedition with the ethnologist Arthur Groom with camel-loads of wild pituri leaves. He became a rich man for a while. Latz searched the Macdonnell Ranges for years in vain, looking for *Nicotiana excelsior*, until a fire burnt the spinifex grasses on some limestone rises, and large stands of *Nicotiana* came up soon after. The seeds had been buried there all the time, just waiting. Aboriginal people, Latz said, seem to have been making use of the nicotine in these wild tobacco plants since long before Drake brought tobacco to Europe.

The others were still asleep as I wriggled out of my sleeping bag at daybreak and quietly wandered over the soft sand, studying the delicate lacework of last night's tracks: skink, goanna, snake, kangaroo mouse, beetle, millipede. The slanting early sun drew tiny shadows along the contours that would soon evaporate like dreams as the fine sand rolled back to evenness in the slight breeze. Drawing a square of the etched desert in my notebook, I thought of the excitement of going out into the meadows in Suffolk after a fresh fall of snow: the busy thoroughfares of the night revealed. People sometimes describe a desert as 'trackless', but of course there is no such thing. The art of desert living, especially for small creatures, is to conserve and retain as much water as possible in their bodies, so they tend to live down cool burrows and emerge only at night. Along a sandy ridge overlooking our camp I found the fresh tracks of a dingo that shadowed our camp, hoping to find scraps but always keeping out of sight.

By the time I returned, Latz had a billy boiling on the campfire and Ramona was swimming in the river. The more Latz talked about Aboriginal culture, the more I began to realize how much had been lost. He and his childhood friends at Hermannsburg learnt to be desert botanists from an early age. All nomadic people living in central Australia had to be first-rate botanists and ecologists just to survive. They needed to know which plants, fruits or seeds to eat, which parts of them would be nourishing, which plants were poisonous or could be used as hunting poisons, which plants needed cooking, which plants were medicine for particular ailments, which had religious significance and were used in ceremonies. They needed to know how to extract water from the roots and hollows of trees, or the stems of plants, and how to find proteins or sugars in grubs hidden inside trees. The larvae of a large cossid moth, often found in the trunks of river red gums, constitute an important part of the traditional diet. As a child, Latz remembers collecting, with his Aboriginal friends, about twenty-five witchetty grubs from one tree in an hour or so of leisurely work, locating their boreholes and fishing them out with the hooked wiry stem of the curly windmill grass. River red gums also supplied the Aboriginal *coola-mons*, carrying bowls carved out of the boles or crooked roots, and sometimes the bark. Hardly a single one of Latz's Arrernte childhood friends from Hermannsburg was still alive. He remarked sadly, 'The grog got them all.'

Latz and Dave elected me to carry the plant-pressing boards, and we set off across the scrubby desert, heading towards a distant mound spring my companions thought might be sprouting some interesting plants after the rains. We picked our way through spinifex, the dense, bristling tussocks of porcupine grass that domi-nate the central Australian deserts and positively thrive on fire. Mulga, by far the most widespread tree or shrub, grew in dense stands on the hard, gravelly, red earth. Both plants are central to Aboriginal life in the deserts: mulga for its nourishing seeds and tough wood, spinifex for a plastic adhesive and filler that is made by grinding and heating its resinous stems. Mulga wood is easily worked when green, but seasons into unsplittable toughness, so is by far the most important material for making implements: spear blades, boomerangs, shields, digging sticks, adzes, fighting clubs, spears and sacred *tjuringas*. Even ash from the burnt twigs is mixed with pituri. As an acacia, mulga produces plenty of seed in legu-minous pods. Cleaned, roasted and ground into a paste that looks and tastes like peanut butter, they are quite as nutritious.

We advanced slowly, botanizing as we went, now and again folding a specimen plant between the collecting boards while Latz wrote notes and assigned it a number. He was up to 15,418 that day. That is how many plants he had collected over twenty-five years.

'About forty of them have been new to science,' he added. There is even an acacia named after him: Latz's Wattle, *Acacia latzii*. All these plants and trees were strange to me, and I tried to work out what difference it made to the way I saw them before and after Latz or Dave taught me their names. Knowing their names, being formally introduced to them, seemed to bring me one step closer to them. It was like meeting people.

Picking our way down aisles between bushes, avoiding the webs of the brilliant-green, gem-like orb spiders slung between them, we ate the sweet little black fruit of the conkleberry and found bush bananas, bush tomatoes and the desert incense bush, whose scent attracts moths at night. The salty mound spring, when we reached it, seemed to be sweating in the heat, water oozing and trickling down tiny gullies where the purple cryola, favourite food of the all but extinct hare wallabies that once lived here, coloured the gravel. A tiny desert wren sang like a squeaky gate. Dingos had been here too, licking the salt and water, printing tracks. The small white volcano holes of spiders stood out in the sandy seepage pan round the spring under desert samphire, another useful food plant, and we sucked the little red berries of the ruby salt bush, which Aboriginal children gather as sweets. Beyond the spring, we came into a big natural bowl full of yalka, a kind of sedge with grassy leaves, whose roots end in small, nutty-tasting bulbs. You roast them lightly by rolling them about in a wooden bowl with hot charcoal. Everywhere in the sand, the holes of snakes, skinks and goannas stared back. Almost everything we saw had a use. A willowy ironwood tree was being wrapped by an army of processional caterpillars. Latz said that in Aboriginal medicine, the silk they spin is valued as a second skin to seal and dress burns.

'Suppose you couldn't see a single tree. How would you find water?' I asked Latz and Albrecht. 'You would have to kill a wallaby or something, rub the meat with plenty of salt and stake it out. You can always find salt in the desert. Then you hide up and watch. Sooner or later a crow comes down and gorges itself on the salted meat. The salt makes it thirsty, so it flies off to the nearest waterhole.

Crows always fly in a straight line. You follow, keeping to that line. Eventually you'll find water.'

That night around the fire, Latz sat writing up his plant notes by head torch. He talked about the Finke and how dangerous it could be when it flooded, bringing a surging bore alive with rampant uprooted trees and branches. As it first charges down the dry, sandy bed, the river feels its way with a slender foot-long tongue of water that slips over the sand ahead of the wall of the flood. River red gums wait for this moment to open their seed capsules and shower millions of their tiny yellow seeds into the swirling brown water; stranded along the outer limits of the flood, they germinate in the organic debris. Women and girls use the seed capsules to decorate their hair by folding over the ends and cramming them with a twig into the nut cavity. They also tuck bunches of the leaves into their arm- and leg-bands to rattle rhythmically during ceremonial dances.

Some day, said Latz, he would like to raft right down the Finke River in flood, from its beginnings south of the Tanami Desert, all the way to the Simpson Desert, and on down the Macumba River into the vastness of Lake Eyre. The fire was having its effect as we gazed into it and dreamt or remembered. Camping 200 miles away in sandhills on the edge of a plain covered in the most elegant desert oaks, Ramona and I had sat before a campfire a few days earlier as giant white centipedes three or four inches long emerged one after another out of the desert darkness and raced madly round and round the fire in a frenzied dance. Energized by the fire, they skipped almost right over our toes, which we instinctively withdrew, though blissfully ignorant of the poisonous, painful bite they could administer.

Latz began to talk of the great deserts: the Simpson, the Gibson and the Tanami, where he loved to go for weeks at a time, sometimes accompanied by the artist John Wolseley on walk-about from his studio home in Leatherarse Gully. There had been photographs on Latz's kitchen wall of Wolseley in wide-brimmed Akubra and cotton jacket, seated on a canvas chair at an easel outside a wiltja of canvas sheeting stretched from a mulga bush. On one of their expeditions together, Wolseley had asked Latz to take him into the Gibson Desert, which he wanted to paint. They went west of Haast's Bluff and made camp, where Wolseley proceeded to spend a week drawing and painting a rare desert plant before once raising his glance to the horizon. He was getting the hang of the place, engaging with it, working from detail as he always did, trusting to his instincts as artist and naturalist to provide the connections and an overview all in good time. On another occasion, he buried painted canvases in the desert, returning a year later to unearth them. This was Wolseley's way of working: to camp in a place, often for weeks or months on end, keep a journal every day, and record every detail of the natural phenomena he encountered and observed. Through the patient acquisition of an intimacy with the land, Wolseley had evolved a kind of fusion: a language of painting that was much closer to the Aboriginal ways of seeing and feeling and at the same time full of scientific detail and limitless curiosity.

The conversation drifted round to cockatoos. We talked about our mutual friend back in Sydney, Tony Barrell, who had made a documentary about a flamboyant Queenslander, the brother of Joe Cocker, and entitled it 'I'm a Cocker Too'. Cocker's nephew Jarvis had agreed to help him make the sequel next time he toured Australia. Tony said he would call it 'I'm a Cocker Too 2'.

It was late. The budgerigars were all asleep in the big red gum up above, and somewhere along the river bed, the mopoke was calling again. We fell silent and Latz leant back, dozing off, dreaming, roosting in his chair before the embers like the fire-bird he really was inside: the red-tailed black cockatoo.

Utopia

It was Sunday, the appointed day of the bush-plum hunt, and Ramona, Theo, Kemarre and I had been up half the night preparing a big picnic stew to take with us, according to the custom. Ramona and I had driven the 150 miles out of Alice a day or two earlier to the remote Aboriginal community at Utopia, where we were staying with her friend Theo, the nurse at the Urapuntja health clinic. 'Utopia it ain't,' the man at the petrol station in Alice had said. Theo said the place took its name from the cattle station that was once here and either expressed the early settlers' naive optimism or a well-developed sense of irony. A book written in Latin by Sir Thomas More and published in 1516 with a title that translates as 'Nowhere City' wouldn't be the first thing that came to mind out here unless, of course, you had a lot of time on your hands.

A few Indian-looking cattle still wandered the bush around Utopia disconsolately searching for the odd blade of desert grass, but the whole area had been grazed into oblivion years ago. The Utopians, mostly of the Alyawarre and Anmatyerre groups, are famous for their painters, in particular a group of female artists who included the late Emily Kame Kngwarreye. Her work takes pride of place in the National Gallery of Victoria in Melbourne and in leading collections all over the world. Although art is now the main economic activity in Utopia, and Aboriginal art has become a lucrative department of the international art market, nobody in Utopia appeared to be getting particularly rich. Emily was said to have earned thousands of dollars a day from her painting, yet always gave away her earnings to an extended family of some eighty relatives who had come to depend on her. She ended her life living on the same old bed under her tarpaulin wiltja in Utopia. At Alice, the famous painter Clifford Possum Tjapaltjarri now lives in a humpy in the dry bed of the Todd River, all his painting money dissipated among countless relatives.

Kemarre, a Lutheran missionary in his early thirties, lived alone in a caravan in the badlands beyond the health clinic and was here to translate the Old Testament into Alyawarre, one of the two main languages of the people here. We found him delightful company: kind, funny, a good linguist, and well versed in Aboriginal ways. He had got as far as Exodus, with the help of an old Alyawarre man, Frank Taylor, who sat down with him in the caravan for four hours every day to work through the text. That left thirty-seven books to do. Kemarre, one of the four main Alyawarre skin names, had been temporarily conferred on the missionary and was likely to stick. Kemarre's real name, David, could on no account be mentioned because someone by the same name in the community had recently died. By the same token, a book about the women painters of Utopia lying open on Theo's kitchen table contained several pages covered up because they bore the name or photograph of a dead person. Such are the conventions of Aboriginal society.

One such convention was that on a bush-plum hunt, it was the natural role of the whitefellas to provide the transport and the meat, preferably prepared in advance and pre-cooked in a stew. As nurse to a community of 2,000 Alyawarre and Anmatyerre people scattered about the Utopia area in some twenty-five outstations and small family groups, Theo knew just about everyone. Her dog Mitchell, a species of black cattle dog with alert, pointed ears, lay outside on the front doormat. There were dogs everywhere in Utopia, most of them half dingo, and hungry.

We put the stew and picnic things in two Toyota trucks and drove over to Kurrajong Camp to pick up the others. The dogs came out to meet us: thirty or forty mangy, skeletal, aimless creatures that ran nearly under our wheels, rolled in the dust, nibbled their fleas and cruised the camp in a pack looking in vain for some action. Four men sat on the roof of an extinct Falcon 500 propped up on wheel hubs. More cars rusted away under some ironwood trees. An old Holden full of dead firewood that stuck out of the windows like snipers' rifles was parked in the sun.

We found Mary Kemarre sitting in her wiltja on a big bed supported on a rusting roof rack raised on ten-gallon oil drums and wheel hubs. 'You got the tucker?' she said. 'Yeah, plenty,' said Theo. The children led us proudly to a clutch of new puppies living down a hole in the ground beneath one of the beds. They reached into the hole up to their armpits and brought out the blind puppies one after another, clutching them inexpertly by a leg or a tail, hauling them into their embrace for us to admire. A well-marked tabby cat with an unusually long tail lay with her kittens under another bed under the trees. 'Some of this country is important dog-dreaming, so nobody can touch the dogs,' said Theo. The dogs had the status of sacred cows. 'The police came out to shoot some of them but the elders told them to go away.' Kemarre said that during the church services, which are always held outdoors, there can be sudden, explosive dog fights and everyone scatters. The women sleep with the dogs to keep warm on cold nights, hence the expression 'two-dog night' or 'three-dog night' as an indication of the temperature. All the dogs had names too – Army, White One, Red One – and everyone was obviously very fond of them, even though they hadn't much notion that they might be suffering or carrying disease. 'Why,' said Theo, 'when 850 million dollars a year are spent on the Aboriginal health care programme, is no money at all spent on sending vets to care for the dogs, which we're told are "culturally important" to Aboriginal people?'

Mary, who was clearly the senior woman in the camp, called her friends over, and we sat and talked and stroked the puppies before setting off. We were quite a gang. Kemarre, who spoke fluent Anmatyerre and Alyawarre, was our translator. One of Ramona's daughters, training to be a doctor, had worked all the previous year at the Utopia clinic, so we were warmly welcomed. Besides Mary and Theo, our hunting party consisted of Audrey, Lily, Tracy, Kylie, her infant Serrick and Audrey's sister Sarah. The women had all been dancing and singing in a ceremony until late in the night and were still full of elation and laughter. Large numbers of empty yoghurt pots were hastily thrown in a plastic bag as coolamons for fruit-gathering, and we all piled into the two trucks and set off. 'Kwaty,' said Mary, pointing to some tiny clouds forming over to the north in the clear sky. She thought it might rain in a day or two. *Kwaty* means 'water' as well as 'cloud', and in Alyawarre, 'raining' is *kwatyrntweyel*: 'water dancing'.

We drove along a rough track into open sand plains dotted with spinifex, mulga bushes, ghost gums and termite mounds. The women missed nothing, spotting goanna tracks from the moving truck and even discussing how fresh they were and whether the big perenti lizards would be worth chasing. Rounding a bend past a corkwood copse, I had to swerve to avoid an extinct Holden smack in the middle of the track. Then, all together, the women cried, 'Akatyerre', and commanded us to stop. Along the sides of the track, bush raisins were growing, and everybody piled out and began filling the yoghurt pots with the shrivelled brown fruit. The desert raisin, a foot-high shrub with purple flowers and soft leaves, is actually a member of the tomato family, *Solanum nemophilum*. Like so many of the desert plants, it depends entirely on periodic fire for its survival and will simply disappear in the absence of regular burning.

Back in the Toyotas, we struck out across country, snaking between termite mounds of ochre adobe standing up two or three feet like Gaudí parapets, and concrete-hard. We also had to avoid the risk of punctures from splintered tree roots or spinifex. When William Dampier first landed in Australia on his voyage in the *Roebuck* in 1699 and saw termite mounds, he thought they were rocks. He writes: 'There were several Things like Hay-cocks, standing in the Savannah; which at a distance we thought were Houses, looking just like the *Hottentot's* Houses at the *Cape of G. Hope*: but we found them to be so many rocks.'

Again, a cry went up from the women, pointing towards a distant stand of trees and bushes. '*Alkwa*': bush plums. We threaded our way off piste through more of the termite stalactites towards the ten-foot bushes, which, sure enough, were covered in ripe black fruit the size of small olives. *Santalum lanceolatum* is an important food for Aboriginal people all over central Australia, and its fruit contains high concentrations of Vitamin C. It is also an important totemic plant for the Arandic peoples, even though, as T. G. H. Strehlow relates in *Songs of Central Australia*, its sacred place, the bush-plum holy of holies, was desecrated by the early European settlers.

The women broke off mulga branches and used them as brooms to sweep the sandy ground encircled by the trees with meticulous care before spreading out picnic blankets and building a fire. We all collected dead mulga wood, and the fire was laid in no time. Once our hearth had built up plenty of glowing embers, Mary and her friends set the stew on it. Mary assumed command, taking control of the cooking quite naturally, as though she herself had been slaving over a hot stove most of the night before. The sweeping of the ground seemed to me an eloquent expression of the extent to which these nomad people regarded the desert as their home. They swept the red earth with as much care as I might sweep my kitchen at home. Aboriginals have a morbid fear of snakes and will always clear the ground around a camp, however temporary, so that tracks will show up in the dirt. Mary and Kemarre told the story of a recent open-air church service in their camp. The congregation was singing lustily from their Lutheran song-book, when someone spotted a snake track. The service instantly came to a halt while the reptile was hunted down and killed. The Aboriginal way with snakes is to stone them with deadly accuracy.

As the stew began to bubble on the glowing mulga, Mary detailed

Ramona, Theo, Kemarre and I with yoghurt-pot coolamons to pick plums. Our performance, under the critical eyes of the women, was not impressive. The fruit kept sticking to our fingers instead of dropping into the pot, and we soon covered ourselves in the adhesive purple flesh of ripe bush plum. Our companions, I noticed, showed a sudden surprising absence of enthusiasm for the fruit, preferring to relax round the fire and pass round a soup spoon, sampling the meat with the air of connoisseurs. When at last we returned with our plastic coolamons duly filled, their contents were decanted briskly into saucepans and billy cans. The fruit was sweet but slightly bland, and you spat out the tiny stone. Little Serrick ate rather too many of them, but discipline, in Aboriginal families, is never administered by the mother but by the father, the aunts or paternal grandmother, who is more powerful than her maternal counterpart. A mother would never cause her child to cry. In this group, Mary's authority was absolute. As an older woman, she had high status and was in charge of certain dreamings that she had inherited with the land to which they were connected, down the female side of the family. She also took charge of the increase ceremonies, which ensured the renewal of plants and animals and the continuance of the camp and family group, thriving and hunting successfully. As we all sat round the fire enjoying the stew, Kemarre interpreted for us. At one point Mary complimented him on his Alyawarre. 'You are losing your English, Kemarre,' she said.

After lunch, Mary and the others took up more yoghurt pots and went to work on the trees, stripping them of plums with astonishing skill and speed, filling whole billy cans in minutes. Knowing how hard the fruit were to pick, the effortless skill, the sheer nonchalance of the women, filled me with admiration. One moment they were relaxing and feasting beside the fire, the next they had become hunter-gatherers with 40,000 years of experience behind them, seizing the opportunity of these uncommon ripe plums. Moving from tree to tree, we picked every plum that afternoon. I remembered Latz telling me that opportunism would always take precedence over everything else in the desert, and that he once saw a man pause in the very act of stalking a kangaroo to bend down and gather some bush raisins he had stumbled across. It struck me that our afternoon's gathering had been done with the minimum of fuss and effort, yet with complete efficiency and a great sense of fun. As we bent down the branches and stripped them of plums, I thought of our family rosehip- and blackberry-picking expeditions in the Chilterns, of how my father would use the crook of his walking stick to bend down the higher branches, and the musical sound of the postbox-red rosehips tumbling into a saucepan.

On the dusty journey home, Ramona, squeezed in the back with Lily, Kylie and Mary, was handed the sticky, dusty baby to cradle. It ate bush plums all the way home as I swung the Toyota about like a dodgem car between the termite mounds, jointly directed by all the women in their soft, low voices. What looked to me like an endless high-rise termite city was country they evidently knew intimately. Termites, far and away the most successful animals in Australia, are the only ones that can eat and digest the most successful plant, spinifex, in its mature, tough form. Mary pointed out the faintest outline of the new moon, no doubt the reason for the previous night's ceremony and dancing, and when I remarked that in England it curves the opposite way, she replied, 'You have wrong-way rubbish moon.'

Theo had several magnificent paintings by Utopia women on her walls, including a Bush Plum Dreaming picture by Kathleen Ngala and another by Gracie Petyarre, one of the five Petyarre sisters, all notable painters, springing from the loins of the same father but born of five different mothers. A real live huntsman spider loitered in one corner of the Bush Plum Dreaming painting. By the time we got home, we ourselves were bush-plum paintings of a kind: purple, sticky and well daubed, objects of some interest to the Utopian flies.

At Leatherarse Gully

Realizing that sleep might be out of the question in the stifling heat of the Whipstick Forest, I settled for a restless night on a mahogany four-poster beneath a tented wedding cake of mosquito netting hooked into the ceiling of one of John and Jenny Wolseley's railway wagons at Leatherarse Gully. The place is hidden away in the abandoned goldfields outside Bendigo, two hours north-west of Melbourne. The retired wagons are wooden guard's vans raised on brick piers in a gypsyish encampment in a clearing beside a tin-roofed bungalow that serves as kitchen and dining room. A winding path through the forest leads to Wolseley's studio. I snuffed the candles and lay listening to crickets, nightjars and a hillbilly band of banjo frogs in the soupy dam where the artist sometimes wallowed in the afternoon. Opened wide on either side of the big bed, the heavy sliding doors allowed the passage of the night air. Across the clearing, I made out the dark forms of swamp wallabies among the box bushes just as our dinnertime wine got the better of me, and I dozed off.

Dawn came up from a glow behind the mallee woods that soon outshone a clear, almost-full moon. Out of the stillness swelled the distant chanting of currawongs. A bell-bird started up like a car alarm. For a few drowsy moments I thought I was waking in my own railway wagon in Suffolk. 'Which train is Roger in tonight?' Wolseley had asked Jenny at bedtime. I got up and wandered through my quarters. Bedrooms at either end opened on to a central compartment with the guard's chair before an iron brake wheel and a periscope that enabled him to look both ways along the roof of the train, a useful contraption in the days of steam engines and the smuts that flew straight into your eye whenever you stuck your head out of a train window. There were bookshelves, candles and a small writing desk. On the wall, Rouget's *The Beekeepers* and a photograph of a 1930s Delaware & Hudson locomotive that hauled the weekly Ghan from Adelaide to Alice Springs, pausing halfway at a desert waterhole for the passengers to swim. Wolseley's friend Peter Latz, whom we had visited outside Alice Springs, used to travel on it with his mother once a year from Alice Springs and remembers how the guard would pass through the carriages half an hour in advance, asking the passengers to be changed and ready in their costumes for the twenty-minute stop. When the driver blew his whistle, the dripping passengers would climb back aboard.

Lines of ants were already on the move as I stepped outside, and the sun baked the reddish, sandy earth between the acacia bushes in this undulating, stony terrain left behind after the Bendigo gold rush of the 1850s. The goldfield was once one of the richest in the world and led to the creation of Bendigo's Victorian elegance, so much admired by John Betjeman. The railway van still bears its original red ochre lead paint outside, the wooden boards over-printed here and there with obscure stencilled shunting-yard lingo: 'Forward Seymour Loco', '4697 D only'.

In its gold-mining days, the Whipstick Forest was an industrial landscape, busy with people and steam-driven machinery. It is still full of leats, artificial running streams dug out to carry water to the gold miners panning the soil or running their rock-crushing steam engines. In this respect it resembles Dartmoor, another once-peopled mining landscape now pretty well abandoned. The gold miners reshaped the Whipstick with their craters, derelict huts and rusting machinery. Scarcely a tree was left standing, but now they have grown back: ironbarks and white gums, grey box, and dense coppice woods of mallee gum trees.

The mallee is the basis of the one industry that continues here: it is coppiced every few years to make eucalyptus oil. Shadbolt's famous Eucalyptus distillery once stood a few hundred yards up the track, one of several now abandoned in the woods. These days the leaves are stripped off the coppiced poles and carted off to town to be boiled up and distilled for oil. It can be a dangerous business with all those inflammable gum gases around: stills have been known to explode. I crushed a leaf, put it under my nose and imagined myself with a towel over my head, face to face with my reflection in the surface of a steaming jug of water as a child, getting sweet relief from a cold.

Even at home, Wolseley cannot altogether shake off the air of the encamped explorer: he seems more at ease out of doors than in. He is tall, relaxed, genial and still distinctly English, with a mischievous sense of the ridiculous in everything, including nature. Preparing mangoes for our breakfast, he flicked the peel on to the veranda deck to an expectant stubby-tailed lizard that appeared from a hole in the wainscot. The reptile devoured it and lingered tamely in the hope of further titbits. It was a foot long, wonderfully plump, and watched us with intelligent, black sparkling eyes as we ate. I noticed hanging on the kitchen wall a salvaged fragment of oft-painted plywood, the 'wrinklescuro' of the paint, as Wolseley called it, revealing a map of its history in successive under-colours. In the garden, odd scraps of iron sheet rusted to the flimsiness of leaves were gently returning to the orange earth. Such leisurely processes of nature and mutability in the Australian landscape have formed the core of Wolseley's work in Australia since its beginnings in 1976, with *The Gippsland Wallpapers*. He spent months at a time living in abandoned farmhouses in Gippsland and the Otway Ranges in Victoria, and found that, as he writes in his journal, 'this new landscape doesn't seem to fit into small rectangles any more; as it did when I was an English gent painting copses and meadows in

Somerset.' At first, he resolved the problem by drawing and painting graffiti directly on to the fading, peeling wallpapered lath-and-plaster walls of the Gippsland ruins, later removing entire sections of them to exhibit in the gallery.

After breakfast we meandered down a woodland path to the studio. It was once the main residence at Leatherarse Gully, another bungalow with a low tin roof and veranda, with a water-butt at one corner. Outside by the door stood a glass-topped museum case full of Wolseley's finds on his painting expeditions in the Australian wilderness: dingo skulls, the tail of a native cat, the skulls of the long-beaked ibis and the stork, nuggets of primeval rock, the out-sized feet of emus, a camel skull and another that wasn't a dingo but might be a mastiff. Beside the feral display was a tiny kitsch, absurdly tame concrete pond surrounded by gnomes, some fishing, some just thinking: the quintessence of suburbia.

Inside the studio, it was sweetly cool. A vintage air-conditioner clanked away in a corner. On the wall were photographs of some of the camps, nearly always in remote parts of Australia, where Wolseley spends several months of each year botanizing, observing birds, insects, rocks and skies, drawing, painting, recording what he finds, cooking over a wood fire, snoozing in a hammock or swag, walking, collecting botanical, zoological or geological specimens, taking photographs and writing assiduously in his journal each night by candlelight. In one photograph, his friend Peter Latz sits at some faraway bush camp dinner table holding up a desert yam. Another shows Wolseley at an 'Art Camp' he says he was 'roped into' once, out beyond Alice Springs. A group of handsome women in middle age stand in the dry, sandy bed of the Finke River. Dressed in shorts, shirts and Akubra hats, they pose under a river red gum admiring a work of art they have assembled in the sand: a giant clitoris composed of river-bed rocks wrapped in pink cotton, an Antipodean riposte to the priapic Cerne Abbas Giant.

Wolseley moved about the studio among the objects of his never-ending curiosity, telling extraordinary stories about everything in it like Merlin in the upstairs room of his cottage in the

Forest Sauvage in T. H. White's *The Sword in the Stone*: 'There was a real live corkindrill hanging from the rafters, very life-like and horrible with glass eyes and scaly tail stretched out behind it. When its master came into the room it winked one eye in salutation, although it was stuffed.' Wolseley's habitat was likewise marvellously crammed with papers, books, maps, hats, drawings, specimens and works-in-progress pegged up on the walls or suspended like washing. Drawers in a map chest were labelled 'Wallace', 'Sedimentary Paper', 'Emotive Fragments'. Laid out carefully on a table were various buried paintings, or parts of them, bearing the ghostly impressions of the roots of grasses or trees, or nibbled by termites. These were the results of the artist's habit of occasionally burying his work in situ, usually somewhere remote, and returning up to ten years later to exhume the remains, nature having by then collaborated, leaving comments and a signature. In a Perspex box sat a leaf of the recently discovered, ancient Wollemi pine from the Blue Mountains north of Sydney. Evolution and the vast span of geological time are recurrent themes in Wolseley's work. There were sticks, bits of charcoal and charred fragments of wood: the land-flotsam of successive desert and forest camps and wanderings. Set out on a table-top were two of the adobe nests of mason wasps attached to the dried carcass of a lizard, the wings of a pardelote and a frogmouth, something like a nightjar, and a row of the cone-like seeds of casuarinas, which Wolseley had been drawing repeatedly for months. Leaves that had half decayed into a lacework of veins were juxtaposed beside the wings of butterflies and birds, which, in turn, were mirrored by aerial photographs of the Spice Islands. A section of white-gum trunk had been drilled out all over to take a hedgehog of pencils. Hanging like Cheyenne headdresses from the picture rail, bundles of parrot and other bird feathers had been bunched and taped together, with notes attached on luggage labels. The spiky branches of bushes lay on sheets of white paper beside collections of lichens or seeds in the ordered trays of delicately dovetailed specimen drawers. Looking perfectly at home against such a background were several drawings of the displays of bower birds.

The walls were honeycombed with more drawers, racks and shelves of books on taxonomy, natural history, geography of one kind or another, back numbers of Kenneth White's *Cahiers de Géopoétique*, the works of other painters or explorers, more maps, well-thumbed field guides and yards of poetry. Rows of Wolseley's notebooks were crammed with watercolours, drawings, notes, pressed leaves, feathers and seedpods. Images were pinned all over every available inch of whitewashed board wall, some drawn, some photographed, some torn from magazines: an owl in flight, a squirrel leaping, a bee-eater taking off, bracket fungi on a tree-trunk, sailing boats, leaf drawings, fruit drawings, dried fruit, sprigs of leaves and more of the 'crackotura' of the ancient sun-baked paint-strata on bits of the flimsy walls of some long-gone plywood caravan. But, among all these, my eye was compelled towards a small formal painting of a child in a flowery summer frock, an early work by Wolseley's father, Garnet Ruskin Wolseley. A distant cousin of John Ruskin, he had been a prize-winning Slade School artist and one of the Newlyn group of painters in Cornwall.

John Wolseley was thirty-eight when he arrived in Australia in April 1976 for a short visit. Nearly thirty years later he was still here, still fascinated by the enigmatic Australian wilderness. He was by no means the first of the Wolseleys to try his fortune in Australia. His great-grandfather, Frederick York Wolseley, came over from Ireland in 1854 aged seventeen. Eric Rolls believes he was probably the inventor of barbed wire: an irony for the ancestor of a champion of all that is fenced out. In *A Million Wild Acres*, Rolls records that around 1867 Wolseley enclosed 10,000 hectares of the Pilliga at Arrarownie on the Borah Creek with a twelve-wire fence eighteen miles long to protect his sheep from dingoes. Wolseley's fencers wound wire barbs into the sprung fencing every six inches. He moved on and invented the Wolseley hotbox, the first shearing machine. It transformed Australian sheep farming. He employed a brilliant engineer, Herbert Austin, as his factory manager, and they eventually diversified, launching, in England in 1896, the first Wolseley motor car. Austin later started his own motor company in a disused printing works at Longbridge in 1905.

Frederick York Wolseley handed on Arrarownie to his seventeen-year-old nephew, Erle Wolseley Creagh, who had been banished to Australia for some minor misdemeanour by his uncle, Viscount Wolseley. Eric Rolls knew people in the Pilliga Forest still alive in the 1970s who could remember him. Wolseley Creagh bred horses, milked goats, lived off his orchards and fig trees, and read the newspapers. Rolls describes how, at the end of the day, 'he washed his hands in the tin dish on a stand outside the door and went in to play his grand piano. Before the last Aborigines left the creeks, a group of them came each evening to hear him play. They walked quietly into the house and sat in a half circle around the piano.'

However, it was yet another of his ancestors whose life drew John Wolseley to Australia. William Trevelyan Wyndham sailed south in the 1850s and lived the life 'of an early hippy', as Wolseley put it, mixing with the Aboriginal clans of northern New South Wales, learning their customs and languages. As a wild colonial boy, he lived by hunting and fishing with the Aboriginal people on South Keppel Island. In 1888 he bought a farm near the mouth of the Boyne River in Queensland. He grew rare plants, planted an orchard of oranges, bananas and pineapples, sailed his forty-foot gaff-rigged cutter *Pelican*, discoursed to the Royal Society in Sydney on the Aboriginal bark canoes of central Queensland, corresponded with the Smithsonian Society of America on Australia's indigenous languages and was buried in his orchard in 1898.

The thermometer outside the door stood at 40°C already, and the air-conditioner was running gamely at full blast. Bloopy, the Wolseleys' red heeler kelpie cross, with kelpie ears, a long dingo nose, speckled paws and ginger flanks, lay panting on the floor. She was too old for such heat. I helped Wolseley unroll a big charcoal *frottage* tree drawing ten feet by five and pin it on to a soft-board wall. Three animal skulls sat on an adjustable Vemco architect's drawing board: rabbit, dog and wallaby. We examined the suture lines between the cranial plates through an eyeglass. Everyone should have an eyeglass and a microscope, I thought: it is much better than TV. We looked at the side of the dog's skull and saw how the sutures meandered like rivers, how the surface of the bone was pocked and puckered like the surface of the moon. The big charcoal picture, we discovered, could either go way up or, even better, go upright and look like valleys and ridge-tops. Wolseley was comparing the skulls and their rock-fault jigsaw with some feathers of the frogmouth he had laid out beside them on the drawing board. They were brown and speckled, resembling tree bark. Under the eyeglass you could see the wave forms within them and the analogous sutures meandering along their central veins.

Wolseley pointed out how the skull and lower jawbone of the wallaby have surprisingly sharp sets of incisors for biting straight through grass rather than tearing at it, as cattle do, and how, further back, there's a set of grinding mandibles for chewing it. Marsupials, he said, are infinitely kinder grazers to the delicate native Australian grasses than cattle and perfectly adapted to the delicate soil structure the earliest settlers would have encountered. Over lunch in the minescape of the abandoned goldfields, we looked up Eric Rolls's classic description, in one of his essays, of the fragility of the Australian land as it once was:

The surface was so loose that you could rake it through the fingers. No wheel had marked it, no leather heel, no cloven foot – every mammal, humans included, had walked on padded feet. Our big animals did not make trails. Hopping kangaroos usually move in scattered company, not in damaging single file like sheep and cattle . . . Every grass-eating mammal had two sets of teeth to make a clean bite. No other land had been treated so gently.

In the hot sun of the afternoon we trod, in our Vibram-soled boots, over the ashes and black earth where a recent fire had raged through the Whipstick Forest, leaving no more than skeleton trees and bushes of pure carbon. Fire had revealed the forest in its abstract forms. We had driven out in Wolseley's beaten-up station wagon, whose back door had refused to shut ever since he reversed it into a tree. He grasped a large drawing board with several sheets of white cartridge paper bulldog-clipped to it and looked about for charred wood that seemed promising. Suddenly he charged and swooped like an entomologist with a net, dashing the board face down in a series of sweeps across a succession of bushes burnt to charcoal. 'I get into a kind of feng-shui trance and then dance through the bush, moving the board over the burnt trees, letting them do the drawing,' he explained. Next he selected a fallen ironbark tree and further imprinted the paper by pressing and scraping the board against its blackened bark. Wolseley called this 'using the tree as a pencil'. The result of all this vigorous activity was a free drawing that expressed the life of the forest with surprising accuracy. The charcoal marks on the paper suggested insects or the flight of birds, and the ironbark created the fish-scale pattern you notice in the drifted sand when you fly over a desert, or in wood ash washed out by rain: a common motif in Aboriginal art.

Unclipping the first sheet and working with the next layer, Wolseley approached the carbon ruins of some casuarina scrub and bashed the paper against the clusters of burnt seeds. They left dancing charcoal dots like musical notations. Wolseley calls this aleatory way of working *frottage*, from the French verb to rub. It began, he said, when the easel accidentally fell face forward on to the top of a burnt bush, and he realized the marks it made were more interesting than his half-finished conventional drawing: the landscape was drawing itself. At the time he was drawing, painting and camping in the Royal National Park, south of Sydney, over a five-month period in the aftermath of the serious bushfires of Christmas 2001. Encouraged by the results of the new technique, he tried the same thing on a bigger scale, with another artist holding the other end of a twelve-foot length of art paper as they galloped and wove through small charred trees down a ravine, registering the black abrasions of tree-trunks and the charcoal stipples and scrapings of saplings and shrubs.

The effects of the afternoon's work in the Whipstick were dramatic: the *frottages* had all the urgency and energy of the racing bushfire itself. The abstract marks on the paper were, as Wolseley pointed out, not images but traces: signs and markings of what was once there, like abrasions, stains, negatives, watermarks or fossil imprints. It is a kind of sign language of burnt trees, each of which has been reduced to its essential mineral structure by the fire. Back in his studio, Wolseley would generally select the most interesting of the charcoal impressions and rework some of them, adding exquisite watercolours and drawings of seeds, birds, flowers, plants, insects and, quite often, his own notes, all garnered in the same place. He would paint in watercolour the ruby interior of a hakea-seed capsule, a swift moth emerging from its chrysalis in the sand after night rain, the scarlet breast of a regent parrot picking white moth-caterpillars off the green-amber new growth of a dwarf Angophora, green flames of new growth exploding from the tops of grass trees like Roman candles or the epicormic growth of buds bursting out of the burnt bark of eucalypts. The astonishing thing, he said, was how quickly signs of life returned to the bush following a fire.

Wolseley said it took him a long time to understand the colours of the Australian landscape. He at last realized that the key to it was not green at all, but shades of grey with scarcely a hint of green. Mix greys out of white and black, and sometimes a little ochre, and you have the forest perfectly. Out in the bush, he often makes his initial drawings and notes in a pocketbook whose cartridge sheets open like a concertina. The form suits Wolseley's breadth of vision and discursive style, and he often translates its cumulative effect into a similar form on a larger scale. He calls these impressionistic, unfolding works 'reporellos', an allusion to the endless catalogue of Don Giovanni's lovers unfolded and revealed by his servant Leporello to Donna Elvira in the first act of Mozart's opera. In his notebook he describes the making of one such giant burnt-wood drawing after the Christmas 2001 bushfires in the Royal National Park:

I unrolled the 5 foot by 30 foot roll of 300 gsm Saunders' and trapped a 12-foot length at each end with 2 × 1 strips of pine nailed together. When Carol lifted up one end and I the other the paper felt firm and purposeful, held tight like a sail in the wind. Pure white, a giant litmus paper ready to receive the tiniest powdering in the air, or record the heavy impact of burnt tree trunks. A skein of straw-necked ibis moved across the pale sky like a lengthening and contracting rubber band. Carol and I moved down the ravine. The length of paper also became a variable line – a snake-like contracting or tautening as we moved between the burnt saplings. We had different kinds of encounters with four or five different types of tree – some we gently brushed against – and then there was a more coercive meeting with a big banksia whose scaly, knobbly bark left a passage of black scales on the paper as if a huge reptile had passed over it.

As we moved through the burnt forest, occasional zephyrs of hot wind stirred up tiny spouts of wood ash, dispersing them like smoke. Half cooked ourselves, we talked of fire: how it has shaped the Australian landscape, whose natural condition is so frequently drought. It was the first thing Captain James Cook and his botanist Sir Joseph Banks noticed when they were blown north off their course to Tasmania from New Zealand in the *Endeavour* on 19 April 1770 and sighted the Australian mainland. 'We saw either smoke by day or fires by night wherever we came,' Cook writes in the log, and he constantly refers to 'this continent of smoke'. The Australians the white explorers and early settlers encountered invariably carried firesticks. 'Firestick farming' describes the way Aboriginal people manipulated and changed their environment on a massive scale through the use of fire. But they never farmed in the conventional sense. The Neolithic passed them by. They used fire to keep their hunting grounds open and freshly grassed by frequent, light burning on the open plains, creating open wood pasture of widely spaced trees through which they could move easily, denying the cover of under-brush to their quarry. The early settlers were all struck by the resemblance of this lightly wooded landscape to English parkland. The Aborigines left fires burning, in camp hearths or hollow trees, everywhere they went, to be taken over by others or for the replenishment of faltering firesticks. 'It seems impossible', says Eric Rolls, 'to exaggerate the amount of burning in Aboriginal Australia.'

Far from harming the land, Aboriginal fire actually stimulated new and more varied growth. Eucalypts positively thrive on fire, their thick bark protecting the living cambium and the epicormic buds hidden beneath it, ready to sprout again almost immediately. They can send up new coppice shoots, as mallee does in the Whipstick, from underground lignotubers, and their roots plunge far too deep to be burnt. A fire is often the trigger that will send their woody seeds raining from the forest canopy. By allowing in the sunlight and generating fertile ash, fire can stimulate germination, increase the variety of other plant species or trigger the growth of useful food plants like wild tomatoes and bush bananas. Aboriginal fires were mostly grass fires, aimed at keeping the land open and accessible. By aiming their fire towards an area that had already been burnt recently, they naturally curtailed it. Their fires were a kind of spring cleaning, a hallowing of the land. Once they ceased their fire farming, the volume of fuel, especially on the floors of forests, greatly increased, and so did the scale of bushfire.

Back at Leatherarse Gully, in a part of the Whipstick which had escaped the recent fire, we drank iced tea and swam gratefully in the soupy brown waters of the Wolseley dam, clad only in Akubra hats. It was so hot that even the leeches couldn't be bothered to attach themselves to our clay-stained bodies. That night, we lit the small flames of candles and dined outside with the crickets. If a bushfire came, said Wolseley, the correct thing would be to stay inside the house and hope it was not too hot and would pass by. Pumping water from the dam to douse the roof and walls beforehand can help. Perhaps the threat of fire helps explain the downright simplicity of so many houses in the bush, as if they never dared to hope that they might survive for very long.

Next morning we walked out through the forest, dead branches crackling underfoot, and admired the giant anthills of the bull ants from a respectful distance. Each one was a low dome of fine gravel some six to eight feet in diameter spangled with tiny pearls of quartzite to form an ant volcano, from whose navel erupted hundreds of the armoured insects all gingered into frenetic activity by the rising temperature of yet another scorching day. Twigs were neatly arranged in a necklace around the black-holed omphalos of each gleaming tumulus. Wolseley said the original gold diggers were known as 'gold-ants'.

Hot wind swayed the tops of the ironbarks and bark peeled off the eucalypts in the heat, hanging in seductive, inflammable ribbons. Perhaps in the hope of a cooling effect on us, we talked about England and some of its artists. Wolseley spoke appreciatively of Cecil Collins, who always rose late and worked mostly in the evenings between five and seven thirty, his hand and mind having steadied by then. 'I know about the dawn without having to be there,' he once said. Collins liked the versatility of the verb 'to draw': drawing someone out, the drawing of breath, of inspiration, of water, or of a curtain to conceal or reveal things. Wolseley described an oak refectory table at his ancestral home in Somerset that dates back to 1558. It is nineteen feet long, he said, four to five inches thick, worn down by the playing of an ancient family version of shove-ha'penny in which coins are flicked the full length of it. He mentioned his Trevelyan grandfather, and his habit of dining each night in a tree house wallpapered with daily shooting tallies. Here, having donned a pheasant mask, he liked to be fed through the beak by his butler via a straw. Listening to Wolseley's stories, told in his deep, kindly English voice, was like looking at one of his pictures, in which layer after layer of the landscape is revealed by the accretion of detail and anecdote.

Entering a clearing, we stood in the crazed, baked mud of a parched dam with only our hat brims for shade. A thirsty wallaby moved listlessly behind a white gum. Further on, we met the spirit of Essex: the lichen-encrusted body of a sky-blue Ford, the chrome upper-case characters spelling out ZEPHYR across the wide beak of its bonnet. Half sunk in sandy earth, it stood near the edge of the site of Mr Flett's eucalyptus oil distillery, now reduced by the termites and ants to a few brick chimneys and sagging tin roofs, rusting railway track, tangled cables, cog wheels and pulleys, a wooden gantry rigged as a crane, a tilted rainwater tank.

On the way home we followed one of the rusting wire fences of the Whipstick improvised from the steel windlass cable that once hauled up barrels of gold-dirt in the mine shafts. If Wolseley has a totem animal, it must surely be the mole. Again and again he returns to the body of the earth: making camps in remote caves, sampling the colours in Aboriginal ochre mines, painting the iron-ore mine at Mount Newman, working for weeks in the giant meteorite crater at Haast's Bluff, or digging into the desert and burying his work for a year or more at a time before returning to exhume it. He talks about painting landscape 'as it is experienced in the ground', subsuming himself into the landscape through what he refers to as 'this "camping alone" business' in order to achieve a direct intimacy with it. 'Often', he writes in his journal, 'I isolate a small piece of landscape, or part of a lizard, or a petal, or an item of litter, and I meditate about it on the paper. On such a small area I can be "slight", and tentative, and investigate the shapes or colours in a gentle exploratory way – abstracting areas of detail and writing associated thoughts and feelings as they come.'

If there is a mystical quality to John Wolseley's journeys into the Australian wilderness and his experience of the camps as recorded and distilled in his work, it is only an expression of the poetic, respectful response to a deeply loved land that prevailed for thousands of years, long since trashed by the people who raised the tall buildings in Sydney. The mole's-eye view John Wolseley offers is that of a thoughtful naturalist, not of a mining corporation.

The Pilliga Forest

Now and again in a lifetime a friend introduces you to a writer and you discover a soul-book, a work that engraves itself on your heart: one you read over and over, falling in love with it more deeply each time. This is what happened to me with *A Million Wild Acres* by Eric Rolls. It is an ecological history of the Pilliga Forest beyond the Liverpool Plains of northern New South Wales, originally published in 1981, written by a poet, farmer and naturalist with a countryman's ear for a good yarn and a laconic wit that could only come out of Australia. Its central story is about the coming of the white settlers and how they changed the entire nature of a forest and, by extension, a whole continent.

'Pilliga' comes from the Aboriginal Kamilaroi word *peelaka*, a spearhead, and may refer to the shape of the elegant river oaks, a species of casuarina, or of the indigenous white cypress pines, *Callitris*. The Pilliga Forest lies beyond the Great Dividing Range in New South Wales and ranges from Narrabri in the north to Coonabarabran in the south. Extending inland across the plains, it begins at the village of Baan Baa and reaches as far as the country town of Baradine to the west. It is chiefly a mixture of eucalypts, acacia and various kinds of cypress pines.

Eric Rolls contends that before the coming of the European

settlers the whole of Australia was much more like a vast English parkland in appearance than the dense forest people like to imagine. With the exception of areas of high rainfall and groves of rainforest strung along the eastern valleys and in the ravines of the Dividing Range, the Aborigines kept the land open and grassy by regular burning off. It carried relatively few trees to the hectare, although some were very old and tall. The arrival of European settlers put an end to the fire farming of the Aborigines, and the forests of Australia as they appear today began to spread into the lowland bush. Rolls's controversial interpretation of the Australian forests and their history suggests that most are no more than a hundred to a hundred and forty years old. Everywhere he finds his contemporaries referring to 'the great primeval forests of Australia', yet the historical records, he finds, tell another story:

'Everywhere we have an open woodland,' wrote Charles Darwin on his 1836 visit. 'Nowhere are there any dense forests like those of North America,' explained *Chambers Information for the People* in an article on Emigration to Australia written in 1841. Such statements are made over and over in early writings. De Beuzeville was aware of them. He reasserted them in his *Australian Trees for Australian Planting*. 'Even along the . . . gullies and the contiguous streams,' he quoted, 'the country resembled the "woodlier parts of a deerpark in England".' In the seventy-two forests declared in New South Wales in 1879 the tree count of those assessed varied from two and a half mature trees to the hectare to eighty on the tablelands and coast. The Forestry Commission, in experimental plots in the Yerrinan section of the Pilliga Forest, found that sixty-year-old white cypress pines thinned in 1940 to two hundred to the hectare produced the best timber over the next thirty years, but, if thinned to six hundred to the hectare, they produced the most timber. Nowhere, in a search lasting months, did I find reference to former stands of timber as thick as those modern thinned stands.

Burning raised the fertility of the land, and when the fresh new grasses and herbs came up they attracted the kangaroos and other grazing animals the nomads hunted. They could be driven across open ground, often by the use of fire, and trapped or killed. Dense forest would provide them with cover and was in any case unsuited to the use of long spears, which the trees and bush would obstruct or break. Boomerangs too would be too easily lost. When John Oxley, the first white explorer, came to the Pilliga in 1818 he saw 'a very thick brush of cypress trees and small shrubs', but most of it was a 'forest' of huge ironbarks and cypress pines, three or four of them only to the hectare.

The ecological history that followed the settlers was complex. Even before they settled, their cattle preceded them, breaking up the delicate, thin crust of the earth and trampling it. The fragile Australian land was not designed for the cloven hoof. Kangaroos spread their weight on their long, soft haunches and powerful tails, and when they cross country are mostly airborne. Cattle and sheep turn good land into dust that, when the rains come, washes away into the rivers. First pastoralists, then small farmers, came and went on their allocated runs and farms, often abandoning them because of poor farming, bad luck, drought, disease or skulduggery. By the 1870s the failed and abandoned farms and cattle runs were being overrun by seedlings of gum and cypress pine in their tens of thousands. The Aborigines and their regular cycles of fire had all but disappeared. The little rat kangaroos that used to nibble down seedlings were destroyed by introduced foxes, and the native grasses were being overwhelmed by the vigorous new species the farmers brought with them. Cypress pines took over the land.

Rabbits came late to the Pilliga Forest and didn't achieve great enough numbers to suppress the seedlings, as the rat kangaroos had, until the 1890s. There was little more growth of pine or scrub until 1951, when a huge fire germinated seeds soaked by heavy rain in 1950. At the same time myxomatosis destroyed the rabbits, and, as Rolls writes, 'the lovely tangle that is the forest today came to life.'

The highest praise I can sing for *A Million Wild Acres*, which I have never really stopped reading for long, is that it defies classification. Les Murray calls it 'a deeply disobedient book' in his 1985 essay 'Eric Rolls and Golden Disobedience'. In the scope and economy of its narrative, he compares the book to an Icelandic saga. Rolls's 'golden disobedience', he suggests, is towards literary convention, in his innate freewheeling ability to transcend the conventional boundaries between fiction and non-fiction, and between the 'human' and 'natural' worlds. In attempting nothing less than a complete account of his large subject, says Murray, the book's enterprise may be seen as Proustian. Rolls introduces us to a gigantic cast of timber-getters, sleeper-cutters, rabbiters, trackers, rogues, outlaws, charcoal-burners, pig-hunters, farmers and cattle-drovers. As Les Murray notes, 'They appear with the sudden naturalness of old friends mentioned in a fireside yarn', yet they hardly stand out from the presentation of the interrelated non-human world, and everyone is accorded the dignity of a name, including the walk-on players. It is a naturally democratic book, and Eric Rolls emerges as part of the place, struggling with the competing demands of his farm as he writes the book. The writer himself comes to seem a million wild acres, speaking for a forest crammed with human histories and natural histories. Rolls's great book works through the accretion of striking detail, portrait and anecdote, so the Pilliga Forest grows in the imagination like an Aboriginal dot-painting: Les Murray calls Rolls's way of writing history 'almost pointillist'. It is by no means extravagant to call this book, as many people do, an Australian classic, according to Italo Calvino's definition of a classic as a book that has not finished saying what it has to say. That must be what drew me to reread the book again and again and eventually compelled me to go to meet its author and explore some of the Pilliga for myself. The first time I met Eric and his wife Elaine Van Kempen we spent several days up the big river fishing in *Sojourner*, the wooden boat that is kept under their house beside the Camden River on the New South Wales Coast at Camden Haven, and we wandered the old-growth coastal forests of big eucalypts together. This time, two years later, I was returning to make the journey inland with him back to his old haunts in the Pilliga Forest.

Going to meet Eric, I took the train out of Sydney at the height of one of the most serious droughts for years. The *Sydney Morning Herald* said over a hundred bushfires were burning that day, and the forecast was for even hotter and dryer weather. Bushfires are part of the weather in Australia. We went through the Sydney suburbs: Stanmore, Petersham, Ashfield, Strathfield, Meadowbank. The jacarandas were in full flower in every garden: pale mauve against the deep green of avocado trees, paperbarks in flower, date palms, scarlet hibiscus and the intense blue morning glory clambering everywhere.

In the newspaper was the story of a Sydney man killed in his garden by a eucalyptus the council had forbidden him to cut down. Approaching the coastal hills of Hawkesbury sandstone, we began to climb through enormous stretches of eucalyptus woods, the blue of their foliage accentuated by the blue-grey haze of smoke that hung over them from the bushfires. The valleys disappeared in smoke, and it flattened the horizons. The train snaked through the lovely flowering woods in the heat, sounding its horn eerily into the sudden darkness. We entered a tunnel, emerged into bright sunshine, then plunged again into another tunnel of smoke. More tunnels, more secret valleys of ferns and pines, wattle and eucalypts, then we were crossing the steep, wooded grandeur of Pittwater in brilliant sunshine. Across on the far shore, wooden boathouses, landing stages and sheds stilt-walked into the glittering fjord, half hidden in the trees, and rows of knee-deep salted sticks delineated the oyster beds like allotments.

Bushfires burnt here and there all the way north for the six hours of that journey, visible in the main as smoke hanging in the cuttings or across valleys further off, or as the blackened, smoking trunks of gum trees. At Camden Haven it was 43°C. In spite of the continuing heat, Eric and I drove west two days later from the coast through

Kempsey and the Broken Bago State Forest, all bare, baked earth and charred trunks of eucalypts where the fires had swept through. Having invited fire by emitting the volatile oils of their leaves in the heat, the eucalypts would now protect themselves with almost immediate new growth from the hidden epicormic buds beneath the under-bark. That is what 'eucalyptus' means: 'well covered', from the Greek. You might call them 'hidden buds'. In a forest fire, said Eric, only five per cent of the eucalyptus wood is burnt. In a grass fire, all the grass is burnt. In 1830 the Broken Bago was all rolling grassland with dense rainforest along the river banks. Now the tangled rainforest has mostly gone, except in the deepest ravines, and a tall eucalypt forest has grown up. From the coast to Kempsey, we passed huge Moreton Bay figs standing in the fields, parrots on the wing and wooden bungalows. In the logging town of Wauchope we paused to inspect a giant tallow-wood trunk marooned beside the road like a whale on a beach. It was said to be a thousand years old, contained 1,842 cubic feet of timber and had been hauled out of the forest, a notice proudly announced, by the firm of Bartlett's of Wauchope.

As we wound up through the mountains of the Dividing Range, dense and dark with smoke, the temperature dropped to 11°C. Now and again the immediate air cleared and we saw that the valleys were all filled with lakes of blue smoke. Every so often we passed a dead kangaroo or wallaby, picked threadbare by eagles and crows. We followed a lorry crammed with live sheep up interminable hairpin bends. One animal had fallen helpless to the floor, its leg sticking out awkwardly through the slatted side. 'All these animals were once driven to market in Sydney along the drovers' roads,' Eric said. 'Estate Agents or Auctioneers would advertise farms for sale in the Dividing Range and all the way to the Namoi River as "only four hundred miles from Sydney" or "an easy three weeks' droving to Sydney". They reckoned these places were nice and handy for the stock markets.'

Descending the western slopes, we entered lovely open, rolling parkland where cattle grazed in the shade of the blue gums that were dotted about it. The drought had bitten hard: all things shrivelled to a drab kangaroo-brown. Swaying herds of thin, listless brown cattle grazed along the road verges, attended by stockmen in shorts and Blunstone boots parked up in the shade of trees in their utility trucks, with flasks, radios and a dog or two.

The temperature was over 40°C at Tamworth as we crossed the bridge over the Peel River, where Eric, fleeing his farm during heavy floods, was once nearly washed off into the surging river in his car. Some of the houses were perched on stilts, like fishermen's shacks. The Australian Stock Company, incorporated by Act of Parliament 'for the Cultivation and Improvement of the Waste Lands in the Colony of New South Wales', established its head-quarters here in the early days of land settlement. Driving into town, looking towards the great sweeping expanses of the Liverpool Plains beyond it, Eric spoke of the Kamilaroi Aboriginal people who used to roam them, from Tamworth to the Pilliga region south of the Namoi River. Kamilaroi, once a widespread Aboriginal language, has now died out. Aboriginals, he said, were all great linguists, often speaking five or six different languages of the neigh-bouring tribes, all very different from their own. The Kamilaroi had a most intricate, subtle, complex language with dozens of words meaning 'to see'. There was a word for seeing things as you approached home ground, another for seeing something far away, another for seeing something within the camp itself. Eric said there were more cases and tenses than in English. There were even three kinds of imperative: normal, emphatic and taunting.

In *Language in Danger*, Andrew Dalby relates how R. M. W. Dixon, a kind of linguistic archaeologist who has recorded many disappearing languages, managed to find two people who could still remember about a hundred words of Kamilaroi between them around 1972. Tom Binge and Charlie White were living in an Aboriginal settlement in southern Queensland. Dalby describes how more linguistic work was done by others and collated with notes taken in the nineteenth century by missionaries like the Reverend W. Ridley, who published *The Kamilaroi Language* in 1886.

Eventually, with poignant irony, a Kamilaroi dictionary was posted as the first-ever dictionary on the internet, just as the language became fully extinct. Eric demonstrated the sucked-in or blown-out aspirates that separated two vowels in Kamilaroi when they occurred together. He could remember old white men of no learning around the Pilliga who could still pronounce the place names authentically as the Kamilaroi did. But most of the British were such bad linguists, he said, that they probably misheard names like *Coonabarabran* and corrupted them.

A road sign on the way into town read 'Welcome to Tamworth, Traditional Home of the Kamilaroi People'. Eric gave it a wry look and spoke of the white squatter stockmen and how they disposed of the Kamilaroi Aborigines who harassed them on the plains in the early days of settlement. This is how he tells the story in *A Million Wild Acres*:

It happened about 1827 or 1828 near a cattle station called Boorambil. The Aborigines might have issued a challenge to the white stockmen as they sometimes did to settle their own differences, with day and hour formally stipulated. The whites had no intention of exposing themselves. When they saw the long line of painted warriors approaching, all the stockmen who had gathered (some said seven, others sixteen) took cover in a well-built hut with slots in the walls to poke rifles through. When spears and boomerangs thrown against the walls in derision failed to bring the whites out, the Aborigines stormed the hut and tried to unroof it. They persisted for hours. Perhaps two hundred were shot, most of the young men of the tribe.

Eric said the warriors had even tried to climb down the chimney of the hut, but every one of them was killed.

A flock of fifty straw-necked ibis flew over as we began crossing the forty square miles of the Liverpool Plains. This vast sweep of land was once some of the best alluvial soil anywhere. Now it is over-exploited and badly affected by salt. On the Beehive Feed Lot, cattle were being fattened for Japanese export beef. They were hot and dusty, flicking their tails unhappily, and there was no shade for them. Eric said the beef was no good either. Here and there conical hills stood up, the cores of old volcanoes. Beyond them, in the far distance to the west, we made out the topsy-turvy outlines of the astonishing Warrumbungle Mountains, like Hokusai waves in a choppy sea. They were the sort of mountains I always thought were confined to fairy stories, jumbled and free-form, a line taken for a drunken walk, their quasi-Aboriginal name somehow ono-matopoeic. Wrecked trees and wrecked cars lay about the huge five-hundred-acre stock enclosures of the farms. We crossed Cox's Creek and the great Namoi River, both of which flood the plains from time to time, and passed into black pine country. A road train loaded with swaying green bales of lucerne went by the other way. The farmers, cattle and sheep were all in crisis with the drought, and there was talk of mass slaughter. The radio spoke of little else.

As we approached Coonabarabran, Eric pulled off the road into woodland, and we walked over to a stand of the local white gums that characterize the place. They were fine trees up to sixty feet tall, with straight, smooth white trunks and limbs. As we came closer to one of the trees, we saw how it was decorated with the most exquisite black-ink doodling, the work of the larvae of a small moth, *Ogmograptis scribula*, as it ate its way through the soft tissue beneath the thin bark. The grub meanders about, etching a little map of its own individual gastronomic tour. But its course is not as random as it seems, because halfway through its larval life the insect loops round and retraces its steps, consuming the hormones it has excreted on the way to complete its development. It then pupates and flies away as a moth, leaving behind the arcane insect jotter-pad Eric and I now contemplated. The zigzags on the bark resembled the jerky lines that denote highs and lows of atmospheric pressure on the graph paper of a barometer. It was quite clear why people call *Eucalyptus rossii* scribbly gum. A close relation, *E. signata*, likewise autographed, grows along the coastal strip of New South Wales.

★

We drove through the white cypress pines and ironbarks of the Pilliga Forest itself and arrived at Baradine, Eric's old home town from his farming days. The place had a Wild West feel: a classical town hall complete with Doric columns presided over a wide main street, entirely deserted in the afternoon heat, a single pub with balconied rooms above, filling station, café, barbershop, agricultural stores and a cluster of utes parked end-on. This is where Eric farmed for twenty-two years at Cumberdeen, a dozen miles from town, and before that at Bogabri for another twenty-two years, to the east of the Pilliga on the Namoi River. The Cumberdeen farm held too many memories for him to go back and see it now.

Out to the west of Baradine lies the pastoral land once known as the Pretty Plains. A ten-mile strip of special soil runs through it: a deep-red and grey sandy loam over a lime subsoil that grows cattle and kurrajong trees beautifully, said Eric, who grew both through his Cumberdeen years. Such a variety of trees and shrubs grow scattered about the paddocks that when Eric lists them in his book, their names are like an incantation:

> Kurrajong, Wilga Budda, Boonery,
> Whitewood, Quinine Bush, Hickory, Gum,
> Ironbark, Supple Jack, Needlewood, Angophora,
> Pilliga Box and Bimble, Cypress Pine, Belar,
> Wild Lemon, Wild Orange, Currant Bush, Beefwood,
> Deane's Wattle, Bull Oak, Boobialla, Motherumbah.

We decided to keep moving and headed straight out into an area of the forest called Merriwindi for a dozen miles along a wide, sandy road before we turned along a track to Trap Yard Dam. These dams were dug out as water reservoirs. But they are not the lush green oases you might imagine. They have caked, muddy banks sloping to brown water puddled by wild horses, wild pigs and cattle. The first you see of a dam as you approach is the windmill above the trees and the corrugated-iron tank on a wooden tower once used for filling the fire-fighting trucks. The wind pumps

and tanks are now all defunct, but the dams are the places to see
animals and birds, especially in a drought at nightfall. They have
interesting names: Friday Creek Dam, Etoo Bore, Tarranah Waterhole, Station Creek Dam, Log Road Dam, Wooleybah Bore, Bibble-
windi Dam, Yellow Spring Creek Dam, Sawpit Road Dam, Dead
Filly Tank, Dingo Hole Dam, Bungle Gully Bore. They relate to
the intricate system of creeks that suffuse the Pilliga map like the
tiny veins in a bloodshot eye.

Next day we drove out to see Eric's friend Gerald Harder at his
sawmill, the Cartref. It stood just outside the forest in an open field
with an old ironbark in it that had shed a mighty bough: a challenge
for anyone with a saw. Gerald, in blue shorts and a white yachting
T-shirt, was in his early thirties, blond-haired and fit-looking. He
worked with Barry in a sawmill they built when they could see that
the farming was no longer paying. A series of flat-roofed, open-sided
tin sheds, supported on wooden poles and bolted white pine struts,
housed the saw benches and planes. A pair of big John Deere tractors
powered all the machinery. They had built the mill themselves by
stages, buying or bartering components and materials as they could
afford them. The skids and rollers for the saw cost Gerald two cases
of beer, one of which he helped to drink, and they had saved and
bought their saw blades one by one. The tin came second-hand off
the roof of an old hospital.

They were cutting two-by-fours out of the tough, dense white
pine the timber-getters delivered at $1,000 a truckload of fifteen
cubic metres. They can sell on the machined timber at $500 a cubic
metre, but there's a lot of waste on the relatively slender trunks of
white pine. As you square them up, you lose the edge strip: the
rounded part of the trunk under the bark. And the circular saw
blade itself is a quarter-inch thick, so every four cuts you lose an
inch of timber and generate mountains of sawdust, although not
enough to interest a power-station in collecting it for burning as
fuel. The Pilliga is too remote and the sawmill too small, so they
end up incinerating it themselves, as if the place needed warming

up any more. The potent scent of white pine flooded the mill. Gerald's dogs, all collies, sniffed the air. His timber is in great demand, especially by the Japanese building trade, who need it to make strong wooden frames for houses. White pine contains turpentine, a natural pesticide, so white ants won't eat it.

We shared a late breakfast of tea and teacakes with Barry, Gerald and his wife in the kitchen up at the farmhouse, an old wooden homestead now leaning at a precarious angle at one end. Its wooden piers were sinking unevenly into the ground. Every now and again, said Barry, there was a loud report like a gun as one of the roof spars or a structural beam sprang clear of its fixings and poked through the outside wall like a broken collarbone. They then had to jack up the house four inches at a time, straighten it up and ease it back on to supporting chocks. The little homestead was on the move, inching crabwise across the Pilliga. This was one definition of moving house. Australians, being practical people with mainly timber-framed dwellings, often took their houses with them when they moved. Gerald did a lot of house moving on contract. 'I just take a chainsaw, climb up on the roof and start cutting her in half,' he said. He even made it sound easy, slicing the house into sections like a carcass, lifting them with a crane on to a low-loader and putting it all back together again somewhere else. This is exactly what Eric and Elaine had done with their fine timber house on the banks of the Camden River at Camden Haven. They found the site, bought a house they liked somewhere else and trucked it to the riverside, where they raised it up on stilts to give themselves an extra storey, a fine balcony and a boathouse, where Eric keeps his beloved wooden *Sojourner*.

Sawmilling was hard work, but better than farming, said Gerald and Barry, because it gave them more freedom to take a day off now and again. They went dinghy sailing on some inland lakes across the plains or chased brumbies in their utes at up to fifty miles an hour. 'They can be dangerous brutes, especially the stallions,' said Gerald. 'They'll kick out sideways at the ute or bite at you as they run.'

Kurrajong trees, a lovely deep green, threw their shadows across Gerald's land like big poplars. Their leaves make good cattle fodder, and their seedpods are so high in caffeine that the explorer Leichardt used them to make coffee on his expeditions: *Brachychiton populneum* belongs to the same family as the cocoa bean tree. The Kamilaroi Aborigines would pull up the yam-like tap roots of the seedling trees and cook them as vegetables. They also made good canoes and shields from the timber.

The sun was mounting, and the tin roof of Gerald's listing farmhouse seemed to wobble in the heat as we drove away past the big ironbark with the fallen bough. Our dust trail led back through the forest to Roy Matthews's sawmill, the Gallagher Insultimber Partnership at the edge of Barradine. Ironbark, *Eucalyptus leucoxylon*, grows strongly in many parts of the Pilliga woods and refuses to conduct electricity. It also lives up to its name in strength and hardness, so almost the busiest machine in Roy Matthews's sawmill was the electric grinder. A queue of big circular saw discs hung up on the wall beside it: each saw must be sharpened three times a day. The job used to be done by hand, with files, and Eric records in *A Million Wild Acres* how Bert Ruttley, who worked for Jack Underwood at the Rocky Creek Mill for thirty years, would wear out four files every weekend, gulleting the circular saws to lengthen their worn teeth.

Ironbarks were always traditionally felled by the journeymen sleeper-cutters who lived or camped in the forest. Roy built up his business making electric fence posts, much smaller in section, from the trees rejected by the sleeper-cutters as too small or twisted. Now that the last of the sleeper-cutters had left the forest, Roy's ironbark came into the sawmill as truckloads of tree-sized logs. A big forklift moved in and carried several new logs to a conveyor. It carried them into the steel jaws of the de-barking machine, which flayed off the bark ready for the saws. Using sophisticated computer controls, the saw operator cut the ironwood into slabs one and a half inches square and just the right lengths, to be sold all over the world for a whole variety of specialized electric fences. There was very little waste. The bark was all chipped and bagged for sale to garden stores, and the sawdust went to the power-station for burning as the five per cent renewable fuel that must now be mixed with coal by law in Australia. Offcuts fell on to a conveyor and went straight to the chip mill to be ferried off by lorry on the first stage of their journey to Japan, where they would be made into some of the very finest paper.

The ironbark fence posts were stored in pigeonholes that named and classified the different sizes of spacing posts, the 'droppers' that separate the wires, leaving just the right calibre of gap between them, tailored to particular animals or birds, ranging from seven-foot deer posts for Japan and Korea to something called the 'Rabbit Peg Tie-down' for the home market. The 'Melbourne' was a big eight-foot slanting dropper for spacing kangaroo fence. I spotted the puzzling 'Frog' and 'Penguin', and the six-foot 'Emu'. Moving along the rows, I found the evocative 'Six-Foot Special Feral Stake', the Australian Dog Fence, useful for stopping wombats according to Roy, and a selection of droppers and posts for electric dingo fences powered by solar panels. Ironbark fence posts will last at least twenty-three years almost anywhere, wet or dry, from Denmark to New Zealand, even under snow for months at a time.

Fences have a special importance in the history of Australia, where people managed very well without them for 40,000 years. Their sudden arrival, running in straight lines across the contours of sacred land, advertising its expropriation with the menace of barbed wire, must have puzzled and offended the native people, as perhaps they still do.

When Roy started milling ironbark in 1979, forty sleeper-cutters were still at work out in the Pilliga. In earlier days there had been several hundred. The Pilliga Forest gave men with no capital the opportunity to work and live independently as timber-getters and sleeper-cutters. As the railways expanded across Australia, more and more sleepers were needed, and ironbark was tough and long lasting. Men would set up camp in the forest near a creek for water, then often build a house and raise a family, strapping an axe to the crossbar and riding bicycles out to new stands of trees when their home patch was cut down. Eric showed me the ancient, frayed, two-foot-six-inch butts of ironbarks the original sleeper-cutters had felled with axes, working at a comfortable height to swing the axe and avoid bending down to cut the tree from its base, regardless of the waste of good lumber.

Having felled and trimmed the trees, the sleeper-cutters sawed them into the regulation eight-foot lengths. So strong was their spirit of independence that they would rig up a strip of tough inner tube tied to a springy bent stick driven into the ground as a 'chinaman' or 'dummy' to draw the other end of the two-man cross-cut saw and work alone. Once the tree was sawn into sleeper lengths, it had to be barked by bruising blows from the back of the axehead. Eric described the result memorably: 'A newly barked log looks like a woman stepping out of a hot bath into cold air, exposed, goosefleshed and a little surprised.' Then the log was split or sawn into sleepers nine inches by five. Ironbark splits well, so a selection of wedges was often driven in with a mall made of a rare, tough, highly valued timber known as Gunnedah ironbark.

The lives of the Pilliga sleeper-cutters as recorded by Eric Rolls in *A Million Wild Acres* contribute to a mythology of the forest. Les Murray, whose own father was a bullock driver and timber-getter in the forests of New South Wales before he married and became a dairy farmer, compares the book to some of the Icelandic sagas in that it 'presents a complex system greater than any of the agents in it'. Murray calls it 'a sort of dynamic tableau, measuring some thousands of square miles by about 160 years'. But he finds an interesting difference: 'In Rolls's presentation, things human and non-human are all happening interrelatedly, and the humans barely stand out.' What interests Les Murray about this is that 'as the sagas only occasionally do, he treats his human and non-human agents pretty much on a par. This par we may call ecological consciousness, and see it as a new form of a very ancient sense of the inter-relatedness of all things.'

East to Eden

I am travelling to Kazakhstan, propelled by a story told to me by Barrie Juniper that is something between the Book of Genesis and the *Just So Stories*: How the Apple Began. Beside a black mulberry tree he planted thirty years ago outside the porters' lodge at St Catherine's College Oxford, I met Barrie, a don of the college, luminary of the Oxford Plant Sciences Department and apple guru. Ruby stains of the fallen mulberries smudged the paving stones. I had heard of Juniper's pioneering work in tracking down the origins of the domestic apple to the Tien Shan Mountains of Kazakhstan and had come to sit at his feet and learn more. Over lunch, he outlined the long journey of the domestic apple from the wild fruit forests of the Tien Shan along the so-called Silk Road to the west. In the course of that journey, Juniper has discovered, the wild apple of the Tien Shan, *Malus sieversus*, evolved into the domestic apple, *Malus domesticus*, and eventually found its way to Britain with the Romans.

Barrie Juniper spent years searching for the ancestors of the domestic apple. He reckoned there were now some 20,000 varieties in the world including over 6,000 recorded in Britain. Many of the old varieties that haven't died out altogether have become rarities, so Juniper realized that mapping out their genetic identities through

DNA samples was a matter of urgency. In 1998 he travelled to Central Asia with some Oxford colleagues in search of the ur-apple. They went to Kazakhstan, to Alma-Ata, now known as Almaty. Alma-Ata is usually translated as 'Father of all Apples', although there is a school of thought in Kazakhstan that believes it is more accurately rendered as 'Where the Apples Are'. It had taken Juniper over a year's struggle with Kazakh official protocol to get permission to visit the outlying regions of the Tien Shan Mountains in search of wild apples, but eventually he and his companions set out from Almaty in the summer of 1998 under military escort to the remote mountain slopes known as the Djunguarian Alatau. Here they found forests of wild fruit: wild pears, plums, apricots, hawthorns, rowans and apples. The apples were all *Malus sieversii*, and their fruits varied enormously in size, shape and flavour, from the hard and the tart to apples that tasted and looked remarkably like our own familiar cultivated apples.

They collected apple specimens and took them home to Oxford, where they analysed their DNA and discovered that *Malus sieversii* shows a far closer affinity with the domestic apple than with any other wild species. But how could all the thousands of varieties of the domestic apple have descended from the wild fruit forests of the Tien Shan? To add to the mystery, *Malus sieversii* is reluctant to hybridize with other species. So how did all these variations on the theme of the eating apple arise? What makes the apple such a chameleon? The answer, in a word, is that apple trees are hetero-zygous. Plant the pips of a hundred apples from the same tree and the new generation of trees can differ, often dramatically, from their parents and from each other. This is how new kinds of apples have arisen by chance over the centuries: people taking a fancy to this or that new fruit, then propagating from that particular tree by taking cuttings from the shoots and grafting them on to other trees. All Bramley seedlings are descended from a single tree in someone's back garden in Northampton. And so on, down thousands of years, so every single kind of eating apple in the world is a direct descend-ant of the apples that evolved in the forests of the Tien Shan.

After lunch, Barrie Juniper and I sat down in the fellows' common room over coffee and the *Times Atlas*, which we opened at Central Asia. He began to explain how he thinks the domestic apple evolved; a story that ranged from the Yangtze Valley, to Neolithic Mesopotamia, to the orchards of Oxford. According to Juniper, *Malus*, the botanical family to which all apples belong, first evolved about twelve million years ago. To judge from the twenty-odd wild species that still exist in central and southern China, it probably bore a small fruit with hard but edible seeds not unlike those of its close relation, the rowan tree. The seeds would have been spread by birds. A small group of species penetrated north-west through the fertile country that is now Gansu Province into the area that was to become the Tien Shan Mountains as they arose in the same geological upheaval that created the Himalayas. Juniper believed that just one or possibly two of these 'bird apple' seeds was lifted over the rising hills to the Tien Shan and the valley of the Ili River, most likely in the crop or faeces of a migrating bird. The spread of the inhospitable Gobi Desert then prevented any migration of apple seed back to the east, and although they were walled in by glaciation to the west, the ice never reached these mountains.

In the foothills and valleys of the Tien Shan range, the new apple found itself in a genuine paradise. Bears, deer and wild pigs lived in the spreading woodlands, eating the wild fruit in autumn and selecting the sweeter, juicier apples while bees laboured in the pollination department of the same evolutionary project. The bears, living in the abundant caves of the Tien Shan, were avid fruit-eaters, and pips could pass through their guts unharmed to germinate in the dung. As Juniper pointed out, the baseball-glove claws of bears are perfectly suited to the grasping of apples. He had seen how enthusiastically they will vandalize a tree bearing a favourite sweet apple, dragging off whole branches in a kind of rough pruning. Out on the steppe, huge herds of wild horses and donkeys also browsed on the ripe apples and helped them spread westwards and south along the range towards what is now Almaty. Like the bears, they kept on selecting the larger, juicier, sweeter apples, so that as it spread west, the apple gradually became larger. At the same time this evolutionary pressure changed it from a 'bird' fruit with edible seeds to a 'mammal' fruit with poisonous seeds. The bitter taste of apple pips is cyanide, and the smooth, hard, teardrop seed coat evolved as the perfect streamlined vehicle to pass intact through an animal's guts.

Juniper believed that by the time the 'new' apple had populated the northern slopes of the eastern Tien Shan and reached near Almaty, it had evolved into something like its present size and culinary appeal. Later, as human populations began to travel back and forth along the old animal migration routes between east and west, they helped to spread the new fruit. People call these routes 'The Silk Roads', but they were in use five or six thousand years before the discovery of silk, which lent its name to the route only during the period from AD 0 to 400. In the early days, said Juniper, camels would have been the means of transport along the routes, but, although they are as fond of apples as any other herbivore, their digestive system is so efficient that not even apple pips will survive it. Then, around 7,000 years ago, something momentous happened on the plains of Kazakhstan. The horse was domesticated, and soon started to travel the trading routes. The more direct northern trade routes led from Shanghai and Xian via Urumchi in north-west China to Almaty, Tashkent and Bokhara, then through Anatolia all the way to the Mediterranean coast. During winter the Tien Shan Mountains were impassable in the snow, so traders took the long way round to the south. But when the snows melted in July, the caravans turned north and until the first snows in November travelled through the Ili Valley and the Tien Shan range via Almaty, passing through fruit forests on the way.

Thanks to the relatively inefficient digestive system of the horse, the seeds of apples pass through the gut unharmed, so horses were very effective disseminators of a random variety of seedlings that grew up into flowering trees that, in turn, were naturally pollinated into yet greater permutations of genes and fruiting characteristics. Apples would also have been a highly portable source of food for both horses and traders, and must surely have travelled many hundreds of miles stashed in saddlebags. By the time the Romans introduced the domestic apple to Britain, they had learnt the secret of grafting.

Barrie Juniper chanced on the early origins of grafting while riding his bicycle through Oxford one afternoon. He met Dr Stephanie Dalley, an orientalist, who told him about something she had seen on the wooden cuneiform tablets she was translating. They were 3,800 years old and had been discovered at Mari, on the banks of the Euphrates in Syria. Some of them depicted the grafting of vines in the valley of the Tigris and Euphrates, where the Babylonians are known to have experienced the problem of soil made salty through irrigation. The tablets revealed that by that time gardeners and orchardists knew how to graft grapes on to salt-tolerant rootstock. If they could graft grapes, they could almost certainly graft apples too.

A favoured apple tree could be reliably propagated only by cutting scions from it and grafting them. Scions could be preserved and carried by driving the ends of the stems into a hard fruit such as a quince. Thus, the favoured fruit variety could be transported west and reared in the orchards of Babylon, and later in Greece, then Rome and eventually in Britain.

In his biography of Alexander the Great, Robin Lane-Fox describes how the enterprising general took gardeners skilled in grafting from the Tigris basin home to Greece, and is known from written accounts to have trained his soldiers to fight in naval exercises in which apples were fired in broadsides as 'blanks'. The Romans learnt to cultivate the apple from the Greeks and eventually brought it to Britain. At St Romain en Gal in the South of France, a Roman mosaic shows the progress of the apple year, from its grafting to its harvesting. The Romans grafted *Malus sieversii* on to the wild *Malus sylvestris* so that the bottom half of the tree could eventually be utilized as the ideal timber for making the cogs of waterwheels or windmills. Barrie believed the Saxons must have inherited the relict orchards of sweet Roman apples and named many places after them. He has found at least forty-seven apple place names: towns and villages such as Appleby and Appledore. The Celtic prefix *af* or *av* also signifies 'apple', as in Avalon or Avignon.

Barrie thought I was mad even to consider reaching the Tien Shan Mountains of Kazakhstan or Kyrgyzstan without months of preparation and frankly warned me that in the face of the endless protocol entailed in securing visas and permission to visit the mountains, I would probably give up. He and his Oxford colleagues had written over 200 emails and letters in their original quest to reach the Tien Shan fruit forests. He was very nearly right. There were times when I almost did give up, as I cycled across London to the Kazakh Consulate opposite the V&A in Kensington again and again, or sat waiting there in queues in an airless office at the bottom of the basement stairs hoping for my elusive visa.

But finally there I was, flying into Almaty at two in the morning to meet Luisa, Barrie Juniper's friend and interpreter. Luisa is learning to drive and has taken a lesson on the way out to the airport with her instructor, Johnny, who drives us back into town at breakneck speed in his Lada along wide, empty boulevards of limes with whitewashed trunks. Outside the wine factory, topiarists have sculpted the limes into giant bottles. Kazakhs, I later discover, love topiary and never pass up an opportunity to flex the shears on almost any tree. On Republic Square, outside the old House of Government building, stands a row of Central Asian elms, shaped into perfect domes like a row of soldiers in dark-green busbies. Everywhere you go in Almaty there are trees and tree-shaped fountains.

Johnny's Lada is dwarfed by the great sweeping forecourt of the Almaty Hotel. So is my singularly tatty rucksack, which a porter insists on carrying in without a trace of irony. The Almaty is a huge old-style Soviet hotel opposite the Opera with tiers of balconies like the decks of an ocean liner. By some miracle worked by Luisa on the unsmiling receptionists, I get a room three floors up, wonderfully tatty, complete with plugless bathroom, jammed balcony

French window, TV, broken fridge and large desk. We arrange to meet in the morning, and I fall asleep instantly.

I wake to sunlight and traffic and the brilliant surprise of the snowy tops of the Tien Shan Mountains, the Heavenly Mountains, that form the steep backdrop to the city to the south. The sun breaks over the ridge, casting a pale duck-egg shade on the snow in the topmost combs. Everything in the backlit city is silhouetted and dramatic. People move along the streets like shadow puppets. The air smells fresh and cool. The city itself is steeply raked up the mountainside, rising from two to three thousand feet in the straight lines of its original Soviet grid, with the 15,000-foot mountain wall behind. My first impression is of a Ruritanian city built in a forest: trees are everywhere, wonderfully unkempt and wild-looking, shading the streets and parks, fed by the mountain rivers and streams that race through the city.

During the 1870s and 1880s, when the place was still called Alma-Ata and the city was being planned by the Russians, the city engineer, a German by the name of Baum, stipulated that every citizen must plant five trees in front of his house. The scheme was such a roaring success that there are now some 138 different species of tree in Almaty. Baum is of course 'tree' in German. Mr Tree was particularly active in the leafy district of the city known as Kompot, which means 'fruit salad', and it was probably Baum's idea that every street there should be named after a fruit tree. Plum Street, Cherry Lane and Apricot Gardens are no more eccentric than our own Birdcage Walk or Petticoat Lane. Many of the Almaty streets are shaded by ramshackle avenues of magnificent oaks in the prime of life, no doubt once twinklings in the eye of Baum, or acorns in his pocket. There are fine apple orchards all over the city, as well as the wild apple woods on the slopes of the Alatau Mountains that rise like a wall behind it. You can sometimes go up there in winter, apparently, and find apples buried under the snow, perfectly preserved by the layer of autumn leaves beneath.

Outside in the wide expanse of the Republiky Alangy, a wedding party is assembled on the steps of the Monument to Independence in bright sunshine. A little folk-band with an accordion, a two-stringed dombra and a drum like an Irish bodrun plays Kazakh tunes. Some of the wedding guests dance together, while others pose for photographs, all dressed to the nines in suits and ties or bright dresses. Luisa flags down another Lada, and we race to meet the Director of the Almaty Botanical Gardens and distinguished member of the Kazakhstan Academy of Sciences, Professor Isa Omarovich Baitulin. Lunching together on borsch and tea, we make plans for a visit the next day to the wild apple forests of the Talgar Valley, some thirty miles to the east of Almaty. After so much preparation and difficulty, I can hardly believe this is happening. Isa cuts a magnificently handsome figure with the oval face, high cheekbones, narrow eyes and olive skin of the Mongol Kazakhs. To our amazement, this fit and agile man turns out to be in his eighties. But he has spent much of his life outdoors, studying the fungi that live in close association with the roots of trees.

Isa speaks little English and I feel ashamed of my small Russian and no Kazakh, but we find we can converse quite happily through Luisa, or in the botanical Latin of the names of trees and plants. Isa says this is a good time to walk in the wild fruit forests because the harvest is not over, and much of the wild fruit will still be on the trees. At the end of May, he says, the whole mountain is white with so much blossom it could be snow. There are wild apricots, blackcurrants, raspberries and mulberries in the fruit forests too, and in the south of Kazakhstan wild woods full of walnuts and pistachios. The wild apples follow the valleys, growing at a height of 3,000–4,000 feet. In Almaty, he says, we are already at 2,800 feet and the Jungar Alatau Mountains behind us rise to 16,000 feet. He talks about the great Soviet scientist Nicolay Vavilov, who was the first to suspect that the original ancestors of all domestic apples lived on the Tien Shan Mountains and in 1936–7 led the first botanical expedition into the wild fruit forests. Vavilov felt sure the domestic apple was descended exclusively from *Malus sieversus*, the wild apple of the Tien Shan, but without the modern genetic techniques of DNA profiling he was unable to prove his hypothesis, as Barrie Juniper did some sixty years later. By the end of lunch we have all relaxed after our initial formality and arrange that Isa will come with a Russian jeep in the morning and we shall set off for the wild fruit forests.

Five of us pile into Ali Khan's red Russian jeep in brilliant early sunshine and set off for the Talgar Valley and its wild fruit forests. Our route runs via Talgar, a large village in the hills about forty miles south-east of Almaty. In 1936 Fitzroy Maclean, whose book *Eastern Approaches* had informed my own journey, travelled exactly the same way on his first excursion out of Almaty, finding a place on a lorry heading out of the city. On reaching Talgar, he set off into the hills on foot, followed by the NKVD secret service agents who tailed him everywhere, but they were local men, and Maclean ended up being entertained to lunch with them in a peasant cottage in the hills.

Ali Khan, our driver, is Isa's son and a judge, although apparently he's resting just at the moment, busy trying to start up a tourist agency for visiting scientists. Isa Baitulin has invited Dr Kuralay Karibaia, a jolly, brown-haired woman dressed in jeans and a red-and-black baseball jacket. Kuralay manages a United Nations Global Ecology Fund project to conserve the fruit forests.

Ahead of us are the snowy peaks of the Zaeleiskoe Alatau and the 16,500-foot Mount Talgar. The jeep is a Yaz with a canvas roof and very hard springs. There are no seat belts, only a handle on the dashboard to grip. They all insist on giving me pride of place in the front seat, but in all honesty I would rather be in the back where it is marginally safer, and where Isa, Luisa and Kuralay sit squeezed together. After a mile or two we are all covered in dust. We bump along wide, dusty roads lined with the whitewashed trunks of poplars or oaks, zigzagging to avoid the vast potholes.

Soon we're in the suburbs, jogging past single-storey cottages with bright wooden windows, pine-boarded or cob walls, shallow-pitched tin or felted roofs, and little balconies and porches raised on wooden stilts. The walls are mostly ochre and the doors and windows bright blue, and all have orchard gardens bursting with lush, fruiting trees, mostly apples and pears but also apricots and walnuts. Along the verges, we see little kitchen tables and chairs set out with jam jars of wild fungi, milk or honey for sale. Others display such curious combinations as a packet of cigarettes, a melon or two and a bottle of lemonade; petrol or motor oil and a clutch of potatoes. A girl squats in the shade of a poplar beside a neat heap of melons. Another sells besoms of bark-bound brushwood. There are bucketfuls of apples and baskets of tomatoes, onions, gourds and pumpkins beside every whitewashed tree.

We are by now on the open steppe, bowling along the very same route taken by Fitzroy Maclean on his first, covert, journey to Almaty in 1936, in the days of the Soviet Empire. Beyond the avenues of roadside trees, Kazakh horsemen are herding their cattle, some of them tiny dots on the distant plains of endless brown grass and dust. Dogs and foals run across the steppe. Lively streams skirt the road on either side, and in the foreground are commercial apple orchards of oft-pruned trees no one has got round to replacing. Isa calls them middle aged. Cattle graze beneath the apples while their cowhands stretch out in the shade and sleep. We pass a man wheeling a slopping milk churn on wheels. A transhumant bee-keeper's caravan full of hives ready to be towed up by tractor into the forest is parked by a barn.

At Talgar, a large village in Maclean's time and by now almost a little town, we weave through lanes of baked mud surrounded by ochre walls and blue windows, an escort of terriers and mongrels prancing round the jeep. Then we swing in through the high gates of the Forestry Headquarters and find ourselves in a yard full of huge logging trucks and more dogs which rouse themselves from under them to come to meet us. The five old bull-nosed Russian Army lorries are endowed with every conceivable winch, crane and towing device, and their wheels are taller than a man. The two head foresters emerge from the office in suits and ties, and there are formal introductions, watched by an old baboushka in the caretaker's gatehouse, her bed just visible behind the door. The Chief Forester is introduced as Medeo.

The foresters clamber into their jeep and lead the way out of Talgar, thundering uphill past an open-air bazaar where more lorries are unloading potatoes and onions. Along the dirt road into the foothills, every rubbish heap grows a crop of pale-blue chicory. I am in that bemused state when you no longer comprehend what exactly is going on but quite happily luxuriate in the sheer richness of everything, the sounds of Kazakh and Russian, the rose-capped mountains, the bustling villages, the shadows of poplars, as you would in a dream. We splash through a river bed and pass a lovely old wooden village mosque, like a village hall with a gleaming silver minaret atop its roof. We catch the rich smell of woodsmoke and baking bread as we drive by farms with blackened cob ovens in the yards sheltered by stilted tin roofs. We traverse the foothills through orchards, planted by the Soviets, laden with ripe pink apples. We go pitching and rolling over the rounded foothills into the minor valleys of mountain streams, lurching through the fords, charging straight back up the next hill. I notice that the handle I'm clutching on the dashboard is the one part of the well-painted Yaz that is worn completely smooth to the bare steel.

Stopping to admire an orchard, Kuralay jumps up to pull down a branch, and we scrump an apple or two. This is exactly what Maclean did when he passed this way in the thirties. Climbing and winding our way through hamlets and farms, we press on, past a garden shed like a tiny mosque with a roof of beaten tin that was perhaps once an oil drum, past marigolds in every cottage garden and the magnificent bulging torsos of cob-built bread ovens, their skin toasted and fissured, the fresh loaves laid out to cool on their roofs like sleeping cats. The fierce, high fences round every little farmstead, and the dogs chained in the yards to dead hulks of cars that serve as garden sheds and kennels, set me wondering about the intriguing bandits in the hills that people have mentioned now and then. We pass a tractor with a whole family crammed in the tiny cab, a small boy somehow perched above the steering wheel and a beaming farmer behind it.

My ears pop as we climb higher, and the air feels much cooler. We breast the top of a ridge and suddenly there they are before us: the wild apple woods. The whole of the mountainside we are approaching is covered in them, beginning with an open, wild wood pasture that shades by degrees into the dense forest that runs on up the slopes. Curiously, it feels like country I have always known. I feel excited, of course, yet entirely at home and at one with the landscape. I have the odd feeling I have lived here all my life. At first we pass through wild savannah scattered with groups of tall apple trees or single specimens, their complex multiple trunks twisted together like sinews. The trees are all thirty to fifty feet tall, spreading and unpruned, except here and there by animals, still bearing plenty of fruit in a good year. They cast sharp shadows across the dazzling yellow grasses of the meadows. One of the trees is massive, its branches apparently full of fruit, but as I approach closer I realize I am not seeing apples but yellowing autumn leaves caught in glancing sunlight. The bark is worn smooth by the hides of cattle and horses. Wisps of their hair stand out like implants. The wild apples flock more densely around the slight valleys of the hundreds of streams that run off the mountains and irrigate the meadows. We are high up, the sky is very blue, and the air smells very clean and thin. To the south is the wall of the Heavenly Mountains, and if I face the other way all I see for hundreds, even thousands of miles is pale-brown steppe with low, rocky hills in the foreground.

After rattling across several miles of this high savannah we pull up before a mound of wooden beehives, an old Mercedes van and a curvaceous, wood-framed caravan sheathed in sheet steel that could have come straight out of *La Strada*. I fully expect to see Anthony Quinn ease himself out of it, yawning and stretching in long johns and a buttoned vest after a strenuous night. And I am not disappointed. It is Valery who comes out, looking every inch as good, his eyes slitted against years of steppe and desert sun, shining brown skin stretched over the high cheekbones, his face benevolently lined. He is probably still in his thirties, but so weathered, skinny and obviously tough that I felt he would always look the same. He wears the soft black suede boots of the horseman, skilfully made from a single piece of hide, stretching over his calves, trousers tucked in a touch rakishly, and a black V-neck T-shirt. He keeps a dozen big rabbits grazing in a run, a few goats and a small flock of sheep. Some chickens emerge from under the van as we talk and resume their pecking about. Valery shows us the wild flowers on the meadow that feed his bees. In spring the hills are ablaze with wild tulips, but in the dust of autumn all we see is the pale blue chicory. Valery has sixty-seven hives, each yielding some ten to twelve gallons of honey each year. He says he produces about a ton of honey from every fifty hives. Each colony will have consumed about 265 pounds of honey for itself over the year: the ten or twelve gallons are what is left over. By feeding sugar to the bees, you can take more of their honey, but that is not generally Valery's way. In the height of summer, there will be over a thousand beehives scattered about these hillsides, the bees feeding off the wild herbs and in the fruit forests.

I wonder if Valery has a wife, and what he does for comforts. He clearly likes the life, and says so. He says the Talgar hills have their own completely different climate. In winter there can be three feet of snow for weeks. In Almaty it can be five below zero and here it may be a warm 20 degrees. We are a bit of a delegation, and it feels wrong to ask him too many personal questions: we're intruding on a peaceful, almost monastic life in one of the most beautiful places on earth. In spring, says Valery, there's an explosion of bees and flowers. These saffron meadows burst into flame with tulips, and the hills are a huge snowfield of wild apple, apricot and hawthorn blossom.

I'm sad to leave the solitary Valery, whom I instinctively like. When we shake hands, it is the two-handed lingering double-clasp kind with a deep look into the eye. The look says, 'We come from vast distances apart on this earth, yet I feel a natural, spontaneous respect for you. It is very moving, that we far-flung people from different tribes are clearly first natural friends, not enemies at all.' I very nearly catch myself making the little speech, but restrain myself in time. Luisa and I buy a litre jar of Valery's best wild apple-blossom honey to share. When Valery hands it over, it feels like a blessing – the palpable proof of the goodness and beauty of the place, and the wild apples. I experience the same feeling when I look around the faces of my new friends: the first thing I see in them is their beauty, and I rejoice in the diversity of human genes that made them, as the flower genes seeking each other in the pollen made the honey.

Further on through the woods, we stop by a little clearing and pick sweet hawthorn berries the size of fingertips. Unlike their English counterparts in the same *Crataegus* family, they are sweet, but you still have to spit out the hard pips. Isa and Kuralay then turn their attention to a dense relict grove of cultivated blackcurrants, a giant variety from China lacking the toothy tartness of our native currant but a welcome addition to our gastronomic wildwood tour.

Our sticky mouths and fingers stained orange and purple, we dip and thread our way through the fruit forest, past a solitary yurt in a wooded glade, then two or three tented settlements or simple farmsteads. Outside a very simple wooden hut, barely more than four or five packing cases slung together, sit a little family with their horses and cattle tethered near by. Two small girls are braiding their mother's waist-length hair, proudly brushing it for her as it shines in the sun. Climbing a steep holloway past exposed roots of elms, apples and apricots, we come to a cottage and farmstead in the woods. Here, says Isa with a little bow, we are invited by the foresters to lunch.

The cottage is set deep in the fruit forest. Leaves and branches arch together overhead, so the place is cool and dappled. We go in up open steps of pine and through a wooden porch raised to the floor level of the house on stilts. Each of us pauses at the foot of the steps to wash our hands at a little cistern contraption supported on a post driven into the ground, with a basin beneath. I was to become familiar with these elegant, water-saving devices wherever I travelled in the countryside across Central Asia. The steel cylinder, shaped like a miniature samovar, holds two or three litres; you punch a piston plug upwards with the back of one of your hands to let the water down as you wash them. It is like milking a cow. A soap dish and hand towel also hang from the post.

We all step out of our shoes in the porch and leave them there with dozens of others belonging to the household. The custom reminds me of my prep school, where we each had our own shoe bag hanging from a peg in the cloakroom, and changed into 'house shoes' for lessons. Padding about in stockinged feet on the fine carpets spread over the wooden floors everywhere feels at once more intimate and informal. A serious-looking woman in a long red skirt and green silk headscarf ushers us into a room at a corner of the house: it contains a bed along the innermost wall, pine-boarded walls and a floor adorned with rugs, some felted in bold, zigzagging Kazakh designs. A large, low table occupies most of the remaining floor space except for a great many cushions and a samovar by the fireplace, tended by the wife and daughter of Medeo, the forester whose house this is. The women silently take turns at squatting beside the samovar and dispensing a continuous supply of chai.

The table is spread with a spectacular array of dishes of all colours: bowls of *kymys*, the fermented milk of mares, sour milk, bowls of wild mushrooms of two or three kinds, sliced tomatoes and cucumbers. We seat ourselves on the floor, cross-legged with our backs against the wall along two sides, wedged and propped by cushions. Isa sits at the head as the senior man, and I sit at his left hand as the principal guest. Medeo sits to the right of Isa, Luisa next to me, then Kuralay, then all the women of the house and two more foresters. The cottage, we learn, is called *Saimasai*, meaning 'Stream in the Little Valley'.

Our lunch begins with a prayer by Isa. It is long and involved and seems rather more than simply grace. We sit with our hands cupped open, as if to receive heavenly food. Then chai is poured, sour milk added, and passed around. Isa proposes we drink vodka, wine or brandy. Luisa and I both choose wine and taste the fruity, full-bodied red Kazakhstanskaya. First we eat lamb shashlik in tender strips with a dried, hard cow cheese and bread, and savoury doughnuts that we dunk in sour milk.

Now come the toasts, proposed by each of us in turn in the true filibustering tradition of an oral nomad culture, Luisa gallantly translating, and abridging, the sentiments so eloquently expressed. Isa goes first, with a rousing speech about the glories of Mother Nature that ends with the sentiment, endorsed by all present, that 'to work for Nature is a noble endeavour that knows no boundaries. Nor should it, for it is our common purpose to work for the ecology of our world.' As glasses are refilled all round, Kuralay rises to deliver another long and lyrical paean to Nature, culminating with the assertion that 'nature's bounty is very great and we all owe it to her to work ceaselessly on behalf of diversity and its expression in the natural world.' We could, I feel, all have been sitting round at some Gaia conference at Dartington or Findhorn.

Now it is my turn. Topping up my glass for courage, I speak of Kazakhstan's two great gifts to the world: the cultivated apple and the tamed horse. However, I say with a flourish, I have today discovered a third: the best hospitality in the world. And so it goes on, with more toasts, and yet more elaborate and sincere compliments, all expressed in the declamatory tones of a bard reciting an epic poem. Since the Kazakhs are the proud possessors of a great tradition of oral poetry, passed on by the bards, or *akyns*, in competitive recitals known as *aiytis*, it is not surprising that oratory seemed to come quite naturally to those present.

After all this high drama, Isa declares an interval, during which we will take the afternoon air outdoors, work up more appetite, dream up more toasts and await the presentation of the next course or two. Kuralay sets off into the woods on horseback and returns like a bee to the hive with saddlebags full of wild apples. I wander up a steep path and sample some sweet feral fruit, slipping the apple pips into my trouser pocket for later planting in Suffolk. Buzzards mew somewhere above the trees, and horses graze, tethered, under the shade of an orchard.

Back at the cottage, I sketch the outdoor summer kitchen, a Central Asian institution I am to encounter everywhere I go. Such places never fail to bring out the untutored architect in me, and I can't help dreaming of constructing some variation on the theme. Let loose on a personal garden city like Letchworth, Welwyn or Hampstead Garden Suburb, I would end up with something between a shanty town and an allotment. Cooking al fresco in an open-sided kitchen built in the garden close to the vegetables and compost heap, with its own wood-fired ovens, charcoal grill and range of sinks draining straight into an irrigation system growing melons, courgettes and gourds, seems to me a fine idea. Set apart from the house, the summer kitchen keeps all the smoke and cooking smells away from it, and allows the space and ventilation to spit-roast a whole lamb over a glowing, open fire, as the women and girls are busy doing now, or to bake quantities of bread in the splendid clay oven. Smoke billows out of the cob chimney as the women in headscarves and floral skirts and children in embroidered pillbox hats bustle about preparing and cooking the forthcoming courses.

The shallow-ridged tin roof of the summer kitchen covers the cob-built ramifications of oven, bakery and grill, and extends forward over a raised wooden working deck to form a veranda with three elegant arches of coppiced hazel that must have been bent and secured when still green. Balcony rails of hazel also run along the front of the kitchen, with wooden steps to its entrance and a wicket gate to keep the dogs out. I watch humming-bird hawk moths play round the marigolds in a flower bed in front. All the building materials for this little palace except the reused corrugated tin on its roof are local, simply dug up or cut down in coppice woods that will soon grow back again.

Just across the garden from the summer kitchen is the sauna, another half-cob, half-wooden shed, heated by a wood-stove with a water tank perched above it. In its cool, shadowy, whitewashed interior I find a bench on which to sit naked in the steamy heat, a plastic bowl and mug, a large jug and a bunch of leafy oak twigs for the traditional mild self-flagellation. Here again, the drainage pipe runs off conveniently into an irrigation trench in the vegetable garden.

An hour or so later, the lamb is served. It has been slaughtered specially for our visit, as is the custom. At the head of the table, Isa carves the head, deftly dissecting and sharing out the various symbolic organs. First, the ears for the children, 'that they may listen carefully and hear well in the forest'. Then the tender cheeks for the women, and the eyes for the two most senior foresters, to help keep them watchful for approaching dangers. I wonder what I might get, and am rewarded with a scallop of pinkness from just above the forehead, which they all assure me is the seat of the imagination. As head man, and perhaps as a professor, Isa spoons himself a liberal helping of the brains, then carves us all huge portions of the rest of the beast, including the greatly relished fat from around the tail. Kazakhs have a liking for fat-bottomed sheep, bred for the rump of fat either side of the tail.

We now add to our plates portions of a kind of pasta to make *beshbarmak*, which roughly translates as 'five fingers' because the dish is traditionally eaten by hand. Isa also insists I accept the choice globules of prized fat from around the sheep's ample bottom. More wine ensues, with a magnificent forest fruit salad, honey, fresh green walnuts, melon, cakes, more chai, and further, supplementary toasts and votes of thanks. Then, abruptly, Isa says grace and the meal is over, with many a double handshake and invitation to return as we all line up outside for a group photograph, then clamber back in the jeep and bounce away downhill in our swarming cloud of dust.

South to the Walnut Forests

I set out early with Luisa and Johnny in the driving-school Lada for the Barakholka, the sprawling flea-market bazaar, and the bus station beyond it in the west of Almaty where the taxis leave for Kyrgyzstan. We were met by a jostling crowd of drivers before a phalanx of cars, all loudly competing to drive me across the border into Kyrgyzstan and Bishkek, its capital. The journey is 150 miles and takes five hours by bus at a fare of £1.50. Taxis cost more but are faster, less crowded, and less prone to delays and breakdowns. Johnny claimed to be a connoisseur of taxi drivers and had kindly offered to help me pick a good car and negotiate a fare. Out of a selection of physically abused cars, Johnny picked out a big, square yellow Mercedes with a massively crazed windscreen with two big holes the size of boulders on the passenger side. Its driver, Nurgazy, was a sharp and streetwise 25-year-old with a close-cropped head of black hair and a round face like an apple behind a natty pair of wrap-around sunglasses. Johnny seemed to think he would be a good bet. An older man was already installed in the car, and Nurgazy said he would take me to Bishkek for 2,000 tenge, if I didn't mind waiting for a third passenger, or I could pay 3,000 and we could go straight away. I opted for the latter, less than £15, bade farewell to Johnny and Luisa, and jumped in.

Nurgazy was indeed a great driver, if utterly anarchic. The Mercedes had once been luxurious, and I settled into the black Rexine of the deep back seat. I had it to myself and was glad of it. As soon as we were out of town the road deteriorated into a random pattern of craters on a wide, bumpy highway lined with elms and robinia. Nurgazy sped along at a constant 60 miles per hour or more, overtaking everything in sight and nudging other drivers out of his way by dint of the sheer bulk and headlong speed of the Mercedes. He wove between the potholes with the grace and skill of a dancer, simultaneously channel-hopping on the radio, losing patience with anything that wasn't either house or accordion music, turning it up to full volume. 'I am the God of House', obviously number one in the Kazakh house charts, rang out across the steppes as we sped along with the Heavenly Mountains to our left and a huge, flat, treeless horizon to our right.

Soon we were alone on the road. Herds of cattle or horses grazed the dry, brown grasses of the open steppe, with now and again a huge flock of fat-tailed sheep and a solitary shepherd on horseback. Long fissures gaped open in the parched earth. We saw distant yurts closer to the mountains, and the occasional low shed or haystack, but they were the only signs of habitation. Before long even these were left behind, and we were far out at sea in the infinities of the old nomads. My fellow passenger in the front seat, a wizened, olive-skinned man in the pillbox hat of an Uzbek, had lost most of his teeth and kept turning round to address me in Kyrgyz. Somehow I gathered that he was a tobacconist on his return journey to the great Osh Bazaar in Bishkek, where he had a stall. His name was Abit, and when he showed me his passport I was amazed to see that a man I had assumed was in his early seventies was in fact no more than fifty. Looking me confidentially in the eye, Abit delved into his bag and offered me some black seeds in a pear-shaped wooden receptacle plugged with a bundle of tiny sticks lashed together with cotton. He indicated in mime that the seeds would propel me into a heightened state of consciousness. I politely declined, although fascinated by the pear-shaped box and curious about the seeds.

Once in Kyrgyzstan, the road changed dramatically. It halved in width and began winding up through low, grassy hills. We passed a yurt in a grove of wild apples above the road and began to see old snub-nosed Russian lorries laden with straw. We were moving closer towards the wrinkled mountains, climbing steeply through bare crags. In the distance across the steppe, plumes of smoke rose where the dry grass was being burnt to improve its fertility.

As we approached Bishkek, the empty road was suddenly busy and the open steppe landscape altered to one of small fields full of vegetables, melons and little orchards. Cattle and horses stood in tiny paddocks. Cottages, tents, sheds and yurts crowded together in the shanties of the outskirts. Groups of men squatted at the roadsides chatting or just watching the world go by. Warm, dusty air filled the car through the holes in the windscreen. The road was so bad I grew used to Nurgazy swinging the wheel suddenly to avoid big, open manholes. Kamikaze pedestrians came at us from all sides, apparently throwing themselves in our path. It wasn't the traffic that slowed us to a standstill so much as sheer numbers of people on the streets outside the enormous Osh Bazaar, where we set down Abit, smiling his toothless farewell, his bags of cigarettes tied up with twine, and somewhere about his person the box of black seeds. He disappeared from view almost instantly among the crowds and stalls.

Good as his word, Nurgazy drove me to Togolok Moldo, a street in the centre of Bishkek named after a wandering bard, where I had arranged to meet Zamira, who was to be my interpreter and guide. We had exchanged several dozen emails before I left England, so felt almost like old friends when we met at last. Zamira's smile would have won me over instantly anyway. Zamira was always smiling, or at least her eyes were, always apparently calm and happy. She never once complained of any of the many discomforts or difficulties of our travels. For a woman in her early twenties, she was amazingly composed, and for one who had never set foot outside Kyrgyzstan in all her life, she spoke astonishingly good

English. Zamira's whole family were linguists, speaking about a dozen different languages between them.

The journey I planned was to the south of Kyrgyzstan, to Jalal-Abad via Osh in the Ferghana Valley, Kyrgyzstan's second city after Bishkek and an ancient crossroads for the Silk Road caravans. It still boasts a huge market and is the base for mountaineers heading into the Pamir range. With more time, I might have chosen to make the spectacular 435-mile journey south by road, but it takes between twelve and nineteen hours and I wanted to reach Jalal-Abad and the walnut forests while the nut harvest was still in full swing, so decided to go in one of the small planes that fly over the 16,000-foot wall of the Kyrgyz Alatau Mountains that rises straight up behind Bishkek. The planes thread their way south along the glaciers and steep gorges to the Ferghana Valley, where the walnut and wild fruit forests are. Flights sometimes varied according to the availability of petrol, but the airport promised a plane to Osh at six that evening.

Somehow thirty-six of us jammed into the tiny plane. The temperature climbed alarmingly in the steamy cabin as more and more people clambered aboard, laden with cardboard boxes and carrier bags that they calmly stacked to the roof in front of the emergency exit and in the minuscule gangway. Nobody had bothered much about checking the baggage anyway, and I began to wonder whether some of us would end up strap-hanging. We took off and climbed steeply towards the mountains over fields and foothills, long skeins of smoke rising and hanging where farmers were burning off grass far below. Then we were skimming snowy tops that rose to 23,000 feet, lakes and tarns winking up from the purple shadows of valleys and the glistening sinews of glaciers and mountain rivers racing through gorges. A soft mist gathered about the peaks, and, as evening drew on, wave upon wave of the darkening shapes of mountains advanced towards us. It was almost dark as we approached Osh, following the winding mirror of the Ak-Buura River flowing out of the Pamir Alay Mountains.

★

I was awakened early by the massed cockerels of Osh. There had been heavy rain overnight, and as I lay in bed I could hear the first traffic splashing through deep puddles in the potholed streets. Unfamiliar birdsong floated in, and a thin steam rose off the windowsills. I found myself in a faded hotel suite of two bedrooms, bathroom and huge sitting room full of ancient threadbare sofas draped in rugs. I felt very much at home; even more so when the hotelier brought in a breakfast tray of fresh, hot bread, honey, butter and chai. I even enjoyed the stampede of silverfish that fled the bathroom and the rusty water of the shower. I knew for certain I was going to like Kyrgyzstan.

Zamira was already up and busy arranging a taxi to Jalal-Abad. Everyone was helpful and relaxed, the hotel almost empty. We were soon out of Osh and ambling through a landscape of small fields of maize, cotton and rice, past shepherds and cowherds in the road with flocks of fat-tailed sheep or cattle we always narrowly missed. Gangs of women in headscarves and bright floral frocks picked cotton, dressed, in fact, remarkably like the women you used to see on the covers of Richard and Linda Thompson or Incredible String Band albums, or almost any of the handsome women you would meet in Suffolk at the Barsham Fair in 1970, or at the Hood Fair in Devon about the same era. Everywhere women were hard at work, hanging out washing, harvesting, shelling walnuts, building hayricks or even making mud bricks to bake in the sun while the men stood about chatting languidly in every village or squatted together at the roadside wearing their traditional tall Kyrgyz hats of embroidered felt, the *ak kalpak*, or the ornate pillbox hats of the Uzbeks. By now the sun was strong and warm, so I could only conclude that the thick felt *kalpaks* were intended to insulate heat out as well as in, along the same lines as the heavy woollen Berber *djeleba* of the Sahara. The effect, when a group of men all wearing *kalpaks* stood about talking, was of a miniature snowy mountain range.

Picket fences of willow sticks surrounded the cottage gardens, and melon-sellers sat beside the road. Each village was an oasis of poplars, the universal building material. The poles are tall, straight, and the wood is easy to work. So long as it is kept dry, poplar will last for years. You even find it in timber-framed houses or barns in Suffolk, often in the roof. Here the barns were all of poplar frame, whole trees forming the floor joists, rafters, and the uprights and diagonals of the walls, which were in-filled with cob bricks. Piles of these bricks, which were simply wet clay, straw and cow dung mixed and rolled together into the size and shape of loaves, lay baking in the sun. The mortar the mostly Uzbek villagers of the Ferghana Valley used was also clay, and the cob wall would eventually be daubed in clay plaster, liberally mixed with cow dung to make it waterproof. Just painting a cob wall with a coat of cow dung is enough to waterproof it.

At Ozgon we stopped to explore the ancient minaret and the mausoleum where the rulers of the Qarakanids, a long-extinct warlike people of Turkish origin, lie buried: just the sort of places Robert Byron, in his *Road to Oxiana*, sought out so single-mindedly in 1936 from Persia to Afghanistan. The place brought back strong echoes of Byron's description of another of the great mausoleums, the Gumbad-I-Kabus in Persia, also a symphony in brick where the body of the Kabus, suspended from the roof in a glass coffin after his death in 1007, was said to shine and glint like a lighthouse across the steppes of Central Asia. The giant doors of the Ozgon mausoleum, intricately carved from plane, opened under 900-year-old lintels of cedar. Three enormous domes of red brick floated on brick columns rendered all the more like trees by dense decorative patterns of leaves and fruit. The minaret too was a forest of earthen leaves. Distant groves of poplars punctuated the huge fertile rice-growing plain below Ozgon, and we glimpsed stretches of the rivers that meandered into the great Surdarya River, flowing west through Uzbekistan and Kazakhstan into the parched and shrunken bed of what was once the Aral Sea.

Under a beating sun, we climbed out of Ozgon into an arid landscape of yellow hills, red earth and rock. Below us in the valley cattle and horses sought shade among the waving bamboos of the rice fields. We were passing an endless stream of people walking, walking, walking in the dust both ways along the road. Drovers on horseback looked unconcerned as we sped past more cattle, more sheep and big dark brown woolly dogs. A huge steel oil barrel lying on its side by the road had been turned into a cabin with windows set in its walls, a stove-pipe and a front door. A Kyrgyz Diogenes sat outside minding a flock of turkeys in a maize field behind. 'Too many people here and not enough land or water,' said Zamira. Three quarters of the villages in the Osh region still have no access to drinking water, and typhoid is on the increase. With a dense rural population of 400 to the square kilometre there is also a desperate shortage of housing. Yet everywhere people were working hard and the cob-and-poplar barns were full of maize. Women in striking patchwork dresses of red, yellow, green and blue picked cotton with young boys, and by a village stream shaded by pollard willows a small girl led an enormous cow on a rope. The swish of willows and the shady stream felt for a moment like home, like Dorset, but then we were off again, slaloming potholes in our cloud of dust, climbing gently all the way to Jalal-Abad.

We headed for the quaintly named district of Sputnik to look for Zakir Zarimsakov at the offices of Jalal-Abad's Forestry Department. I had first heard about Zakir from Barrie Juniper in Oxford. 'Quite simply the best botanist you could hope to meet. Knows every tree and plant there is in Kyrgyzstan. You might just be lucky and find he's in town and willing to help.' By a small miracle, one of my messages had reached him. They did have telephones at the Forestry Office, and email too, but people would keep stealing the telephone cables for the copper they contain, so they often went incommunicado for days. In Jalal-Abad you always kept your telephone covered with a cloth, not out of modesty or for security but to keep out the dust.

Zakir arrived and showed us into his office. He was a fit-looking, well-built man in his forties, and every line in his weathered face ended in a smile. Working in shirtsleeves and open neck, he had an air of relaxed authority that communicated a warm informality to his staff. A big map of the upper Ferghana Valley was pinned on the wall, the areas of walnut forest shaded in green: by far the greatest, and probably the oldest, wild walnut forests in the world. Green tentacles of forest ran up the valleys of the Ark-Terek range and followed the contours around an average elevation of 9,000 feet. A collection of walnuts of all sizes and forms lay on Zakir's table like bowls on a green. Hand-labelled jam jars of them stood in rows on top of a cupboard. The miracle of the walnut forests and wild fruit woods, said Zakir, is that they were planted by God, not man. In southern Kyrgyzstan there are one and a half million acres of them. Gathered round the map, we began to outline a possible journey through the mountain forests. Zakir, it turned out, would be only too happy to join us a couple of days later for an exploration of the woods, travelling by Russian jeep and on foot, staying in farmhouses, cottages or cabins along the way. In the meantime, it was agreed, Zamira and I would arrange a jeep and driver, and set off next morning for Ortok, a village 6,000 feet up in the fruit forests to the east of Jalal-Abad.

We had arranged to be collected by Gena and his Lada jeep, ready to set out for Ortok and the walnut forests. A toot on the horn, and there he was, down in the street. Dressed in T-shirt, navy tracksuit bottoms and the Chinese trainers everyone seemed to wear, Gena was lean and fit, and in his early thirties. He was good-looking too, in the high-cheekboned, narrow-eyed way of the Kyrgyz people. But he also had the deadpan look and the slightly hooded eyes of Buster Keaton, and we were to discover his talent for clowning. As a tank driver in the Russian Army for six years, he had seen plenty of action and certainly knew how to handle a jeep.

Gena's full name was Egdenberdi Oljobaeb, and he was to be our cook as well as driver. He owned a small café/restaurant and billiard hall in town, and he and his partner Rafjan had saved up and bought a Russian jeep together so they could hire themselves out as drivers for cross-country journeys or expeditions. We took the bumpy road towards Ortok and the mountains, passing groves of pistachio bushes and almond trees all over the dry, brown hillsides. In every village, men stood about in *kalpaks* while the women laboured in the cotton fields. Gena at the wheel of his Mark Two Lada was soon in high spirits, singing snatches of song and swerving deliberately whenever he could to scatter flocks of turkeys. Poplars and pollard willows lined the road as we began winding up the valley of the Kork-Art River, gleaming in its wide stony bed and in the rice fields it watered.

We had climbed into the most beautiful stretch of parched and rolling yellow hills, which seemed to go on for ever into the intensely blue sky. Mothers and farm children sat making bricks of mud and straw, which would be baked in the sun and then used to build the cob walls of new barns. Sparrows blew in clouds along elm hedges that could have bordered lanes in the Somerset Levels. Skylarks rose up like messages on kite strings. Below us the silver river ran faster than it had before and snaked about between luscious green rice paddies. Haystacks whizzed by, and on the hillsides mynah birds strutted about the backs of dark brown cattle. As we went still higher, thickets of wild apple and hawthorn, whose succulent berries we had bought in the bazaar, began to appear in the hills. In a clearing I caught sight of a yurt, a horse, a tethered calf and two women firing up a bread oven.

There were wild apples here too: beautiful, rugged trees, their branches arched over with the weight of rosy fruit, just like their cousins in Kazakhstan. Zamira and I braced ourselves as Gena hurled the bucking jeep up the stony track, gripping our steel panic-handles as we climbed steeply, then levelled off on the ridge.

There were the first walnuts: a few occasional clumps of big, gnarled trees growing among the apples, wild hollyhocks, yellow butterflies and old man's beard. Then, as we rounded another spur, clouds of vivid walnut green surged up the hillsides like the dense up-curling smoke of a bonfire. Softening the contours of the mountains, the canopy of the walnut forest mantled the entire landscape between 3,000 and 6,000 feet. Only the higher slopes, with their stubble of juniper, rose out of the great sea of green to the distant snowy mountain-tops over towards China in the east.

We were now in the walnut forest on a dusty holloway that wound for a dozen miles along the steep sides of gorges high above streams or rivers below. In the winter rains and snow, said Gena, such tracks are treacherous with mud or ice. Everything up here becomes thick red mud and nothing can move for it. Now it was a thick layer of the lightest, most powdery dust imaginable. The walnut trees dwarfed any I had ever seen before, even in France or Italy. Some were as much as ninety or a hundred feet tall, and most were sixty feet, all with immense, sculptured trunks. Beneath the canopy, the wood felt airy and open like wood pasture, with little sunny glades and paths, and a great sweep of silver-grey trunk before the first branches between fifteen and twenty feet off the ground. We saw the pale flanks of cows flickering through the woods as they wandered in and out of shadow and sunlight. A boy called and waved to us from a treetop as we passed, and three women, a mother and two daughters, led a donkey laden with sacks of fresh nuts down a rocky path. The forest had all the steepness and cathedral scale of a Chiltern beech hangar combined with the fruitfulness and bustle of an English orchard at harvest time. A cockerel stood in the track. Gena deliberately near-missed it by inches. 'What if we hit it?' I asked. 'We pay the farmer. They're only about fifty som.' It was nearly lunch-time when we rounded a steep hairpin and dropped down into Ortok. We arrived outside the forestry office, almost the first wooden building in the single village street, a wide mud road, deeply rutted, fringed by tall poplars and single-storey wooden dachas.

Set back behind a front garden full of vegetables, wallflowers and marigolds, the forestry office acted as village post office, having a short-wave radio as the only means of communication with the outside world. Here we met Kaspar Schmidt, a Swiss forestry academic whom I had contacted in advance from England through Barrie Juniper and Peter Savill in Oxford. Both had met Kaspar here the year before. In cooperation with Zakir and the Forestry

Department, Kaspar was working on a Ph.D. study of the walnut forests and their culture, and had come up to stay in Ortok to try to find out from local farmers how the forest impacts on their lives and subsistence. He had helped arrange a place for our little party to stay, and took us up to meet Buruma at her farmhouse on a hillside in the village.

Buruma, round faced and olive skinned, was sitting shelling a big heap of walnuts in the farmyard. She wore a long red dress, pink headscarf and grey felt waistcoat, and was assisted by her mother, a frail, deaf, ninety-year-old lady who never seemed to move from her station in the shade of an even older, more wrinkled fruiting hawthorn tree. Walnuts lay spread out to dry on sacking all round the yard, even on the raised porch, and Buruma's tiered rows of beehives rose up the hillside beside the house. Everyone in Ortok had beehives, whitewashed to keep the bees cool inside and to help guide them home. The farmhouse and its yard were perched on a terrace in the steep hillside above a gorge and a river, looking across to a dense walnut forest canopy that covered the opposite side of the valley, rising over the hilltop and beyond sight to the head of the valley. Whenever I see a forest like this, steep and luxuriant, I think of Nestor Almendros's camera panning majestically over the French chestnut forests to a soundtrack of Vivaldi's mandolin concerto at the beginning of François Truffaut's *L'Enfant Sauvage*.

While Buruma prepared lunch, I went exploring. The house itself was a single-storey wooden structure, entered up a set of wide wooden steps into a porch with a *tapchan* covered in coloured woven rugs and cushions. The collection of shoes and galoshes just inside the door supplied clues about the inhabitants: boy, girl, mother, grandmother. The father was away in the woods for the walnut harvest. The elegant galoshes lined with felt were the perfect mud-proof footwear for slipping on and off with ease at the threshold, according to custom. Each time I did this I had to lace or unlace my walking boots and was always left behind by the others.

Across the yard at the edge of the terrace, with a fine view of the woods, was the wonderfully economical bathroom: a post with a tin-roofed soap dish on top and a two-litre piston-operated water cistern hanging from a peg. The value such an economical washing system set on water seemed to me the very height of civilization. In the morning, when we needed hot water for shaving, Buruma filled the cistern with warm water. A hand towel hung on a nearby apple tree growing out of the centre of a lorry tyre, which could be filled with water during dry weather, allowing it to percolate into the roots. Everything on the farm, down to the plank-built drop-latrine at the far corner of the land, effectively a composting system, was turned to the economy of nature in an entirely unself-conscious way. Buruma would probably never have heard the word 'green' applied to anything other than a walnut leaf, yet life and farming in Ortok was essentially organic in character. Bees foraged in the wild fruit forests. The people went out and harvested walnuts, apples and all sorts of other wild fruit and fungi from the forest. Their cattle, horses, donkeys and flocks of turkeys grazed it, and they manured their domestic orchards and gardens from the farm-yard. The farm dogs lived in an ingenious tin-roofed two-storeyed kennel constructed of simple poles of poplar lashed together, with walls of woven wattle and daub. They had made the daub by mixing clay, straw and cow dung with water, slapping it on inside and out. I admired its simple architecture, equalled only by the kennels of hollow tree-trunks I had seen in southern Poland.

For lunch, Buruma had laid out bowls of fresh green walnuts, honey, yoghurt, nan, chai, and, greatest delicacy of all, walnuts in syrup. The soft, unripe fruits steeped in sugar and their own dark juices were the candied equivalent of the Catalan dish of *calamares en su tinta*, in which the squid are stewed in their own ink. These were the first of a great many succulent Ortok walnuts we were to enjoy.

After lunch Zamira and I walked down through the village and took a steep path uphill through the forest. Gena wandered off to feed the farmyard turkeys, gather some walnuts for his family and take his siesta on some grassy bank. As soon as we entered the woods I realized they were full of people. The almost vertical track rose through towering walnuts, their grey, cracked bark swollen and blistered into burrs. They were heroic, dishevelled trees, and they were laden with walnuts. During late September and October thousands of people in the Ferghana Valley migrate to the forest and set up camp for up to six weeks to harvest the walnuts. We had entered the world of Thomas Hardy and *The Woodlanders*. The sounds of woodland work were everywhere. People called to each other across the valley or through the leaves. A boy greeted us from high up in a tree and shook down a hail of nuts. Further on Zamira even encountered an old schoolfriend of hers from Bishkek in the fork of another venerable walnut. He had come to help his relations in their woodland camp with the harvest, and she carried on a conversation with him thirty feet above us. He sat astride a bough and called down to us without a hint of vertigo. People climbed the trees to shake down the nuts, many still sheathed in the bright-green fleshy tegument, while other family members and relations combed the forest floor and picked them up. Everyone carried a shoulder bag or sack, and, like them, we shelled and ate walnuts as we went.

A little way into the woods, not far from the top of the steepest part of the ascent, we saw a camp in a little clearing on a level place. Our path branched and led that way, and, as we passed, the older of two women sitting shelling walnuts outside their tent invited us to come and rest and have a cup of tea with them. We gladly assented and stepped into their neatly organized camp, with bright rugs on the ground before the entrance of a good-sized ridge tent, tall enough to stand up in down the middle and roomy enough, by the look of it, for four or five to sleep in. We sat in the saddles of several logs beside the morning's harvest of walnuts spread out to dry in the afternoon sun. We introduced ourselves, and Aitbu sent her teenage daughter Gulbarchyn to find wood for the fire. Both women wore long quilted dresses to their ankles, Aitbu's dark blue and purple in a bold floral pattern, Gulbarchyn's crimson, showing off her plaits of long black hair. Aitbu's family were from Ortok, and they had harvested this particular part of the forest since she was a child.

Gulbarchyn returned with a bundle of sticks and lit the fire in a blackened open fireplace of clay and stone, with a circular ledge a foot above the fire pit that accommodated the *kazan*, the heavy steel cooking pan, shaped like a big wok, in which every Kyrgyz family cooks nearly every meal. Around the fire was an ingenious arrangement of spits and bits of bent iron designed to suspend things over it. Gulbarchyn filled a large kettle from a water drum, and Aitbu set out a cloth on the ground with a bowl of honey, another of fresh shelled walnuts and several flat loaves of nan. I cannot think of a more delicious combination than wet walnuts and mountain honey. Added to this was the pleasure, all too rare now in England, of eating food in its natural season and in its own place.

By now, having shelled and eaten a good many nuts, my hands and Zamira's were nearly as black as everyone else's. Everyone in Ortok had black hands, stained by the potent dye in the walnuts, especially in the sappy green husk that mantles the woody nutshell. Sit peeling these off for a few hours and your hands soon took on the dark tan leathery look that marked out the inhabitants of the Ortok woods. As Gulbarchyn poured out the chai, we were joined by her brother Asylbek, carrying yet another sack of walnuts. The whole family were musicians, and they all sang and played together in a family band. In their love of folksong and horses, and instinctive respect for poets, the Kyrgyz kept reminding me of the Irish. Before we rose to go, Gulbarchyn shyly presented me with a walking stick of wild plum she had been whittling by the fireside, and the little family invited us to supper with them in the camp next day.

On the hilltop, we undulated along a ridge track, very dusty and eroded from the passage of horses, carts, tractors and pickup trucks. Beneath the cathedral of great walnut trees an under-storey of wild apples, cherry plums and the sweet fruiting hawthorn, *Crataegus ponticus*, grew in thickets and clearings. Many of these apples were the same species I had encountered in Kazakhstan, *Malus sieversus*, but we also found a good many groves of *Malus kyrgyzorum* with its small, tangy rosy-veined fruit. We picked wild apples as we went and sampled them, and I pocketed all the pips to take home as seed to try to raise in Suffolk. Most were sweet enough, with enough sharpness and tanginess to be interesting. Every now and again we encountered another family camp, and were invariably invited in for tea, bread and honey, and fresh walnuts. Combined with the apples, it was a healthy-enough diet, and we had no need of Mars bars to keep us going. The talk was invariably of walnuts, which were as varied in size and form as the honey was in flavour. Everyone we met insisted on giving us their prize specimens. The really big ones were called Bomba ('the bomb') and were much sought after.

Nearly all the men wore the *kalpak* and climbed giant trees in nothing more hi-tech than wellington boots to shake down the nuts. They scorned the use of ropes, harnesses or climbing gear of any sort, relying on nothing more than their bare hands. Everywhere in the woods we heard the sound of scuffed dry leaves and the thunder of nuts drumming to the ground in sudden cascades. You would hear a whistle somewhere above you and look up, and there would be someone perched in the canopy, half hidden by leaves, rustling and swishing a branch to dislodge the obstinate nuts, setting the whole tree a-tremble. Or you would hear a song floating over the forest high up and think of angels, until a fresh shower of nuts came down and keen-eyed children appeared out of the under-shrub to scrabble about for the bright green nuts. Of course, there were accidents and sometimes fatalities. People fell out of trees every year, and there were broken bones or worse. Walnuts are not the most reliable of trees to climb. Their branches are susceptible to rot and can often break off. Some of the trunks rise straight up for twenty or even thirty feet before the first branches, so aren't easy to climb. Others, with their warty, creviced bark erupting into hand-holds of knots and burrs, began branching almost at ground level like irregular stepladders, as if defying anyone *not* to climb them. The only consolation was that the deep, springy leaf mould of the forest floor might soften your fall.

I felt oddly at home in the walnut forest, with its mosses and lichens and venerable, contorted trees, perhaps because I live with a walnut tree outside my bedroom window in Suffolk, or perhaps because the forest had a similar character and atmosphere to an English oak wood. Ortok and Hintock, the village in *The Wood-landers*, even sounded like echoes of each other. The woodland paths were like green lanes or droves, and the next camp, in the wide verges of a grassy droveway, had exactly the feeling of an English gypsy encampment. Four tethered horses grazed before the main khaki tent, almost a small marquee, probably originally used as an officers' mess by the Russian Army on field manoeuvres. I had never seen such an impressive collection of vintage tents, and admit to coveting nearly all of them.

Zamira and I must have looked an unlikely couple wandering through the woods so far away from anywhere, and were the object of frank and open curiosity wherever we went. Who was I? How old was I? How many children did I have? When I told them 'one', they didn't believe me. Children existed only in the plural here: nobody could possibly have just the one. To have a single son would be like keeping a single chicken, or growing a solitary potato. As if to underline this, Kurmanbek's prodigiously extended family sat in a semicircle in the entrance of the tent and brought cushions for us and yet more tea and walnuts. His young children Timirlan, Jangyl and Dilaram took us into a little glade to meet their donkey foal. It was barely three days old, and the children seemed to have complete charge of the animal and its docile mother. Kurmanbek's wife said they had been camping for ten days and would stay a month longer. It was a good year for walnuts. Other years weren't so good, especially if there were spring frosts after the trees flowered and the young nuts began to form. The families brought every-thing with them: all their livestock, dogs, cows and horses, even their *induk* – their turkeys. Flocks of these sleek, magnificent birds ran free through the woods, in exhilarating contrast to the concentration-camp conditions in which they are almost invariably kept in Britain. But was it really worth while to endure the hardship of camping out to harvest a few nuts? 'Most certainly it is,' they all agreed with a passion. It wasn't just that it was a family custom to get away each autumn from the daily round to a kind of dacha in the forest. It was also a great social occasion, when families would meet others in the evenings round the fire and share a meal or drink vodka together. And, in any case, it was pleasant, sociable work, and the returns were good.

Between them, the family would gather one or two tons of nuts in the course of the season, and in a really bounteous year, as much as five tons. Some of the woodlanders would even stay on until the end of November.

We circled back, turning for home at a hilltop crossroads of the green lanes marked by an ancient walnut tree, presiding over travellers as an old oak might do in similar places in parts of Wales or England. Riders with bulging panniers of walnuts passed us on the holloway that plunged downhill and slowed their horses to converse with us as they went. In every camp we passed, harvesters were upending sacks into green mounds of the day's nuts, ready to be husked and spread out on the ground to dry in pools of pale brown. I felt moved and elated by the universally cordial atmosphere that suffused the forest: we shook hands with everyone we met, so that the black stain of the walnut juice became a badge of friendship and hospitality in this place. Everyone gave us walnuts, always carefully choosing their very best. Our pockets swelled, our hands blackened. The sound of autumn leaves, scuffed or falling on to the leaf mould, deep and crisp and uneven, lisped through the trees.

The Forestry Department maintained a dacha as a hostel at one end of the village for visiting workers and students of the forester's art. Kaspar and some of his fellow woodfolk entertained us to dinner there. We ate wild pistachios, followed by *plov*, a rice pilaf of meat and vegetables cooked in the *kazan*. As is the custom, we all shared the same pan. Kaspar had gone off on horseback through the woods that afternoon on another of his ethnographic expeditions among the hill farmers. I had been amazed at the sheer numbers of people we saw living and working in the forest. It was like stepping into the Middle Ages, or into the pages of *The Woodlanders*. Kaspar said 10,000 people were camped out in the Ferghana Valley for the walnuts just now. The harvest was an essential feature of their lives, economically and culturally. Besides picking walnuts, they gather wild apples and cherry plums for jam, and all manner of berries and medicinal herbs.

Kaspar explained how things work here. There are almost 12,500 acres of walnut forest around Ortok producing at least 350 tons of nuts most years. But walnuts are susceptible to late-spring frosts, which wither their buds and flowers, and a bumper crop comes only about once every five years. The wild apples, cherry plums and berries of the forest generally render a really good crop every three years. By talking to farmers in the villages surrounding the forest, Kaspar was trying to work out how it could be saved from the increasing human pressure that was already damaging and reducing it and could eventually erode it out of existence. The main problem, he said, was cattle grazing and haymaking, both of which were officially forbidden in the forest, but had been widespread ever since the relative anarchy and poverty that came with independence and the end of the Soviet Union at the beginning of the 1990s. By grazing the sapling walnuts, livestock prevent the forest from regenerating naturally, and the haymakers' scythes have a similar effect. Grazing and haymaking both hamper plant conservation.

But the gathering of nuts and fruits also disturbs the natural process of forest renewal by depriving it of seeds. Increased hunting has further depleted the wild life of the forest. All these difficulties arise from the huge growth in the population of the Ferghana Valley over the past twenty years. The hamlets that surround the forest have suddenly mushroomed into densely populated settlements of 5,000 to 8,000 people, most of them keeping livestock, and sixty to seventy per cent of them unemployed. Everyone needs fuel wood, and gathers wild fruit and nuts, and the high value of walnut as timber tempts some to illegal tree-felling.

Walnut timber has always been highly valued, and there is plenty of evidence of past depredations to the Ferghana Valley forests. During 1882 alone, records show over 30,000 bullock carts of walnut timber sold in the great Uzbek bazaar of Margilan. Over the past eighty years the forests of southern Kyrgyzstan haven't altered much in extent, but during the period between the first forest survey of 1894–7 and 1926, the forests were widely clear-felled for timber, or to provide more arable land, and their area reduced by half. French and English timber merchants came prospecting for walnut burrs to manufacture veneer. They are extremely valuable, and at the time the price of a pound of burr was equivalent to the price of a pound of silver. You can still see the scars on some of the older trees where these European timber dealers cut off burrs and left the trees standing. From 1896 to 1926 some 500 tonnes of walnut burr were exported from the Kyrgyz forests to England and France. During the Second World War walnuts were again felled to provide gunstocks for the Russian Army: 140,000 cubic metres of timber between 1938 and 1942, in fact. The Soviets kept precise records.

They also cared enough about the value and interest of the forests to send two scientific expeditions to the region. N. I. Vavilov, leader of the first of these in 1935, believed, correctly, that all the world's walnuts originated in these forests and those of the mountains of Afghanistan and China. He concluded that since the Central Asian wild fruit forests contained a genetic fund of international significance, their conservation would be of far greater long-term value than any short-term benefits from economic exploitation. The 1945 expedition of the USSR Academy of Sciences was led by the eminent scientist Vladimir Nikolaevitch Sukachev and comprised no fewer than three academicians, twelve doctors and professors, twenty-four professional scientific assistants and 152 other scientific employees. Its findings led to the creation of the Southern Kyrgyz Fruit Reserve, covering all the forests in the Ferghana Valley. Cattle grazing, haymaking, tree-cutting and hunting were all prohibited in the forests, and the gathering of walnuts regulated. These conservation measures seem to have worked well enough under the Soviet regime, but the foresters have experienced increasing difficulty enforcing them since independence in 1991.

In all the twenty-five or thirty thousand years since the forest first developed, it has probably never been under such pressure. So many of the questions we discussed that night seemed to be universal dilemmas for nature conservation everywhere. The walnut forests were, after all, a kind of commons in which ordinary local people could reasonably feel they should have a share. Their needs are immediate: food, the harvest work and its modest wages, subsistence for their livestock, and what we would call in Britain 'air and exercise' – a more urgent version of the need for a change of scenery that we would call a holiday, camping or an allotment. Only a couple of generations ago, until the 1920s, the local Kyrgyz people were nomads or transhumant herders, accustomed to moving uphill into the mountains for the summer grazing and living under the stars. The Uzbeks were small farmers who had always supplemented their modest economy by foraging and grazing animals in the wild forest.

Yet these wild walnut and fruit forests comprise no fewer than 183 different tree and shrub species, 34 of which exist only in Central Asia, with 16 endemic to southern Kyrgyzstan. In turn, there is a huge variety of flowering plants and medicinal herbs, and a fauna that includes brown bears, snow leopards, wild boar, roe-deer, badgers, marmots, porcupines, golden eagles and a great number of other birds. A number of the forests' species are now thought to be at risk of extinction. Four of the beautiful, delicate wild roses could be lost, along with their exotic names: *Rosa webbiana*, *Rosa laxa*, *Rosa wasilczenkoi* and *Rosa beggeriana*. Also becoming worryingly scarce are seven of the wild honeysuckles that clamber about the woods, two species of wild pear, and five of the many different willows. I seemed to have heard this story before.

Beyond its undoubted conservation value, the forest performs a vital geographical function in acting as a giant sponge to absorb the rains and even out the flow of water through the many mountain rivers. Without the forest roots to hold the soil together, and trees to take up and contain water, landslides, mudslides and floods would all increase in winter. The climate of the whole valley would alter too, deprived of the humidity of the woods and the leaves of walnuts precipitating dew and rain.

At bedtime I fished out walnuts from every pocket like a squirrel and stashed them at the bedside. Then I put the wild apple pips from my trouser pocket in a labelled plastic bag. I thought I might try sowing them in a corner of my vegetable garden in Suffolk and raise an orchard. Gena, with whom I shared the room, had a sack of walnuts to show for his afternoon's work, although he claimed to have eaten more than he kept. Walking home up the side of the valley in the dark, we had passed cattle asleep in the middle of the caked mud road. As we crossed the farmyard, a puppy approached us, uncertain whether to be fierce or friendly. The turkeys roosting in the big walnut tree by the house were silhouetted in the moon-light. Somewhere up in the village, a donkey creaked dolorously into voice. Buruma brought warm water, and I washed off the dust of the day at the post and cistern, then lay on a hard mattress under a beautiful floral quilt. A small dog barked across the valley, and the farm cockerel sounded as if it was bursting into tears. The cool mountain air drifting in through the open bedroom window reminded me that we were 6,000 feet up. Drugged by a million walnut leaves, I slept well.

I was sad to leave Ortok and all its woodlanders. Buruma gave me a jar of her superb walnuts in syrup. She had picked them while they were still soft and green, before the shell began to form, boiled them in syrup and bottled them. We had eaten them at breakfast each morning, and I wasn't sure I could live without them. Gena fed the turkeys a few parting crusts, and we all shook hands with the deaf ninety-year-old grandmother on her chair under the apple tree. Up in the village, we met Kaspar and trooped past the lupins in the front garden into the foresters' cottage to find the radio operator wearing headphones the size of coconuts in front of an elaborate bank of amplifiers and tuning devices, fiddling with the controls. He was picking up interference, he said, and I wondered if it might be the starlings on the aerial outside. No, he said, it was the Americans flying troop planes out of Bishkek into Kabul. We sent a radio message to Zakir back in Jalal-Abad telling him to expect us later in the day.

Turning to wave goodbye to our hosts as we drove away in Gena's jeep, we found them already obscured by the plume of dust. We seemed to bounce down the mountainside in no time, past walnuts, past apples and wild blackcurrant bushes, past mud barns and haystacks, half-hidden yurts in the trees, scampering turkeys and waving men in *kalpaks*, men stripping bark off poplar spars to make the rafters of a barn, schoolchildren dressed in white, all the way to the valley of the glistening Kork-Art whose wavelets galloped over its wide pebble bed. Under a brilliant sun, we drove between round, yellow hills with rosy pink earth showing through in the threadbare places and the cattle paths. We passed old Soviet chicken farms, now rows of derelict sheds, and the old jam factory the Soviets built to utilize the wild apples and cherry plums. In the valley, where the rice is grown, I discovered why it sometimes tasted gritty. Some farmers were busy winnowing the crop on the road, coning off one side of it for a fifty-yard stretch with an infant sat down at either end, presumably calculating that, although drivers would certainly run over cones, they might just think twice about children.

At the walnut market in Jalal-Abad boys played billiards at dozens of green baize tables in open-sided, tin-roofed sheds while men and women emptied sacks of walnuts on to piles in the concrete yard. A man with a giant set of scales weighed the sacks and deals were struck in some obscure way. Gena said the best walnuts were fetching 27 som a kilo, but if they were merely average, you would only get 20 to 23 som. People were also trading expensive shelled walnut kernels, and wholesale quantities of the sweet wild hawthorn fruit of *Crataegus ponticus*. Everywhere, black, stained hands gestured as the haggling connoisseurs bustled round each new heap of nuts.

Shaydan and Arslanbob

The road up to Shaydan was even rougher than the Ortok road. This time we had Zakir with us as we headed up the valley of the wild Kara Unkur River, past fields of fluffy ripe cotton full of women in bright headscarves harvesting. Cotton has to be watered five times before it is gathered in, and the four million tons of it grown each year in Uzbekistan has led to the drying up of the Aral Sea at the other end of the great Sur-Darya River that rises here from its mountain tributaries. Even little Kyrgyzstan grows 76,000 tons of cotton a year, and its heavy demand for water, in contrast to crops like sunflowers, often leads to strife among farmers in the fields. Higher up, we passed through hills dense with wild pistachios, the male trees bare by now, the females still in full leaf. We stopped in a village to buy nan from women at the roadside, and onions, potatoes, cabbage, garlic and rice from a bazaar for cooking *plov* in Gena's *kazan* later.

At last we found ourselves in a high, rocky valley full of wild apples and almonds, dog-roses and berberis bushes, with the great snow-covered peak of Balbash-Ata and its neighbouring mountains rising behind it. Innumerable rivers came rushing down. We crossed over one of them, the Karangul, then turned off the track, crossed an alpine meadow and forded the racing Shaydansay River.

Beside it, a boy was scrubbing a carpet on the grass, drenching it with buckets of mountain water. We were never far from the hissing or tumbling of rivers here as we roamed the valleys, and I relished the sound of their names too, as we went: the Yassy, Kara-Alma, Kyzyl-Ungur, Arslanbob-Yarodar, Kazan-Mazar, Alash-Sai and Maili-Suu.

At the end of a lane through planted orchards of apple and walnut, we passed a farmhouse with tiers of beehives set on a hillock behind it, and came to a long wooden dacha looking out across the valley. A millstream, diverted from the main river, danced along a channel in the orchard behind it. A pair of Uyzes, old Russian jeep versions of the Dormobile, were parked outside, armoured and jacked up on high wheels as if once designed for use as landing craft. A group of forestry students from the university in Jalal-Abad were here with their teachers for some fieldwork. The wooden lodge, nearly 4,000 feet up, was maintained by the Forestry Department as a base in the mountains for experimental research work in forestry, chiefly the culture of walnuts and apples.

The university teachers were Zakir's old friends and welcomed us warmly. We heard shouts and the slap of hands on flesh. The young male foresters were down on the meadow before the lodge, stripped to the waist for an informal wrestling tournament. A circle of admiring young women formed an audience. The students were impressively strong and skilled, their wrestling full blooded and spectacular. Seeing the fierce determination in their narrowed eyes, I couldn't help imagining the army of Genghis Khan, which passed this way and must have amused itself in similar ways, encamped on summer evenings. We were quartered in dormitories in the lodge, which, being miles from anywhere, was lit by electricity generated by an ingenious waterwheel in the millstream. It was improvised from the back wheel hubs, axle and transmission shaft of an old lorry. Steel paddles had been welded on to the wheels, thirty-two on each, which were mounted under the spouts of two steeply inclined twenty-foot steel tubes, the stream having been split in two and funnelled into them from the concrete mill-race ten feet above. The resulting pair of powerful jets spun the wheels at high velocity, and the whirring transmission shaft turned a pulley and belt-drive running up to a dynamo mounted in a protective box astride the stream. Wires on poles led back to the lodge. So intent was I on examining this machine that I lost my sunglasses in the mill-race, where they were instantly flipped and minced in the waterwheels, as sardines are by dolphins. Inside the lodge, they could tell if it had rained in the mountains by the waxing or waning of the electric lights. In late summer, when the stream's flow is relatively low, the lights are dim, but everyone eats outside and goes to bed early anyway.

Zakir took us on a tour of the orchards, full of beehives for the summer. As the snows melt in spring and the spectacular flowers of the alpine meadows come into bloom, the beekeepers move up the valley with their hives. Zakir, who knows these hills and meadows intimately, has listed well over 150 different flowering plants contributing pollen to the Shaydan honey, which he says is generally reckoned the very best in all Kyrgyzstan. I was reminded of the fine feta from the Vlach village of Samarina, whose sheep enjoy the highest, most variegated wild flower grazing in Greece. The cheese is so good that Vlachs come from as far away as New York to buy supplies of it.

Passing over the fact that all beehives are monarchies, the industrious habits and efficiency of bees must have appealed to the communists. Honey would always have featured strongly among the peasant farmers of Russia, but among the nomads and transhumant herders and shepherds of Kyrgyzstan it is likely that beekeeping was introduced as part of the Soviet de-nomadization programme that began in the 1920s. In the Soviet Union as a whole, beekeeping was a significant part of agriculture. The records for 1986, for example, show 40,000 tons of it harvested in the main Soviet countries and another 21,000 tons harvested in countries like Poland, Czechoslovakia, Romania, Hungary and Bulgaria.

We passed through an orchard of Star Crimson and Janatan apples, the latter a version of the American Jonathan. In other orchards they were growing varieties with names like Reinette Simerenko and Kandil Almatinsky to see how they would thrive at this altitude. Zakir and his foresters had planted 89 different kinds of apple tree here and found that only 17 of them did well. Wandering through plantations of apricot, almond, pear and poplar, we came to a field planted out with rows of three-foot walnut saplings raised from seed, all labelled with the names of the 288 varieties Zakir and his colleagues had identified. The genetic variations were enormous. We saw tiny, precocious trees they call 'fast fruit' that were already bearing fully fledged walnuts at the age of three. Others took seventeen years before bearing fruit, as they tend to do in England. Zakir proudly showed us his invention for raising seedling walnuts that allows them to be transplanted without damage to their roots. Walnuts, when they germinate, put down remarkably long tap roots, which are susceptible to damage by transplanting. Zakir's idea was to sow the walnuts in a deep bed of compost in a concrete tank four feet deep. Once the saplings have put down roots and are ready for planting out, he floods the tank, turning the compost into a liquid slurry, and gently lifts out the little trees with roots intact.

While we examined the walnut nursery, Gena had been busy vegetable poaching in a nearby field and reappeared back at the lodge with an armful of corn-cobs for dinner. I helped him gather firewood and light the fire under the *kazan*, which he placed on a ledge carved out specially in the clay bank. We made the fire in the hollow beneath it, and Gena sliced up onions, garlic, potato and cabbage to make a stew. We spread out rugs and cushions in the orchard beside the millstream as it grew dark and watched the stars come out, very clear and apparently close in the mountain air. We lay listening to the water and the sounds of cooking inside the *kazan*. Flames leapt and cupped themselves around it in the dark. 'We call tomorrow *Jura*, Uzbeki for Friendship Day,' said Zakir. 'Sundays are when men get together and go out to the countryside and cook on an open camp fire, talk and drink tea all day long. We air our domestic problems, talk politics, put the world to rights and cook some more. Then we go home again to our families.' I thought of the English equivalent: going fishing, or up to the allotment. Gena brought the bubbling *kazan*, and we ladled out plates of vegetable stew. In another part of the orchard, a circle of students sat round their fire and sang to a dombra. 'This is a new era for our trees,' Zakir said. 'The older foresters were all trained in Russia, growing firs and pines, so they got used to planting trees close together. Then they came back and did the same thing with walnuts in Kyrgyzstan, so we got a whole generation of tall, straight trees with hardly any fruit on them. They all had to be thinned out, of course. If there's one thing a walnut can't stand, it's too much competition. They need plenty of light.' Lounging on our cushions like Romans, we nibbled the corn-cobs Gena had roasted over the fire and munched fresh Star Crimson apples. We tracked a satellite across the sky and noted the irony of Kyrgyzstan's poverty when it is so rich in all the things the world so longs for: clean air, clear mountain water and wild, organic fruit. That all the fruit here is exceptionally tasty was noted by the Australians, who have taken scions from Kyrgyz apples to propagate and cross-fertilize with their own. Gena felt the Ferghana Valley people were open to exploitation by the Turkish traders, who come to buy walnuts and under-pay the women to shell or husk them. Zakir complained that too many animals were allowed to roam the forest, preventing its natural regeneration with their browsing. Zamira was already half asleep. The owls began calling up and down the valley. Entirely sober, deeply contented, we stumbled off to our bunks.

Next morning, after a good steaming in the wood-fired sauna, we breakfasted on *kasha*, rice pudding, yoghurt, bread and honey from the next-door farmer. It was superb honey. It tasted of lemons, nuts, thyme, wild roses and maple. We reclined splendidly cushioned in the shade of the orchard again. Bees came in their dozens and settled around the honey bowl on our picnic tablecloth, wandering about its rim, feasting and gorging themselves. And why shouldn't they? It was the fruit of their own labour and they were simply claiming back stolen property. As if in acknowledgement of this, nobody minded a bit, and we were soon surrounded by the little gatecrashers to our *petit déjeuner sur l'herbe*: big, chunky, striped hive bees that knew the meaning of hard work. They are so industrious up here that the beekeepers harvest honey from the hive three times a year, in May, July and late August or September. The Kyrgyzi call them *ary*. Once gorged, they went staggering unsteadily about our breakfast things, occasionally tumbling sideways as they taxied for take-off. Gena brewed tea on the mud-hearth fire and we prepared to set off.

Fording the Shaydansay River again, we bumped, swayed and teetered our way higher up the valley to over 6,000 feet, then walked along the river to a grove of ancient Tien Shan birch and Turkestan maple trees that formed a gateway to an alpine meadow with a sacred spring at its centre. Standing beside the spring was a wishing tree, an old hawthorn, *Crataegus turkestanica*, a tattered thing, decorated with hundreds of ribbons, shreds of bleached, coloured cloth, even a tiny prayer, rolled tightly in a scroll and hung by cotton on a branch. Thorns are important medicine trees in Kyrgyzstan. The berries or flowers are made into a tea to alleviate heart disease. A big walnut trunk had been hollowed into a drinking trough beside the spout of mountain water. The place was so remote, it seemed surprising that anyone would ever come here, let alone so many.

Once again I had the curious sensation of being in a place that felt very much like home, and yet it was full of trees and plants that were all subtly different from those I knew in England. There were birches, but they weren't tall, slender and silver-barked. The birches that grew near the river were thick-set, ancient things whose trunks burst out in warty boles. This was *Betula turkestanica*, and many of these trees could be a hundred years old, said Zakir. We often found ourselves conversing in Latin: our common language was plants and trees, and their Linnaean names. Everything at this altitude grew very slowly, so even quite modest-looking bushes and trees were much older than they appeared. The valley walls and the open wood pasture we walked through were full of wild cherries, dog-roses, the Kyrgyz wild apple, cotoneaster bushes, wild Sogdian plum trees and berberis, whose seven or eight different varieties provide an important crop of wild berries, traditionally consumed by the Kyrgyz people for their high content of Vitamin C. The sharp-tasting black berries make a very good jam, and Uzbeks like to add them to their cooking. Zakir reckoned the honeysuckle that clambered up the trees on prodigious, sinewy trunks, *Lonicera tianschanica*, was probably over a hundred years old too, and some of the weather-beaten trees of thorn and juniper could have been clinging to the ledges along the valley walls, inching themselves up, for 400 years.

A pair of black eagles cruised high above us up the valley, towards the snowy tops of the Ferghana range with its great peaks, Babash-Ata, Alyysh-Tau and Chichekty-Tau, sheltering the valley from the cold northern airstreams. The Ferghana Valley is also protected from the hot Afghan air to the south by the Alai Gorge and the Pamir Mountains, and from the dry winds off the Mongolian deserts by the Alaykuu range. The high Chaktal and Atoinok ranges complete the horseshoe that creates a benign microclimate of moderate summer temperatures, mild winters, plenty of rainfall in spring and short bursts of it in early summer. This provides the walnuts, and the extraordinary variety of plant species associated with them in the fruit forests, with the ideal conditions of life. The unusually rich vegetation contains no fewer than 183 different trees and shrubs, including 51 species of wild rose.

As we climbed higher up the valley, and clambered up its steep wall, Zakir pointed out how the trees grew naturally in distinct bands according to altitude: walnuts further down the valley, Turkestan birch and maple by the river banks higher up, wild roses, honeysuckle and berberis on the valley floor and its margins along the rising walls. We climbed up through tangled woods of thorn trees and wild apples, and emerged into a higher zone of junipers. Three different species grow on the mountainsides. In the massive, furrowed fork of one old tree, and among its roots under its dark canopy, we stumbled across a children's den: a bunch of found horseshoes tied on to a branch, a pair of tattered grown-up ladies' shoes, a little empty wooden box with its lid open, two rust-pocked white enamel bowls and a bit of tin for a wall. This tree, a Turkestan juniper, would be at least 400 years old, Zakir thought. Around 8,500 feet, even the junipers cease to grow, although in some slightly more sheltered places they even reach up to 10,000 feet.

The sun felt relentless up here, and, as we rounded a big rock, a pair of tawny snakes moved out of our path. '*Kulvar*,' whispered Zakir in Uzbek as they slid off. We were climbing up to take a look at two enormous old walnuts standing either side of a spring. Zakir said people called the trees 'diviners' because they are always a sign of water, especially in otherwise arid places. A little covey of partridges, *keklik*, shot up and wittered across the valley.

After a picnic lunch in the orchard, with more honey, and more bees, we set off in the jeep along a dirt road through the forest for the village of Arslanbob. The walnut woods were full of the sound of singing, harvesters calling to each other, the sibilant rustling of shaken trees and hailstorms of falling nuts. Every so often we would catch a glimpse of a little encampment in the trees, or the Indian rope trick of smoke from a campfire. Deep in the woods, we encountered a battered, dusty Russian Army lorry parked up in a clearing with a range of household goods on display in the open back. It was nothing less than a mobile woodland shop, selling food and drink, soap, vodka, ironmongery, rugs and fabrics. You had the choice of paying in som or walnuts, and I discovered that walnuts were generally accepted everywhere in the forest as legal tender. Now and again huge trucks like this came ploughing along the dirt road in storms of dust, with standing room only behind the cab, passengers clinging on wherever they could, like ants on a leaf in a gale.

At Uzbek Gava, a quiet village full of lush apple orchards and ripe, rosy fruit, the dusty, orange road became a holloway so deeply tunnelled that the knotted roots of the mighty walnuts either side of it were exposed like the innards of some grotesque creature from a bestiary. The root systems of these trees have the same complex, wandering habit as their branches and must create all manner of crypts, vaults and subterranean mazes for the creatures that live beneath the forest floor. At the next village, Sharap, we had climbed to 5,600 feet. Someone had been digging the crimson clay out of a cliff face to make mud bricks, which, like blushing loaves, lay drying in the sun beside the poplar frame of a barn or farmhouse under construction.

We paused in a meadow that rose to pure apple woods of *Malus kyrgyzorum* and collected fruit and pips. By now Gena and Zamira were adept at eating an apple and retaining the pips in their mouths. Every now and again they solemnly presented me with a precious regurgitated handful to be stored and labelled in a paper bag or envelope. Some of the wild Kyrgyz apple trees around these dusty hills stood alone, twenty or thirty feet tall, in meadows beside the road and were magnificent specimens still bearing plenty of the festive, bright-red fruit, which we found sweet, tangy and over-flowing with juice. Gena brought down the topmost fruit in the traditional way, by throwing sticks. Zakir, who is in charge of the forests of southern Kyrgyzstan, turned a blind eye.

At Arslanbob, right under the imposing snowy heights of Babash-Ata, we stayed in the outlying farmhouse of Safora and her daughter Erissida. They swung open a farm gate built like a portcullis to let us in to the walled yard and welcomed us with the now familiar Kyrgyz version of the cream tea: fresh wet walnuts, *airan* or *kefir*, the farm's yoghurt, nan, more walnuts in syrup, apples, buns, fresh cream and chai. The two women immediately made us feel at home. Our tea-time conversation centred on walnuts as brain food. We all agreed that since the shelled kernel looks like a brain, the principle of sympathetic magic would indicate that it must be good for brains. That, at any rate, was what all the woodland folk in the walnut forest believed. Zakir said the Romans wouldn't allow their slaves to eat walnuts in case they grew too clever. Gena said, 'If I eat enough walnuts, perhaps I could become a doctor of science like you.' Zakir explained how the humus from falling walnut leaves helps foster other plants. But photosynthesis in the living leaves produces an ether called juglone, which evaporates into the air on warm days and can affect your brain, so you shouldn't sleep under a walnut tree by day. Because it is a mild organic pesticide, many insects tend to avoid walnuts. Zakir said this is one reason for planting them in the yards of farmhouses: horses can stand in their shade, less bothered by flies. Gena added that people sometimes rub the leaves on their faces to keep off flies, but I couldn't decide if he was serious or just wanted to see us all blackening our faces with walnut leaves.

Later, after dinner of chicken broth with noodles, Erissida gave me a big towel, and I went across the yard to take a sauna. Every household seemed to have a wood-fired sauna and took the business of bathing very seriously. I followed a garden path past the cowshed towards a column of woodsmoke; this was issuing from under the Chinaman's hat atop the stack of a simple tin-roofed structure with thick walls of insulating cob. You went first into a narrow ante-chamber, with just a bench, duck-boarded floor and a row of wooden pegs along the wall. I climbed out of my dusty clothes and opened a second well-insulated door into the torrid semi-darkness of the inner sanctum, a room of six or seven feet by ten, with just enough headroom under the close-boarded ceiling. A single electric lightbulb in the changing room shone through a strip of misted window and reflected off the whitewashed cob walls. The semi-darkness only heightened the atmosphere of sanctity. In one corner stood a milk churn full of cold water. To the right, a wood-fired boiler, fed through a steel door in the changing room, wheezed and popped with a recent ration of split logs. Directly on top of the boiler was a steaming tank of hot water, topless, like me, and next to it a steel drum full of hot stones. The stove was a lanky contraption with two chimney pipes, one running up through the stones, the other through the hot-water tank. The two pipes then joined in a welded confluence into a single pipe issuing through the roof towards the ozone layer. It was like being in an engine room. Before me along the back wall a big enamel bowl stood on a long, low wooden table. Beside it were two large enamel mugs for use as ladles and a hosepipe with a tap. A second bowl contained pale-green water steeped with bunches of mint, which I flicked on to the hissing stones. A delicious mint-tea pungency began to fill the sauna. I was soon sweating, partly from the heat and partly from filling up bowls, topping up the milk churn and ladling cold water over my body to prevent it melting. I worked at it like a stoker on the footplate of a steam engine and resolved one day to build myself a wood-fired sauna, even making a few soggy drawings of the plan and elevation.

I was woken by a chorus of the massed donkeys of Arslanbob with descants by the cockerel in the yard. It was another still, sunny day. After a feast of pancakes and honey, Safora gave me the recipe for preserving walnuts in syrup as we sat outside the front porch in the shade of the farm's big walnut tree. You must pick your walnuts while they are still green and soft, before the shells have begun to form. First, you perforate them with a fork and soak them in brine for twelve hours. You then wash them several times to take away the salt. Finally, you boil the walnuts in water with enough added sugar to make syrup. The longer you boil, the thicker and more delicious the black syrup.

At the other end of the yard stood two old Russian lorries, one of which bore the legend *Animal Wild* painted in big letters on its side and a cut-out picture of a tiger on its radiator. Erissida said it belonged to her neighbour Mansur, a Tartar woodturner and beekeeper. He used the lorries to carry his hives about the country in springtime, in pursuit of wild flowers and blossom. I imagined him as a modern Giles Winterbourne, perfectly in tune with his beloved bees, as Winterbourne was with his trees, roving the wood pastures and alpine meadows in search of early tulips, wild roses and apple blossom behind the wheel of *Animal Wild*.

Thirty or forty crows circled up on a thermal as Zakir, Zamira and I began walking up Babash-Ata through the foothills. Gena had gone to buy food and prepare it for our return. Mountain water raced all about us, irrigating a system of small fields of potatoes, onions and maize separated by low walls of stones picked from the land. The air cooled as we climbed, and the trees began to vary like goods on the ascending floors of a department store. First we passed wild cherries, then tough-looking elms, *karagachi* in Kyrgyz, *Ulmus ulmifolia* in Latin. Higher up, we reached Turkestan maples, *Acer turkestanica*, old trees like smaller-scale English planes, surviving on almost bare rock. At 7,500 feet, halfway up the mountain, we found ourselves on a sudden high plateau and stepped on to a desert of pale, silver stones. A single magnificent tree stood at the shimmering centre of what must once have been a glacier. It was a walnut, the finest I had ever seen, and in its deep shade lay a whole flock of some 200 sheep.

As we walked over to meet the tree, three figures separated themselves from the shadowed flock and advanced over the unsteadying pebbles. For a moment there was a hint of High Noon about the scene, but we exchanged greetings and shook hands. They offered us tea with their grandfather, nodding towards a camp on the hillside half hidden in the shade of some rocks. Not wishing to disturb the sheep from its shadow, I viewed the walnut from a respectful distance. Its roots must have located a spring, for in the midst of nothing but barren stones it rose some fifty feet into an immense crown of dense leaves. Its great trunk, which must have measured at least twelve to fourteen feet in girth, had been polished smooth by sheep and lanolin. Walnuts, said Zakir, need moisture in the air around them as well as in the soil, which is why they have been thriving for millions of years in the uniquely humid microclimate of the Ferghana Valley. I wondered again how it is that trees are able to feel their way towards water, even when their roots have to travel some distance to reach it. By what process do they sense its nearness? Those little hairs on roots, which do all the work of absorbing water, may just be antennae of a kind.

At the camp, the women worked quietly at a makeshift kitchen beneath a tented awning on poles. Rice and walnuts hung in plastic bags from a bush. Rugs, quilts and cushions were laid out for us before the entrance of a felt-walled shelter with a ridged canvas roof, half yurt, half tent, with willow lattice walls inside. The old man placed a kettle on the wood fire and sat down with us. His white goatee contrasted with the deep tan of his lined Mongol features. He wore baggy black breeches, an Uzbek pillbox cap and tall boots of soft black leather. Their long pointed toes gave him the look of a magician, and as the family assembled, squatting in a line beside him, a tiny boy crept up and nestled into the old man's chest, burying his head shyly in his arms. They had three hundred goats and six hundred sheep, he said, and they milked the sheep. We drank the thick, neat sheep's milk and sat talking about the history and holiness of the mountain, about winter feed for the goats, about the milking of sheep. The tea never actually appeared: the old man seemed to have forgotten the kettle as it boiled away, and everyone took his or her lead from him, politely ignoring it.

We climbed higher into a fine alpine meadow of close-cropped herbs and grasses, with here and there a weather-worn Turkestan maple standing hunched and alone among giant boulders, lichened wood and stone looking very much alike. Zakir said the meadow would be a mass of tulips in spring, which comes late up here, in June, or even July. We had reached 9,000 feet when we saw the white streak of a 250-foot waterfall tumbling out of the mountain ahead of us. But a ravine and a wild river defeated all our attempts to ascend to it. We crossed the river, discovered the ravine was all cliff and decided to go down instead. Eventually we had to wade back through the icy torrent to reach the spot on the banks of a gentler, glassy tributary where Gena had nobly ascended bearing lunch, spreading it out in a picnic beneath the shade of apple trees.

Next morning I rose early, awakened by massed choirs of the Arslanbob cockerels and donkeys. The cows were standing quietly with a calf in the cowshed after gentle overnight rain. Dogs ran through the dark walnut woods that surrounded the farm and rose steeply uphill immediately behind the yard. From inside the privy at its far corner I peered through the cracks in the door between the rough wooden boards at the waking chickens, ducks and other farmyard animals, feeling a bit like one myself. Erissida and her mother were asleep in the hayloft in the roof, having ceded the living quarters on the ground floor to us. At night when we cleaned our teeth at the little tin udder on the post outside the door, they disappeared quietly up a ladder into the gable like birds settling in the eves. Now Erissida made her way across the yard, released the ducks from their shed and settled to milking the two cows. I could just hear the waltz of the milk jetting into the ringing pail and fell in love with Erissida there and then in the impossible way of the traveller far from home. It was her sheer competence, courage and resilience that appealed to me. Added to that, we could only really communicate through smiles and gestures, or through the interpretation of Zamira. And I liked the hippie-ish sloppy Joe pullovers she always wore. It was hopeless and impossible, and anyway she was probably married. I never asked because I didn't want to know.

At the top end of the village we picked up Zakir's colleague Davlet Mamachanov, who probably knows more about walnuts than anyone alive. Davlet has identified 286 distinct varieties of walnut growing naturally in the forests of the Ferghana Valley and spends a lot of his time walking the woods in order to collect nuts to cultivate and study. Making an early start, we drove out along the great silver, dashing, white-water Kara Ungur River on its way north and west to the Aral Sea. We went on dirt roads and along river beds, crossing other rivers and sometimes even driving straight up them in sheets of spray, as I thought people in jeeps only did in television commercials. We also bumped over a lot of rocks and scattered plenty of chickens, turkeys, dogs, sheep and cattle as we dashed through the occasional village. Gena was in heaven, showing off his experience as a tank driver in Belarus with the army. Without his obvious skill, I would have been terrified.

Things I could have happily sat for hours sketching flashed past: all manner of barns, sheds, privies, summer kitchens, *tandurs*, verandas and roadside kiosks, all bleached and faded by the sun. Nothing had been painted for twenty years. The poplar frame of poles, infilled with willow wattle and daubed with cob, or walled in cob bricks and plastered in mud, was an infinitely versatile, free-form way of building. Free of any apparent planning laws, the vernacular self-builders were free to express themselves. I saw a little summerhouse on stilts with windows all round an approximate hexagon, with a beaten-tin roof. The butcher's shop where we paused to buy mutton for our lunch was no more than a hole in a wall, a tiny kiosk with a cavernous, shadowy inside, a big blue-painted set of scales on the counter, and a series of meat hooks along the outside wall like a row of clothes hooks bearing the dismembered components of a sheep or two dangling and drying in the heat, objects of considerable interest to the local flies and wasps.

The further we sped away from Arslanbob, Erissida, the milking pails and home, the more the nomad instincts in my companions came alive. Gena carried a beautiful Tajik knife, its beaded handle inlaid with mother-of-pearl, undulating like a curled lip. He had the butcher dice up some mutton for a stew and wrap it in newspaper. He was going to cook it in the *kazan*. Opposite the butcher's, people were loading up a dusty blue bus with sacks of walnuts on their way to market at Korgon Bazaar. Huge lorries with standing room only in their open backs trundled past, flouring the meat with dust. For a few miles, we gave a lift to a beautiful young woman with gold teeth. Stately turkeys sailed the roads.

Everywhere old buses and covered trailers left over from the Soviet era were now in use as houses or summer cottages for the walnut harvesters. Transport then, as now, was mostly communal, so we saw few scrap cars. At a road block Zakir and Davlet were instantly recognized and we were waved through, but everyone else was checked for walnuts. Anyone driving in or out of the forest must show a valid licence to gather them and declare their cargo as though it were another country, which indeed it was.

Reaching the confluence of the Sary Dash and Kurslangur rivers merging into the nascent Kara Ungur, we followed the lively Kurslangur along a track beside it. Walnuts cloaked the steep walls of its humid valley. At the village of Kurslangur, squat tin-roofed houses sheltered under a crumbling sandstone cliff, and walnuts were drying in wire-netting cages. Beyond the village, we left the jeep and began walking up the head of the valley beside the turquoise river, boiling through rocks and waterfalls. Gena found a fire pit for his *kazan* and began preparing an elaborate stew for lunch.

The walnuts in the steepest parts of the river gorge were coppiced, and Zakir explained how the coppicing is done naturally by the violence of winter avalanches and rockfalls levelling the old trees, from whose rooted stools fresh coppice shoots then grow. The result was a quite different-looking wood, more like an English bluebell copse of ash: straight, smooth-barked poles growing in profusion from gnarled mushroom-tops of ancient mother wood. Zakir cut walking sticks from some of them for us. We found the *chag*, a medicinal bracket fungus of the walnut, and swung our way back down to the river from tree to tree. Herbal medicine is still an important part of life in the Ferghana Valley. Everywhere we went Zakir was given bee propolis, or queen substance, which he took home for his convalescent son Muhammad, who was known to suffer from asthma.

Further up the gorge we had to negotiate a dramatic moraine beneath a cliff and came face to face with a steel plaque commemorating the death of a 21-year-old Russian woman climber, killed at this spot. Her fall haunted me as we climbed up into the old woods among huge walnuts as bent and twisted as the oaks on Dartmoor. We pocketed nuts of all kinds as we went, Davlet running about under the trees like a human squirrel, filling small polythene bags with nuts; he labelled these, often stuffing in elaborate notes too. 'What is the perfect walnut?' I asked him. Davlet continued breaking open the shell of a pale walnut, picking out the meat as he thought about this. 'Well, it is big, like the one we call Bomba, the bomb, but it must be well filled inside too, and its shell must crack open easily, with a ridge around the middle for strength and a sweet kernel that rattles about in the shell a little, so it is no trouble to extract. The kind of walnut you have to hammer open, or whose kernel can be winkled out only with a pin or the point of your knife, is no good.' He paused and rummaged in his rucksack, produced a Bomba the size of a squash ball and opened it. 'These look good and sell well in the market, but the kernel itself nowhere nearly fills the nut. A smaller, better-filled nut with a fairly thin shell, like one we call the Ugyursky, is actually far superior.' He was right: the Bomba was like the boxes of muesli you see in the supermarket, twice the size of their contents, all talk and no trousers. Davlet had the scientist's hunger for data: what is the total weight of our English walnut harvest? I had no idea. How many hectares do we have under walnut cultivation? Again, total ignorance on my part. I resolved to do better and send Davlet the information.

We had climbed to 6,000 feet, passing through a windy canyon and a zone of the woods rich in plums of different kinds. Warm air from below was being drawn up the canyon by the presence of a glacier above. Zakir knew of at least seven species of plum here: yellow, golden, pink, crimson, two shades of violet and black. *Prunus sogdiana* was the commonest, named after the Sogdians, the earliest inhabitants of the region. It was one of those exotic names with a strangeness I just couldn't get out of my head, like the aged, sturdy birch trees *Betula turkestanica* that grew along the mountain rivers, or the beautiful, dense bushes *Exochoda tianschanica*, whose woody seeds the children threaded into strings of beads. Another was one of the many different wild roses, delicate-leaved and slender-stemmed, *Rosa kokaniko*. Somehow the names added to the beauty of the plants like the foliate illuminations on the initial letters of medieval manuscripts, or honeysuckle spiralling up a living tree. People's names, like Beeban Kidron or Atom Egoyan, get stuck in my head the same way, as though the memory, about its daily housework, doesn't quite know where to put them and ends up carrying them about distractedly.

We ascended through immense walnuts sixty feet tall to a little square wooden hut framed in the natural arch of an old tree that had bent over like a wooden Durdle Dor just before it. Two fathers and their teenage sons were living in this curious shelter, whose domed roof of hay topped off with polythene they had roped down to eight rough poles sunk in the ground. They all wore old army boots, camouflaged fatigues and woollen tea-cosies, so they could have been the SAS on an exercise, especially as they were smudged all over with walnut juice. Their hands, with which they shook ours heartily several times, were unusually black. Beside the hut lay the cause of their temporary melanism: a huge midden of empty nutshells and a sea of fresh, gleaming kernels laid out to dry. While Davlet, Zakir and Zamira were all absorbed in yet another walnut-tasting, I was invited into the shade of the hut, and noticed our hosts slept under blankets in the four nests they had impressed into a heap of hay. It was a rough life, but they all seemed happy and evidently serious about their nut-gathering. On the way down, we met one of the beekeepers we had encountered earlier bringing a honeycomb and some of the precious queen substance as a gift for Zakir. Like the local nabob he was, he accepted it graciously. Zakir, after all, had in his gift the allocation of the various permits and licences, and the delineation of each woodland territory of nut trees. Considering the extent of his power over the forest, he was miraculously kind and gentle with everyone, always modest and friendly, listening with tolerance and patience as his woodland constituents unburdened themselves of their many hardships and complaints.

Further down the gorge, the smoke curling up through the trees from Gena's cooking fire came into sight and quickened the appetite. The *kazan* was bubbling with a stew of mutton and potato, which we devoured sitting in a circle around it beside the river. Before beginning our meal, Zakir led us in the traditional gesture of thanksgiving to Allah in which the hands are raised and passed over the face, as if washing it in mime. We were entertained by a dipper, the dainty *chulduk*, flitting from rock to rock in a water ballet. But this peaceful interlude was interrupted by the sudden thunder of a trio of American troop planes flying low across the mountains towards Afghanistan. Gena said they would be ferrying reinforcements from the camp on the airfield at Bishkek into Kabul.

When we looked back to the river, there was no longer any sign of our friend the *chulduk*.

After lunch we took the jeep up a winding track out of the valley and south-east in the direction of Ortok. Breasting a hilltop scrub orchard of wild apples, we confronted a switchback descent to a water-splash ford across a river. The dirt road eventually brought us to the foot of a storybook land of dramatic red-and-ochre cliffs of vertically stratified rock that I took to be some kind of sandstone conglomerate strongly impregnated with iron. One of the mighty geological contortions for which the southern Tien Shan are famous had dislocated the strata through ninety degrees into the vertical, creating a castle in the air unassailable except on foot, cradling a walnut forest in its plateau. It was a scene from Hieronymus Bosch. People were labouring up and down a narrow path that wound up into the woods, those on the descent carrying sacks of nuts. Those who had been allocated licences to harvest here had certainly drawn the short straw, yet they all seemed content enough.

After a bout of Gena's enthusiastic off-road driving, it was good to wander across a nearby hillside through the wild apple trees. The view suddenly opened up: dense golden-green walnut forest covered the hills and valleys everywhere as far as the horizon, unbroken except where the spires of poplars indicated the distant groves of Arslanbob. Gena and I discovered a charming thatched hut with walls of wattle and daub standing in a wild orchard the other side of a stream. We vaulted over the water to reach a fine crop of the red, ripe apples of *Malus kirghisorum* and filled our pockets. A little deeper into the walnut woods, a family was encamped with all its livestock. A fine chestnut stallion, his front fetlocks hobbled, grazed in a clearing, and in the long, straight shadow of a tall walnut lay an orderly row of two dozen Muscovy ducks, snoozing away the afternoon, shifting position now and again to follow the shade.

Back in the old Soviet days in 1965, when forestry was taken seriously, the Russian scientist Victor Schevchenko planted an orchard at Yaradar, a forest village in the Dashman Massif not far from Arslanbob. He chose the hardiest, best-fruiting trees from the wild fruit forest and began a long-term experiment to see how they might perform under cultivation. He planted walnuts, apples, pears and cobnuts. The apples had names like Kyrgyzka, Zimnya, Rushida, Guardysky and Dolono, and, out of the ninety-six varieties Schevchenko planted, Zakir and Davlet had decided that eight were worth recommending for the table. Of the seventeen original pears, they selected six. Scions of the choicest walnut trees growing in the forest had been grafted on to vigorous rootstock of black walnut, *Juglans nigra*, and planted out twenty feet apart in rows of half a dozen or so: Arcterek in the first row, Guardysky, Panfilovsky, Rodina, Bostandiksky, and the finest of them all, Uygursky, from the forest village of Gava. The Uygursky walnut, in the informed opinion of Davlet, comes closest to perfection. He ought to know, having thought long and hard about the 286 wild varieties he has identified. Breaking one open as we wandered the orchard that morning, he revealed the pale, cream kernel, how snugly it fitted the shell and how readily it detached itself. In the market, the pale kernels are considered far superior to the brown ones and fetch a higher price. By contrast, Davlet shook one of the giant nuts from a row of eleven Bomba trees to show how the kernel rattled inside.

Spring in the Ferghana Valley is often an uncertain time. Cold weather can come just as the trees are flowering and a frost can wither the young nuts on the tree. Some years there is scarcely any walnut harvest at all. Late-blooming varieties of *Juglans regia* such as the Uygursky naturally stand a better chance of avoiding late-spring frosts, so Davlet and his colleagues have been looking out for such trees and breeding hardier young stock from them in the orchard nursery for planting back into the forest. It was delightful to see Davlet Mamachanov in his element, the proud father of his trees, showing them off. The desk in his office resembled a crowded billiard table: walnuts covered every available square inch of it, and along the shelves were ranged rows of little labelled plastic bags and glass dishes containing more specimens: *Bomba, Uygursky, Ostrovershiny, Oshsky, Pioner, Gavinsky, Slad Koyderny, Alal-Buka,*

Bostandiksky, Panfilovsky, Guardysky, Kazakstansky, Ubileyniv, Rodina, Kistevidniv. A large-scale map of the fruit forest on the wall marked the position of unusually interesting or productive trees.

Back in Jalal-Abad next day, we walked through the parched remains of what had until recently been a fine orchard of walnuts and other fruit, originally planted by Zakir. Here too were rows of various apples, wild and domestic, and a collection of assorted pistachio nut bushes. Since independence in 1990 the Forestry Department and this eighty-acre garden have been starved of funds. They had been forced to get what money they could by growing sapling walnuts and fruit trees and selling them to the public. The wilting orchard had grown into the image of the nation state: paths that were once gravelled and shaded by lush leafy tunnels were now overgrown with brambles and weeds, the trees struggling to survive, unwatered, in the heat of the town. The orchards had become the refuge of homeless people, and a little village of bivouacs and benders was springing up among the trees. Some enterprising individuals had even cultivated parts of the garden with onion patches, like unofficial allotments. It was desperately ironic that Zakir's orchards were failing for want of regular watering in a land so rich in wild rivers and streams. By contrast, the walnuts that filled the garden of the Zarimzakov family at home were deep green and well watered.

We all went for a farewell lunch together in the shade of a spreading oriental plane tree and a walnut at Madumar Ata, Jalal-Abad's longest-established and most popular restaurant. Madumar Irsalev, its founder, was born in 1900 and was still cooking here at the age of ninety. The place had begun life thirty-five years ago as a modest café. Now it was so big and prosperous that the proprietor's family recently built a magnificent mosque just across the street. We entered past a vast, man-sized samovar and washed our hands at a small basin before taking our outdoor table beneath the trees. Gena had telephoned ahead and ordered the dish for which the restaurant is famous: giant potato pancakes filled with the choice

mutton and fatty tail-fillets so beloved of this enthusiastically car-
nivorous people. By reducing cholesterol levels in the body, walnuts
would be the ideal palliative to such a fatty diet. Beyond a general
belief in the health-giving properties of walnuts, my companions
were not aware of the cholesterol connection.

Zakir had held his son's wedding reception at Madumar Ata.
As with almost any wedding in Kyrgyzstan, he had been obliged to
invite over a thousand sisters, cousins and aunts, and the lavish
array of presents had included no fewer than twenty-three carpets.
We toasted each other repeatedly with glasses of chai and all felt
very sad at the prospect of parting and going no more a-roving together through these tumultuous forests, so delightfully inhabited,
so brimming with human warmth and candour. The impulse for
hospitality to utter strangers never ceases to delight me.

In the back of a Mercedes taxi heading out of Bishkek two days
later, I felt sad to be leaving my friends. I was going to miss them.
But I also felt elated to be alone again. As we sped towards the
frontier, I tried to make sense of the lives I had shared, however
briefly. All the Kyrgyz people I had met were very poor. Their lives
were hard, their country was the poorest in Central Asia, and their
government was hardly liberal. Yet they seemed far from miserable.
I thought of Erissida in her long pullover, waving goodbye at the
farm gate beside her mother; of Davlet, showing us proudly round
his beautiful orchards; and of the young foresters, stripped to the
waist, wrestling in the sunset meadow beside the river at Shaydan.
At our last dinner at Zakir's home, I had received from him a
magnificent Tajik knife in a sheath, its handle inlaid with mother-
of-pearl, and, from Gena, a beautiful *kalpak* and a walnut bowl
filled with herbs – hypericum and oregano. Next day, he had driven
me and Zamira to Jalal-Abad's tiny airfield, where cows were
discouraged but people wandered freely about the grassy aprons
gathering herbs. We had all become such firm friends that the
parting was emotional, we really did hug each other like bears. I
now clutched a second bag filled with the walnuts we had gathered

in the woods, and those Davlet had given me, carefully labelled by variety and origin. Everywhere we went, we had kept some of the best nuts as seed: from the forests of Kurslangur, Arslanbob, Jay-terek, Gava and Ortok. In my rucksack were several film cans filled with the carefully labelled pips of wild apples, and squirrel-stashes of walnuts also destined to be sown later in my Suffolk garden, as a living reminder of the wild fruit forests I had encountered on my travels.

PART FOUR

Heartwood

Suffolk Trees

Back home, and almost the first tree I met was a tall, brooding Devonshire Quarrendon grown from an apple pip from Ted Hughes's orchard. I am near the Suffolk coast in Middleton, near Yoxford, where the poets Michael Hamburger and Anne Beresford have lovingly tended forty or fifty apples, pears and plums for half their almost fifty years of marriage. When they moved in they inherited the old orchard, and one thing led to another. Besides publishing nearly twenty volumes of poems, criticism and translation since 1945, Michael Hamburger has worked as prolifically in his orchard for twenty-five years, as one might work on a long poem. He has also confounded the ordinary conventions of horticulture by growing dozens of new apple trees from pips instead of by grafting, with excellent results.

Down a lane by the marsh that borders the Minsmere River I came on a rambling farmhouse that seemed to subside into the wild profusion of climbing plants surrounding it. Someone was playing the piano indoors. Michael and Anne welcomed me into a house overflowing with books and apples and led me into a library, deliciously scented by neat rows of recently plucked fruits on racks beneath the bookshelves. My hosts mentioned that the poet Schiller couldn't write a word without the scent of gently rotting apples wafting up from his desk drawer. I suspect the same may be true of them.

'This one's Berlepsch, a cross with James Grieve, but it keeps longer,' said Hamburger, handing me a German apple he originally brought to Suffolk as pips and propagated in a flowerpot outside. Rubbing shoulders with *Essays on Thomas Mann* were ranks of the tasty little pineapple-flavoured Ananas Reinette, and beside them under the window was a battalion of my own favourite apples, the nutty Orleans Reinette.

Another part of the library was reserved for the English classics: Ribston Pippins, each of which contains five times more vitamin C than a Golden Delicious, and Ashmead's Kernel. Apples of every shape and complexion, from bottoms to gargoyles, khaki to streaked crimson, balanced in trays on old typewriters or perched on planks atop baskets of kindling in such profusion that gusts of their perfume followed us through the open door as we stepped into the orchard via a long greenhouse crammed with fruiting oranges and grapefruit also grown from pips.

As Barrie Juniper explained to me before I began my apple quest, pips aren't supposed to grow true to their parent fruit variety, because apples must cross-pollinate to produce fruit; indeed the apple's tendency to dream itself into ever new forms is the very basis for the evolution of the 6,000-odd varieties of British domestic apples that have been named over the centuries. That Hamburger's pip-sown apples actually look and taste like their parents, or at least close, must be good fortune.

To grow an apple tree from a pip to its first fruiting takes about twelve years. It is a labour of love, and it soon became apparent as we toured the orchard that the key principle in Hamburger's planting selection was the same as Adam's in paradise: his wife's predilections. Because the seed trays and their labels had sometimes been sabotaged by mice, some of the new trees were nameless. It was tempting to christen them as Thoreau named his favourite wildings around Walden Pond: Beresford's Favourite, perhaps, or, for those delicious apples that refuse to grow to a uniform size and shape, Tesco's Despair.

15 *October*

Today I sawed off a dead lateral branch of the big walnut, leaving three feet at the stump end to lean my ladder on. The wood is still sound. I will turn it on the lathe and make bed-ends. Taken out of its original context as part of the tree, it now has an independent existence as wood.

9 *January*

A wild, windy night and a bright, clear, blustery day. I walk out along Cowpasture Lane and up the hill to the pollard hornbeam. With its wide bolling and outstretched boughs, it is what the Basques would call a *trasmocho* tree. It has grown into the shape of a church bell, and you can swing up into it and sit reading, enfolded in its foliage. Crossing the stream at the ford, I stand leaning on the wooden bridge to one side, losing myself in the muscular surge of fresh rainwater. I pass three dreys in the complex old pollard oaks in the lane. Each tree is different in habit and even in the details of its leaves and acorns. These are descended from ancient wild wood trees, rather than planted woodland trees. The dreys are ingeniously thatched on top with the pale-blond dried leaves and stalks of the maize that is grown in wide bands along the edges of the woods and the lane as pheasant cover. The pale maize thatch roofs cover the darker weave of oak twigs and leaves.

Turning off the lane, I make a long trudge into the wind into the oak woods to reach the badger sett, still very active and well trodden, with claw marks in the clay everywhere. The whole wood creaks. The curious thing is how quiet and calm it can be inside a wood during a wind. The wood shelters itself. All you hear is the wind in the fringes and in the treetops, a sound with the quality of a shingle seashore not far away. Close beside me two birches sing like a squeaky hinge as they rub together. This is an unusual sett, tunnelled inside an unusual hill fort of earth, the diggings from a decoy pond near by in the woods, left here years ago. Beaten badger paths radiate into the wood, out across a plank bridge and into a big meadow that slopes down to the railway embankment. In the long shadows of the late-winter sun it is easy to distinguish them and follow one downhill to a gap in the railway fence, where the animals obviously like to scratch themselves on the wire, leaving little clumps of their shaving-brush hair on the grass. I return to Cowpasture Lane in the shadow of the embankment and scuttle home, glad of the shelter of the lane's hedges.

I remember the whole of Suffolk as a landscape of many elms until the mid to late seventies: cumulus clouds of their canopies on every horizon, elms in the hedges and at the corners of fields, pollard elms like milestones in the green lanes. Probably the most ancient use of elm has been to pollard it for animal feed. I used to cut elm branches for fodder for my own goats. They relished the nourishing leaves far above grass. Let out into the fields, they would rise on their hind legs and strut like circus animals to reach the luscious branches. On our common, a clear browse line was discernible on all the overhanging hedgerow elms at seven or eight feet, just beyond the cows' reach. Outside the Hall Farm, looking west from my gate, stood three giant elms improbably close together as if arm in arm, like the Seven Sisters, the tuft of elms that once encircled a walnut in Tottenham and gave their name to the road that runs north-east from Holloway. At sunset our three village giants cast their immense shadows along the green all the way to the church a quarter-mile away. They seemed too mighty to succumb, yet they died the same summer as the Rookery Farm elm, leaves withering at first as the scolytus beetles got to work in their galleries beneath the bark. Eager chainsaws felled the skeleton trees, their brittle branches collapsing as they crashed, burying their shattered stumps deep in the shuddering clay. They lay like flensed whales as the firewood men swarmed over them with chainsaws, slicing the marvellous timber into cutlets to be split with the axe or the hydraulic log-splitter running on the power take-off of a tractor. The elms had stood like the triple spires of Gaudí's cathedral in Barcelona. Robbed of their grandeur, the mile-long inland sea of grass we call our common was diminished by their loss, and still is to this day. I still see their ghosts when I look that way, and cows still gather sometimes around the cratered remains of their stumps as if to shelter.

As the elms died one by one along my hedgerows during the 1970s, I left them standing as green sails of ivy grew up them and eventually blew them down. The ivy sheltered insects and roosting birds, and kept the wood-pigeons fed with berries in the winter. Many of the dead trees went down in the great storm of October 1987. I sawed them into four-foot lengths and stored the soundest outside the workshop. Much of that elm ended up spinning on my lathe late at night, and lives on as bowls or the occasional row of Shaker-inspired coat pegs. Even when I had consigned great jumbles of the sawn, split logs to the woodshed as firewood, I couldn't resist reprieving some for the lathe, often at the last moment in the very act of casting them into the fire. I have even posted split elm logs into my wood-stove and then felt so haunted by an after-image of their grained beauty that I have pulled out the already charred wood, doused it and borne it to the workshop instead. Turning elm blunts the chisels and the gouges so often that you spend almost more time at the grinding machine than the lathe, but to see the flowing wave patterns of the grain revealed as you hollow out a bowl and watch the wood begin to gleam like a horse chestnut fresh from its shell is a rare pleasure. What better way for the elm to live on?

At the common's far end, a single seventy-foot mature elm still thrives, possibly shielded from invasion by beetles by the big leaves of the horse chestnuts that surround it like bodyguards. And I can now count twenty-seven elms of around thirty feet

growing vigorously in my own hedgerows, the wind folding back
their branches, turning the leaves inside out, flashing their silver
backs.

A New-laid Hedge

It dawned sunny and cold but not quite frosty: perfect weather for hedging. I set off through the long meadow to the wood in the far corner of my land. It is the sort of place that might have been christened 'Botany Bay' or 'Van Diemen's Land' in the nineteenth century to denote its remoteness on a farm. Of course, it is not at all remote, just mildly inconvenient to reach on foot if you're laden with tools. So I hooked up the old elm-boarded trailer to the tractor and loaded up with chainsaw, fuel cans, triangular bow saw, two billhooks, trimming hook, sharpening stone, a pair of sturdy leather gloves, leather kneepads, protective glasses and a wooden beetle for driving in stakes. My task was to lay the wood's perimeter hedge of maple, hazel, dogwood and hawthorn. I probably should have plashed it several years ago: some of the trees were tall and unwieldy.

Working from the outside of the wood and hedge, I began at the left-hand end, working along the hedge to my right and laying the cut trees and hazel stems to my left. I cut through each stem as close as possible to the ground with a diagonal stroke of the billhook that severed the stem almost right through, but left the bark and enough connective tissue to allow the sap to flow. Once cut in this way, the stems or trees are called pleachers. No doubt an expert sizes up the hedge trees in a flash and makes the crucial decisions about what to cut out and what to leave almost instinctively. I spend quite a lot of time considering each tree in line and imagining how it should fit into the evolving weave of the laid hedge. Removing some of the side branches makes it possible to weave the pleacher in and out of the stakes you drive in every eighteen inches or two feet. There is plenty of hazel in the hedge, and coppice hazel growing in the wood too, so I wasn't short of stakes. Hazel or ash is best, an inch or two thick, sharpened with the billhook. I drove them in with the beetle and gently wrestled the pleachers into the twiggy basketwork. With each new pleacher I laid and wove, I was building more tension into the structure and increasing its stability. The tensile strength in a plashed hedge is actually the sum of the imparted strength and energy of the hedger. The more you can follow the grain of the wood and work with it, the easier the hedging. Cutting with an upward stroke of the billhook, going with the grain, is far easier than cutting downwards, as you have to at the base of the pleacher.

Hedgers always worry about frost because it kills the living cells of wood exposed by cutting. Some even light small fires along the hedge to keep it warm. But the work must be done in winter when the hedge reveals its architecture. Since it involves pruning the trees, a temporary reduction of their substance, this is labour for a waning moon, the low tide of the sap. John Clare's version of the doggedness and the misery of the hedger in *The Shepherd's Calendar* suggests his own experience of plashing in the rain:

> The hedger soaked wi the dull weather chops
> On at his toils which scarcely keeps him warm
> And every stroke he takes large swarms of drops
> Patter about him like an april storm.

Hazel is the most amenable to cutting and plashing, as though it has evolved into the habit. Hawthorn and ash are also pliable enough. The laid pleachers must always slope upwards. The river of sap will only flow uphill. Already, in February, the maple was so full of early-rising sap it wept copious tears when I cut it, the sap trickling down the pleated bark or splashing on to my boot. I tasted it optimistically, but, although a little sweet, it was also brackish, like human tears, and it was impossible not to think of all the sad times when my own tears, or those of loved ones, have run down my cheeks and I've licked them away. Impossible too not to imagine that the tree itself was mourning its own wound: this mutilation, subjugation to a human will.

Some of the maple had grown too big to be cut with the billhook, so I used the chainsaw to cut a wedge at the base of the trunk and gingerly eased each tree over, supporting its weight to protect the fragile hinge of sapwood, cambium and bark. What peace when I switched off the engine and resumed work with the billhook. I could hear myself think again. Thinking is one of the great pleasures of working outdoors with hand tools. In *The Woodlanders*, Hardy calls this kind of labour 'copse-work' and explains its effect on the Hintock village minds:

Copse-work, as it was called, being an occupation which the secondary intelligence of the hands and arms could carry on without the sovereign attention of the head, allowed the minds of its professors to wander considerably from the objects before them; hence the tales, chronicles, and ramifications of family history which were recounted here were of a very exhaustive kind.

Evening drew on and I leant over the hedge in the dimming light to take hold of one of the green hazel wands and thrust it sideways and downwards into the weave where it is most dense, folding over the slender tips into a barb that will shove through but won't spring back. There was a half-moon in a clear sky with an intense orange sunset lighting up the line of trees along the green lane on the far side of the meadow. Their shapes were black before it, the fretwork of branches and twigs all picked out in deep red as the huge Suffolk sun dropped behind them. The hedge was very dark when I looked back at it, but the back-lighting showed up a damaged, mossy blackbird's nest, the mud inside it baked and crazed, so I wove a framework of supporting hazel sticks, adding some crimson dog-wood for effect. I decided I would work along as far as a single wild service tree that had grown into a twenty-foot hedge tree since I planted it as many years ago. A foot a year is quite respectable growth in the competitive tangle of hedge roots that must slow up the tree, at least until it has thrust its roots deeper than its neighbours.

There was great satisfaction in topping off the new-laid hedge with the woven binders: long, slender eight- or ten-foot wands of hazel plaited decoratively but also entirely functional. They hold down the springy pleachers and draw an elegant line along the hedge, protecting it from cattle, which will tend to lean into it or massage their necks against it. Last of all, I went along cutting off the tops of the stakes to an even height just proud of the binders. Professionals take a lot of pride in the resulting white-sliced dotted line.

Hedgers usually make bonfires of the brushwood, but I often deny myself that pleasure and try to follow an older custom of wasting nothing, so pile it on to the trailer, throw a rope over it and add it to the dead hedge I've built beside an old pollard crack willow at the edge of the common. The hedge affords protection to the house and garden from the fierce westerlies that blow across the great inland sea of common, beating the grasses into waves of silver light. The same winds dry out the stacked brushwood, which settles imperceptibly – as a pheasant or a leveret, when surprised, settles itself stealthily into the ground. Once the brushwood has dried and compacted itself, I slice it up like a loaf into kindling and begin all over again. Brushwood faggots from the hedge were much used in bread ovens.

In his *Natural History of Selborne*, Gilbert White gives a revealing account of the value that was placed on the smaller denominations of wood, the 'lop and top', brushwood or *spray* that is now regularly fed into a wood-chipper or burnt on a bonfire:

A very large fall of timber, consisting of about one thousand oaks, has been cut this spring (viz. 1784), in the Holt forest; one-fifth of which, it is said, belongs to the grantee, Lord Stawel. He lays claim also to the lop and top; but the poor of the parishes of Binsted and Frinsham, Bentley and Kingsley, assert that it belongs to them; and, assembling in a riotous manner, have actually taken it all away.

The earliest hedges may have been palisades of thorn shoved in between two rows of stakes to pen stock, or perhaps to create a defence. Sheltered from browsing herbivores by the dead hedge, it would not have been long before a living hedge of saplings sprang up from seed and superseded it. The dry moats of hill forts like Maiden Castle in Dorset would probably also have bristled with coppiced blackthorn. In *Rogue Male*, set in Dorset near by, Geoffrey Household describes the remote hollow lane where his hero goes to ground as protected by 'sentinel thorns'. He too uses the dead thorns defensively: 'Then I unpacked the billhook and slashed at the dead wood on the inside of the hedges. I jammed the bicycle cross-wise between the banks and piled over it a hedge of thorn that would have stopped a lion.'

Down in the wood, I used a long-handled hook to cut back some of the blackthorn army that was slowly suckering its way out of one of the other perimeter hedges. I spared most of it, because blackthorn makes a magnificent show of snowy blossom when the cold north-east winds blow in late March, known as the 'blackthorn winter'. It also provides an intoxicating harvest of sloes for sloe gin at Christmas. They are always best fully ripened after the first frost, then posted one by one down the gullet of a bottle of cheap supermarket gin with added sugar, as geese are forcefed for pâté in the Dordogne. Blackthorn makes beautiful, plum-dark walking sticks and gives deep cover to birds. In my wood, nothing grows beneath it except lords and ladies, dog's mercury and the occasional primrose or celandine at the margins of its impenetrable, spiny thicket. The rabbits love its bare earth floor and have excavated a busy warren in the safety of its forbidding tangle. Linnaeus dubbed blackthorn *Prunus spinosa* because everything about it is prickly, tart, sour and generally stroppy. He might have called it *noli tangere* – don't touch. But its old Latin name is *bellicum*. Its hard, dense wood is said to fashion the original cosh: the knobkerrie, or shillelagh, although Robert Graves asserts in *The White Goddess* that the weapon is in fact an oak club. However, he goes on to say that blackthorn is the traditional timber with which Irish tinkers fight at fairs, and its Gaelic name, *straif*, may be the origin, via Breton and the Northern French *estrif*, of 'strife'. The blackthorn staff, says Graves, was the witches' instrument of sorcery. I prefer to think of the sloe eyes of romantic heroines, or of Dylan Thomas's 'sloeblack, slow, black, crowblack, fishingboat-bobbing sea'.

I have learnt to treat blackthorn with respect. Now and again it pierces my leather hedging gloves like a snake bite. It is the viper of trees. The spines are syringes loaded with some obscure poison that causes the deep puncture wound to bruise and throb painfully for days. Hedging can be far more dangerous than it seems. It often puts me in mind of my late friend Billy Bartrum, a farm labourer who was blinded in one eye by blackthorn as a young man while hedging. As savages in our first woods at Headstone Lane, we would eat a single mouth-puckering sloe for a dare or an initiation. Andy Goldsworthy collects the thorns of hawthorn or blackthorn to sew his leafy constructions together. I still have one of his exquisite leaf boxes of sycamore, pinned with thorns, on a shelf. It soon faded from green to brown and is now sixteen years old, still perfectly intact.

Many of our modern would-be managers of nature are under the delusion that blackthorn is some kind of weed, just because it spreads, like elm, by suckering roots. Nothing could be less true. Cobbett extols its virtues as the very fiercest of hedges: one of the few that stock will not simply eat their way through. In the wood, I use the blackthorn brushwood to protect the stools of the hazel I have just coppiced. The porcupine mounds allow the new shoots to come up unmolested by deer or rabbits. It is a species of barbed wire and, you might imagine, far too dangerous ever to have made faggots. In fact, it makes a superb fuel, burning with such instant, vicious incandescence that it was ideal for the microwave of the old cottagers: the brick or cob bread oven. On a bonfire it displays the same explosive power, towering into flame and heaving thunderous sighs from inside a white-hot core. Even when green, it can be persuaded to burn. In January I had found myself lying full length on the frosty tussocks of a glade blowing like a dragon into the orange wigwam of flame at the core of a tangled blackthorn bonfire. I was clearing some of the front rank of spear-bearers marching out into the wood from the hedge. The technique is to crawl in at rabbit-level among the molehills with a triangular bow saw and cut through the tough little trunks an inch up. The inside of a blackthorn thicket is the best place to be if you want to understand the value of such places, fashionably dismissed as 'scrub', as cover for wild mammals, insects and birds.

I had broken the ash handle of one of my billhooks during the day through some mild abuse: using its flat side to beat in some of the hazel stakes. Already weakened by woodworm, it snapped. That night I thrust the blade into the fire to burn out the embedded remains of the old handle, resolving to make a new one in the morning. The split ash logs I was burning were clean, white and straight-grained, so I took one outside next day and took my axe to it, splitting off a triangular piece roughly the right size for a handle. Then I rough-carved it with a pocket knife, turned one end on the lathe, and fitted and pinned it into the steel socket in the blade. Locking the blade in the vice, I grasped the handle, sculpting and smoothing it to the shape of my grip. These hedging tools are both swords and ploughshares. They are not so far removed from the halberds and pikes of the old battlefields, and it is easy to see how readily a peasant army could have been raised and armed.

Although I have only four meadows and a small wood, there is nearly a mile of hedgerow on my land. There was still a maze of mostly small fields and hedges when I came to the village in 1970. There were four miles of them within a half-mile of my doorstep. Now almost all are gone, except for my own eccentric oasis, the nearby woods and our green lanes. Before 1960 few of the parish hedges shown on the 1936 Ordnance Survey had been uprooted, and I calculate from the maps that there were some thirty-seven miles of them. Today no more than eight miles of them survive, of which three run round the perimeter of the common. Another three miles line the lanes and a few of the byroads. On the farmland itself, just one and a half miles of hedges survive. People talk about managing hedges, as if you had to be constantly working at them like the Forth Bridge. If you want them to be stock-proof, laying them every twenty years and cutting them each year is the best way, but if containing animals is no longer the main object, or there's a fence to do it, neglect can often be the most enlightened policy. Most of my hedges are jungles of the various trees, draped with blackberry, dog-rose, bryony, honeysuckle and wild hop, all scrambling about the branches. Birds are highly attracted to this sort of cover, so the hedges are full of nests and birdsong.

Each hedge has a distinct character. One was dominated by elm until the disease killed the trees one by one. They stood like masts for years, as sails of ivy hoisted themselves in their rigging, then caught the full force of whichever November gale came along next and crashed. Hawthorn, dogwood, sloe, maple, crab apple, rose and bramble leapt in and filled the gaps, but now the elm is tentatively reasserting itself, growing from its original roots and overtopping the brambles, which may well be acting as a shield against the beetles that carry the spores of the Dutch elm disease fungus. The beetles mostly fly below twelve feet, and if all they encounter is a wall of bramble, they will just go elsewhere. Most of the other hedges are a mix of hazel, maple and ash, with here and there a holly, crab apple, bullace or an oak, and an under-blush of dogwood, the hips of wild roses or the exquisite little pink berries of the spindle tree.

Laid hedges are certainly more stock-proof, and their trees grow into interesting, contorted shapes. Very old laid hedges can be works of the hedgers' art: a kind of tree jazz, improvised down the generations. A laid hedge is also sturdier and more stable. But the modern farmer's or conservationist's natural impulse towards tidiness and management is mostly one to resist when it comes to hedges. Unless you can lay them by hand, far better to leave them alone to be as wild as they like and grow into their own shapes. I know of nothing uglier or more saddening than a machine-flailed hedge. It speaks of the disdain of nature and craft that still dominates our agriculture. Even after years of benign neglect, plashed hedges stand as monuments to the best traditions of good husbandry.

Coppicing

Keith Dunthorne, my thatcher friend from our next-door village, had invited me over for a day's coppicing with him in his hazel wood near Bungay. Every thatched roof requires quantities of coppiced hazel spars to secure it like hairpins. So each winter Keith harvests the fast-grown pliable stems he will need for the coming season's work. I rise early and roust about in my workshop for the right billhook, then start up the humming grinder to hone the blade. Sparks strike the cold early-morning air, and I temper the hot edge in rainwater with a fizz. I throw a triangular bow saw into the back of the car, thick leather gloves, goggles and a hard hat with a visor.

When I arrive in Keith's yard he too is loading tools into the open back of his truck, and I help break open some hay for the horses. Next to the bales in the open-fronted barn sheafs of reed are stacked fifteen feet high, end out. This is Norfolk reed from the Broads, the real thing. For Keith, it is a matter of principle to insist on using it instead of the cheaper imported material from Romania or Hungary. It means his price for a roof will be a little higher, but it helps keep the few remaining reed-cutters on the Broads in work.

Keith is agile, slender and wiry, with the weathered good looks and steady eye of a man who is confident in his skills. In his battered trilby and lace-up boots, he has the romantic air of a Romany. He puts fuel cans and his Stihl chainsaw in the back with his favourite hook, very sharp and thin bladed. Between us on the bench seat of the Toyota Hiace sits his lurcher, Zeka. She is docile and affectionate, with a dark-grey curly coat. We follow the Waveney along its water-meadows, and the dog never stops scanning them for anything that moves. Near Bungay we turn off into the winding lanes of an estate, pass the hall and slip into the old wood, pulling in the truck down a brambled, grassy concrete road the Americans constructed during the war. It was their policy to store the bombs and armaments hidden inside woods in camouflaged concrete bunkers well away from the vulnerable airfields that chequered Suffolk and Norfolk. Woods were, as ever, places of concealment.

Keith and I sit in the cab steaming the windscreen with tea from our flasks. Vapour rises off dewy trees into the sunny February day as we leave Zeka asleep in the van and set off into the line of hazel coppice in helmets and visors. Keith wears no gloves: his hands are leather. He has been coppicing the wood for twenty-five years now, working from its south flank, cutting successive swathes of ash and hazel about ten yards wide from east to west of the wood. The result is that each new band of coppice regrowth is stepped back, zoned by height towards the south to allow in the maximum of sunlight to stimulate new growth. Some coppicers pile the leavings of brushwood over the newly cut coppice stools to protect new shoots from browsing deer or rabbits. The shoots will always find their way to the light through the mounded twigs. Keith doesn't bother and finds the trees regenerate perfectly well. The wood seems to have escaped damage from deer. This may be because it is relatively small, and there is evidence that deer prefer to browse in bigger woods, where they may feel safer and there is more to eat.

Keith cuts down the twelve- or sixteen-foot hazels with his chainsaw almost level with the ground. He finds it makes no difference whether the stools are cut horizontally or at an angle, as recommended by the traditionalists to allow rainwater to run off.

I follow with the billhook, stripping off the side shoots and stacking the resulting poles in loose bundles on the wood floor. As we move through the wood, I make neat piles of the brushwood. In medieval days, and probably until well into the last century, none of this would have been wasted. It would have been bundled tightly into faggots and stored in the barn to dry thoroughly. Faggots were burnt in the bread oven, heating it with a short, fierce blaze.

We drag the poles through the wood to the truck and load them in the open truck so they overhang at the back. It is gruelling work, all the more so because of the awkward, unnatural twisting effort of hugging the rods together at the same time as hauling them through snagging brambles.

Apart from the chainsaw, we are following a very old tradition in this wood. The billhooks we are using would have looked much the same two hundred years ago, although they varied in design, as they still do, in each part of the country. The art of coppicing goes back at least 6,000 years in Britain to the Sweet Track in the Somerset Levels, a Neolithic wooden walking track over a mile long running across wet or flooded peat to link what was then the island of Westhay to Shapwick Burtle, a ridge of higher ground. Poles of ash, oak and lime were cut down, transported to the Levels and pegged together in a sophisticated piece of early engineering in the winter or early spring of 3807 or 3806 BC. A series of trestles, driven into the wet peat, supported an oak walkway of split trunks. A whole web of wooden tracks has been discovered in the Levels. Another, the Eclipse Track, was built differently out of a series of woven coppice hurdles in 1800 BC, and the Walton Track, also on the Levels, was composed almost entirely of hazel rods. Close examination of the widths of the tree rings in the wood of these tracks makes such historical accuracy possible. The ring patterns are compared with those in other wood samples of known date. Early coppice, cut with a stone axe, is recognizable by the heel of torn cambium and bark at the base of each rod left where it was wrenched and twisted off the stool. The ancient Somerset tracks have all been preserved in the airless conditions of wet peat.

There is evidence that early coppice was grown for fodder, and that the tops of the stems were cut off for their foliage. Pollard ash is still harvested for fodder today in parts of Sweden and elsewhere in Europe. The coppiced rods would have provided a second harvest. Quite how trees evolved their ability to sprout new stems when coppiced is something of a mystery. They often coppice themselves naturally: hazel will grow new shoots when old stems die, and I have seen trees broken off at the base by an avalanche sending up new coppice stems. One intriguing possibility, recently suggested by Oliver Rackham in *Ancient Woodland*, is that the first large-scale coppicers were the giant elephants of the Pleistocene Era, like the one found at West Runton near Cromer, an animal the size of a London bus whose devastating browsing would have exerted a powerful evolutionary argument for spontaneous regrowth.

By the time of the Sweet Track, people had discovered that trees are far more productive if they are coppiced on a regular cycle. Since the earliest account of a medieval wood in 1269–70 at Beaulieu Abbey in the New Forest, coppice cycles have varied from as little as four years to twenty-eight, depending on the species and the use of the wood. But prehistoric people also knew how much more useful, versatile and manageable the regrowth shoots from a stump were than single trees. Interpreting the historical records, Oliver Rackham has pointed out that woods often represented a form of savings account, to be coppiced and sold as a crop of under-wood on a rainy day. Some woods were coppiced all at once every so often, others by harvesting a succession of glades on an annual rotation, as we were doing.

Keith's agreement with the estate doesn't allow him in to coppice the wood until after the pheasant-shooting season. Now he is anxious to cut the hazel as soon as he can before the sap begins to rise and spoil the wood for thatching brorch, or spars. The presence of sap will attract woodworm, which love its sweetness, so you must cut your hazel while the sap is sunk for the winter.

We take a break for tea at twelve, then lunch at two so we can sit in the cab and listen to the Archers. I peel open a tin of sardines and carve off chunks of bread with my Opinel. We sit munching and sipping, watching a pair of tree-creepers working an ash trunk for insects, wandering up or down the tree vertically with no apparent effort. The wood shows all the signs of its antiquity: hazel and ash with maple, hornbeam and oak standards here and there, floored with dog's mercury and bluebells in spring. As we eat, Keith tells me its story, and how he came to be coppicing it. Twenty-five years earlier he approached the owner, an old gentleman who was happy to see him take over the coppicing for thatching spars and firewood, to keep the ash and hazel stools in good order. Come Christmas, Keith would always visit him, taking a bottle of whisky and his one pound annual rent for the coppice rights.

Recently the son inherited the estate, a young fellow in the City who brought in a managing agent from Norwich to oversee it. The agent met Keith in the wood and asked him to suggest a commercial rent for it. Keith pointed out that he had always paid in kind, so the agent said, 'All right, make us some sheep hurdles. Let me know how many you think you can make us each year.' Hurdles are a lot of work, so Keith declined the proposition, as he did another that he should supply the firewood to the estate as rent. The agent has now stipulated that Keith can take only hazel poles, and no firewood of a thickness greater than his arm. He must cut down the firewood and leave it for the estate to carry out and sell.

As the late-afternoon sun slants through the brown wood, it turns it to purple with an underglow of crimson. We finish loading the truck, lash down the great springy bundle of rods, swig the last of our tea and head home.

Towards the end of March, Keith had finished the year's coppicing and cut the loose rods of hazel into bundles of twenty ready to be split into brorches. He had also cut six-foot bundles for liggers, the riven wands he uses to secure the ridge capping of the thatch in a distinctive pattern, leaving his signature on the roof much as a baker might decorate a loaf. All the new hazel was stored neatly under cover in the barn.

Keith's yard was almost walled by tall canvas-covered stacks of thatching reed bundles laid in a geometrical criss-cross like a reed *mudhif* guest house of the all-but-extinct Iraqi Marsh Arabs on the Euphrates. A pair of gypsy wagons shrouded in tarpaulins stood beside the reed stacks. Across the garden was a third, its stainless-steel stove-pipe glinting in the sun, and its front doors ajar to let in the air and spring sunshine. In other corners of the yard, old trailers, a threshing machine and a blue Fordson tractor, all sheltered under yet more faded green or blue canvas, so the effect was of being in an encampment.

Zeka appeared from behind the barn and came bounding towards me, sniffing my corduroys with approval and wagging not just her tail but her whole body, making a hill of her back. The first time I met her four years earlier she had run so far away from home that she landed up two miles away in my fields. She rolled over when I approached her, and I led her into my kitchen, where she soon made herself at home before the Aga while I rang the number on her collar. To my surprise it turned out to be Keith's. I found Keith and Canny drinking coffee at the open door of a little lean-to office at one end of their barn listening to news of the Iraq War on the BBC World Service. It was an odd scene: the Toyota Hiace parked outside with its cab doors wide open, its radio filling the Suffolk air with news of fresh disasters from the desert, sunshine pouring in through the open barn doors, lapping at the half-shadow where Keith now resumed work splitting hazel. The sweet-smelling wooden bundles were stacked almost to the crossbeams, the pale cut ends peering in their hundreds from out of the shadows. He sat in an old chair in the middle of the barn's centre bay surrounded by the stacked bundles of hazel spar-gads, neatly sorted according to thickness and cut into twenty-eight-inch lengths. Once he had split and sharpened each brorch, Keith folded it in two with a twist to make a V-shaped sprung scissor that he would drive into the reed to peg it into the thatch.

As with all the old crafts, each county has its own variations on every detail, and Keith's Suffolk 'brorches' would be 'sprays' in the

Chilterns, 'buckles' in Worcestershire, 'spars' from Dorset to Devon and 'spekes' or 'spicks' in Wiltshire. In Worcestershire they would be of willow, more flexible than hazel, but not so long-lasting. And not so long ago, when thatchers still had apprentices, the splitting of these pegs would have been part of their work. In *The Woodlanders* it is Marty South who sits up late at her fireside making thatching spars for Mr Melbury in her attempt to earn enough from the piecework to escape having to sell her long hair to Mr Percombe, the barber, who looks in at her cottage:

In the room from which this cheerful blaze proceeded he beheld a girl seated on a willow chair, and busily working by the light of the fire, which was ample and of wood. With a billhook in one hand and a leather glove much too large for her on the other, she was making spars, such as are used by thatchers, with great rapidity. She wore a leather apron for this purpose, which was also much too large for her figure. On her left lay a bundle of the straight, smooth hazel rods called spar-gads – the raw material of her manufacture; on her right a heap of chips and ends – the refuse – with which the fire was maintained; in front a pile of the finished articles. To produce them she took up each gad, looked critically at it from end to end, cut it to length, split it in four, and sharpened each of the quarters with dexterous blows, which brought it to a triangular point precisely resembling that of a bayonet.

In Hardy's time, all sorts of journeymen were on hand to supply or assist the thatcher, whereas the modern craftsman has become increasingly isolated and has to do everything himself. The isolation had already set in by the 1930s, when H. J. Massingham writes of his local thatcher 'taking upon his own shoulders donkey work that in the old days was done by the thatcher's boy or apprentice'. Later on in *The Woodlanders*, Hardy describes the manufacture of spars in Mr Melbury's timber and copse-ware yard: 'Winterbourne thereupon crossed over to the spar-house where some journeymen were already at work, two of them being travelling spar-makers from Stagfoot Lane, who, when the fall of the leaf began, made their appearance regularly, and when winter was over disappeared in silence till the season came again.' In Ronald Blythe's *Akenfield*, Ernie Bowers, the thatcher, describes how he and his father would thatch up to 600 ricks of straw a year for the Suffolk farmers after harvest. 'Every parish', he says, 'had its own thatcher in the 1920s. But in the 1930s things changed. Most of the good thatchers were getting on the old side and beginning to drop out. I can remember five or six great thatchers of the old school dying then. Nobody replaced them. They were men of the old time – of the old life.'

Later in the day, Keith turned to splitting liggers. Splitting a length of the hazel with a small, sharp billhook reveals the white sapwood inside, the tree's innards, and doubles it into a pair of liggers. The pile of curly shavings and offcuts accumulating on the floor was the kindling Keith and Canny used to light their fires. Keith leant each pole on a leather pad strapped to his knee and drew the old Parkes billhook towards him, guiding it on its journey, subtly twisting it to right or left as it travelled up the grain to keep the two halves exactly equal. I tried it myself and worried that the billhook might travel up my groin. I sat in Keith's old kitchen chair facing the sunlit open doorway of the barn, got the billhook started into the end grain of a pole and drew it unsteadily up the grain. The first foot went well, but then the blade seemed to veer off with a will of its own, like a gramophone needle jumping out of its groove. My attempt was relegated ignominiously to the firewood pile, and so were two more. There's nothing like trying something yourself for swelling your respect for a craftsman who really knows what he's doing. 'Keith made it look so easy' is the standard way to say this, but he really did, and for him, he assured me, it really was.

Always working with the same billhook, Keith bevelled off the ends of each ligger to make a join. The secret of the splitting, he said, is all about feeling for the grain as the blade slides along it. Drawing a new bundle of twenty wands from several stacked to his left against an old pram, he said he could split a bundle an hour, so he will do eight a day at most, each hazel pole yielding seven or

eight brorches. Working over the winter, Keith makes 20,000 to
30,000 brorches and liggers a year. Of course, he could buy them
ready-made by someone else, or imported from Central Europe, as
many thatchers do, but Keith enjoys the seasonal nature of his work,
and its varied rhythms from month to month. He even sells his
own brorches when he has some to spare. In *The Woodlanders*, Mr
Percombe asks Marty how much she gets for her spar-making:

> 'Eighteenpence a thousand,' she said reluctantly.
> 'Who are you making them for?'
> 'Mr Melbury, the timber-dealer, just below here.'
> 'And how many can you make in a day?'
> 'In a day and half the night, three bundles – that's a thousand and a
> half.'
> 'Two and threepence.' Her visitor paused.

Canny said that she has been a Wood several times over. Her
surname was Shaw, meaning a wood, and she originally married a
man called Wood. Now she lived with Keith, who was a Dunthorne,
and quite plainly one of nature's woodlanders. Working with him
that February day, a master craftsman who still went into the woods
with only his dog, and the *Archers*, for company, I remembered H. J.
Massingham, writing about his own thatcher in the 1930s: 'He lacks
the townsman's favours, but owns a fortune in his inward peace.'

As I was about to leave, Keith disappeared into the shadows of
the barn and returned with a hazel staff, more of a magician's wand
than a walking stick, and presented it to me. I could not imagine a
more beautiful gift: even in the tree's fingertips, in the branched
wand of the water diviner, there is a special magic in all hazel. It
has come from the wood, of course. From bottom to tapering top,
the rod had grown naturally fluted and spiralled by the strangling
effect of the honeysuckle stem that still encircled it like an asp,
the tourniquet causing the freckled hazel bark to fatten along its
line in a continuous swelling like a banister rail, a helter-skelter
of sap-engorged bark perfectly matched to the human grip. The

wooden vortex that grew along the woodbine ligature asserted the tree's will to live. Keith took the Parkes billhook to it and bevelled off the top. My four-foot-six Jack-and-the-beanstalk Merlin-staff was a masterpiece of nature, the voluptuous embrace of the honey-suckle exciting the hazel into a wild frenzy of cell division. Waving it, I felt, might turn a toad into a princess.

Tools and Workshops

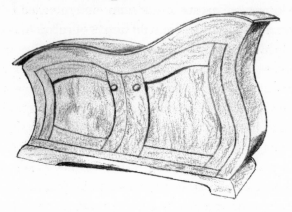

On the wall behind the lathe in my workshop is a newspaper photograph of David Pye, the late Professor of Furniture Design at the Royal College of Art. Dressed in navy boiler suit and scarf, he is entering his workshop from a garden through half-open French doors. Light from the anglepoise lamp over his lathe reflects off his round spectacles. He looks serious and thoughtful. Two of his trademark hand-carved, fluted wooden dishes stand on a bench in the foreground beside a Golden Virginia tobacco tin and a clutch of wood-handled gouges. A massive baulk of timber, anchored to the lathe on steel brackets, is obviously his homemade tool rest for turning outsized bowls. Rows of chisels and callipers are slotted into a rack on the wall behind a second workbench cluttered with wood shavings, tins of Brasso, oil cans and a blade-sharpening grinder. Above them hang more tools: a collection of adzes, axes and hand saws. Two more side axes are stuck into a chopping block. Framing the scene very close to the lens in soft focus are the graceful wooden handles of three planes.

Probably most workshops come to look something like this. Mine certainly has: the heavy workbenches standing like oxen, the wood floor pimpled with spilt glue and odd lighting contraptions in every corner. Pye's workshop has high white plaster walls and elegant moulded ceilings. It is evidently within his house. My workshop is illuminated by a set of stage lights and tells of a lifetime's accumulation of tools. I went to farm auctions and bought impossibly long wooden stack ladders nobody needed or wanted any more for a few pounds. I bought a 1948 Fordson Major tractor with a useful little six-cylinder Perkins diesel engine in perfect working order. It had been used just after the war for towing bombers about on the American airfields round here. I also equipped myself with a full armoury of trailers, ploughs, harrows, cultivators and hay-cutters to go with it. At the farm sales, it was impossible not to rescue machines with names like the Nicolson swathe-turner and such things as enormous hay rakes originally designed to be drawn by horses, wooden bullock carts, or the kind of miniature tipping trailer known as a tumbril, one of the most useful things any farm could possess.

I never met David Pye. He lives on the wall as a mentor. His book *The Nature and Art of Workmanship*, published in 1968, taught me to think about wood, and whatever I make of it, in a new light. Pye didn't just write or teach about the making of things: he was a maker himself. He originally trained to be an architect of wooden buildings, then served with the navy during the war and afterwards taught for twenty-six years at the Royal College. He inevitably pondered the problematical word 'craft', and thought about the ideas of William Morris and John Ruskin on the crafts and workmanship. Pye wrote a passionate critique of some of Ruskin's ideas in 'The Nature of Gothic'.

Here is a very modest example of the workmanship of risk. I spent from three o'clock this afternoon until the light ran out at half past five making what David Nash calls a 'cut-and-warp column' out of a length of green cherry for my friend Terence Blacker's birthday. The column is three feet tall, and I had to put in thirty incisions of my chainsaw all round it, using the machine as delicately as a paintbrush. The idea was to saw almost right through the wood cutting in towards its centre, leaving only a slender central column supporting leaves of cherry three eighths of an inch thick.

Each circular cut involved rotating the log four times to present the best angle to the saw, so you could say there are 120 saw cuts altogether. It was punishing work, and the sweat flowed freely. I worked outside at an improvised anvil of hefty two-foot oak and willow logs, cross-sections of tree-trunks heavy enough to take a firm hold of the workpiece. First, I squared off the four sides of the bark to make a straight-sided column that tapered a little towards the apex.

A cut-and-warp column is a good example of David Pye's 'workmanship of risk' because at any moment things could go wrong. Tip the whizzing blade of the chainsaw a half-inch too far into the centre, and you could undo all your painstaking work by cutting short the column. You walk a tightrope from beginning to end of what feels more and more like a performance as you go on. Your glasses steam up in the cold air. You enter a trance of concentration, and the sweat runs down your back or springs itchily into your scalp inside the safety helmet and streams down your forehead behind the gauze visor. Your eyes begin to water in the frosty air. After the first few incisions you get into a rhythm and instinctively feel how deep to plunge the saw blade into the wood. By making a series of circular incisions no more than a quarter of an inch apart, you are left with a column of wooden leaves apparently suspended in air, in fact cantilevered on the slender central column of continuous heartwood. The bar of your chainsaw is three eighths of an inch thick, so with each cut you remove as much wood as you leave standing in the column, and introduce a new element, air, into the wood. Thus you begin to open the tree to the air, allowing the sap to evaporate, breathing it in yourself as you do so.

With each new incision, the piece grows more fragile, and the potential for disaster, if you were to make a mistake, that much greater. As time goes by and the piece gets more interesting, your investment in it as well as your anxiety both increase. The trick, of course, is not to allow anxiety to creep in at all but to maintain a kind of Zen composure, complete confidence, and the poise and instinctive skill that result. That, at any rate, is the theory. At last you make the final cut and carry the column into the house for the first time, cradling it like a baby. You set it down on a table and scrutinize it from every angle, from close up and from the other side of the room. It is nothing like as beautiful as anything David Nash might make, but it still feels good, and it will feel even better when you present it to your friend.

Clive's workshop is a little shed up a concrete farm track opposite the cowsheds at Crabb's Farm. There's a tall cylindrical stove in one corner that burns his wood shavings. He refuels it by poking a length of two-inch pole inside from the top before filling it with shavings and packing them down tightly all round, so that when he gently removes the pole there's a natural chimney, and a draft, up the centre of the stove. Wood shavings burn with intense heat.

Clive is packing up his tools today, leaving the workshop, his craft and his partner for a new life in Oxford as a forester. The tools are housed neatly in old leather-clad wooden chests that look as if they're designed for going to sea. The chisels lie in neat rows, the set squares fit snugly under brass clips, and the morticing tools nest in their niches. The big electric machines are ranged around the walls: a morticing machine, a pillar drill, a circular saw, a bandsaw and a plane. Standing in the middle of it all is the Art Deco armoire Clive has just finished making in English oak. It will be his last piece of furniture, and he must deliver it to Framlingham after lunch. The doors of the top half, the wardrobe part, mirror each other in the cat's-paw burrs that figure the wood.

A chubby extractor fan tube snakes out of the wall. I cast an inquiring eye on a set of clamps hanging up beside it. Clamps are what all joiners collect: you can never have too many. But Clive has promised them to his friend Caspar to use while he's away. I have the kind of weakness for wood other people have for puppies or chocolates. Outside in the farmyard is Clive's stash of timber: planks of oak, beech, sycamore, cherry and elm. He even has several lengths of London plane, an underrated wood with its deep blush of salmon. Inside the workshop are a few precious lengths of English holly, pure grained, smooth, white and heavy. It is all for sale, says Clive.

Perhaps it is some hidden pheromone in the wood itself that turns my brain, but, as in a dream, I find myself buying the stuff. First, the entire trunk of a beech, neatly stacked to season with spacers between the boards. Next, I spot a stack of burr oak, thickly planked by Freddy Buggs, the local Stoke-by-Nayland sawyer. Instantly lost in the psychedelic wonders of its rioting grain, I imagine the burr oak bowls I could turn on the lathe, and the kitchen table I could make, set with pale plates and eggcups. Clive lifts off the tarpaulin covers with a flourish, revealing more and more curiosities. I have soon added to my order four massive hunks of deep-red turkey oak, a pair of elm boards and a quantity of fine, pale sycamore for turning plates. It is the wood that was always used for milk pails, because it imparts no taste. I am also quite unable to resist the holly in the workshop. I have spent far too much money on timber I am going to have to transport and store under cover. I have no immediate need of any of it, but it is unusual timber, selected by a connoisseur. I convince myself it is an investment.

After lunch we all help Clive lug the armoire into his van and watch him set off to Framlingham on his final delivery as a joiner, then go over to Polstead, a few miles away, to see Dylan Pym. He is a joiner too, and his workshop stands on the edge of the orchard of the cottage where Maria Martin lived. Polstead was always famous for its cherries, but on 18 May 1828 Maria Martin was murdered by a jealous lover, William Corder, and buried under the floor of the Red Barn. Huge crowds came to Bury St Edmunds on 11 August 1828 to see Corder hanged in the last public execution in England. That summer alone over 200,000 people made the pilgrimage to Polstead, removing pieces of the barn as souvenirs year after year until 1842, when it was burnt down by an arsonist. In Bury St Edmunds market at cherry harvest time, the fruit sellers' cry was ever after 'Polstead Cherries! Red as the blood of Maria Martin!'

Dylan's workshop is a boarded two-storey shed surrounded by open-fronted sheds full of seasoning timber, including the planked trunks of oaks up to three feet wide from the local woods. Inside, a blackboard on the wall is chalked up with lists of the numbered components of chairs and their dimensions and a schedule of work from day to day. Dylan's banjo rests on a windowsill, and an impressive collection of clamps is ranged along a wall. Vapour rises past them from an eight-foot plywood steam box bubbling gently, supplied by an old electric Burco boiler. I notice the dribbles of tannin staining the plywood around the steamer's ventilation holes. Dylan is making chairs of English oak. He opens the little plywood door at one end of the oblong steamer and pops in a slender six-foot length of inch-square green oak. It is going to be the curved back of a chair like a Windsor smoker's bow. Dylan explains that timing is the all-important thing in wood steaming. This particular component, he says, needs cooking for exactly twenty minutes. No more, no less. He then falls into earnest conversation with two potential clients and forgets the deadline altogether. After half an hour he remembers and opens up the box. Steam and the acrid smell of tannin billow out, and I help slide out the oak and fit it to a steel backing strap, with handles at either end, then swiftly bend it over the U-shaped form and clamp it tight. Minutes later, as soon as it has cooled, Dylan loosens the clamps and lifts off a perfect U-shaped chair back with plenty of spring in it. He hooks it up on a beam to join a row of others, destined to make a set of chairs. By using green wood from a single tree, with the same moisture content, Dylan ensures it will bend and behave consistently. He leaves the steamed components hanging up for a year to dry and season thoroughly, turns the legs on his lathe, hollows out the seats with an adze and a spokeshave, then assembles the chairs.

I set out this morning with my friend and neighbour Terence Blacker in search of wooden flooring for the barn he is rebuilding as a house. First we go to Coton and turn down a track in the heavy rain. We arrive outside a dripping woodshed packed to the eaves with reclaimed pine from demolition sites. Two youths with crow-bars are prising old nails out of some boards. Val Hancock, a man of medium but muscular build wearing dusty glasses, emerges from behind a large circular saw. Sawdust frosts his shoulders, chest and curly hair. He leaves the saw running, and we have to speak against its hum. It is almost as though it is running under its own momentum, or a millstream runs beneath the floor to power it. The interior of Val's sawmill is landscaped with sawdust and shavings. Foothills arise at one end of an electric plane and keep on rising all the way to the back wall. I notice a giant bandsaw too and catch myself involuntarily checking Val's hands for a full complement of fingers.

Val shows us yellow pine, Douglas fir and pitch pine, running a plank or two through the plane to show off the figure. The pitch pine has the tightest grain. It is heavier, harder, tougher stuff, with a powerful aroma of resin. Val has built his own sawmill, a huge wood-framed hangar supported on laminated timber girders, out of an old public library somewhere in South London. It is deeply ramshackle and admirable in its defiant spirit of enterprise. Val is doing well too, with a sudden floorboard gold rush of well-heeled computer people and graphic designers busy on their home improvements. I am quite shocked when he tells us the prices, but reflect that the quality of this older, highly seasoned timber is far higher than that of most new wood. Most of Val's pine has grown slowly in the wintry forests of the Baltic, Siberia or British Columbia. As a result it is close grained and dense, and will make good floors. Val reveals that he is actually milling pitch pine floorboards out of the roof trusses and other structural beams of Victorian and early-twentieth-century warehouses.

We visit several places like Val's, hidden away up tracks all over Suffolk. As we drive further south, the prices rise. Near Bury St Edmunds someone is charging £150 for the sort of unremarkable doors you could find *gratis* on any London skip until recently. Even a modest elbow of oak, a support for a crossbeam, is not far off £100. Clearly times have changed. At Olde Worlde Pine somewhere near Clare we find an impressive selection of fourteen-inch oak boards, elm from a mill in Somerset, French oak, ash, yellow pine and pitch pine. The French oak is less expensive because of a glut caused by all the trees knocked over by the big storm in 1999. They tempt Terence with stories about elm: how the floor will move every day according to the weather, how it will be a living thing, shifting like a minor earthquake in a thunderstorm or lying still on calm, cool, dry days. Terence is much moved by this description, I can see, and we drive away deep in discussion of the merits and aesthetics of oak, elm, ash and pine.

On down to Polstead, where we meet Dylan Pym and Jude, and Dylan's workmate Carl, in their timber-framed and boarded workshop in the orchard of Maria Martin's cottage. They are working on some 'chesty' cupboards, part of a kitchen of English chestnut. We climb a steep staircase into the upstairs office and sit around in Dylan's superb chairs of deep-brown English oak with steamed spindle backs and arms, rather in the Shaker style. 'We're totally into steaming here,' says Dylan, who is a kind of wood-working Jamie Oliver: genial, relaxed and always ready to pick up the banjo that stands in the corner and play. Dylan shows us his six-foot steaming box and the Burco boiler that powers it. Steaming, he says, is all about speed. Once it is out of the steamer, you have less than two minutes to get the hot wood strapped into its bent shape and clamped on to the form.

We inspect the beautiful English and French hardwood seasoning in the yard outside. Dylan says trees that grow towards the light slowly spin towards it, so that for ever after they will tend to twist, even when you saw them into planks, plane them, season them and store them flat. If their nature is to twist, that is what they will always do.

Ash

My ash bower is a kind of folly, an Aboriginal wiltja that stands at the top of my long meadow in Suffolk. It consists of a double row of lively ash trees bent over into Gothic arches like a small church. I planted it twenty years ago. It is eighteen feet long by nine feet wide, with four pairs of trees six feet apart along each side curving up to meet just under seven feet off the ground, so you can walk up and down inside. In the summer heat it is a cool, green room roofed with wild hops and the flickering shadows of ash leaves. I sometimes sling a hammock inside. I even installed a bed last year, exactly like the one I slept on in my swag at Peter Latz's place in the shadow of the ghost gum and the caterpillar hills. Or the one that sheltered the puppies beneath Mary Kemarre's wiltja on the bush-plum hunt. Every so often, it needs pollarding and reshaping. I make no claims for the originality of its conception: it was directly inspired by David Nash's *Ash Dome*. It is what they call in film or art magazines an *hommage*, although I prefer to hold up both hands and call it pure plagiarism. For all that, it gives me enormous pleasure and interest, and it has grown into a mild obsession.

Years ago, once they had reached seven or eight feet, I bent the saplings together in pairs and grafted each one to its partner. They began to grow together, uniting into a single organism with two sets of roots but a single vascular system. In other words, they began to share the same sap. Then, as the lateral branches grew long enough, I did the same with them, peeling off a section of the bark and bast of both branches with a pocket knife to reveal the cambium at the point of contact, then binding them tightly together. Again the branches grew together as one flesh to form a swollen scab of bark.

The result of all this wood-welding is a remarkably stable structure, engineered in exactly the same way as a timber-framed house. The first wooden houses were indeed A-frames, or cruck built, just like this. Their mortice-and-tenon joints, secured with oak pegs, were the equivalent of the grafted stems and branches. In parts of Indonesia and Malaysia subject to flooding, houses are elevated on stilts of living trees on a similar principle to the ash bower.

The structure is really a composite pollard, or a laid hedge on stilts. It is constantly sending up new shoots, reaching for the light like a hedgerow ash. Every two or three years I must pollard or lay its canopy. This is what I have to do today under the waning moon. If the moon can cause the tides to rise and fall, why should it not do the same to the sap in plants and trees? That is the logic behind the notion that the husbandry of increase, such as sowing and planting, is best done during the waxing phases of the moon. Conversely, harvesting, the work of decrease, including coppicing and pollarding, belongs in the time when the moon herself is decreasing.

I prop a ladder against one side, lay two scaffold boards along the basketwork of the roof and rope them down. They spread my weight, so I can move about up there with a billhook, pollarding some vertical shoots, cutting others into pleachers, bending them over, weaving them in. Wrestling the tallest of them, I feel how much muscular, tensile strength there is in ash. Bent over and woven or tied down, the pleachers have the pent-up power of strongbows. Every now and then I descend and stand back to ponder my next few moves. Which rods to cut out and which to lay? Should this tall one go lengthwise or crossways? The pondering and choosing resembles chess, or a game of outsized pick-a-stick. I use a rope to haul over some of the pleachers, tying it high up, guiding it from solid earth for better footing.

The elephant-grey bark begins to gleam in a light rain shower. I love this skin of ash, almost human in its perfect smoothness when young, with an under-glow of green. It wrinkles and creases like elephant skin at the heels and elbows of old pleachers where they have healed. It bursts out in pimples or heat bumps where the epicormic buds are about to break out into new shoots. The oldest and best-laid hedges are often in sheep country in Wales or Cumbria, where the hedgers have had to respond to the challenge of animals determined to find a way through. Laid branches of ash or hazel will often form solid elbows uniting the stools of several trees together where they have grafted naturally through close contact and the rasping action of the wind on the hedge.

The bower is floored in lords and ladies, ground ivy and mosses, and its eight trunks cross-gartered with wild hops, our English vines. They thatch its roof with their big, cool leaves, dangling bunches of the aromatic, soporific female flowers from the green ceiling like grapes. As spring comes on, the bower fills like a bath with frothy white Queen Anne's lace. The great strength of ash lies in its suppleness and in the straightness of its grain, and it makes the very best firewood, even burning green before seasoning.

Almost within sight of the bower, on the common beyond the moat and along the green lanes, are dozens of ancient ash pollards. Because of the extra effort of regrowing new poles at each pollarding every twenty years, the pollard trees grow slowly but live longer, like coppice stools. Left alone to grow naturally, an ash will live no more than 200 years, but pollards as much as 500 years old rise like grey, lichened dolmens in the hedges of Cumbria. In Bradfield Woods in Suffolk there is a giant ash coppice stool still slowly rippling outwards from its ruined core that might well have been living over a thousand years. Even at the age of twenty the trunks of the bower are beginning to show some of the early signs of what will accrue with age: they are green with algae, and lichens are beginning to form around their damp feet. They are putting on ankle socks of moss. There is something goat-footed about ash trees: the shaggy signs of Pan.

I imagine these eight trees as they may be in 200 years: their long embrace a living expression of arboreal solidarity. By then lichens will have very gradually colonized the trees, and may be a good indication of their age, since they exist in a different dimension of time. Lichens do better in the wetter conditions towards the west and the Atlantic. In Cumbria they call the 500-year-old pollards that line field boundaries, tracks and streams at the heads of the side valleys leading off Borrowdale, Stonethwaite and Seathwaite 'cropping ash'. They seem to grow out of the stone, and are encrusted with some of the richest lichen communities in England besides those in Cornwall and the New Forest. Lichens do well on ash because its bark is less acidic. They like poplar, sycamore and willow for the same reason, and thrive less well on the acid bark of trees like pine, oak, birch or alder.

The existence of a complex flora of different lichen species on a tree is a sign of its age, and may be evidence of a link with the wildwood. A great many moths, like the peppered moth, mimic the lichens of bark in their intricately camouflaged wings: evidence of just how widespread and abundant lichens must once have been. The legendary lichenologist Francis Rose, whose pioneering work in the New Forest led to the discovery of some 344 different lichens living there, developed such acute ecological sensitivity through his years of fieldwork that he was able to predict, from close study of a map, or just from a car window, where relic populations of certain rare lichens associated with ancient woodland would be found. During the 1970s Rose refined his concept of 'ancient woodland indicator' lichens to publish, in 1976, an index of thirty key species, most of them subtle variations on *Lobaria pulmonaria*. Finding any twenty of the species on the list would give a very good indication of unbroken ecological continuity in a wood stretching back at least to the Middle Ages, and quite possibly to pre-Roman times.

Lichens are incredibly sensitive to place and famously averse to pollution. One of the typical lichens of ash trees is the delicately branched *Evernia prunastri*. Seen under a magnifying glass, the lichen looks like the tiniest bonsai tree. In his definitive New Naturalist book on lichens, Oliver Gilbert demonstrates how, the further you move away from the polluted centre of a big city such as Newcastle-upon-Tyne, the bigger and more luxuriant are the specimens of *Evernia*. Nine examples collected on a straight line running from seven and a half to thirty miles from the city centre show a massive increase in size.

Pollards slowly develop their own very rich ecosystems. Each of the ash pollards on our green is a world of its own, tenanted, like the common, by a great variety of individuals, each intent on a particular form of sustenance. Snails live in the crevices of the hollows, probably grazing by night on lichens, like the herbivorous bark lice that live on the trunks. Ants run up and down in continuous two-lane traffic, perhaps to milk aphids in the canopy. Spiders sling webs across the crevices, and all kinds of moths, both caterpillars and adults, roost or feed concealed in the tree.

Along our local lanes, ash pollards stand as monuments to centuries of woodmanship. Climbing wooden ladders to a bole eight or ten feet up, and standing in it to cut off the poles, is hard work. The axe was often the preferred tool, since it cuts cleanly and is easier to swing from a standing position in the tree. Sawing by hand means squatting or kneeling in the bole. Ashes thrive on the heavy clays of High Suffolk. Two hundred yards from here a dozen pollards rise from the common in a double row like hambones, their knuckles a kind of battleground, swollen like boxing gloves. Yet there is also a fruitfulness about their swelling as they launch yet another eager generation of smooth grey poles: they have the topknot look of date palms or pineapples.

In the next village, Thrandeston, a superb ash pollard stands alone at the crossroads on the green. It is fissured like a rock, over two yards in girth, and hollow, as old pollards usually are. But I worry that its twenty poles are due for pollarding before they split the tree in two in the next big gale, and who will cut them now?

Lichens have painted the south- and west-facing flanks a soft pale green. Moss cools the roots. A little further along the quiet roadside on my route to our market town of Diss is a trio of such magnificence they are almost a shrine to me. Three giants' fists thrust defiantly into the misty Suffolk sky. The biggest is over eight feet in girth, with an enormous open hollowed bolling like a madly exaggerated cartoon of a Doric column. This horny mass of scar tissue measures six foot six across its outspread palms. Inside the musty, hollow trunk the wood is tanned almost black and figured with bird's-eye patterns of tight curls and fine, stippled waves. As if to confirm the ash tree's antiquity, the road bank beneath it is pinned with celandines and dog violets.

Such massive mushroom bollings are called *desmocho* by the Basques in the beech and oak woods of the western Pyrenees around San Sebastián. But they have two ways of pollarding, and the other is called *trasmocho*, in which the four-foot stumps of three or four of the original main lateral branches form a composite bolling. But already, as pollarding goes out of fashion, *desmocho* has been lost from the language and all pollards are called *trasmocho*. The Basques always synchronize their pollarding with the waning phase of the moon. My friend Helen Reed, who grew up in Thrandeston, has travelled all over Europe in search of pollard trees. Wherever she found them, she studied the techniques of their culture and harvesting, and, as in the case of the Basque pollards in the steep woods of Aiako Harria and the Forêt de Sare, recorded the vocabulary of the craft. Helen discovered two main uses for pollard trees on the continent of Europe: the supply of fodder and fuel, mainly in the form of charcoal. The cutting of leafy branches for browse wood goes back to prehistoric times. I have done it myself to feed goats, as others did in my village, mostly with elm before the last ravaging by disease. It is highly nutritious and herbivores relish it. The remains of several old elm pollards are still gently decaying in my hedges, but new trees are rising again from the roots.

On the Åland Islands between Denmark and Finland, Helen

found some 7,000 ash and elm pollards, all between one and two hundred years old, still being harvested for their browse wood. Using an axe or billhook, the islanders cut the new shoots on a one- or two-year rotation when they are in full leaf. They bind them into bundles and hang them on the fences to dry like hay. The eight-foot pollards are set out in wood pasture so that the patches of meadow between them measure twice their height. The farmers store the dried bundles in their barns and feed them to the cattle in winter. Once the cows have eaten the leaves, the branches are fed to the rabbits, which strip the bark for its sugars. The bare sticks then dry out thoroughly and are made into faggots to fuel the bread ovens. The islanders always cut with a sharp blade in preference to a saw, because the teeth may spread infection in the sawdust that clings to the teeth. Sweden probably once had as many as four million pollards, now reduced to about 70,000. The most productive possible use of grazing land, says Helen, is to grow pollards for winter fodder and to graze the sward beneath them.

The bollings of pollards in England were generally the property of the landlord, but the tenant farmer was entitled to harvest the pollard wood. Firewood was always being stolen in the country. Most woods were gated and padlocked against carts, and the man-orial court records show frequent instances of fines for stealing under-wood. Poor people in the country had few comforts and, desperate for the warmth of a fire in winter, often stole fuel from the hedges and were beaten for it. Oliver Rackham has uncovered evidence of a wood-poaching crime wave, and harsh beatings meted out by the courts, during the bitter winters of the decade from 1590 to 1600.

I live beneath the protective boughs of a sheltering ash. The tree springs up as a single trunk of nine-foot girth for five feet and then divides into three, each of its branched trunks four feet in girth arching high above me. I love its natural flamboyance and energy, and the swooping habit of its branches: the way they plunge towards the earth, then upturn, tracing the trajectory of a diver entering the water and surfacing. In March the tree is a candelabra, each bud emerging cautiously, like the black snout of a badger, at the tip of every branch. Sometimes an ash will send out its branches in florid, Baroque spirals for no apparent reason except exuberance. On his way from Tintern Abbey to Ross on 16 June 1866, descending a steep lane to the River Wye, Gerard Manley Hopkins saw such a tree: 'Then the fields rose high on each side, one crowned with beautiful trees (there was particularly an ash with you could not tell how many contradictory supple curvings in the boughs).' *Fraxinus excelsior* captures the majestic essence of the tree very well. I look out from my desk window to a stand of tall ashes in whose bare waving tops dozens of fieldfares perch for hours and roost each winter. When the November winds blow, the elastic branches rattle against each other, and all that is left on the big tree by the house are bunches of the winged ash keys that fill the gutters.

Now the roof of the ash bower is folded down on itself, ready to bud and thrust into new life in spring once the sap stirs in the roots and surges up through the hinges of bent sinews that lead into this maze. There is something practical about the way ash goes about healing itself: the way the bark curls over the starburst of radial cracks in a half-severed stem at the heel of a pleacher, just like a human scar. All over Europe, people have always believed in the healing powers of the ash. Writing in 1916 in his Dartmoor classic *Small Talk at Wreyland*, Cecil Torr gives this account of the healing of a child in his tiny hamlet on the edge of Dartmoor:

A child was born here on 20 November 1902, and had a rupture. Some while afterwards I asked the father how the child was getting on, and the answer was – 'Oh, it be a sight better since us put'n through a tree.' And I found that they had carried out the ancient rite. The father had split an ash-tree on the hill behind his house, and had wedged the hole open with two chunks of oak. Then he and his wife took the child up there at day-break; and, as the sun rose, they passed it three times through the tree, from east to west. The mother then took the child home, and the father pulled out the chunks of oak, and bandaged up the tree. As the tree-trunk healed, so would the rupture heal also. I asked him why he did it, and he seemed surprised at the question, and said – 'Why, all folk do it.' I then asked him whether he thought it really did much good, and the reply was – 'Well, as much good as sloppin' water over'n in church.'

Rolling itself into a neat rustic architrave around a wound, the ash tree, in its workmanlike resilience, foreshadows its practical virtues as a timber. William Cobbett characteristically values the utility of ash over its beauty:

Laying aside this nonsense, however, of poets and painters, we have no tree of such various and extensive use as the Ash. It gives us boards; materials for making instruments of husbandry; and contributes towards the making of tools of almost all sorts. We could not well have a wagon, a cart, a coach or a wheelbarrow, a plough, a harrow, a spade, an axe or a hammer, if we had no Ash. It gives us poles for our hops; hurdle gates, wherewith to pen in our sheep; and hoops for our washing tubs; and assists to supply the Irish and West Indians with hoops for their pork barrels and sugar hogsheads. It therefore demands our particular attention; and from me, that attention it shall have.

Ash is remarkably pliable and tough. Coopers made the hoops Cobbett refers to by cleaving coppice ash in two and bending the flat side round the barrel or washing tub. I have made one more ash folly a few yards away from the bower, bending three slender ten-foot coppice poles into a spiral, lashing them to ash stakes driven into the ground to hold them in position until, as I hope, the tree adapts and eventually grows into a corkscrew. I question myself as I do such things. Is this too much like getting circus animals to jump through hoops? I reason that I've done the tree no harm, and in time it will grow into something beautiful as ash always does, the badger-noses on the new shoots leading the way. It doesn't need me to teach it to dance; it is naturally playful, a contortionist with ancestral memories of tumbling with the hedger's no less wilful strength. When the bower eventually comes of age long after I am gone, the wooden spinning top might still be going round too.